"This wonderful collection addresses all the important questions: How modern is genocide? Can various cases be compared? Why has genocide been committed by such different kinds of states, from liberal democracies to vicious dictatorships? And how can we balance claims for justice with the need for objective scholarship? Everyone should read this book. It is an emotionally wrenching experience, and one that will make every reader think about modern human history in ways few of us learned in school."

> – Daniel Chirot, Professor of International Studies and Sociology, University of Washington

"The comparative study of genocide is an evolving field characterized by great complexity and often competing approaches, dispositions, and interpretations. The editors of *The Specter of Genocide* clearly succeed in preserving the specificity of the individual cases while also demonstrating the necessity and worth of comparative analysis. Without ignoring the past, the volume focuses on the age of modernity and the direct relationship between ideology, state power, and total war and the perpetration of genocidal acts. It is sure to find broad application in scholarship and in the classroom."

> – Richard G. Hovannisian, AEF Chair in Modern Armenian History, UCLA

The Specter of Genocide

MASS MURDER IN HISTORICAL PERSPECTIVE

Genocide, mass murder, and human rights abuses are arguably the most perplexing and deeply troubling aspects of recent world history. This collection of essays by leading international experts offers an up-to-date, comprehensive history and analysis of multiple cases of genocide and genocidal acts, with a focus on the twentieth century. The book contains studies of the Armenian genocide, the victims of Stalinist terror, the Holocaust, and imperial Japan. Several authors explore colonialism and address the fate of the indigenous peoples in Africa, North America, and Australia. As well, there is extensive coverage of the post-1945 period, including the atrocities in the former Yugoslavia, Bali, Cambodia, Ethiopia, Rwanda, East Timor, and Guatemala. The book emphasizes the importance of comparative analysis and theoretical discussion, and it raises new questions about the difficult challenges for modernity constituted by genocide and other mass crimes.

Robert Gellately is Strassler Professor in Holocaust History at Clark University. His previous books include *Backing Hitler* (2001) and *The Gestapo and German Society* (1990). He coedited, with Nathan Stoltzfus, *Social Outsiders in Nazi Germany* (2001) and, with Sheila Fitzpatrick, *Accusatory Practices* (1997).

Ben Kiernan is A. Whitney Griswold Professor of History and Director of the Genocide Studies Program at Yale University. He is the author of *The Pol Pot Regime* (1996; 2nd ed., 2002) and *How Pol Pot Came to Power* (1985) and the editor of *Genocide and Democracy in Cambodia* (1993).

The Specter of Genocide

MASS MURDER IN HISTORICAL PERSPECTIVE

Edited by
ROBERT GELLATELY
Clark University

BEN KIERNAN
Yale University

CAMBRIDGE
UNIVERSITY PRESS

PUBLISHED BY THE PRESS SYNDICATE OF THE UNIVERSITY OF CAMBRIDGE
The Pitt Building, Trumpington Street, Cambridge, United Kingdom

CAMBRIDGE UNIVERSITY PRESS
The Edinburgh Building, Cambridge CB2 2RU, UK
40 West 20th Street, New York, NY 10011-4211, USA
477 Williamstown Road, Port Melbourne, VIC 3207, Australia
Ruiz de Alarcón 13, 28014 Madrid, Spain
Dock House, The Waterfront, Cape Town 8001, South Africa

http://www.cambridge.org

First published 2003

Printed in the United States of America

Typeface Bembo 11/13 pt. *System* LATEX 2$_\varepsilon$ [TB]

A catalog record for this book is available from the British Library.

Library of Congress Cataloging in Publication data

The specter of genocide : mass murder in historical perspective / edited by Robert Gellately,
Ben Kiernan.
   p. cm.
Includes bibliographical references and index.
ISBN 0-521-82063-4 – ISBN 0-521-52750-3 (pb)
1. Genocide. 2. Crimes against humanity. I. Gellately, Robert.
II. Kiernan, Ben.
HV6322.7 .S654   2003
304.6′63′09 – dc21   2002031553

ISBN 0 521 82063 4 hardback
ISBN 0 521 52750 3 paperback

Contents

Contributors

Elazar Barkan: Professor and Chair of Cultural Studies, Claremont Graduate University

Omer Bartov: John P. Birkelund Distinguished Professor of European History, Brown University

Leslie Dwyer: Researcher in Bali, Indonesia, and Recipient of a MacArthur Foundation Global Security and Sustainability Research and Writing Grant for Collaborative Research

Marie Fleming: Professor of Political Science, University of Western Ontario

Robert Gellately: Strassler Professor in Holocaust History at the Strassler Family Center for Holocaust and Genocide Studies, Clark University

Greg Grandin: Assistant Professor of History, New York University

Isabel V. Hull: Professor of History, Cornell University

Ben Kiernan: A. Whitney Griswold Professor of History and Director of the Genocide Studies Program, Yale University

Edward Kissi: Assistant Professor of History, Clark University

Gavan McCormack: Professor of History, Australian National University

Robert Melson: Professor of Political Science and Codirector of the Jewish Studies Program, Purdue University

Degung Santikarma: Researcher in Bali, Indonesia, and Recipient of a MacArthur Foundation Global Security and Sustainability Research and Writing Grant for Collaborative Research

Jacques Semelin: Professor at the Institut d'Etudes Politiques and Senior Researcher, Centre National de la Recherche Scientifique, Paris

John G. Taylor: Professor of Politics, South Bank University, London

Eric D. Weitz: Director of the Center for German and European Studies and Arsham and Charlotte Ohanessian Chair, University of Minnesota

Nicolas Werth: Researcher, Institut d'Histoire du Temps Présent, Centre National de la Recherche Scientifique, Paris

Jay Winter: Professor of History, Yale University

Acknowledgments

This volume originated as an international conference on genocide organized by Robert Gellately and Ben Kiernan. The conference was supported by the Harry Frank Guggenheim Foundation and held in Barcelona, Spain, in December 2000. Some of the essays published in this volume were presented at that conference, and those that were have been revised and sometimes also greatly expanded. In addition, we solicited a number of essays to broaden the picture and the discussion of genocide and mass murder in the modern world. This entire project could not have gotten off the ground without the support of the Harry Frank Guggenheim Foundation, and we particularly want to thank its two leading lights, Karen Colvard and James Hester. Five anonymous readers of the manuscript for Cambridge University Press made many very helpful suggestions for the improvement of the manuscript, and we wish to thank them as well. It is our hope that this volume will be useful in the classroom and that it stimulates further reflection about and research into this deeply troubling topic.

Introduction

1

The Study of Mass Murder and Genocide

ROBERT GELLATELY AND BEN KIERNAN

The twentieth century has been well described as an "age of extremes."[1] There were two world wars, major revolutions, colonial and anticolonial conflicts, and other catastrophes. All too often mass murder of noncombatant civilians marred these conflicts. The murders were usually state-sponsored or officially sanctioned.[2] Indeed, by midcentury the pattern struck some scholars as so alarming that they began groping for new words to describe it. The Polish jurist Raphael Lemkin introduced the concept of genocide in a small book published during the Second World War.[3] Later he helped prod the United Nations into formulating its Convention on the Prevention and Punishment of the Crime of Genocide in 1948. The convention defined genocide broadly as "acts committed with intent to destroy, in whole or in part, a national, ethnical, racial or religious group."[4] These acts included killing or causing serious bodily or mental harm to members of the group and also deliberately inflicting conditions on a people such as "to bring about its physical destruction in whole or in part." The convention condemned measures like the prevention of births so that a people would die out and forcible transfer of a group's children to another group. Because the Genocide Convention is a good starting point for discussion of the phenomenon, we analyze both its nature and its implications.

In 1945–46 the victorious Allies convened the International Military Tribunal at Nuremberg. These trials were partly justified in law as setting the precedent of holding leaders and other perpetrators responsible for crimes against humanity and war crimes. At about the same time, the

---

1 The concept is from Eric Hobsbawm, *The Age of Extremes: A History of the World, 1914–1991* (New York, 1994).
2 T. Bushnell et al. (eds.), *State Organized Terror: The Case of Violent Internal Repression* (Boulder, 1991).
3 Raphael Lemkin, *Axis Rule in Occupied Europe* (Washington, D.C., 1944).
4 The text of the convention is reprinted in the Appendix (pp. 381–84).

3

establishment of the United Nations opened the possibility of creating an international court that could try such crimes as genocide. During the next decades, however, the Nuremberg precedent was something of a dead letter. The International Criminal Court was created only in 2002, opposed by the United States, China, India, and Iraq, among others. Worse, state-sponsored mass murder had even begun to increase toward the end of the twentieth century. New varieties of international crimes came into being during the 1980s and 1990s, encapsulated by the repugnant term "ethnic cleansing." Though used before, the term was now given new currency.[5]

This book was conceived in the context of continuing reports of genocide, ethnic cleansing, and a wide range of other mass crimes still occurring in various parts of the globe, including East Timor, Rwanda, and the former Yugoslavia. We survey here a wide variety of mass murders and genocidal activities, but we make no claim to have covered all the cases. It is our hope that these studies will contribute to understanding the social, political, and psychological dynamics of the murderous side of the modern world.

Why has it taken so long for many scholars to get seriously involved in genocide research? Throughout the twentieth century individual scholars and survivors wrote and spoke out about the mass crimes against civilians they witnessed. Nevertheless, the sustained study of genocide and other forms of mass murder has been remarkably slow to start, although it accelerated in the 1990s.[6] For example, only fairly recently have most (but not all) specialists agreed that the mass murder of the Armenians by the Young Turks was genocide, perhaps even the first twentieth-century case. The Armenian minority in Ottoman Turkey had been subject to sporadic persecutions over the centuries, and these were stepped up with pogrom-like massacres in the late nineteenth century. With the outbreak of the First World War, the Young Turk government proceeded far more radically against the Armenians. Inspired by rabid nationalism, Turks drove the

5 In Yugoslavia during World War II, Chetnik leaders had proposed "cleansing the lands of all non-Serb elements" and of "all national minorities." See Norman Cigar, *Genocide in Bosnia: The Policy of "Ethnic Cleansing"* (College Station, Tex., 1995), 18. For a more general examination, see Andrew Bell-Fialkoff, *Ethnic Cleansing* (New York, 1996).
6 See, e.g., Frank Chalk and Kurt Jonassohn, *The History and Sociology of Genocide: Analyses and Case Studies* (New Haven, 1990); Helen Fein, *Genocide: A Sociological Perspective* (London, 1993); George J. Andreopoulos (ed.), *Genocide: Conceptual and Historical Dimensions* (Philadelphia, 1994); Samuel Totten, William S. Parsons, and Israel W. Charny (eds.), *Genocide in the Twentieth Century: Critical Essays and Eyewitness Accounts* (New York, 1995); Kurt Jonassohn with Karin Solveig Bjornson, *Genocide and Gross Human Rights Violations in Comparative Perspective* (New Brunswick, N.J., 1998); Levon Chorbajian et al., (eds.), *Studies in Comparative Genocide* (London, 1999); Israel Charny (ed.), *The Encyclopedia of Genocide* (Oxford, 1999).

Armenians from their homes and massacred them in such numbers that out-side observers at the time remarked that what was happening was "a massacre like none other," or "a massacre that changes the meaning of massacre."[7]

Although we do not have reliable figures on the death toll, many historians accept that at a minimum between 800,000 and 1 million people were killed, often in unspeakably cruel ways. Unknown numbers of others converted to Islam or in other ways survived but were lost to the Armenian culture. At the time a number of influential people spoke out against these atrocities, most notably the distinguished historian Arnold J. Toynbee, but only in the past several decades have scholars devoted anything like sustained attention to this human catastrophe. Two essays in this volume deal with important aspects of the topic, but much more remains to be said.[8] There is more than enough evidence to suggest that the mass murder of the Armenians was a genocide, as that crime was subsequently defined in the United Nations Genocide Convention of 1948. In this volume we treat this mass murder and other state-sponsored genocides as belonging to the same category of crime. Any surviving perpetrators of the Armenian genocide could certainly have been held to account in an international criminal court – if only international enforcement of the Genocide Convention had not had to wait for the convening of the Ad Hoc International Criminal Tribunals for Yugoslavia and Rwanda in The Hague in the 1990s, or the first permanent International Criminal Court in 2002.[9]

The study of mass murder and genocide took a major turn because of reactions to the atrocities committed by the Third Reich. On the one hand, the number of people killed in the Second World War in Europe as a whole was truly staggering, greater than in all the other wars fought in Europe since 1870. More than half of those killed in the Second World War were civilian noncombatants. In addition to the victims of bombing raids, millions were put to death as part of deliberate Axis plans to kill them because they belonged to groups or nations arbitrarily defined as "enemies." The wartime killing in Europe could not be pushed aside, as too often happened when mass murder occurred in some distant land. The persecution of the Jews reached genocidal proportions in the heart of Europe. The Nazis even had plans for serial genocides. Had they succeeded, other nations would have been wiped out as identifiable cultures. As Gellately shows in his essay

---

7 See the remarks of contemporaries cited in Norman M. Naimark, *Fires of Hatred: Ethnic Cleansing in Twentieth-Century Europe* (Cambridge, Mass., 2001), 37.

8 For a full-scale study and the literature, see Vahakn N. Dadrian, *History of the Armenian Genocide: Ethnic Conflict from the Balkans to Anatolia to the Caucasus*, 3rd rev. ed. (Providence, 1997).

9 For a brief account, see "For Crimes of International Law, a Guide," *Boston Globe*, July 23, 2001.

in this book, survivors would have been exploited as hapless helots. The Japanese also had far-reaching plans in the Pacific, which Gavan McCormack discusses in his essay. In both cases, the plans were stopped before they could be fully implemented. The war crimes of both states were publicized in postwar trials. At Nuremberg in 1945–46, the Nazi murder of the Jews was prosecuted as one of several "crimes against humanity," but, as a leading historian of the Holocaust puts it, the crimes against the Jews as such "never assumed a prominent place" at Nuremberg.[10] The term "Holocaust" began to be widely used only in the 1960s and later, and sustained professional study of what happened to the Jews began later still.[11]

It is true, however, that the 1948 United Nations convention against genocide was formulated in the shadow of Auschwitz. Lemkin had wanted to criminalize and prosecute what he described as "the criminal intent to destroy or to cripple permanently a human group. The acts are directed against groups, as such, and individuals are selected for destruction only because they belong to these groups."[12] Nevertheless, for many decades no charges of "genocide" were ever brought, so that in the 1950s and 1960s, when the Genocide Convention was discussed at all, it remained more of a rhetorical than a judicial device for use in the Cold War against the opposing superpower. Soon enough even accusations of genocide faded away.[13]

In the past two decades or so, a conjuncture of events has sparked renewed concern about genocide, mass murders, and grave human rights abuses of all kinds. The American public in particular grew far more attentive to the Holocaust beginning in the mid-1970s with a gradual introduction of Holocaust Remembrance days and other forms of commemoration.[14] By the latter 1980s various cities had opened Holocaust museums, and in 1993 the United States government dedicated a new U.S. Holocaust Memorial Museum. By that time scholars around the world were engaged as never before in the study of the Third Reich. Historians and jurists alike began to see patterns in state-sponsored mass murders, so that during the past two decades, just as the study of the Holocaust greatly increased, so too can we see many more studies of various cases of mass murder and human rights abuses.

---

10 Michael R. Marrus, *The Holocaust in History* (Hanover, 1987), 4.
11 For numerous relevant contributions, see Michael Berenbaum and Abraham J. Peck (eds.), *The Holocaust and History: The Known, the Unknown, the Disputed and the Reexamined* (Bloomington, 1998).
12 Cited in Andreopoulos, *Genocide*, 1.
13 See Peter Novick, *The Holocaust in American Life* (Boston, 1999), 101.
14 Israel introduced a Holocaust Day of Remembrance on April 7, 1959. Such a day was introduced in the United States in 1979. See James E. Young, *The Texture of Memory: Holocaust Memorials and Memory* (New Haven, 1993), 270–72.

The attention of the West to mass murder of all kinds was also fueled from the 1960s and 1970s onward by reports of the systematic mass murder and genocide committed by the Suharto regime in Indonesia and East Timor, and by the Pol Pot regime in Cambodia.[15] These cases, the worst postwar mass murders in Asia, heralded a new chapter in the modern history of genocide. In this book, Leslie Dwyer and Degung Santikarma analyze the wave of killings that swept the Indonesian island of Bali in 1965. From Africa came news of other mass murders, such as those in Burundi in 1972 and in Ethiopia from 1974, which Edward Kissi's chapter compares with those in Cambodia. A major turning point was reached in 1994 with the genocide in Rwanda. Initial reports of what was happening were downplayed until investigators brought out the truth, alas, mainly after the genocide had been brought to an end by Rwandan opposition forces. Robert Melson discusses the Rwanda case here. Those events, and hardly less horrific conflagrations in East Timor (again) in 1999, Bosnia in 1991–95, and elsewhere, helped to stimulate far more concern about mass murder and human rights abuses in our contemporary world. In this volume John Taylor examines what happened in East Timor from 1975 to 1999 as a case of counterinsurgency leading to genocide. Jacques Semelin looks at events in the former Yugoslavia in the 1990s and develops the concept of "mass crime" to include killings, destruction, deportation, and other large-scale persecutions. In his comparative chapter, Kiernan draws attention to some common ideological themes behind these diverse twentieth-century tragedies, stressing land-related issues – territorial expansionism and a preoccupation with cultivation – along with widely studied factors such as racism and religious prejudice.

Recent research into the history of mass murder and genocide has also been fueled by evidence from the archives of the former Soviet Union after its demise. For a long time, many Europeanists had been blind to the gravity of the human rights abuses committed over generations in the Soviet Union since the Russian Revolution. Plenty of news circulated from the 1930s about the fates of the kulaks ("rich peasants") and Ukrainians. Thanks to perestroika and the new openness in the 1980s, and certainly after 1991 when the USSR dissolved before our eyes, research by historians in newly (if still only partly) opened Soviet archives brought out more stories that could not be denied or brushed aside. We are finally learning the full scope of what happened in the Soviet Union, not only in the 1930s, but during

15 Robert Cribb (ed.), *The Indonesian Killings, 1965–1966: Studies from Java and Bali* (Clayton, Australia, 1990); Ben Kiernan, *The Pol Pot Regime: Race, Power, and Genocide in Cambodia under the Khmer Rouge, 1975–79* (New Haven, 1996).

the war itself, and even well into the postwar era. We would point to the milestone studies recently published by historians in France like Nicolas Werth, who provides us here with an up-to-date account of the mass murders committed in the Soviet Union under Stalin.[16] Several other Western scholars have also made important contributions to the history of these events.[17] Together they show beyond a shadow of a doubt that even though some officially sponsored murder campaigns in the USSR did not always lead to genocide – as defined by the United Nations Convention – in a number of cases there was systematic mass murder of many millions. Certain peoples in the multinational Soviet Union were "ethnically cleansed," others persecuted to the point where their cases could (now) be prosecuted under the convention. The implications of these recent studies must be considered by anyone trying to account for mass murder in the twentieth century.

Thus only in recent years has the new field of genocide studies come into being. This development has led in turn to the investigation of hitherto little-known or long-denied cases of mass murder and genocide. One such case, what happened in Guatemala, is detailed in this volume by Greg Grandin. The full story of the U.S. aid to killer regimes in Chile and El Salvador, on the other hand, has yet to be written.

As historians, sociologists, anthropologists, political scientists, and others get involved in a new field like this, one that is remarkably complex, it is not surprising that they adopt multifaceted approaches and different "models" of explanation. In this volume we offer a multiplicity of theoretical approaches. It is worth briefly sketching out some of the main ones. We point to the diversity and mention several disputes, even among contributors in this volume, but we do not try to resolve them here.

THEORETICAL POSITIONS

The basic question in all studies of mass murder and genocide is, Why is an "enemy" – however defined – "exterminated"?[18] Scholars from various fields have taken many different routes in trying to answer that question, but two main approaches stand out. One suggests that genocide, like war, massacre, mass rape, and other such atrocities, is anything but new and hardly

---

16 See Stéphane Courtois et al., *The Black Book of Communism: Crimes, Terror, Repression*, trans. J. Murphy and M. Kramer (Cambridge, Mass., 1999).

17 See, e.g., Terry Martin, "The Origins of Soviet Ethnic Cleansing," *Journal of Modern History* 70 (December 1998): 813–61.

18 Courtois et al., *The Black Book*, 747.

an invention of the twentieth century. These scholars insist that such horrors have occurred throughout history in all parts of the world.[19] Mass killings are as old as time. We certainly can find many examples in history, during war, imperial conquest, religious unrest, social upheaval, or revolution, when widespread death and destruction were deliberately inflicted upon a foe, including innocent civilian noncombatants. As we detail here, even "extermination" was a familiar concept before 1900.

Nevertheless, if this first group of scholars tends to underline continuities in the human condition as explaining the recurrence of mass murder, another group emphasizes change over continuity. In this book, Omer Bartov, Marie Fleming, and Eric Weitz focus on the specific modernity of genocide. In their essays here they insist that there is something very new about many (if not all) of the twentieth-century mass murders, such as those inflicted on the Armenians or the Jews. Many of us would agree with the point made by Isabel Hull in her essay in this volume. On the basis of what happened to the Herero tribe in German South West Africa before the First World War, she argues that the vastness and totality of recent genocides or "final solutions" aimed at what she terms "problem populations" is such that they can be pursued only by an institution like the modern state. For her the question is, Under what conditions do governments and their agents decide on the utterly utopian goal of totally destroying a "problem population"? In German South West Africa, the representatives of the state on the spot began to move well beyond a "war of pacification."[20] Long after the Herero were any real threat, the local German military commander issued an extermination order. Hull suggests that there were links between the kind of behavior that emerged in early twentieth-century German Africa and the Nazi "final solution to the Jewish question," but her thesis is not of a simple continuity from Africa to Auschwitz.

The link between European imperialism and mass murder can be found in older literature.[21] Yet there is a need for basic research on many other parts of Africa and Asia. Developments there need to be integrated into our studies of more modern cases of mass murder. Just how we can do this remains for another book. In this volume, Elazar Barkan offers an account of the genocides of indigenous peoples, which has become a controversial topic.

19 See, e.g., Chalk and Jonassohn, *The History and Sociology of Genocide*.
20 For this phraseology, see Trutz Von Trotha, " 'The Fellows Can Just Starve.' On Wars of 'Pacification' in the African Colonies of Imperial Germany and the Concept of 'Total War,' " in Manfred F. Boemeke et al. (eds.), *Anticipating Total War: The German and American Experiences, 1871–1914* (Cambridge, 1999), 415–35.
21 See, e.g., J. A. Hobson, *Imperialism, a Study* (1902; Ann Arbor, 1965); Hannah Arendt, *The Origins of Totalitarianism* (1951; New York, 1973).

It is not always important to get bogged down on the question of whether or not these premodern or early modern mass murders can or cannot be defined as genocide. Although we again suggest the UN legal definition as a starting point, we need to move beyond definitions to study all such events in order to uncover their underlying dynamics. Mass murders in past centuries, however, should be seen as much more than mere antecedents to what happened in the twentieth century. It is not particularly useful to suggest that human nature – whatever that is – "explains" these horrors. We can study long–term trends, precursors, and antecedents but also look at differences. Why do some conquests and conflicts turn to mass murder, and others not? We also need to ask, as Glenda Gilmore has pointed out, both why there was no genocide aimed at the blacks in the United States, and why African Americans were nevertheless more concerned than most whites at the Nazi persecution of the Jews.[22]

The issues about continuities and changes in the history of mass murder and genocide are not going to be resolved any time soon, and there is no good reason why they should be. There is plenty of room for discussion and for varying approaches and different methods.

A common goal of all researchers is to piece together who ordered the killings to commence in any given case. If in the twentieth century these mass murders were usually state-sponsored or at least officially sanctioned, who made the decisions? What were their motives? These questions are particularly relevant if we want to hold leaders responsible for genocide or other grave human rights abuses before international courts. The problem for historians and jurists is that leaders and their agents try, usually with considerable success, to cover up their crimes and to destroy the evidence. Moreover, some states continue to deny crimes, including cases of mass murder and even genocide, committed by their predecessors. They also limit access to their archives and even persecute or threaten researchers. When scholars are finally granted access to archives, they often find that evidence has been "laundered" or destroyed. So reconstructing the decision–making process is often no easy task.

Those scholars who focus mainly on the leaders of the mass murders adopt a "top down" or "intentionalist" approach. There are a number of intentionalist essays in this volume. They posit that leaders, and particularly

---

22 Glenda Gilmore, "'An Ethiop among the Aryans': African Americans and Fascism, 1930–1939," paper to an international colloquium on Comparative Genocide, Barcelona, December 7–10, 2000. The colloquium was held by the Genocide Studies Program (Yale University) and the Center for Holocaust and Genocide Studies (Clark University) and sponsored by the Harry Frank Guggenheim Foundation.

dictators who intend to carry out mass murder, are more or less capable of bringing about their wishes, both using force and mobilizing sufficient support by winning converts to their cause. The argument is that without key decisions or orders from the top, without the role of a Hitler or a Pol Pot, to name two examples, the genocides now identified with their regimes would not have happened. It is therefore critical to study the emerging pre-occupations and ideologies of such unusual figures and their small close-knit circles, in order to be able to identify, predict, and prevent future outbreaks of extreme violence.

Another group of scholars represented in this volume, while not disagreeing with the importance of leaders, is interested in the implementation or enforcement process. They adopt a "bottom-up," sometimes called "functionalist" or, more accurately, an "interactive" approach. They investigate how the intentions or orders of leaders – often located in distant capital cities – were translated into reality. These scholars argue that it is insufficient to point to the will or orders of the dictator to account for how the orders get followed. Jay Winter argues in his essay on World War I here that the consent of the broad masses of the people was somehow crucial and that this consent was not created or manufactured by a proverbial Big Brother "from above." As he puts it, "The truth is more frightening: the Great War provided much evidence of the propensity for populations to generate internally a commitment to carry on a war of unprecedented carnage." According to Gellately, the same point holds with regard to the Nazi regime in the Second World War. He suggests that the persecution of social outsiders between 1933 and 1939 won more support for Hitler's regime than it lost, and that the early successes in the Second World War turned Hitler into Germany's most popular leader of all time. That support encouraged Hitler to launch his campaigns of mass murder.

Scholars often disagree in their assessments of the motives of the face-to-face killers in the field. A number of essays in this volume adopt an interactive approach and focus both on what happened at the local level and, at the same time, look at the interactions between those "above" (the leaders) and "below" (those who either do the killing or collaborate in some way with the killers). These approaches, as well as a number of recent publications devoted to mass murders, strongly suggest that it is important to investigate, along with the thinking and policies of the leaders, the social and historical background of all kinds of mass crimes.[23]

23 See Christopher R. Browning, *Ordinary Men: Reserve Police Battalion 101 and the Final Solution in Poland* (New York, 1992), and Daniel Jonah Goldhagen, *Hitler's Willing Executioners: Ordinary Germans and the Holocaust* (New York, 1996).

Several accounts of recent mass murders in Africa indicate that one factor that leads to escalation, is a breakdown of previous relationships between emerging perpetrators and victims. In Rwanda, for example, close-knit bonds, even reaching into families over many decades, suddenly were torn asunder. When we turn to such cases, the question that arises is, Why did the killers start? Why did Hutus turn against their erstwhile Tutsi neighbors, even family members? Was it merely the case that both Hutus and Tutsis took over the discourse of their former colonial masters?[24] Was this another postcolonial legacy? Had they lived in greater harmony before Belgians strengthened ethnic distinctions in the latter part of the nineteenth century? Were the killers so easily manipulated and misled by such messages? Kissi, in his discussion of Ethiopia, maintains that tribal or racial animosities may have deep roots, but he also shows how a modern revolutionary regime can choose different approaches.

The "models" we once used to explain the behavior of the killers may now need rethinking. It turns out that even in the Holocaust, certainly the most widely investigated genocide of the twentieth century, our understanding of just who did the killing and why has changed dramatically in the past decade. Although the Nazi SS were key perpetrators, and the most important killing sites were specifically designed death camps, perhaps as many or more people were killed outside the camps. Mass killing certainly took place in "modernized" death camps but also in hands-on, face-to-face encounters.[25] These new studies suggest how "ordinary" people became caught up in the killing. Jan Gross shows, in his book on Jedwabne, what even the citizens of this little Polish town did. They murdered every one of their Jewish fellow citizens, apparently mostly for personal gain. They did so in unimaginably cruel ways, with neither restraint nor much involvement by the German occupation forces. That victims (under the Third Reich, these included the Poles) could also be perpetrators, was demonstrated beyond doubt in Jedwabne.[26]

Recent research has pointed to the importance of focusing more on the victims in our accounts of mass murder. But by definition most victims are dead and unable to testify, and this makes it easier for the perpetrators not only to try to cover up their crimes, but also to erase the history, culture, and even the language of the victims. Whole communities, many of them going

24 See, e.g., Philip Gourevitch, *We Wish to Inform You That Tomorrow We Will be Killed with Our Families* (New York, 1998), 54–55.
25 See Browning, *Ordinary Men*, and Goldhagen, *Hitler's Willing Executioners*.
26 Jan Gross, *Neighbors: The Destruction of the Jewish Community of Jedwabne* (Princeton, 2000).

back for centuries, are wiped off the face of the earth as if they had never existed. We must research these lost people, even though it is difficult to reconstruct what happened in the vortex of the killing process. When we are lucky, we can talk to survivors, hear their testimony, but all too often little or nothing remains. Dori Laub has reminded us in thoughtful essays how important it is to study the surviving victims, and even their children. The experience of coming close to death, being confined or threatened or forced to witness horrific crimes, constitutes for many a trauma requiring years to heal and exerts a powerful influence on their actions and on future generations.[27]

A number of scholars have written about gender issues in genocides, but it is clear that this work is only beginning.[28] The great majority of the perpetrators of mass murder (even serial killers) are male. That finding has led some feminist writers and others to suggest that genocide has been a specifically male proclivity, and some of them have gone on to develop gender-specific theories of evil. From the few studies we have, however, it would seem that under certain circumstances some women are as capable as men of perpetrating horrific crimes and human rights abuses.[29]

The gender of the victims, it has to be said, often did not count for much, especially if the perpetrator's intention was total annihilation. Notably in the Holocaust, there was (supposedly) a strict taboo on sexual relations between Germans and the Jews, and in Cambodia, between peasants and former city dwellers. More recently, though, mass rape formed part of ethnic cleansing operations in the former Yugoslavia. The appalling accounts of the treatment of Muslim women at the hands of Serb forces in Bosnia-Herzegovina seem to indicate that state-sponsored mass rape really was something new and that it carried a genocidal intent. Catharine MacKinnon goes so far as to assert that mass rape of this kind was "a form of genocide directed specifically at women."[30] In Bosnia-Herzegovina and several other areas (like Bali) covered in this volume, mass rape was employed consciously or systematically with the intent of destroying a group.

---

27 Dori Laub, *Psychoanalysis and Genocide: Two Essays*, Genocide Studies Program (New Haven, 2002); Ilany Kogan, *The Cry of Mute Children: A Psychoanalytic Perspective of the Second Generation of the Holocaust* (London, 1995).
28 See, e.g., Adam Jones, "Gendercide and Genocide," *Journal of Genocide Research* 2, 2 (June 2000): 185–211; "Gendercide," special issue, *Journal of Genocide Research* 4, 1 (March 2002); and the Gendercide Watch website <http://www.gendercide.org>.
29 For a brief introduction, see Joanna Bourke, *An Intimate History of Killing: Face to Face Killing in Twentieth Century Warfare* (London, 1999), 294–333. For specific cases, see Gudrun Schwarz, *Eine Frau an seine Seite: Ehefrauen in der SS-Sippengemeinschaft* (Hamburg, 1997), 99–227.
30 Catharine A. MacKinnon, "Crimes of War. Crimes of Peace," in Steven Lukes et al., *On Human Rights: The Oxford Amnesty Lectures 1993* (New York, 1993), 83–109, at 88.

Mass rape is not unknown in history, even in recent times, and to mention a prominent example, was so pronounced in eastern Germany under the invading Soviet armies at the end of the Second World War, that whole villages of women, from young girls to grandmothers committed suicide by throwing themselves in rivers in order to avoid the marauding soldiers.[31] That chapter in the history of mass rape did not end in mass murder of the surviving women, but it was accompanied by many other human rights abuses, including banishment to Siberia.[32]

In more recent conflicts in the Balkans as well as in Asia, however, rape has been used not just as revenge, "reward" for the soldiers, or as random acts of sexual violence. Rape in some instances is no longer an "eternal" accompaniment of war but has come to be used as a systematized weapon of domination. Such strategic uses of organized mass rape seem new, and we can see how it functioned in several countries, particularly in Europe in 1945 and 1946, when it was used to terrorize certain ethnic groups into leaving their homes in search of safety.[33] Attacking women and even young girls was not only another way of shaming the men who may have fled, but it also dehumanized victims and made it easier to kill them. Even when these actions did not result in mass murder, the intention was at times genocidal in the sense that the aim was either to destroy the "problem population" as a living social or ethnic entity or to undermine its biological future.

As the Dwyer and Santikarma essay on Bali in this volume shows, it is often difficult to study these atrocities, because the survivors do not want to talk about what happened. Rape is enveloped by social taboos in all cultures, and many victims of mass rape do not want to discuss it for fear of being victimized yet again, perhaps even by their own families.

LEGAL AND ANALYTICAL CONCEPTS

The Intent of the Perpetrator

Legally, genocide is the most serious crime. It is considered an "aggravated" crime against humanity, for an important reason. The 1948 UN Genocide Convention requires the proven intent of the perpetrator to destroy a human

31 See Norman M. Naimark, *The Russians in Germany: A History of the Soviet Zone of Occupation, 1945–49* (Cambridge, Mass., 1995), 69–140.
32 See Freya Klier, *Verschleppt ans Ende der Welt: Schicksale deutscher Frauen in soujetischen Arbeitslagern* (Munich, 2000).
33 See Naimark, *Fires of Hatred*, 108–38, for an examination of how rape was used by Poland and Czechoslovakia to terrorize native Germans into leaving these countries at the end of the Second World War.

community – "the intent to destroy, in whole or in part, a national, ethnical, racial or religious group, as such." Other crimes against humanity and war crimes do not require proof of such intent, merely of the criminal action itself, such as mass murder.

What is "intent" to destroy a group? There are two different views on this. The everyday meaning tends to confuse intent with "motive." If a colonial power, motivated by conquest of a territory, or a revolutionary regime with the aim of imposing a new social order, in the process destroys all or part of a human group, does that constitute genocide? Not according to most popular definitions of intent. But in criminal law, including international criminal law, the specific motive is irrelevant. Prosecutors need only prove that the criminal act was intentional, not accidental. A conquest or a revolution that causes total or partial destruction of a group, legally qualifies as intentional and therefore as genocide whatever the goal or motive, so long as the acts of destruction were pursued intentionally. In this legal definition, genocidal intent also applies to acts of destruction that are not the specific goal but are predictable outcomes or by-products of a policy, which could have been avoided by a change in that policy. Deliberate pursuit of any policy in the knowledge that it would lead to destruction of a human group thus constitutes genocidal intent. In international law, then, "genocide" describes *both* deliberate mass extermination campaigns specifically motivated by fear or hatred of a victim group, as in the Nazi Holocaust, *and* destruction of human groups pursued for more indirect or political purposes, such as the Indonesian military conquest of East Timor or the Khmer Rouge utopian communist revolution. Of course, there remain important social and political distinctions between these cases, but the legal category of genocide includes them all.

The term "as such" in the UN definition, added to the convention text as a late political compromise, presents thorny legal problems. How are we to interpret this term as it appears in the phrase "intent to destroy, in whole or in part, a national, ethnical, racial or religious group, as such"? Does "as such" refer to the preceding word "group," meaning the destruction of people as a communal group, but not necessarily destruction of individual members? The convention is positive on this. "Killing members of the group" is only the first of the convention's list of five acts, any of which constitute genocide when committed with intent to destroy a group. The fifth, "forcibly transferring children of the group to another group," for instance, may destroy a communal group by dispersal without killing any of its individual members. For this reason the Australian Aborigines were recently held to have suffered genocide up to 1970, as a result of the policy of forcibly removing children from their parents to "breed out the colour."[34] Perhaps 50,000 Aboriginal children were placed with white Australian families explicitly "for the absorption of these people into the general population." Australia's Human Rights and Equal Opportunity Commission's 1997 report, *Bringing Them Home*, concluded that "between one in three and one in ten indigenous children were forcibly removed from their families" between 1910 and 1970. The commission described this forcible removal as a breach of Article II (e) of the 1948 Genocide Convention.[35]

This finding was legally correct, though controversial. Popular perceptions of "genocide" often do not encompass nonlethal destruction of a group, even when intentional. Nor would a colloquial definition encompass acts of destruction motivated by proclaimed positive or humanitarian purposes, such as removing children purportedly to provide better care for them. Legally, both do constitute genocide. The destruction of the group "as such" is in each case pursued with intent. Applying a more colloquial definition of genocide here would deny victims a remedy to which they are legally entitled.

Or does "as such" mean destruction of individual members *because of* their membership of the group? This would entail some form of discriminatory practice. What if all groups are treated similarly, as in Cambodia where everybody was occasionally served small pieces of pork in the compulsory communal mess halls? That might not seem discriminatory. But is it not discrimination against Muslims to force *them* to eat the pork, on pain of death? Or does the law require proof of a test case of a non-Muslim who refused to eat pork and was *not* executed? That Muslims be killed "as Muslims" – rather than as recalcitrants who refused to eat what they were served?[36] Here again, the legal definition of "intent" comes into play. A policy of total national conformity, even if enforced without discrimination, will predictably lead to destruction of minority ethnic or religious groups, "as such." Relentless pursuit of such a policy constitutes, in law, genocidal intent.

The same may be said of a policy of conquest such as the Indonesian occupation of East Timor. Does intent to destroy a group "as such" require

---

34 Quoted in Robert Manne, "In Denial: The Stolen Generations and the Right," *Australian Quarterly Review* 1 (2001): 38–40. See also Raymond Evans and Bill Thorpe, "The Massacre of Australian History," *Overland* (Melbourne), no. 163 (winter 2001): 21–39.

35 Ronald Wilson, *Bringing Them Home: Report of the National Inquiry into the Separation of Aboriginal and Torres Strait Islander Children from Their Families*, Human Rights and Equal Opportunity Commission (Sydney, 1997), 275.

36 See the exchange between Ben Kiernan and Michael Vickery in the *Bulletin of Concerned Asian Scholars* 20, 4 (October–December 1988): 2–33; 22, 1 (January–March 1990): 31–33; and 22, 2 (April–June 1990): 35–40.

the destruction to be motivated by targeting of an ethnic or religious group? Again, intentional mass murder of a political resistance movement, whose nationwide support ensures that its destruction means partial destruction of an ethnic or national group – this too, in law, constitutes genocide.

The Targeted Victim Groups

The intent of the perpetrator is only one end of the genocidal process. Differing definitions of genocide used by scholars and lawyers also cover different victim groups. Much depends on whether genocide victims are targeted in groups of the kind that allow individual members to escape persecution and death by concealing or abandoning one group identity, and taking up another as a member of a nontargeted group. The UN convention, as we have seen, requires victims to be members of a "national, ethnical, racial or religious group." It is most difficult for members of racial or ethnic groups to abandon such markers of their identity or declare their membership of alternative groups. Most Jews in Nazi-occupied Europe, for instance, found it impossible to alter or hide their identity as targets of Hitler's "final solution." It is sometimes easier for individuals to change their citizenship or creed than their racial or ethnic background. During the Armenian genocide, a small number of Armenian Christians adopted Islam and were spared by the Young Turk regime.[37] But generally both national and religious groups are also quite stable, commanding such loyalty from their members that it is an extreme injustice to require people to abandon such groups (even) to save their own lives. For these reasons, genocide is the ultimate crime against humanity because it is legally defined as the targeting of people for destruction on the basis of what are presumed to be more or less inherited, perhaps genetic, shared group characteristics that the victims cannot divest nor be reasonably expected to divest, irrespective of their intentions or actions.

On the other hand, membership of social classes, such as "the bourgeoisie," is more easily divested and less unjustly prohibited. The forced abandonment of one's membership of such groups is not necessarily so demanding a condition for survival as forced abandonment of one's religious or ethnic identity. It certainly has none of the impossibility of transforming one's racial background. The Soviet persecution of kulaks in the 1930s took millions of lives. Debate continues whether Stalin's intent was to physically exterminate all kulaks as individuals or rather to confiscate their property

---

37 Chalk and Jonassohn, *The History and Sociology of Genocide*, 25.

forcibly and thus destroy them "as a class."[38] The latter policy, which in principle would allow some kulaks to survive by adopting a different class identity, would not constitute genocide in international law. The Chinese Communist Party also exterminated landlords and persecuted their children. Some scholars believe social groups should be protected by the UN convention on the grounds that social group membership, and even property or wealth, is largely inherited and that it is unjust to expect members to transform their socioeconomic lives radically simply in order to be spared extermination. Many scholars believe that for this reason the UN definition of genocide is conceptually deficient. Some, like Helen Fein, have advanced academic definitions that include destruction of social groups.[39] And, of course, in practice the massacre of social groups often proceeds dogmatically, with little real opportunity for targeted group members to win clemency by declaring their adherence to a more acceptable social group.

Political groups are more ephemeral again. Adherence to a political association is usually a voluntary act of adulthood, a democratic right. But extinguishing political freedom by force is not the same as genocide. The extermination of an entire political group – for instance, leftists in Indonesia or Guatemala, or rightists in Ethiopia – does not constitute genocide under the UN convention. A major reason for the convention's failure to protect social and political groups is the Soviet Union's opposition to their inclusion during the negotiations of the late 1940s, to prevent Stalin's mass murders being held to be genocidal. The United States, which has also directed mass exterminations of political groups – for instance, in Vietnam, Chile, and El Salvador – has similarly benefited from the convention's failure to protect them.[40] These victims are protected by the international law on crimes against humanity, although some scholars prefer a definition of

---

38 For different views on this, see Robert Conquest, *Harvest of Sorrow: Soviet Collectivization and the Terror-Famine* (New York, 1986); R. W. Davies, Mark Harrison, and S. G. Wheatcroft, *The Economic Transformation of the Soviet Union, 1913–1945* (Cambridge, 1994), 64–77; V. Danilov et al. (eds.), *The Tragedy of the Soviet Village: Collectivization and Dekulakization: Documents and Materials, 1927–1939*, vol. 3: *The End of 1930–1933* (Moscow, 2001), 842–87; R. W. Davies, M. Tauger, and S. G. Wheatcroft, "Stalin, Grain Stocks and the Famine of 1932–1933," *Slavic Review* (Fall 1995): 642–57; James Mace and Leonid Heretz (eds.), *Oral History Project of the Commission on the Ukraine Famine* (Washington, D.C., 1990); and works listed in *Holodomor v Ukrayini 1932–1933 rr.: Bibliohrafychnyi pokazhchyk* (Odesa-Kyiv, 2001), 656.

39 Fein, *Genocide: A Sociological Perspective.*

40 Barbara Harff and Ted Robert Gurr estimate that 475,000 Vietnamese civilians in National Liberation Front of South Vietnam (NLF) areas "died as a direct consequence" of actions by the U.S. and Saigon regime in 1965–72 alone. "Toward Empirical Theory of Genocides and Politicides," *International Studies Quarterly* 1988 (32): 364. See also Christopher Hitchens, *The Trial of Henry Kissinger* (London, 2001).

genocide that also includes destruction of political groups.[41] Valid objections
to the political manipulation of the negotiations leading up to the adoption
of the Genocide Convention do not undermine the conceptual case that
the ultimate crime against humanity is that of exterminating groups whose
members had no choice in that membership. This does not apply to political or even social units in the way it does to religious and especially racial
groups.

Finally, scholars have argued that even the targeting of imaginary groups,
such as alleged "wreckers" (nameless industrial saboteurs) in Stalin's purges,
should be included in the definition of genocide.[42] Here, with the most
ephemeral of all target groups, the spectrum bends into a horseshoe. To sow
arbitrary terror among an entire population, perpetrators may kill rather indiscriminately but still identify "targets" by a common if meaningless label.
These victims are not members of any existing or objective group but are
forced into an imaginary association. They are "political" groups only in the
mind or the propaganda of the perpetrator but are therefore most difficult
of all for their members to abandon. Again, the intent of the perpetrator is
the key factor, but in this case it does not target "a national, ethnical, racial
or religious group, as such," so the result is not categorized legally as genocide. Perhaps it should be. Nevertheless, the UN legal definition is finally
being enforced and developed in several international courts. It remains the
best starting point for discussion of genocide, if only to make conceptual
distinctions between different cases irrespective of labels we choose to apply
to them.

Ethnic Conflict and Ethnic Cleansing

The main differences between ethnic conflict and genocide lie in two areas.[43]
The distinctions, again, focus on the definition of the targeted victim group
and on the perpetrators and their intent. First, in principle at least, ethnic
conflict may at times be no more than a clash of ethnic armed forces; it may
not necessarily be genocidal or even target civilians, though of course it
often does, as in the case of Kosovo in 1999. Second, ethnic conflict implies
a mass popular movement, with at least widespread acquiescence or even

---

41 Fein, *Genocide: A Sociological Perspective.*
42 Chalk and Jonassohn, *The History and Sociology of Genocide,* 25 ("if people define a situation as
   real it is real in its consequences"), 30. See also Chalk, "Redefining Genocide," in Andreopoulos,
   Genocide, 47–63, and Helen Fein, "Genocide, Terror, Life Integrity, and War Crimes: The Case for
   Discrimination," in Andreopoulos, *Genocide,* 99.
43 See, e.g., Daniel Chirot and Martin Seligman (eds.), *Ethnopolitical Warfare: Causes, Consequences, and
   Possible Solutions* (Washington, D.C., 2001).

participation. Genocide does not necessarily require that, though of course it sometimes takes a mass participatory form, as in Rwanda in 1994.

In some cases, then, genocide can be decided, planned, and ordered (even sometimes carried out, in secret) by very few perpetrators. But almost by definition, it claims very many victims. This key imbalance is not central to ethnic conflict, which, again in principle, may even be unbalanced the other way. One may imagine mass participation in ethnically recruited armies fighting wars but without targeting enemy civilians, inflicting military casualties but not producing massive numbers of victims. Even unarmed mass participation sometimes restrains violence on both sides, as in Hindu-Muslim communal divisions in South Asia. So, resolution of the definitional dilemmas of genocide must distinguish it from ethnic conflict. Perhaps genocide could be considered a subcategory of ethnic conflict, if all we need to define is a specific form that targets civilians for destruction. But not if we define ethnic conflict as a broad social phenomenon. Genocide, with its essential feature of perpetrator intent, need only be a political operation.

Likewise, again in principle, "ethnic cleansing" involves the "purification" of a territory, not necessarily of a population. This means the deportation, usually threatening but not necessarily violent, of an ethnic group from the territory. As Fein points out, "Ethnic cleansing requires either a protected reservation within a state or a free exit for the victims to escape; genocide precludes both protection and exit."[44] In practice, but not always, ethnic cleansing precedes and/or accompanies genocide, as in the case of the Khmer Rouge annihilation of the Vietnamese minority in Cambodia in 1975–79. Or, like the earlier Lon Nol regime's massacres that drove 300,000 Vietnamese from Cambodia in 1970, ethnic "cleansing" may be merely a precedent, or a phase in a burgeoning genocidal process. But it is a separate event.

The chapters of this book examine murderous processes that range across these various but conceptually distinct categories. They consider different definitions and interpretations that bring the international history of genocide in the twentieth century into comparative perspective. In part, this is a necessarily sociological undertaking. But chronological perspective is equally illuminating.

---

44 Helen Fein, "Ethnic Cleansing and Genocide: Definitional Evasion, Fog, Morass or Opportunity," paper presented at the Association of Genocide Scholars Conference, Minneapolis, June 10–12, 2001, 1–16, at 13.

EXTERMINATION BEFORE THE CENTURY OF GENOCIDE

The twentieth century introduced new features to the process of mass murder. The concept of total war that burst onto the historical scene, most notably in World War I, brought civilians into warfare in all-encompassing new ways, from mass participation in industrial mobilization at the rear, to the targeting of whole populations by opposing armies. As Niall Ferguson has put it, "at root, the First World War was democratic."[45] With or without elections, the age of nationalism brought entire peoples into new political life as both agents and victims. Technological developments such as mass production of arms, the proliferation of heavy weaponry, the development of poison gas and other vectors of large-scale destruction, lightning communication by radio and telegraph, and rapid mass transportation by rail and road all brought unspeakable violence into civilian life. And new forms of organization such as militarized bureaucracies, totalitarian party-states, and continental military strategies transformed entire peoples and nations into pawns in war games on political chessboards. Peasants became cannon fodder, workers cogs in machines, mothers bearers of child soldiers, children porters of the future, teachers skirmishers for national or international ideologies. All therefore became targets of opposing regimes, similarly composed as armies, with the same new capacity to deliver on their ambitions and threats.

But the twentieth century did not invent mass extermination of peoples. In the early modern world, the technologies used were inferior and the organization of the killing was not as state-controlled or as systematic. Modern totalitarian ideologies were also absent. However, the population losses were equally catastrophic. In Mexico, conquered by Spanish conquistadors in 1519, the estimated pre-Columbian population of 12 million or more fell to just over 1 million by 1600. Tzvetan Todorov has shown that as early as 1600 the Spanish had set in motion three overlapping processes that led to the deaths of millions of Indians. These included deliberate mass murder, death as a result of forced labor and maltreatment, and "microbe shock" by which the majority population was infected and died off. He suggests that the British and French acted similarly wherever they went. They did not wipe out as many as the Spanish did simply because their expansion at that crucial time was not as extensive.[46]

---

45 Niall Ferguson, *The Pity of War: Explaining World War I* (New York, 1999), 435.
46 Tzvetan Todorov, *La conquête de l'Amérique. La question de l'autre* (Paris, 1982), 170–71; English translation: *The Conquest of America*, trans. R. Howard (New York, 1985), 133.

Todorov writes of sixteenth-century Mexico: "If the word genocide has ever been applied accurately to a case, this is it." He distinguishes the Spanish massacres from the Aztecs' own human sacrificial murders. European massacres, he writes, were

inextricably linked to colonial wars, waged far from the metropolis. The more distant and alien the massacre victims, the better: they were exterminated without remorse, more or less as beasts. The individual identity of the massacre victim is by definition irrelevant (or this would be murder); there is neither the time nor the curiosity to know whom one is killing at any moment. In contrast to the sacrifices, the massacres were generally not proclaimed; their very occurrence was kept secret and denied. If the religious murder is a sacrifice, the massacre is an atheistic murder. . . . Far from central power, from royal law, all restraints disappear, and the social bonds, already loosened, snap, revealing not a primitive nature, the animal sleeping in all of us, but a modern being, full of the future itself, which retains no morality and which kills because and when it pleases. The "barbarity" of the Spanish is in no way atavistic, or animalistic. It is very human and announces the arrival of modern times.[47]

It is difficult to read Todorov's account and not identify deliberate policies of mass murder and genocide, although diseases escaping the control of the colonists caused most of the deaths.

North of the Rio Grande, the indigenous population in 1492 has been estimated at over 5 million.[48] By 1892 the survivors numbered only 500,000.[49] The colonies that became the United States saw massive brutality and even deliberate exterminations. In seventeenth-century Connecticut, hundreds of Pequots were slaughtered in more than one incident,[50] and a thousand Narragansetts were massacred in Rhode Island.[51]

A century later, during the Ottawa chief Pontiac's rebellion, British forces turned deliberately to biological warfare. Commander in chief General

---

47 Todorov, *La conquête de l'Amérique*, 170, 184–85. For the toll, see also Kirkpatrick Sale, *The Conquest of Paradise* (New York, 1990), 159–61; Mark Cocker, *Rivers of Blood, Rivers of Gold: Europe's Conquest of Indigenous Peoples* (New York, 1998), 111; and David E. Stannard, *American Holocaust: The Conquest of the New World* (New York, 1992), 267.

48 Stannard, *American Holocaust*, 266–68; Sale, *Conquest*, 316; James Wilson, *The Earth Shall Weep: A History of Native America* (New York, 1998), 20, notes extreme estimates of 2 million and 18 million.

49 Sale, *Conquest*, 349. Stannard, *American Holocaust*, 146, gives a figure of 250,000 for 1900.

50 English forces massacred 400 Indians in one village in 1634; at another, 500 Pequots were killed in one hour in 1637. See, e.g., Chandler Whipple, *The Indian and the White Man in Connecticut* (Stockbridge, Mass., 1972), 74; Stannard, *American Holocaust*, 115, quoting Richard Drinnon, *Facing West: The Metaphysics of Indian Hating and Empire Building* (Minneapolis, 1980), 46–47; Francis Jennings, *The Invasion of America: Indians, Colonialism, and the Cant of Conquest* (New York, 1976), ch. 13; and Alfred A. Cave, *The Pequot War* (Hanover, 1996), 148–53.

51 Wilson, *The Earth Shall Weep*, 95–97; Jennings, *Invasion*, 312; James D. Drake, *King Philip's War: Civil War in New England, 1675–1676* (Hanover, 1999); Russell Bourne, *The Red King's Rebellion: Racial Politics in New England, 1675–76* (New York, 1990).

Jeffrey Amherst urged a field officer in Philadelphia on July 7, 1763: "Could it not be contrived to Send the Small Pox among those Dissafected Tribes of Indians?" His officer, en route to relieve Fort Pitt in western Pennsylvania, replied: "I will try to Inoculate the Indians by means of blankets." On July 16, Amherst reiterated: "You will Do well to try to Inoculate the Indians by means of Blanketts, as well as to try Every other method that can serve to extirpate this Execrable Race." Fort Pitt had already anticipated these orders. Reporting on parleys with Delaware chiefs on June 24, a trader wrote: "[W]e gave them two Blankets and an Handkerchief out of the Small Pox Hospital. I hope it will have the desired effect." The military hospital records confirm that two blankets and handkerchiefs were "taken from people in the Hospital to Convey the Smallpox to the Indians." The Fort commander paid for these items, which he certified "were had for the uses above mentioned." Elizabeth Fenn documents "the eruption of epidemic smallpox" among Delaware and Shawnee Indians nearby, about the time the blankets were distributed.[52]

After independence from Britain, massacres of Indians accelerated in parts of the United States, especially the West.[53] In 1851 the governor of California, Peter Burnett, urged "a war of extermination . . . until the Indian becomes extinct." His successor also threatened "extermination to many of the tribes." From 1852 to 1860, California's indigenous population fell from 85,000 to 35,000.[54] Massacres proliferated and official bounties were paid for Indian scalps.[55] The *San Francisco Bulletin* commented: "Even the record of Spanish butcheries in Mexico and Peru has nothing so diabolical."[56]

A Minnesota newspaper announced in 1863: "The State reward for dead Indians has been increased to $200 for every red-skin sent to Purgatory. This

52 Elizabeth A. Fenn, "Biological Warfare in Eighteenth Century North America," *Journal of American History* 86, 4 (March 2000): 1552–80, at 1554–58.
53 See Anthony F. C. Wallace, *Jefferson and the Indians: The Tragic Fate of the First Americans* (Cambridge, Mass., 1999); Robert V. Remini, *Andrew Jackson and His Indian Wars* (New York, 2001); Anthony F. C. Wallace, *The Long Bitter Trail: Andrew Jackson and the Indians* (New York, 1993); and Gloria Jahoda, *The Trail of Tears: The Story of the American Indian Removals, 1813–1855* (New York, 1975).
54 Stannard, *American Holocaust*, 144–46.
55 U.S. troops perpetrated a massacre of Pomo Indians in the Clear Lake area in 1849; 2,000–3,000 Yana were almost annihilated between 1850 and 1872. In a genocide, the 12,000 Yuki were reduced to fewer than 200; several times a week, white killing parties would murder 50 or 60 Indians on a trip. Militiamen attacked the annual ritual gatherings of the Tolowa people, killing several hundred people in 1853, piling up "seven layers of bodies in the dance house when they burned it" the next year, and killing 70 Indians in "a battle at the mouth of the Smith River" in 1855. In 1859–61, bounties "in payment of Indian scalps" were advertised in local newspapers; after one massacre, "enormous claims were presented to the Legislature." In 1860, Major G. J. Raines reported that "Volunteers" had raided "the home of a band of friendly Indians" known as Indian Island, "murdering all the women and children" on the island. Wilson, *The Earth Shall Weep*, 228–33.
56 Ibid., 233.

sum is more than the dead bodies of all the Indians east of the Red River are worth."[57] Colorado's *Rocky Mountain News* proclaimed in the same year that the Indians "ought to be wiped from the face of the earth." When two soldiers were killed in a clash, the local military commander predicted that "now is but the commencement of war with this tribe, which must result in exterminating them." The *Rocky Mountain News* urged troops to "go for them, their lodges, squaws and all," and called again for "extermination of the red devils." Colonel John Chivington campaigned to "kill and scalp all, little and big." He stated his view that "Nits make lice," prefiguring a Nazi racialist metaphor. At Sand Creek on November 29, 1864, Chivington's troops slaughtered 100 to 500 unarmed women and children and scalped nearly all of them.[58]

When Cheyenne, Sioux, and Arapaho warriors attacked army posts, ranches, and wagon trains, the U.S. Army sent orders to "kill every male Indian over twelve years of age." General Sherman in 1866 urged "vindictive earnestness against the Sioux, even to their extermination, men, women and children."[59] In 1891 South Dakota's L. Frank Baum, author of *The Wizard of Oz*, called for "the total annihilation of the few remaining Indians." After Wounded Knee, when the U.S. Seventh Cavalry massacred 200 women and children, Baum recommended that "we had better, in order to protect our civilization, follow it up ... and wipe these untamed and untamable creatures from the face of the earth."[60] Theodore Roosevelt stated flatly: "I don't go so far as to think that the only good Indians are dead Indians, but I believe nine out of ten are, and I shouldn't like to inquire too closely into the case of the tenth." The extermination of Native Americans and seizure of their lands "was as ultimately beneficial as it was inevitable."[61]

In Australia, the Aboriginal population at the time of British settlement in 1788 is now estimated at around 750,000. About 20,000 Aborigines died fighting, the birthrate fell, and 600,000 perished from introduced diseases.[62] In 1867 a Queensland newspaper urged "a war of extermination" against

57 *Winona Daily Republican*, September 24, 1863. Chris Mato Nunpa provided a copy.
58 Stannard, *American Holocaust*, 129–34; Stan Hoig, *The Sand Creek Massacre* (Norman, Okla., 1961).
59 Wilson, *The Earth Shall Weep*, 277–78.
60 Stannard, *American Holocaust*, 126–27, quoting Baum, *Aberdeen Saturday Pioneer*, December 20, 1891.
61 Stannard, *American Holocaust*, 245.
62 The 750,000 figure is that of anthropologist Dr. Peter White and prehistorian Professor D. J. Mulvaney, quoted in *Sydney Morning Herald*, February 25, 1987. See also Noel Butlin, *Our Original Aggression: Aboriginal Populations of Southeastern Australia, 1788–1850* (Sydney, 1983). Henry Reynolds, *The Other Side of the Frontier* (Melbourne, 1982), 122, plausibly estimates the number of blacks who died violently at 20,000.

Aborigines as "the only policy to pursue."[63] In 1911 the survivors numbered 31,000.[64]

Thus, despite the absence of totalitarian ideologies and state control, the language of extermination was already common by the nineteenth century. It did not always signal purposeful genocide. In another British colony, the Irish Famine of 1846–51 killed a million people in peacetime, and another million emigrated. Britain provided minimal assistance, and none after October 1847. In 1849 British prime minister Russell refused Ireland the 100,000 pounds minimum considered necessary to prevent further possible starvation.[65] The earl of Clarendon, Britain's lord lieutenant of Ireland, decried what he called Westminster's "policy of extermination" of the Irish.[66]

Several decades later, the high tide of imperialism in Africa swamped the Congo. The rapid decimation of the African population by introduced diseases, while European overseers often worked the survivors to death, resembled the early impact of Spanish rule on Hispaniola and Mexico. Adam Hochschild writes that smallpox left "village after village full of dead bodies." Sleeping sickness killed half a million people in 1901 alone. "When a village or a district failed to supply its quota of rubber or fought back . . . soldiers or rubber company 'sentries' often killed everyone they could find." Belgian district commissioner Jules Jacques called for "absolute submission . . . or complete extermination." The Congo's population fell by half, according to estimates – 10 million died from 1885 to 1920.[67]

Not far away to the south, in 1904, General Lothar von Trotha was appointed commander of the German colonial forces confronting the rebellious Herero nation in South West Africa. Von Trotha proclaimed: "I shall annihilate the revolting tribes with rivers of blood and rivers of gold." He deployed 5,000 soldiers to surround the hills where the surviving 60,000 Herero people and their herds had gathered. The German forces

---

63 Henry Reynolds, *Why Weren't We Told?* (Melbourne, 1999), 119, quoting the editor of the *Peak Downs Telegram* in Clermont, Queensland.

64 Colin Tatz, *Genocide in Australia*, Australian Institute of Aboriginal and Torres Strait Islander Studies, Research Discussion Paper No. 8 (Canberra, 1999), 9. The 1921 census produced a figure of 62,000 Aborigines. C. D. Rowley, *The Destruction of Aboriginal Society* (Ringwood, Victoria, 1972), 382.

65 Cormac O'Grada, *Black '47 and Beyond: The Great Irish Famine* (Princeton, 1999), 77, 83.

66 George Villiers, Earl of Clarendon and Lord Lieutenant of Ireland, in a letter to British Prime Minister Lord John Russell on April 26, 1849, denounced Britain's refusal of aid: "I don't think there is another legislature in Europe that would disregard such sufferings as now exist in the west of Ireland or coldly persist in a policy of extermination." The bishop of Derry, in a public letter dated April 9, 1847, had referred to the famine as "wholesale systems of extermination."

67 Adam Hochschild, *King Leopold's Ghost: A Story of Greed, Terror and Heroism in Colonial Africa* (Boston, 1998), 226–33.

seized the waterholes, and sprung their trap. The Herero had little choice but to head into the Omaheke desert. Pursuing German troops massacred almost everyone they found, including women and children (on von Trotha's orders), and poisoned the waterholes in the desert. On October 1, von Trotha issued an "extermination order" (*Vernichtungs Befehl*), which proclaimed: "Any Herero found within the German borders with or without a gun, with or without cattle, will be shot. I shall no longer receive any women or children; I will drive them back to their people or I will shoot them. This is my decision for the Herero people."[68] Only 1,000 survivors crossed the desert to reach British Bechuanaland alive.

The twentieth century had begun.

68 Cocker, *Rivers of Blood, Rivers of Gold*, 333.

PART I

Genocide and Modernity

2

Twentieth-Century Genocides

Underlying Ideological Themes from Armenia to East Timor

BEN KIERNAN

The perpetrators of the 1915 Armenian genocide, the Holocaust during World War II, and the Cambodian genocide of 1975–79 were, respectively, militarists, Nazis, and communists. All three events were unique in important ways. Yet racism – Turkish, German, and Khmer – was a key component of the ideology of each regime. Racism was also conflated with religion. Although all three regimes were atheistic, each particularly targeted religious minorities (Christians, Jews, and Muslims). All three regimes also attempted to expand their territories into a contiguous heartland ("Turkestan," "Lebensraum," and "Kampuchea Krom"), mobilizing primordial racial rights and connections to the land. Consistent with this, all three regimes idealized their ethnic peasantry as the true "national" class, the ethnic soil from which the new state grew.

These ideological elements – race, religion, expansion, and cultivation – make an explosive mixture. Most also appear, in different colors and compounds, in the chemistry of other cases of genocide, including the Indonesian massacres of Communists in 1965–66 and in East Timor from 1975 to 1999, and also in the Bosnian and Rwandan genocides of the early 1990s.

RELIGION AND RACE

In colonial genocides, racial divisions are usually clear-cut, overriding even religious fraternity. The first genocide of the twentieth century pitted the German military machine against the Herero and Nama peoples of South West Africa, whose leaders were mostly Christian-educated.[1] Two days after

---

1 Mark Cocker, *Rivers of Gold, Rivers of Blood: Europe's Conquest of Indigenous Peoples* (New York, 1998), 304, 314–15, 335.

issuing his 1904 "extermination order" against the Herero, General Lothar von Trotha wrote to the Berlin General Staff: "My knowledge of many central African peoples, Bantu and others, convinces me that the Negro will never submit to a treaty but only to naked force. . . . This uprising is and remains the beginning of a racial war."[2]

In other cases, race and religion have played important, intertwined roles. The Young Turk ideologue Yusuf Akçura asserted in 1904 that "the Turks within the Ottoman realms would unify quite tightly with both religious and racial bonds – more tightly than with just religious ones." He added: "The great majority of those Turks whose union is possible are Muslim. . . . Islam could be an important element in the formation of a great Turkish nationality." But because "the general trend of our era involves races," for Islam "to perform this service in the unification of Turks it must change in a manner that accepts the emergence of nations within it. . . . Therefore, it is only through the union of religions with race, and through religions as buttressing and even serving ethnic groups, that they can preserve their political and societal importance." Akçura rejected multinational Ottomanism and argued that Pan-Islamism "would split into Turkish and non-Turkish components." Looking to "a world of Turkish-ness," Akçura praised "the brotherhood born of race."[3] The Armenian genocide, which coincided with Turkish massacres of Greeks, can be portrayed in part as an attempt to eliminate Christian non-Turks from a newly defined Turkish Muslim nation, but the racial element is significant.

Pol Pot's Cambodia perpetrated genocide against several ethnic groups, systematically dispersed national minorities by force, and forbade the use of minority and foreign languages.[4] It also banned the practice of religion. The Khmer Rouge repressed Islam, Christianity, and Buddhism, but its fiercest extermination campaign was directed at the ethnic Cham Muslim minority.[5]

In the German case, Saul Friedlander argues, antisemitism "gives Nazism its *sui generis* character. . . . the Jewish problem was at the center, the very

---

2 Jon Bridgman and Leslie J. Worley, "Genocide of the Hereros," in Samuel Totten, William S. Parsons, and Israel W. Charny (eds.), *Century of Genocide* (New York, 1995), 18–19.

3 Yusuf Akçura, *Uç Tarz-I Siyaset* (Three kinds of politics) (Istanbul, 1911). Barak Salmoni kindly provided a copy of his English translation and preface.

4 United Nations, AS, General Assembly, Security Council, A/53/850, S/1999/231, March 16, 1999, Annex, *Report of the Group of Experts for Cambodia Established Pursuant to General Assembly Resolution 52/135*; Ben Kiernan, "The Ethnic Element in the Cambodian Genocide," in Daniel Chirot and Martin E. P. Seligman (eds.), *Ethnopolitical Warfare: Causes, Consequences, and Possible Solutions* (Washington, D.C., 2001), 83–91.

5 See Ben Kiernan, *The Pol Pot Regime: Race, Power and Genocide in Cambodia under the Khmer Rouge, 1975–1979* (New Haven, 1996), 251–88, 427–31.

essence of the system."[6] In the words of Hitler's October 1941 proclamation, "The Jewish question takes priority over all other matters." Gerald Fleming notes Hitler's "unlimited and pathological hatred for the Jews, the very core of the dictator's *Weltanschauung*."[7] But he also makes a distinction between two different aspects of Hitler's hatred – "the one a traditionally inspired and instinctively affirmed anti-Semitism that due to its racialist/biological component took a particularly rigid form; and the other *a flexible, goal-oriented* anti-Semitism that was pragmatically superimposed on the first."[8]

GENOCIDAL PRAGMATISM

This political flexibility is a feature of other cases too. Genocidal regimes, radical and often unstable, need to make pragmatic as well as ideological decisions, in order to maintain or secure their grip on power. Genocidal power often proves deadly to dissenters, even those of the supposedly privileged or protected race. This was not true in the case of the Armenian genocide, given the small number of civilian victims from the Turkish ethnic majority. However, the Serb perpetrators of the Bosnian genocide regarded dissident fellow Serbs as a special threat, and treated them with the same brutality as the more numerous Muslim victims.[9] In Rwanda, too, the first victims of "Hutu Power" in 1994 were the Hutu moderate politicians, and thousands of Hutu in the south of the country were killed for lacking zeal to exterminate Tutsi.[10] In absolute numbers, most of the victims of the Khmer Rouge regime were from Cambodia's ethnic Khmer majority, though minorities, again, were disproportionately targeted. Under Nazism, Jews were the largest single group to be exterminated, but the numerous other victims were not limited to "non-Aryans" such as Gypsies and Slavs. Hitler also targeted German homosexuals, communists, liberals, trade unionists, and other oppositionists. In the Nazi purge of German culture, books and paintings were burned, literary and film criticism abolished, and modern music banned.[11] The day after the *Kristallnacht* pogrom, Hitler speculated that "he might one day exterminate the intellectual classes in Germany if they no longer proved to be of use."[12] Intellectuals of the Khmer and Hutu

---

6 Introduction to Gerald Fleming, *Hitler and the Final Solution* (Berkeley, 1984), xxxii.
7 Ibid., 31, 69.   8 Ibid., 29 (emphasis added).
9 Norman Cigar, *Genocide in Bosnia: The Policy of "Ethnic Cleansing"* (College Station, Tex., 1985), 83–85.
10 Gérard Prunier, *The Rwanda Crisis: History of a Genocide* (New York, 1997), 231, 249–50; Alison Des Forges, *"Leave None to Tell the Story": Genocide in Rwanda* (New York, 1999), 19.
11 Jeffrey Richards, *Visions of Yesterday* (London, 1973), 292.
12 Richard Evans, *In Hitler's Shadow* (New York, 1989), 81, citing Ernst Nolte.

majorities were also targeted in both Cambodia and Rwanda.[13] The "rejection of the individual in favour of the race"[14] did not privilege individuals for their membership of a preferred race but on the contrary it made them vulnerable to measures to "protect" it.

DEFINING RACE

Nazi "eugenics" also eliminated 70,000 Germans with hereditary illnesses.[15] The late George L. Mosse pointed out the close link, spanning the races, between this euthanasia and the destruction of Jews: "Putting euthanasia into practice meant that the Nazis took the idea of 'unworthy' life seriously, and a life so defined was characterized by lack of productivity and degenerate outward appearance," while similar "ideas of unproductivity and physical appearance were both constantly applied to Jews."[16] Richard Evans adds, "It was not these people's racial identity that marked them out for elimination, but their supposed biological inferiority, irrespective of race."[17] By the same token, Gypsies, although defined in 1935 as "alien to the German species," were in the early years of the war "not persecuted on 'racial' grounds, but on the basis of an 'asocial and criminal past' and a security threat." Some of the more assimilated, known as Sinti, "even served in the armed forces until the order came in 1942 that all Gypsies must be sent to Auschwitz."[18]

"One can see how confused Nazi racism was," Yehuda Bauer comments, "when Jewish grandparents were defined by religion rather than so-called racial criteria."[19] The November 14, 1935, "Nuremberg law" defined a "mixed-blood" Jew (*Mischling*) as "anyone who is descended from one or two grandparents who are fully Jewish as regards race. . . . A grandparent is deemed fully Jewish without further ado, if he has belonged to the Jewish religious community." Raul Hilberg adds that "a person was to be considered Jewish if he had three or four Jewish grandparents. . . . If an individual had

---

13 Prunier, *The Rwanda Crisis*, 249–50.   14 Richards, *Visions of Yesterday*, 289.

15 "The euthanasia program killed some 70,000 people . . . ," quotation from George L. Mosse, *Towards the Final Solution: A History of European Racism* (Madison, 1987), 218, reprinted as "Eugenics and Nazi Race Theory in Practice," in Frank Chalk and Kurt Jonassohn (eds.), *The History and Sociology of Genocide: Analyses and Case Studies* (New Haven, 1990), 356. See also Henry Friedlander, *The Origins of Nazi Genocide: From Euthanasia to the Final Solution* (Chapel Hill, 1995).

16 Mosse, "Eugenics and Nazi Race Theory in Practice," 356.

17 Evans, *In Hitler's Shadow*, 79.

18 Gabrielle Tyrnauer, " 'Mastering the Past': Germans and Gypsies," in Chalk and Jonassohn, *The History and Sociology of Genocide*, 366–77, at 368, 376, 377.

19 Y. Bauer, "The Evolution of Nazi Jewish Policy, 1933–1938," in Chalk and Jonassohn, *The History and Sociology of Genocide*, 345.

two Jewish grandparents, he would be classified as Jewish only if he himself belonged to the Jewish religion [or] was married to a Jewish person. The critical factor in every case was in the first instance the religion of the grandparents."[20]

In Cambodia, Khmer Rouge racism was even more inconsistent.[21] There was no attempt at "scientific" precision, but biological metaphors abounded. The Khmer Rouge considered its captive urban populations "subhuman" (*anoupracheachun*), the same term the Nazis had used for conquered Slavic *Untermenschen*.[22] Democratic Kampuchea referred to its enemies as "microbes," "pests buried within," and traitors "boring in."[23] The Germans had talked of "vermin" and "lice."[24] Pol Pot considered his revolution the only "clean" one in history, just as the Nazis "cleaned" occupied areas of Jews. Both regimes were obsessed with the concept of racial "purity."[25] Pol Pot called himself the "Original Khmer,"[26] but his preoccupations had precedents. And they prefigured biological depictions by Bosnian Serbs of the "malignant disease" of Islam threatening to "infect" Europe,[27] and by the Hutu Power regime in Rwanda, which described Tutsi as "cockroaches" (*inyenzi*), requiring a "big clean-up."[28]

TERRITORIAL EXPANSIONISM

Genocidal regimes often proclaim a need to "purify" not only a race but a territory. Prior to World War I, the Young Turks dreamed of a

---

20 See "The Anatomy of the Holocaust," in Chalk and Jonassohn, *The History and Sociology of Genocide*, 348, 358–66, at 360–61.

21 See Kiernan, "The Ethnic Element in the Cambodian Genocide," 83–91.

22 François Ponchaud, *Cambodia Year Zero* (London, 1978), 109 (*anoupracheachun*); on the Nazi term *Untermenschen*, see, e.g., Hélène Carrère D'Encausse, *Stalin: Order through Terror* (New York, 1981), 91.

23 D. P. Chandler, "A Revolution in Full Spate: Communist Party Policy in Democratic Kampuchea, December 1976," in D. Ablin and M. Hood (eds.), *The Cambodian Agony* (Armonk, N.Y., 1987), 129; and *Ieng Sary's Regime: A Diary of the Khmer Rouge Foreign Ministry, 1976–79*, translated by Phat Kosal and Ben Kiernan, Cambodian Genocide Program, Yale University and Documentation Center of Cambodia (1998), 30 <www.yale.edu/cgp>.

24 Fleming, *Hitler and the Final Solution*, xxxv, quoting Ernst Nolte.

25 The Law for the Protection of German Blood and German Honor, passed on September 15, 1935, claims that "the purity of German blood is a prerequisite for the continued existence of the German people." Quoted by Bauer, "The Evolution of Nazi Jewish Policy, 1933–1938," 348. The horrendous 1978 massacres in Cambodia's Eastern Zone were launched with the call to "purify . . . the masses of the people." An earlier example is in *Tung Padevat* 9–10 (September–October 1976), noting the need for a rural cooperative to be "purified."

26 *Khemara Nisit* (Paris), no. 14 (August 1952).

27 Cigar, *Genocide in Bosnia*, 31, 100.

28 Prunier, *The Rwanda Crisis*, 54, 171, 188, 200; Des Forges, *"Leave None to Tell the Story,"* 51, 249–51, 405–6. See also Scott Strauss, "Organic Purity and the Role of Anthropology in Cambodia and Rwanda," *Patterns of Prejudice* 35, 2 (2001): 47–62.

"Pan-Turanian" empire of all Turkic-speaking peoples. They initially chose to name their country "Turkestan," with its irredentist Central Asian connotations. In 1904 Yusuf Akçura questioned whether "the true power of the Ottoman state" lay "in preserving its current geographical shape." He instead called for "the unification of the Turks – who share language, race, customs, and even for the most part, religion, and who are spread throughout the majority of Asia and Eastern Europe." This meant "the Turks' formation of a vast political nationality . . . from the peoples of the great race" encompassing Central Asian Turks and Mongols "from Peking to Montenegro."[29]

This goal was shelved for a time, but in 1917–18 the collapse of the opposing tsarist armies in the Caucasus allowed a revival of Pan-Turanianism. Young Turk armies pushed into Russian Armenia where 300,000 survivors of the 1915 genocide had taken refuge, "extending the genocide of Ottoman Armenians to the Russian Armenians."[30] In the words of the allied German military attaché von Lossow, this involved "the total extermination of the Armenians in Transcaucasia also," in what he called the Young Turks' attempt "to destroy all Armenians, not only in Turkey, but also outside Turkey." After the defeat and fall of the Young Turk regime, Kemalist forces again invaded the fledgling Republic of Armenia in 1920. The minister of foreign affairs in Ankara instructed the commander in chief of the Eastern Front Army: "It is indispensable that Armenia be annihilated politically and physically."[31] Purification and expansion went hand in hand.

In *Mein Kampf*, Hitler proclaimed that "for Germany . . . the only possibility of carrying out a healthy territorial policy lay in the acquisition of new land in Europe itself. . . . it could be obtained by and large only at the expense of Russia, and this meant that the new Reich must again set itself on the march along the road of the Teutonic knights of old, to obtain by the German sword sod for the German plow and daily bread for the nation. . . . We take up where we broke off six hundred years ago."[32] Holocaust historian Christopher Browning has pointed out that, as with the expansionism accompanying the Armenian genocide, the Nazi "achievement of *Lebensraum* through the invasion of Russia and the Final Solution to the Jewish Question through systematic mass murder were intimately connected."[33] Hitler

---

29 Akçura, *Uç Tarz-I Siyaset.*
30 Vahakn N. Dadrian, *The History of the Armenian Genocide* (Oxford, 1995; rev. ed., 1997), 349.
31 Ibid., 349, 358.
32 Adolf Hitler, *Mein Kampf* (Boston, 1943), 139f., 654, quoted in Deborah Dwork and Robert Jan van Pelt, *Auschwitz: 1270 to the Present* (New York, 1996), 82.
33 Christopher R. Browning, *The Path to Genocide: Essays on Launching the Final Solution* (New York, 1992), 26. For valuable further discussion, see Michael Burleigh, *Germany Turns Eastwards: A Study*

initially envisaged "three belts of population – German, Polish and Jewish – from west to east." Pragmatic considerations gave first priority to deporting rural Poles to make way for German settlers, before expelling or exterminating Jews.[34]

Hitler's deputy Heinrich Himmler wrote in his diary in 1919, at the age of nineteen: "I work for my ideal of German womanhood with whom, some day, I will live my life in the east and fight my battles as a German far from beautiful Germany."[35] According to Rudolf Hoess, in 1930 Himmler again "spoke of the forcible conquest of large sections of the East."[36] Hoess recalled: "Himmler considered his true life's work to be the spread of the continued existence of the German people, secured by a superior peasantry on a healthy economic basis and provided with a sufficient amount of land. All his plans for settlements, even long before the assumption of power, were directed to this objective. He never made a secret of the fact that this could be accomplished only if land was seized by force in the East."[37]

In 1977–78 the Khmer Rouge regime launched attacks against all three of Cambodia's neighbors: Vietnam, Laos, and Thailand. The Pol Pot leadership harbored irredentist ambitions to reunite Cambodia with ancient Khmer-speaking areas that had formed part of the medieval Angkor empire.[38] On the sea border with Vietnam, the Khmer Rouge regime unilaterally declared a new expanded frontier line to which Hanoi objected. Internal Khmer Rouge documents also reveal a demand for "changes at some points in the present [land] border line." In speeches in various parts of Cambodia throughout 1977–78, as all Vietnamese residents were being hunted down for extermination, numerous Khmer Rouge officials announced their ambition to "retake Kampuchea Krom," Vietnam's Mekong Delta.[39]

The 1986 "Serbian Memorandum," which prepared much of the ideological basis for the genocide in Bosnia, urged "the establishment of the full national integrity of the Serbian people, regardless of which republic

---

of Ostforschung in the Third Reich (Cambridge, 1988), and Klaus Hildebrand, *The Foreign Policy of the Third Reich* (Berkeley, 1973).

34 Browning, *The Path to Genocide*, 8–9, 12–13, 22.

35 Quoted in Peter Padfield, *Himmler* (London, 1990), 13.

36 Rudolf Hoess Aufzeichnungen, Institut für Zeitgeschichte, Munich, F 13/5, p. 279/283. Himmler returned to this theme nine years later in a speech to SS leaders a month after the invasion of Poland, where ethnic German warrior-settlers would hold off "Slavdom." Michael Burleigh, *The Third Reich: A New History* (New York, 2000), 446–47. See also Nicholas Goodrick-Clarke, *The Occult Roots of Nazism* (New York, 1992), ch. 14.

37 Rudolf Hoess Aufzeichnungen, Institut für Zeitgeschichte, Munich, F 13/5, p. 295.

38 See Kiernan, *The Pol Pot Regime*, 102–25, 357–69, 386–90. For evidence of Khmer Rouge irredentism against Thailand and Laos, see ibid., 366–69.

39 Ibid., 360–66.

or province it inhabits." Five years later Slobodan Milosevic warned that "it is always the powerful who dictate what the borders will be, never the weak. Thus, we must be powerful." Just as Hitler in 1939 had threatened the Jews with annihilation if war broke out, Bosnian Serb leader Radovan Karadzic asserted in 1991 that Bosnia's Muslim community would "disappear from the face of the Earth" if it decided to "opt for war" by choosing an independent Bosnia-Herzegovina. He added later that "Muslims are the most threatened, . . . not only in the physical sense . . . rather, this is also the beginning of the end of their existence as a nation." Karadzic added in 1992: "The time has come for the Serbian people to organize itself as a totality, without regard to the administrative [existing] borders." The next year, the speaker of the Bosnian Serb parliament proclaimed the need "to grasp our ethnic space," while Belgrade's army chief of staff referred to "our *lebensraum* in Bosnia."[40] Again we see genocide and expansionism, marching hand in hand.

For their part, the Hutu chauvinist leaders in Rwanda advocated a "final solution to the ethnic problem" there.[41] For years their world view had also focused on territorial issues. The genocidal *akazu*, or "little house," was a secret clanlike network of extremist Hutu officials from the northwest of Rwanda, mostly from the Bushiru region incorporated into the kingdom of Rwanda ("Tutsified") only in the 1920s.[42] The 1973 coup by Juvénal Habyarimana, married to a Bushiru princess, initially brought "northern revenge" by "marginalised, fiercely Hutu, anti-royalist Rwanda" over the more liberal and tolerant Hutu communities of southern Rwanda.[43] After Habyarimana's death in a plane crash on April 6, 1994, these *akazu* chauvinists conducted the genocide of Tutsi, until their overthrow four months later. Gérard Prunier describes them as "'the real northwesterners,' the representatives of the 'small Rwanda' which had conquered the big one."[44] Their campaign against the Tutsi and more pluralist southern Hutu suggests that they aimed to extend throughout Rwanda the ethnic Hutu purity of the defunct northwest kingdom of Bushiru. After the regime's overthrow in July 1994, the genocidal Interahamwe forces "not only continued to kill Tutsis in Rwanda but also targeted Banyarwanda Tutsis living in Eastern Congo." These Hutu militias ranged across Kivu province of Congo, massacred the local Tutsi cattle herders known as Banyamulenge, and also "sent elements into the Masisi plateau to gain support amongst the Banyamasisi

40 Cigar, *Genocide in Bosnia*, 23, 40, 42, 63, 79.   41 Prunier, *The Rwanda Crisis*, 200–1, 221–22.
42 Des Forges, *"Leave None to Tell the Story,"* 44; Prunier, *The Rwanda Crisis*, 19, 86.
43 Prunier, *The Rwanda Crisis*, 86, 124.   44 Ibid., 222, 167–68.

Hutu and to eliminate the Banyamasisi Tutsi."[45] Prunier explains that in this way the Interahamwe could also "carve out for themselves a kind of 'Hutuland' which could be either a base for the reconquest of Rwanda or, if that failed, a new Rwanda outside the old one."[46] Meanwhile, Hutu forces from Rwanda joined those in Burundi, and "increasingly operated together against the common ethnic enemy," the Tutsi, who did likewise.[47] Again, a genocidal conflict became an international one.

NARRATIVES OF TERRITORIAL DECLINE

Real or perceived geographic diminution is often the backdrop to aggressive expansionism accompanied by genocide. The decline of the Ottoman Empire from the sixteenth century made fear of further territorial diminution a political preoccupation. By 1625 an Ottoman official warned that without defensive action, "the Europeans will rule over the lands of Islam." An Ottoman official cautioned in 1822: "Let us ... not cede an inch of our territory."[48] But financial collapse in 1874 begat uprisings in Bosnia and Herzegovina, and by Bulgarians, Serbs, and Montenegrins in 1876; the Russo-Turkish War followed in 1877–78, the British and French replaced Turkish overlordship in Egypt in 1879, and in 1896 the Cretan insurrection and Greco-Turkish war led to the Turkish evacuation of Crete in 1898. Yusuf Akçura wrote in 1904: "Russia was in pursuit of possessing the Bosphorus Straits, Anatolia and Iraq, Istanbul, the Balkans and the Holy Land ... [renewing] the age-old competition between Russia and England for [control of] the Islamic collective and the sacred Islamic lands."[49] As historian James Reid puts it, "the collapse of the Ottoman Empire deprived the ruling elite of any security it once had and created a condition of paranoia."[50] This same period saw the first major massacres of Armenians, in which 100,000 to 200,000 perished in Anatolia in 1894–96. The Ottoman collapse accelerated with the Austrian annexation of Bosnia and Herzegovina in 1908, the declaration of Bulgarian independence in 1909 and revolts in Albania in 1910–12, the Italian seizure of Tripoli in 1911–12,

---

45 LTC Rick Orth, "Rwanda's Hutu Extremist Genocidal Insurgency: An Eyewitness Perspective," 41pp., unpublished manuscript (2000), 15, also citing Jeff Drumtra, "Where the Ethnic Cleansing Goes Unchecked," *Washington Post*, weekly edition, July 22–28, 1996, 22.
46 Prunier, *The Rwanda Crisis*, 381.　　　47 Ibid., 378–79.
48 Bernard Lewis, *The Emergence of Modern Turkey* (Oxford, 1968), 25–38, 325, 332.
49 Akçura, *Uç Tarz-I Siyaset*.
50 James J. Reid, "Philosophy of State-Subject Relations, Ottoman Concepts of Tyranny, and the Demonization of Subjects: Conservative Ottomanism as a Source of Genocidal Behaviour, 1821–1918," in L. Chorbajian and G. Shirinian (eds.), *Studies in Comparative Genocide* (London, 1999), 75–78.

and the Balkan Wars of 1912–13. Now "only the Armenians and Arabs" remained as Ottoman subject nationalities.[51] At the outbreak of World War I, the empire comprised little more than Anatolia and the Arab countries directly to its south. In 1915 the Young Turks launched the genocide of Armenians.

For his part, Hitler projected himself as the ruler of a constricted country as a result of World War I. In an extraordinary speech in August 1939, he described Germany and Poland "with rifles cocked": "We are faced with the harsh alternative of striking now or of *certain annihilation sooner or later*." "I have taken risks," he went on, "in occupying the Rhineland when the generals wanted me to pull back, in taking Austria, the Sudetenland, and the rest of Czechoslovakia."[52] Thus, even as he recited his list of territorial gains, Hitler was still proclaiming the threat of Germany's "certain annihilation." This was much less rational than the Ottoman fears. Striking is Hitler's tactical assumption that German *territorial* stability was unachievable. Failure to expand meant annihilation. Actual expansion was denied or dismissed as insufficient to deter enemies.

Pol Pot's regime, too, saw Cambodia's post-Angkorean geographic decline as a millennial theme, uninterrupted by the twentieth-century fact of territorial recovery.[53] The Khmer Rouge view of the past simply stressed "2,000 years of exploitation," in which "royal and feudal authorities" sold off the national territory to foreigners.[54] In his major public speech in 1977, Pol Pot urged his people to "prevent the constant loss of Cambodia's territory."[55] This required both "tempering" (*lot dam*) the country's population to become hardened purveyors of violence and reconquering long-lost territory from Vietnam, such as "Kampuchea Krom."[56] The next year, Khmer Rouge radio exhorted its listeners not only to "purify" the "masses of the people" of Cambodia, but also to kill thirty Vietnamese for every fallen Cambodian, thus sacrificing "only 2 million troops to crush the 50 million Vietnamese, and we would still have 6 million people left."[57]

51 Feroz Ahmad, *The Young Turks* (Oxford, 1969), 154, quoted in Dadrian, *History*, 192.
52 Anthony Read and David Fisher, *The Deadly Embrace: Hitler, Stalin, and the Nazi-Soviet Pact, 1939–1941* (New York, 1988), 241–42 (emphasis added). For an explanation of the psychology of the Nazi belief in "total annihilation," see Elizabeth Wirth Marvick (ed.), *Psychopolitical Analysis: Selected Writings of Nathan Leites* (New York, 1977), 284–85.
53 See Ben Kiernan, "Myth, Nationalism, and Genocide," *Journal of Genocide Research* 3, 2 (June 2001): 187–206; Anthony Barnett, "Cambodia Will Never Disappear," *New Left Review* 180 (1990): 101–25.
54 Kiernan, *The Pol Pot Regime*, 360.   55 Pol Pot's September 27, 1977, speech.
56 See Kiernan, *The Pol Pot Regime*, 103–5, 357–69, 425–27.
57 BBC, *Summary of World Broadcasts*, FE/5813/A3/2, May 15, 1978, Phnom Penh Radio, May 10, 1978.

The leaders of the Young Turks, Nazis, and Khmer Rouge came disproportionately from "lost" territories beyond the shrinking homeland. The
Young Turks' four ideological leaders included a Russian Tatar and a Kurd
(Yusuf Akçura and Ziya Gokalp) and two Azeris; political leaders Talaat and
Enver were from Bulgaria and Albania, while Dr. Nazim and two others
came from "obscure Balkan origins." In the Nazi leadership, *Volksdeutsch*
from Austria and central Europe were disproportionately represented, including Hitler, Rosenberg, Hess, Röhm, Goering, and Kaltenbrunner.[58]
Of the top three Khmer Rouge leaders, Pol Pot's deputy Nuon Chea grew
up in Thai-occupied Battambang province, and Ieng Sary was a Khmer
Krom born in southern Vietnam – as was Khmer Rouge defense and security chief Son Sen.[59] These leaders likely heightened the sense of territorial
threat faced by their regimes.

The Bosnian Serb military commander, General Ratko Mladic, also complained that Serbs were threatened with extinction. In 1992–93, he claimed
that German, Croatian, and Muslim goals included "the complete annihilation of the Serbian people." Mladic added: "We Serbs always wait until it
reaches our throats. Only then do we retaliate. . . . In the thirteenth century,
we were more numerous than the Germans. Now, there are just over twelve
million of us, while they have grown to one hundred fifty million."[60] The
Serbian governor of Herzegovina promised to "correct the injustice with
regard to the borders which Josip Broz [Tito] drew with his dirty finger.
He gave Serbian lands cheaply to the Croatians and Muslims." It would be
"pure Serbian masochism to keep Broz's borders." The Serb response, then,
was mere self-defense, in Mladic's words: "I have not conquered anything
in this war. I only liberated that which was always Serbian, although I am
far from liberating all that is really Serbian. . . . Even Trieste [Italy] is an old
Serbian city."[61]

IDEALIZATION OF CULTIVATION

The myth of racial victimization and territorial diminution are not the only
metaphysical preoccupations of the genocidal world view. Idealization of the
peasant cultivator has been another key element. Enver Pasha claimed that
his Young Turk army had drawn "all its strength from the rural class," adding

58 R. Hrair Dekmejian, "Determinants of Genocide: Armenians and Jews as Case Studies," in Richard
   G. Hovannisian (ed.), *The Armenian Genocide in Perspective* (New Brunswick, N.J., 1986), 92–93.
59 Kiernan, "Myth, Nationalism and Genocide," 187–206.
60 Cigar, *Genocide in Bosnia*, 78. Cigar comments aptly: "This dualistic self-view of superiority and
   accompanying vulnerability bordering on paranoia can be a particularly explosive mix."
61 Ibid., 81, 43–44.

that "all who seek to enrich those who do not work should be destroyed."[62] Before World War I the word "Turk" itself, while meaning "Muslim" in the West, had a connotation in Turkey of "rural" or "mountain people." The Ottoman cities of Istanbul and Izmir, on the other hand, comprised majorities – 56 and 62 percent respectively – of non-Turks: Armenians, Greeks, and Jews.[63] In 1920–21, Enver Pasha briefly flirted with Bolshevism; it is possible that he had long seen such urban ethnic communities as capitalist parasites on the Turkish peasant body.

The leading Young Turk ideologue, Yusuf Akçura, considered the peasantry "the basic matter of the Turkish nation" and the group requiring greatest assistance,[64] a view he combined with his ethnic-based Turkism and his Pan-Turkist territorial irredentism.[65] The leading organizer of the 1915 genocide, Talaat Pasha, became first honorary president of the farmers' association in 1914–16.[66] According to Feroz Ahmad, "in their first flush of glory and while they were at their most radical," the Young Turk leaders had proposed "measures intended to lighten the burden of the peasant," including land distribution, low-interest loans, tithe reductions, agricultural schools, and a cadastral system, and "promised to encourage the development of agriculture in every way possible." It was considered "vital to save the peasant from the feudal lords." Stressing "the importance of the small farmer," Young Turk intellectuals also urged cooperativization.[67] However, the political leadership quickly encountered the stranglehold of the notables in rural areas; the top 5 percent of landowners owned 65 percent of the land. The Young Turks then "took the path of least resistance," accommodating landlord power for "the salvation of the empire" and pursuing only modest reforms to modernize and commercialize agriculture. They promoted "ambitious irrigation projects" including creation of "another Egypt" in Cilicia, and even envisaged eventual "nationalization of agriculture and the joint cultivation of the soil."[68] Dr. Nazim, an architect of the Armenian genocide, boasted in 1917 that "our peasants, who made fortunes through the unwarranted rise in food prices, can pay three liras for a pair of stockings for their daughters." In fact, most peasants suffered increased forced labor

62 Gregor Alexinsky, "Bolshevism and the Turks," *Quarterly Review* 239 (1923): 183–97, at 185–86.
63 Ronald Grigor Suny, "Ideology or Social Ecology: Rethinking the Armenian Genocide," paper presented to the conference on State-Organized Terror, Michigan State University, Lansing, November 1988, 24.
64 *Türk Yurdu*, xii, 1333/1917, p. 3521, quoted in Feroz Ahmad, "The Agrarian Policy of the Young Turks, 1908–1918," in *Economie et societés dans l'empire Ottoman*, Editions CNRS, *Colloques internationaux* no. 601 (Paris, 1983), 287–88.
65 Akçura, *Uç Tarz-I Siyaset*.
66 Ahmad, "The Agrarian Policy of the Young Turks," 284 n. 34.
67 Ibid., 276, 278, 286.   68 Ibid., 279, 282–83, 286.

and land expropriations under the Young Turks, but the regime's ideological claim to foster the peasantry and cultivation is clear.[69]

In Germany, National Socialism's precursor, the *völkisch* tradition, was "essentially a product of late eighteenth-century romanticism."[70] Nazi nationalism sprang directly from the concept of "blood and soil" (*Blut und Boden*). This sought strength for the *Herrenvolk* (master race) in "the sacredness of the German soil ... which could not be confined by artificial boundaries." And in peasant virtues. Hitler declared the farmer "the most important participant" in the Nazi revolution.[71] In *Mein Kampf*, he linked German peasant farmland with German racial characteristics, adding: "A firm stock of small and middle peasants has been at all times the best protection against social evils." He urged that "Industry and commerce retreat from their unhealthy leading position," to become "no longer the basis for feeding the nation, but only a help in this" – to the peasant sector.[72]

In the late 1920s the future Nazi peasant leader Richard Walther Darré took up government contracts in the field of animal breeding. He forged a reputation with his publications on selective breeding, "which became the basis of his subsequent racist anthropological theoretisation."[73] Darré authored the Nazi doctrine of *Blut und Boden*, becoming "the main theoretician of eastward continental expansion and agricultural settlement."[74] According to Richard Breitman, Darré helped to convince Heinrich Himmler of "the need for a new racial–German aristocracy."[75] In Munich, Himmler had studied agriculture "intensely for several years" and was "an impassioned agriculturalist," according to Rudolf Hoess, the man he later placed in command at Auschwitz.[76] In 1930 Himmler headed the Bavarian branch of the Artamanen, a sect advocating return to a Teutonic rural life-style. Hoess, who had fought in the German army in Turkey during the Armenian genocide[77] and was also a member of the Artamanen, later recalled: "It was the objective of the Artaman society to induce and aid ideal healthy young Germans of every party and ideology who, because of widespread

69 Ibid., 286–87.
70 David Welch, *Propaganda and the German Cinema, 1933–1945* (Oxford, 1983), introduction.
71 Ibid., 96–97, 102.
72 Adolf Hitler, *Mein Kampf*, 141st ed. (Munich, 1935), 151–52, quoted in Barrington Moore Jr., *Social Origins of Dictatorship and Democracy* (Harmondsworth, 1973), 450.
73 Gustavo Corni, "Richard Walther Darré: The Blood and Soil Ideologue," in Ronald Smelser and Rainer Zitelmann (eds.), *The Nazi Elite* (New York, 1993), 19.
74 Woodruff D. Smith, *The Ideological Origins of Nazi Imperialism* (New York, 1986), 243.
75 Richard Breitman, *The Architect of Genocide: Himmler and the Final Solution* (New York, 1991), 34.
76 In 1934 Hoess had "wanted to settle on the land," but Himmler recruited him to the active SS and had him posted initially to Dachau. Rudolf Hoess, *Commandant of Auschwitz*, trans. Constantine Fitzgibbon (New York, 1960), 227. See also Dwork and van Pelt, *Auschwitz*, 189–90, 207.
77 Vahakn N. Dadrian, *German Responsibility in the Armenian Genocide* (Cambridge, Mass., 1996), 202.

unemployment, were without proper occupation, to return to the countryside and to settle there once again."[78] Himmler's ideal was "the primeval German peasant warrior and farmer."[79] The editor of the SS newspaper *Das Schwarze Korps*, Gunter d'Alquen, later described Himmler as "a theoretical agriculturalist with an academic education" that influenced "his character formation and its consequences," including "[m]any of the practices he enlarged on subsequently with regard to breeding, selection, and perhaps even what he understood by extermination of vermin."[80] Himmler also used an agricultural metaphor to order that homosexuals be "entirely eliminated ... root and branch."[81] Breitman adds: "He thought he could apply the principles and methods of agriculture to human society.... Darré, like Himmler, had studied agronomy and the two men knew all about the breeding of livestock." Himmler, whom Breitman calls the "architect" of the Holocaust, appointed Darré the first head of the SS Race and Settlement Office; "until they quarreled in the late 1930s the two men both tried to turn the SS into their new stock."[82] When Poland fell, Himmler toured the conquered land with his amanuensis, who wrote: "And so we stood there like prehistoric farmers and laughed.... All of this was now once more German soil! Here the German plough will soon change the picture. Here trees and bushes will soon be planted. Hedges will grow, and weasel and hedgehog, buzzard and hawk will prevent the destruction of half the harvest by mice and other vermin."[83] As Himmler put it, "The yeoman of his own acre is the backbone of the German people's strength and character."[84]

Martin Bormann, head of the Nazi Party chancellery and an old friend and assistant of Himmler, was another "passionate agriculturalist."[85] Many Nazis believed in "the superior virtue of rural life."[86] *Blut und Boden* became the title of a film made for use in Nazi Party meetings, subtitled "Foundation of the New Reich." Historian David Welch asserts that "the peasant provides the constant culture hero for National Socialism."[87] Hitler's minister

78 Rudolf Hoess Aufzeichnungen, Institut für Zeitgeschichte, Munich, F 13/5, p. 279/283.
79 Breitman, *The Architect of Genocide*, 35.
80 Gunther d'Alquen Unterredung, Institut für Zeitgeschichte, Munich, ZS 2, March 13–14, 1951, 95.
81 Quoted in Peter Tatchell, "Survivors of a Forgotten Holocaust," *London Independent*, June 12, 2001.
82 Breitman, *The Architect of Genocide*, 12–13, 34–35.
83 Burleigh, *The Third Reich*, 447–48.
84 Heinrich Himmler, quoted in BBC documentary series, *The Nazis* (1997), part 1, "Helped into Power."
85 Rudolf Hoess Aufzeichnungen, Institut für Zeitgeschichte, Munich, F 13/5, p. 286. See also Jochen von Lang, "Martin Bormann: Hitler's Secretary," in Smelser and Zitelmann, *The Nazi Elite*, 8, 12.
86 David Schoenbaum, *Hitler's Social Revolution* (London, 1967), 161, quoted in Welch, *Propaganda*, 96.
87 Welch, *Propaganda*, 97, 101, 103.

of agriculture saw the issue in a way that Pol Pot himself could have put it: "Neither princes, nor the Church, nor the cities have created the German man. Rather, the German man emerged from the German peasantry.... [The] German peasantry, with an unparalleled tenacity, knew how to preserve its unique character and its customs against every attempt to wipe them out.... One can say that the blood of a people digs its roots deep into the homeland earth."[88] Goebbels commissioned at least seven feature films on the topic of "blood and soil."

Another semi-documentary, *The Eternal Forest* (*Ewiger Wald*) expressed "anti-urban, anti-intellectual sentiments," and "idolatry" of the woods: "Our ancestors were a forest people.... No people can live without forest, and people who are guilty of deforesting will sink into oblivion.... However, Germany in its new awakening has returned to the woods." The film depicts "a pure German race, in which the peasant represents the primordial image of the Volk – a Master Race whose roots lie in the sacred soil fertilized for centuries by the richness of their blood."[89]

This view is related to the Nazis' antisemitism. Historian Jeffrey Richards writes: "The Jew was characterized as materialist and thus the enemy of Volkist spiritualism, as a rootless wanderer and therefore the opposite of Volkist rootedness, and as the epitome of finance, industry and the town and thus alien to the agrarian peasant ideal of the Volk."[90] Hitler proclaimed that "a nation can exist without cities, but ... a nation cannot exist without farmers."[91] He described modern industrial cities as "abscesses on the body of the folk [*Volkskörper*], in which all vices, bad habits and sicknesses seem to unite. They are above all hotbeds of miscegnation and bastardization."[92] Himmler agreed: "Cowards are born in towns. Heroes in the country."[93]

Himmler projected Auschwitz itself as "*the* agricultural research station for the eastern territories." He instructed Hoess in 1940: "All essential agricultural research must be carried out there. Huge laboratories and plant nurseries were to be set out. All kinds of stockbreeding was to be pursued there." Early the next year, Hoess wrote, Himmler visited Auschwitz with plans for "the prisoner-of-war camp for 100,000 prisoners." But he added: "In addition there will be the agricultural research station and farms!" In mid-1942 Himmler observed "the whole process of destruction of a

---

88 Ibid., 101–2.   89 Ibid., 108.

90 Richards, *Visions of Yesterday*, 288.

91 Smith, *The Ideological Origins of Nazi Imperialism*, 242.

92 Quoted in Henry A. Turner Jr., "Fascism and Modernization," in *Reappraisals of Fascism* (New York, 1975), 117–39, at 136 n. 12.

93 Heinrich Himmler, quoted in BBC documentary series, *The Nazis* (1997), pt. 1, "Helped into Power."

transport of Jews," and ordered: "The gypsies are to be destroyed. The Jews who are unfit to work are to be destroyed. . . . Armaments factories will also be built. . . . The agricultural experiments will be intensively pursued, for the results are urgently needed."[94] The German peasant warrior must destroy his ethnic foes.

As in the case of the Young Turks, once in power the Nazis' peasant policy came up against "the requirements of a powerful war economy, necessarily based on industry." But as Barrington Moore adds, "a few starts were made here and there"[95] – including at Auschwitz.

The Khmer Rouge took all this much further, emptying Cambodia's cities and seeing "only the peasants" as allies in their revolution.[96] A Khmer Rouge journal announced: "We have evacuated the people from the cities which is our class struggle."[97] These unorthodox communists wrote: "There is a worker class which has some kind of stand. We have not focused on it yet."[98] "We do not use old workers. . . . We do not want to tangle ourselves with old things."[99] The entire population of Cambodia became an unpaid agricultural labor force, and the economy a vast plantation. In their violent repression of enemies, the Khmer Rouge regularly used metaphors such as "pull up the grass, dig up the roots," and proclaimed that the bodies of city people and other victims would be used for "fertilizer."[100]

The Young Turks, the Nazis, and the Khmer Rouge all had to contend with other ethnic groups occupying the land they coveted. Armenian peasants inhabited large areas of eastern Anatolia, straddling the route to "Turkestan." Poles and Russians were obstructive occupants of the eastern territory on which the Nazis planned to settle Aryan farmers. Touring Poland with Himmler in 1939, his amanuensis Johst dismissed it as "not a state-building nation. . . . A country which has so little feeling for systematic

---

94 Hoess, *Commandant of Auschwitz*, 230, 232, 234, 238.

95 Moore, *Social Origins of Dictatorship and Democracy*, 450.

96 David P. Chandler, Ben Kiernan, and Chanthou Boua (eds.), *Pol Pot Plans the Future: Confidential Leadership Documents from Democratic Kampuchea, 1976–77* (New Haven, 1988), 219. The full quotation reads: "Concretely, we did not rely on the forces of the workers. The workers were the overt vanguard, but in concrete fact they did not become the vanguard. In concrete fact there were only the peasants. Therefore we did not copy anyone."

97 Communist Party of Kampuchea, *Tung Padevat*, special issue 9–10 (September–October 1976): 40. See Ben Kiernan, "Kampuchea and Stalinism," in Colin Mackerras and Nick Knight (eds.), *Marxism in Asia* (London, 1985), 232–50.

98 *Tung Padevat*, special issue 9–10 (September–October 1976): 52.

99 Democratic Kampuchea, *Kumrung pankar buon chhnam Sangkumniyum krup phnaek rebos pak, 1977–80* (The Party's Four-Year Plan to build socialism in all fields, 1977–80) (July–August 1976), 110 pp., at 52.

100 For use of the "fertiliser" metaphor during the genocide of the Aborigines, see Raymond Evans and Bill Thorpe, "Indigenocide and the Massacre of Australian History," *Overland* 163 (2001): 21–39, at 29.

settlement, that is not even up to dealing with the style of a village, . . . is a colonial country!"[101] The Nazis considered Slavic *Untermenschen* to be in conflict with the German peasantry in a different way from archetypal urban Jewry. In Cambodia from 1975 to 1979, the Khmer Rouge demonization of ethnic Vietnamese encompassed both these ideological features: some were considered exploitative city dwellers, workers and shopkeepers consuming rural production without benefiting the peasantry in return, and others, rice farmers occupying land that the Pol Pot regime saw as belonging to the authentic homeland of the Khmer.

Other genocidal regimes have also portrayed themselves as protectors of peasant life against urbanites and rural rivals. The perpetrators of the Bosnian genocide of 1992–94 saw their Muslim victims as city dwellers, in contrast to the rural Serb peasantry.[102] In Rwanda, too, the Tutsi were seen either as urban dwellers or as cattle-raising pastoralists, not hardy peasant cultivators like the idealized Hutu. Belgian scholar Philip Verwimp has noted that the protogenocidal regime of Juvenal Habyarimana in Rwanda (1973–94) shared some of the characteristic features of idealization of the peasantry. Habyarimana's justification of his coup d'etat was "to ban once and for all, the spirit of intrigue and the feudal mentality . . . to give back to labor and individual yield its real value . . . the one who refuses to work is harmful to society." "We want to fight this form of intellectual bourgeoisie and give all kinds of physical labor its value back." "Our food strategy gives absolute priority to our peasants," Habyarimana announced; "the government always takes care of the peasant families, . . . the essential productive forces of our country."[103] Verwimp considers Habyarimana to have been influenced (like the Pol Pot group) by physiocratic economic theories, but he also notes reports that literature about Nazism was found in Habyarimana's home after his death. Verwimp adds: "The dictator considered cities a place of immorality, theft and prostitution . . . [and that] Rwanda is a peasant economy and should remain one."[104]

During the 1992 pregenocidal massacres of Tutsis, Prunier adds, "There was a 'rural' banalisation of crime. Killings were *umuganda*, collective work, chopping up men was 'bush clearing' and slaughtering women and children was 'pulling out the roots of the bad weeds.' The vocabulary of 'peasant-centered agricultural development' came into play, with a horrible double

---

101 Burleigh, *The Third Reich*, 447. 102 Cigar, *Genocide in Bosnia*, 119.
103 These speeches by Habyarimana are dated, respectively, October 14, 1973; May 1, 1974; July 5, 1983; and July 5, 1984. For references, see Philip Verwimp, *Development Ideology, the Peasantry, and Genocide: Rwanda Represented in Habyarimana's Speeches*, Genocide Studies Program Working Paper no. 13 (New Haven, 1999), 18ff.
104 Verwimp, *Development Ideology, the Peasantry, and Genocide*, 18–21.

meaning."[105] In Verwimp's view, the subsequent genocide "was indeed a 'final solution,' to get rid of the Tutsis once and for all, and to establish a pure peasant society."[106]

FROM MASS MURDER TO GENOCIDE: INDONESIAN EXPANSION INTO EAST TIMOR

In one recent case, territorial aggression made the difference between mass murder and genocide. In the 1960s, the Indonesian regime of President Suharto compiled a record of murderous repression of domestic political opponents but not of genocidal racism or territorial expansion. In the 1970s, however, Indonesia's attempted conquest of the former territory of Portuguese Timor brought about a genocide.

In October 1965 General Suharto came to power in a military takeover in Jakarta.[107] A massacre of the communist opposition, members of the Partai Kommunis Indonesia (PKI), immediately began. Suharto later recalled: "I had to organize pursuit, cleansing, and crushing."[108] He ordered an "absolutely essential cleaning out" of the PKI and its sympathizers from the government. As his paratroops moved into Central Java, General Nasution reportedly said that "All of their followers and sympathizers should be eliminated" and ordered the party's extinction "down to its very roots."[109] In a few months, half a million to a million communists were slaughtered.[110]

In legal terms, this was not genocide.[111] There was no particular ethnic or racial bias against the victims. The number of ethnic Chinese killed, for instance, was comparatively small, and limited to two regions of the country.[112] Most victims were Javanese peasants, usually only nominal Muslims.

---

105 Prunier, *The Rwanda Crisis*, 139–42.
106 Verwimp, *Development Ideology, the Peasantry, and Genocide*, 45. See also Philip Verwimp, *A Quantitative Analysis of Genocide in Kibuye Prefecture, Rwanda*, Center for Economic Studies, Discussion Paper Series DPS 01.10, Departement Economie, Katholieke Universiteit Leuven, May 2001, 54 pp.
107 For recent discussion, see Benedict Anderson, "Petrus Dadi Ratu," *Indonesia* 70 (October 2000): 1–7; R. E. Elson, *Suharto: A Political Biography* (Cambridge, 2001), chs. 5–6.
108 Elson, *Suharto*, 125.
109 Suharto's formal order was signed on November 15, 1965. Arnold C. Brackman, *The Communist Collapse in Indonesia* (Singapore, 1969), 118–19, quoted in Charles Coppel, "The Indonesian Mass Killings, 1965–66," paper presented at the colloquium on Comparative Famines and Political Killings, Genocide Studies Program, Yale University/Department of History, Melbourne University, August 1999.
110 Robert Cribb (ed.), *The Indonesian Killings, 1965–1966: Studies from Java and Bali* (Clayton, Australia, 1990).
111 Robert Cribb, "Genocide in Indonesia, 1965–66," *Journal of Genocide Research* 3, 2 (June 2001): 219–39.
112 Charles Coppel writes that the number of Chinese killed in 1965–66 "cannot have exceeded about two thousand, in other words disproportionately low when compared to their percentage of the total population." *Indonesian Chinese in Crisis* (Kuala Lumpur, 1983), 58–61.

Fervent Muslim youth groups did much of the killing, instigated by the army to massacre suspected PKI supporters. The killings were political, concentrated in areas like Java and Bali where the PKI had won large numbers of votes in elections in the 1950s.[113] Paratroop commander Sarwo Edhie reportedly conceded that in Java "we had to egg the people on to kill Communists."[114] In his study of Bali, Geoffrey Robinson states that the armed forces ensured "that only PKI forces were killed and that they were killed systematically."[115]

Ten years later, the Indonesian armed forces launched another slaughter, this time of genocidal proportions. The victims now were of a different nationality and religion, in a territory outside Indonesia's borders, and they specifically included the Chinese ethnic minority. Jakarta's troops invaded East Timor, a small neighboring Portuguese colony about to become independent. The East Timorese were not Muslims, but Catholics and animists. Indonesia, which had never claimed the territory, now planned to destroy the popular leftist anticolonial movement known as Fretilin, which had won local elections in the Timorese villages,[116] and then won a brief civil war. By November 1975 Fretilin had consolidated power in East Timor after the Portuguese withdrawal. Indonesia's December seizure of the capital, Dili, was bloody and successful. But unlike the PKI a decade before, Fretilin waged continued resistance and held sway in much of the mountainous hinterland of the island.[117]

Although its anticommunist political motives remained similar, this time the Suharto regime could not destroy what it termed the "gangs of security disruptors" (GPK).[118] Fretilin was politically predominant in East Timor, and despite massive losses it continued to harass the occupying forces. In its effort to wipe out this resistance, Indonesia now became embroiled in a genocidal campaign to suppress the Timorese people. Of the 1975 population of 650,000, approximately 150,000 people disappeared in the next

---

113 See, e.g., Iwan Gardono Sujatmiko, "The Destruction of the Indonesian Communist Party (PKI): A Comparative Analysis of East Java and Bali," Ph.D. diss., Harvard University, 1992; M. C. Ricklefs, *A History of Modern Indonesia* (London, 1981), 238, 248; and Herbert Feith, *The Indonesian Elections of 1955* (Ithaca, 1957).

114 John Hughes, *The End of Sukarno* (London, 1968), 181. Sarwo Edhie added, "In Bali we have to restrain them, make sure they don't go too far." But Coppel comments: "Although political tension was high and some violence had occurred before the arrival of the paratroops, the worst of the violence occurred afterwards."

115 Geoffrey Robinson, *The Dark Side of Paradise* (1995), 295–97, quoted in Coppel, "The Indonesian Mass Killings."

116 James Dunn, *Timor: A People Betrayed* (Milton, 1983), 100.

117 For a map of the areas still reportedly occupied by Fretilin in August 1976, see Carmel Budiardjo and Liem Soei Liong, *The War against East Timor* (London, 1984), 23.

118 Ibid., 82.

four years.[119] Among the first victims were Timor's 20,000-strong ethnic Chinese minority, who were singled out for "selective killings." Indonesian troops murdered 500 Chinese in Dili on the first day of the December 1975 invasion. Soon afterward, "In Maubara and Liquica, on the northwest coast, the entire Chinese population was killed." Surviving Chinese in East Timor numbered only "a few thousand."[120]

An Indonesian census in October 1978 produced a population estimate of only 329,000. Possibly 200,000 more may have been living in Fretilin-held areas in the hills.[121] In the strongly pro-Fretilin eastern third of the territory, for instance, Indonesian officials secretly acknowledged that "a large part of the population in this region fled to the mountains and only came down to the new villages at the beginning of 1979." Moreover, "as a result of all the unrest, many village heads have been replaced, whilst many new villages have emerged."[122] The experience of two eastern villages is instructive: "With the upheavals," an Indonesian commander acknowledged, the inhabitants "fled into the bush," returning in May 1979, when they were "resettled" in a district town. "But this led to their being unable to grow food on their own land, so that food shortages have occurred."[123] In fact, famine ravaged East Timor in 1979. Indonesian aerial bombardment of homes and cultivated gardens in the hill areas had forced many Timorese to surrender in the lowlands, but food was scarce there. As Indonesian control eventually expanded, counts of the Timorese population rose to as many as 522,000 in mid-1979.[124]

The new racism against the Chinese was thus only part of a broader targeting of the Timorese majority in a determined counterinsurgency campaign. While insisting that "God is on our side," Indonesian intelligence and military commanders in Dili acknowledged confidentially in 1982 that "despite the heavy pressure and the disadvantageous conditions under which they operate, the GPK [Fretilin] has nevertheless been able to hold out in the bush," and can still deploy "a very sizeable concentration of forces in one place." After seven years of occupation, Fretilin "support networks" still existed "in all settlements, the villages as well as the towns." Thus, "threats and disturbances are likely to occur in the towns as well as in the resettlement

---

119 At a meeting in London on November 12, 1979, Indonesia's foreign minister Mochtar Kusumaat-madja gave a figure of 120,000 Timorese dead from 1975 to November 1979. See John Taylor, *East Timor: The Price of Freedom* (London, 1999), 203.
120 Ibid., 68–70, 164, 207, citing *Far Eastern Economic Review* 8 (September 1985).
121 Taylor, *East Timor*, 89–90.
122 Budiardjo and Liong, *The War against East Timor*, 201, 243.
123 Ibid., 212–13.   124 Taylor, *East Timor*, 98.

areas."[125] Indonesian commanders still aimed "to obliterate the classic GPK areas" and "to crush the GPK remnants to their roots and to prevent their re-emergence," so that the conquered territory would "eventually be completely clean of the influence and presence of the guerrillas."[126] Deportations continued; in one sector of the East, thirty villages were resettled in 1982.[127] Two years later, a new territory-wide military campaign attempted what one commander called the obliteration of Fretilin "to the fourth generation."[128]

Traditional swidden agriculture on dispersed hill fields did not favor Indonesian control. The population of each village had to be closely controlled. The military commander of the province ordered local officials to "suspect everyone in the community."[129] He hoped to uncover and block "every attempt by inhabitants or the GPK to set up gardens to provide logistical support for the GPK."[130] Thus, the intelligence commander ordered officials to "Re-arrange the location of gardens and fields of the population":

a. There should be no gardens or fields of the people located far from the settlement or village.
b. No garden or field of anyone in the village should be isolated (situated far from the others). Arrange preferably for all the gardens and fields to be close to each other.
c. When people go to their gardens or fields, no-one should go alone; they should go and return together.[131]

The overriding motive for such measures was military. But the result resembled the ideological inspiration of the close-knit, communal Javanese village. Beginning in 1980, Indonesia also established new "transmigration" villages in Timor for 500 families of Javanese and Balinese peasants, who were much easier to control.[132] Jakarta considered the Timorese agriculturally backward: the first group of 50 Balinese transmigrants were given the task to "train East Timorese farmers in the skills of irrigated farming." John Taylor (Chapter 8 in this volume) comments that the Indonesians overlooked the long tradition of irrigation agriculture in their area of settlement,

---

125 Indonesian documents translated in Budiardjo and Liong, *The War against East Timor*, 182, 215, 222, 227, 194–96, 216, 184.
126 Ibid., 242, 193, 228, 241.   127 Ibid., 243, 213.
128 Taylor, *East Timor*, 151.
129 Budiardjo and Liong, *The War against East Timor*, 212, 214, 218–19, 229.
130 Ibid., 205.   131 Ibid., 220.
132 Jakarta aimed not only to reduce the overpopulation of Java and Bali, but also, as Taylor writes, "'Minority populations' are to be assimilated into national development plans because this will make them easier to control, and because the movement of the population to outer island areas will create pools of cheap labour." Taylor, *East Timor*, 124–25.

making the impact "largely symbolic."[133] Here too, glorification of an imagined superior cultivation trumped Timorese reality. In September 1981 an eyewitness reports that after his unit had massacred 400 Timorese civilians near Lacluta, an Indonesian soldier uttered a remark "which was considered to be part of the wisdom of Java. He said: 'When you clean your field, don't you kill all the snakes, the small and large alike?' "[134]

In early 1999, as a long-awaited UN-sponsored referendum finally approached, Indonesian military and militia commanders threatened to "liquidate ... all the pro-independence people, parents, sons, daughters, and grandchildren."[135] Jakarta's governor of the territory ordered that "priests and nuns should be killed."[136] The Indonesian military commander in Dili warned: "[I]f the pro-independents do win ... all will be destroyed. It will be worse than 23 years ago."[137] In May 1999 an Indonesian army document ordered that "massacres should be carried out from village to village after the announcement of the ballot if the pro-independence supporters win." The East Timorese independence movement "should be eliminated from its leadership down to its roots." The forced deportation of hundreds of thousands was also planned.[138] It was implemented, along with a new wave of mass killing, immediately after the UN's announcement of the result of the August 30 ballot, in which 79 percent of Timorese voted for independence from Indonesia. The killing was halted only after the UN took over the territory itself.

As in other cases of mass murder, the Suharto regime's territorial expansionist project transformed earlier repression – domestic political slaughter of communists – from mass murder into genocide of the Timorese. Thus from 1975 unprecedented massacres of the Chinese racial minority complemented the more widespread violent assault on the East Timorese national group.[139] As in the Armenian genocide, the Holocaust, Cambodia, Bosnia,

---

133 Ibid., 124–25. For another contemporary case, see Robin Osborne, *Indonesia's Secret War: The Guerrilla Struggle in Irian Jaya* (Sydney, 1985).

134 Quoted in Taylor, *East Timor*, 102.

135 Andrew Fowler, "The Ties That Bind," Australian Broadcasting Corporation, February 14, 2000, quoted in Noam Chomsky, *A New Generation Draws the Line: East Timor, Kosovo, and the Standards of the West* (London, 2000), 72; for further details see Annemarie Evans, "Revealed: The Plot to Crush Timor," *South China Morning Post*, September 16, 1999.

136 Evans, "Revealed: The Plot to Crush Timor."

137 Brian Toohey, "Dangers of Timorese Whispers Capital Idea," *Australian Financial Review*, August 14, 1999; John Aglionby et al., "Revealed: Army's Plot," *Observer*, September 12, 1999; and other sources quoted in Chomsky, *A New Generation Draws the Line*, 72–76.

138 Chomsky, *A New Generation Draws the Line*, 74.

139 See also Dunn, *Timor: A People Betrayed*, 283–86. Further research might usefully examine whether the killings of Chinese in Timor expressed antiurban as well as xenophobic prejudices.

and Rwanda, the tragedy of East Timor demonstrates the virulent, violent mix of racism, religious prejudice, expansionism, and idealization of cultivation. Each of those factors is, of course, often a relatively harmless component of nationalist ideology. Taken singly, none is a sufficient condition even for mass murder. But their deadly combination is a persistent feature of twentieth-century genocide.

3

The Modernity of Genocides

War, Race, and Revolution in the Twentieth Century

ERIC D. WEITZ

The twentieth century was a period of the most intense and widespread violence. Two world wars and literally hundreds of smaller-scale armed conflicts pervade any accounting of this recent past. But the violence of the twentieth century is reflected not only in the number and intensity of wars. Woven through and wrapped around wars both large and small were radical and violent population politics – the categorization and then the internments, deportations, killings, and, ultimately, genocides of defined population groups.

For some contemporary observers, the violence of the first total war of the twentieth century and of the fascist regimes that soon followed seemed like a throwback to "medieval barbarism," the breakdown of civilization constructed with such determined effort since the Enlightenment. More recently, some observers have explained the violent conflicts in the Balkans as the resurfacing of age-old hatreds, timeless tribal conflicts that had been only artificially suppressed in the communist era.[1] But more insightful commentators, both in earlier decades and in the contemporary period, have seen in the violence of the twentieth century, both its vast wars and its devastations of defined population groups, the scourge of modernity, the nefarious

The research and writing of this chapter was generously supported by a Faculty Summer Research Fellowship and a McKnight Summer Research Fellowship from the Office of the Vice President for Research and Dean of the Graduate School of the University of Minnesota, and by the Center for German and European Studies, a consortium of the Universities of Minnesota and Wisconsin-Madison that is funded by the German Academic Exchange Service (DAAD).

For their very helpful critical readings of earlier drafts, I would like to thank my fellow participants in the Comparative Genocide Conference; Sheila Fitzpatrick and Ron Suny and the members of their Modern Europe Workshop at the University of Chicago; and Tom Wolfe and other participants in the Anthropology Department Colloquium at the University of Minnesota.

This chapter is drawn from my book, *For Race and Nation: Genocides in the Twentieth Century* (Princeton: Princeton University Press, forthcoming).

1 Notably, Robert D. Kaplan, *Balkan Ghosts: A Journey through History* (New York, 1993).

underside of Western societies since the Enlightenment and the French Revolution. The breadth and depth of twentieth-century violence could be explained, it seemed, by modernity's defining features, the combined force of new technologies of warfare, new administrative techniques that enhanced state powers of surveillance, and new ideologies that made populations the choice objects of state policies and that categorized people along strict lines of nation and race. In some combination, this has been the view of major twentieth-century theorists of modernity. For Max Horkheimer and Theodor Adorno, especially in *The Dialectic of Enlightenment*, National Socialism and the (as yet unnamed) Holocaust represented the fulfillment of the "instrumental rationality" of the Enlightenment.[2] In that classic work of the mid-twentieth century, *The Origins of Totalitarianism*, Hannah Arendt located the horrors of the age in the racism that developed in tandem with the new imperialism of the late nineteenth century, in the rise of "mass society," and in the dissolution of a classically defined and limited political sphere – all markers of the age of modernity.[3] Zygmunt Bauman has recently presented an argument similar to Horkheimer and Adorno's, albeit in a more nuanced version, in his widely acclaimed *Modernity and the Holocaust*.[4] Somewhat less concerned with the high theory of the Enlightenment, more focused on the harmful consequences of state practices that seek to shape the character of populations, Bauman ended in the same place as the two Frankfurt School theorists – modernity is the Moloch to be feared. Bauman's approach also has clear affinities with the writings of Michel Foucault. Only rarely did Foucault deal directly with National Socialism or with other regimes engaged in massive population purges. Nonetheless, his approach undoubtedly leads to the conclusion that the violence and mass killings of the twentieth century constitute the ultimate fulfillment of the biopolitics and surveillance that define modernity. As he commented in one lecture: "In the end Nazism is in fact the outcome of developments in the mechanisms of power, newly developed since the eighteenth century, that have been pushed to their high point."[5] On a less theoretical level, many historians of some of the most egregious cases of violent population politics have forcefully linked mass deportations and killings with modernity.[6]

2 Max Horkheimer and Theodor W. Adorno, *Dialectic of Enlightenment*, trans. John Chumming (New York, 1972).
3 Hannah Arendt, *The Origins of Totalitarianism* (1951; Cleveland, 1958).
4 Zygmunt Bauman, *Modernity and the Holocaust* (Ithaca, 1989).
5 Michel Foucault, "Leben machen und Sterben lassen: Die Geburt des Rassismus," in Sebastian Reinfeldt, Richard Schwarz, and Michel Foucault, *Bio-Macht*, DISS-Texte Nr. 25 (Duisburg, 1992), 46. The text is a lecture Foucault gave at the Collège de France in March 1976 and was first published in *Les temps modernes* 535 (February 1992): 51–58.
6 For Germany, see, e.g., Detlev Peukert, "Genocide and the Spirit of Science," in David F. Crew (ed.), *Nazism and German Society* (London, 1994). For a general theoretical statement that also takes a much

Yet when one attempts to define more precisely the distinctively modern elements of twentieth-century warfare and the radical population politics woven in and around it, the effort always seems to be vitiated by some event or category found in earlier histories. The pointed power of "modernity" as an explanation seems to dissipate into a blurry landscape filled with pre-modern acts of enormous brutality, of clear demarcations drawn between distinct population groups, of forced population removals, of mass killings, of grand spectacles of violence.[7] Wars in which the victors razed an entire city, slaughtering and enslaving its inhabitants, date back to the earliest recorded history. From the Babylonian captivity depicted in the Hebrew Bible to the czarist state's deportation of Chechens in the early nineteenth century, empires used population removals as a key tactic of domination. Modern spectacles of violence, like the crowds that cheered Lithuanian auxiliaries as they clubbed Jews to death, or that watched the mass shootings of Jews in Galicia, seem eerily and distressingly evocative of the Aztecs' long, slow, agonizing murder of their main captive before thousands of onlookers.[8] Even before the twentieth century, population removals and, at times, deliberate genocides constituted a central theme of European colonization, from the Spanish, English, and U.S. campaigns against Native Americans, to the events in Tasmania, where British settlers managed to exterminate an entire population in the 1830s. The Portugese had accomplished something similar in the Canary Islands already in the fifteenth century. Despite still-prevalent myths about the long peace from 1815 to 1914, war has been shown to be endemic to the nineteenth century, especially when one moves out of a Eurocentric stance.[9] At the other end of the chronological spectrum, the wars of the twentieth century, for all the technological prowess that marked them as something new, by no means eliminated face-to-face brutality.[10] And the case of Rwanda in the 1990s has demonstrated that

longer historical view, see Ben Kiernan, "Sur la notion de génocide," *Le Débat* (March–April 1999): 179–92.

7 For many examples, see John Keegan, *A History of Warfare* (New York, 1993), who discusses numerous instances of war as not just politics but as "a culture and a way of life" (7) or "as an expression of culture, often a determinant of cultural forms, in some societies the culture itself" (11). See also Mark Levene and Penny Roberts (eds.), *The Massacre in History* (New York, 1999).

8 German incidents in Ernst Klee, Willi Dressen, and Volker Riess (eds.), *"The Good Old Days": The Holocaust as Seen by Its Perpetrators and Bystanders*, trans. Deborah Burnstone (New York, 1991), 256–68, and Walter Manoschek, "Die Vernichtung der Juden in Serbien," in Ulrich Herbert (ed.), *Nationalsozialistische Vernichtungspolitik 1939–1945: Neue Forschungen und Kontroversen* (Frankfurt am Main, 1998), 209–34; Aztec accounts in Keegan, *History of Warfare*, 106–15, who draws on Inga Clendinnen, *The Aztecs: An Interpretation* (New York, 1997).

9 See Michael Geyer and Charles Bright, "Global Violence and Nationalizing Wars in Eurasia and America: The Geopolitics of War in the Mid-Nineteenth Century," *Comparative Studies in Society and History* 38:4 (1996): 619–57.

10 See esp. Joanna Bourke, *An Intimate History of Killing: Face-to-Face Killing in Twentieth-Century Warfare* (New York, 1999).

hundreds of thousands of people can be killed very quickly with the most basic weaponry. In the modern age, genocide does not require gas chambers or highly organized bureaucracies.

All of these events raise serious questions about the links between the violent population politics of the twentieth century, genocide in particular, and modernity. Crassly stated, is the distinctiveness of the twentieth century solely a matter of the higher body count, the more thorough extirpation of populations than in previous centuries? Is scale the sole distinctive criterion?

I think not. Genocides emerge for a variety of reasons and no single explanation can cover every case. But they almost invariably develop in the context of warfare and extreme social and political crisis, when the normal rules of human interaction are suspended and the practice of violence is honored and rewarded. In the twentieth century two additional factors came into play, namely, the hegemony of race thinking in the West and the seizure of state power by revolutionary movements. A new synthesis was created of warfare, race, and revolution that vastly increased the incidences and scale of genocides. The new synthesis does not account for every case of deportations, mass killings, or genocide – the events are far too common, too ubiquitous, to be subject to any one set of explanations. And certainly not every revolutionary state has engaged in genocide or ethnic cleansing. Nor are revolutionary states the only kind of regimes that practice violent population politics. The notion that liberal regimes never engage in genocide can only be sustained if one completely isolates the domestic practices of liberal Western states from their international activities. Despite these qualifications, the new synthesis I am discussing here covers some of the very large cases – Nazi Germany and the Soviet Union – as well as more recent examples, like Cambodia under the Khmer Rouge and the former Yugoslavia.

Race thinking developed from the mid-fifteenth century onward. It was certainly a contested doctrine, but the inclination to think of the human species as divided into a hierarchy of biologically defined races, to think also of certain social behaviors as reflective of a transgenerational, immutable biological or cultural constitution, either of a superior or a degenerative nature – that approach, it is fair to say, had become hegemonic by 1914. Race was such a powerful, mobile way of understanding difference that ethnic, national, and even class identities could, in particular historical situations, become "racialized," a process enhanced by the character of World War I and by the intense social and political conflicts that ensued.[11]

11 See George L. Mosse, *Fallen Soldiers: Reshaping the Memory of the World Wars* (New York, 1990).

But the truly innovative moment emerged when race and violence became linked to the massive political aims of revolutionary movements and states, a new development of the twentieth century. Revolutions were social projects; they mobilized populations for economic development and literacy campaigns, for political repression and population purges. In the process of mobilization, the regimes and their supporters developed rituals of violence that bound people as perpetrators ever more closely to the systems in question. In this chapter, I want to define more carefully the character of twentieth-century revolutions and, in particular, the practices of violence that resulted in the most extreme forms of population politics, ethnic cleansing, and genocide.

DEFINING REVOLUTIONS IN THE TWENTIETH CENTURY

The shadow of the Great War extends over the entire twentieth century. Out of the war came an aesthetics of death based on industrial-scale killing and a new model of states and politics.[12] More prosaically but no less profoundly, the war left empires in shambles and states in ruin. Boundaries had to be redrawn all across the continent, new states created. The misery of war, at the front and at home, led to waves of strikes, demonstrations, armed rebellions, and civil wars, a European-wide upheaval unknown since 1848.

And out of this war came a series of revolutions, the most profound societal transformations that penetrate to the very essence of individual and collective existence. The French had more or less stumbled into revolution at the end of the eighteenth century; the revolutions of 1848 had all failed. However incomplete their support, the Bolsheviks and Nazis were able to seize and sustain state power long enough to implement transformations so dramatic and deep that only the term "revolution" captures their meanings. The Nazis certainly maintained key elements of the existing economic and state structures and the traditional elites were, by and large, deeply complicit in the practices of the Third Reich. The many profound differences between Nazi Germany and the Soviet Union in this regard and many others should by no means be ignored. Still, the two systems shared a number of general, overarching similarities that warrant comparison and permit the expansion of the term revolution to encompass transformations engineered by the right as well as the left. Furthermore, the two systems had such profound, global effects that their practices were "modular" – replicated and adapted by other

---

12 See esp. Omer Bartov, *Murder in Our Midst: The Holocaust, Industrial Killing, Representation* (New York, 1996).

regimes.[13] The Khmer Rouge, for example, reproduced and radicalized Soviet and Chinese communist policies. And the genocidal practices of the Croatian Ustasha state in World War II, which were themselves modeled on Nazi policies, became a constant referent for both Serb and Croat nationalists in the 1990s.

Among the key elements that revolutions of the right and left shared in the twentieth century were the following:

1. An ideological utopianism promoted the belief that the current regime could indeed create the perfect society that would be the end point of history.
2. The utopia necessitated population purges of one sort or another. Aside from carefully cultivated gender distinctions, utopia would be a leveled, homogenized society. Even when the exotica of cultural differences were celebrated, as in the Soviet Union – epic poetry, folk dances, food items – these lacked all substantive political significance.
3. The creation of utopia required massive popular mobilizations.
4. A breakdown of preexisting norms of behavior and a reworking of the rules of social interaction included the promotion of political violence as the method of progress toward utopia.

Revolutions substantially restructure the political and economic systems of a nation. The huge scholarly literature on revolutions overwhelmingly emphasizes these structural matters, and the writers instinctively think of revolutions as solely left-wing affairs.[14] Typical for the structuralist approach to revolutions is Charles Tilly's rather limpid definition: "A revolutionary outcome is the displacement of one set of power holders by another."[15] But revolutionary regimes, as I am describing them here, have goals even more dramatic than the establishment of a new political elite and a new ideology, or the creation of state-run industries and collectivized farms. In their overarching drive to create utopia, revolutions of the twentieth century, right and left, have sought to create the "new man" and the "new woman." To do so requires a refashioning of individual consciousness, a disciplining and self-disciplining even of the honored members of the population. To these goals, revolutionary regimes bring a distinctive rigor, an ideological commitment, and a deep-seated, utopian temper.

---

13 I am adapting the term modularity from Benedict Anderson, *Imagined Communities: Reflections on the Origin and Spread of Nationalism*, rev. ed. (London, 1991).
14 See, e.g., Anthony Giddens's definition of revolution in *Sociology* (Oxford, 1989), 604–5; Peter Calvert *Revolution and Counter-Revolution* (Minneapolis, 1990), 17–18; Theda Skocpol, *States and Social Revolutions: A Comparative Analysis of France, Russia, and China* (Cambridge, 1979); Charles Tilly, *From Mobilization to Revolution* (Reading, Mass., 1978); and Hannah Arendt, *On Revolution* (New York, 1963).
15 Tilly, *From Mobilization to Revolution*, 193.

The creation of new men and women also requires the implementation of collective population politics on a vast scale. Revolutionary societies would be marked by homogeneous populations of one sort or another. Hence, the revolution entails determining the very composition of society, the inclusion of some groups and the eradication of others who are deemed enemies. Revolutions of the twentieth century invariably deploy the powerful metaphors of "cleanness" and "purity." Typically, Pol Pot lauded the "clean" victory of the Khmer Rouge.[16] Radio Phnom Penh reported that "a clean social system is flourishing throughout new Cambodia."[17] Earlier, both Soviet and Nazi rhetoric were replete with images of strong, virile, healthy men and (from the mid-1930s in the Soviet case) maternal women. Both systems spoke of creating healthy new social organisms and dispensing with the diseased and degenerate aspects of the old.

Cleanliness and purity are terms that, necessarily, signify their binary opposites, the unclean and the impure. Certainly, Nazi propaganda was replete with images of Jewish uncleanliness and filth. But other revolutionary movements and states of the twentieth century were not far behind. The Khmer Rouge claimed that city people were impure and unclean, as were politically suspect "base people."[18] Serb nationalists claimed something similar for Muslims, as did the Soviets for the wide variety of groups, from political opponents to purported class and ethnic enemies, that became subject to purge operations. Those who were considered unclean were an active source of pollution; their unclean state threatened to spread beyond them, contaminating the clean and the pure. Hence they had to be at least quarantined and, in the most extreme cases, eradicated altogether. The Khmer Rouge claimed that villagers "have rid the areas of all vestiges of the old regime, cleaning up the village, wiping out old habits, and taking up the new revolutionary morals."[19] To Serb nationalists we owe the popularization of the term "ethnic cleansing," although variants of the phrase were in use in the Russian Revolution and under the Nazis. From the very beginning, the rhetoric of the Russian Revolution was infused by the biologically charged language of "cleaning out," "social prophylaxis," and "purge" itself.[20] Against the ethnic and national groups deported from the late 1930s into the early 1950s, the

---

16 Quoted in Ben Kiernan, *The Pol Pot Regime: Race, Genocide, and Power under the Khmer Rouge, 1975–79* (New Haven, 1996), 94.
17 Quoted in Karl D. Jackson, "The Ideology of Total Revolution," in *Cambodia 1975–1978: Rendezvous with Death* (Princeton, 1989), 67.
18 Kiernan, *Pol Pot Regime*, 62, 216–17.
19 Quoted in Jackson, "Ideology of Total Revolution," 67.
20 See Aleksandr I. Solzhenitsyn, *The Gulag Archipelago, 1918–1956: An Experiment in Literary Investigation*, vols. 1–2, trans. Thomas P. Whitney (New York, 1973), 35, 42, 77.

Eric D. Weitz

Soviets spoke of "cleansing actions" against "suspect" or "enemy" nations.[21] For some of the powerful revolutions of the twentieth century, the dirt that Mary Douglas famously described as "matter out of place" was, in fact, human matter, and it had to be eradicated through political action.[22] In excluding "dirt," revolutionary regimes were "positively reordering [the] environment, making it conform to an idea."[23]

In each of the revolutions, the disciplined and self-disciplined members of the elect – Aryans, Great Russian proletarians and peasants, "old people" in Cambodia – were seen as "clean" and "pure" and the cultural and the genetic carriers of the future society. Although both the elect and the enemies might be defined by class or national backgrounds, very often these identities were racialized in the sense that the honored and the dangerous characteristics were seen to inhere in each and every member of the group and were considered transgenerational. This approach typifies not just Nazi Germany but also the population purges promoted by some communist states, in which the identification of supposedly nefarious behaviors extended from individuals to families and, in some instances, to entire ethnic and national groups.[24] Saul Friedländer's very insightful coinage of "redemptive anti-semitism" might be adapted to many other cases in which the removal of defined population groups is considered an absolutely necessary precondition for the efflorescence of the honored group.[25] These identities, the honored and the dishonored, are never self-evident, never devoid of the act of ideological construction.

By transforming the very composition of society, by creating the social body in this very basic, existential sense, the revolution defines the membership in the "universe of obligation" or those to whom the "bonds of solidarity" extend.[26] It also defines the limits of these commitments, those to whom the most basic human obligations no longer apply. Those outside

21 See N. F. Bugai, " 'Pogruheny v eshelony i otprveleny k mestam poselenii ...': L. Beriia-I. Stalinu," *Istoriia SSR* 1 (1991): 143–60, and Aleksandr M. Nekrich, *The Punished Peoples: The Deportation and Fate of Soviet Minorities at the End of the Second World War* (New York, 1978).

22 Mary Douglas, *Purity and Danger: An Analysis of the Concepts of Pollution and Taboo* (1966; London, 1996), 36.

23 Ibid., 2.

24 On the mobility of the concept of race, see the discussion in Eric D. Weitz, "Racial Politics without the Concept of Race: Reevaluating Soviet Ethnic and National Purges," *Slavic Review* 61:1 (2002): 1–29. On Cambodia, see esp. Kiernan, *Pol Pot Regime*, who argues that race was a central category of Khmer Rouge politics.

25 Saul Friedländer, *Nazi Germany and the Jews*, vol. 1: *The Years of Persecution, 1933–1939* (New York, 1997).

26 The first is Helen Fein's apt term, which has gained wide usage. See Fein, "Genocide: A Sociological Perspective," *Current Sociology* 38:1 (1990): 1–126. The second term comes from Michael Geyer's presentation at the American Historical Association, 1998.

the charmed circle can no longer be secure even over the most basic rights to life and the integrity of the individual body. For the revolution, to purify the social body of enemies signifies that the entire society moves closer to the Elysian fields, to that imagined state of societal bliss. The enemies have either to be reeducated, expelled, or murdered, and just as their identities are constructed and often hazy, so the lines between these different forms of exclusion are not always completely clear.

Another key characteristic of twentieth-century revolutions is that they entail *popular participation*, whether through force, begrudging compliance, enthusiastic support, or the innumerable forms in between. This is a fundamental, defining feature of twentieth-century revolutionary regimes. The revolution is an immense social *project*.[27] It cannot simply be decreed and it does not happen over night; it has to be created by the hard work of thousands and thousands of people. In other words, the revolution *mobilizes* the population; it prizes participation, both before and after the seizure of power, even when that participation is of a highly manipulated sort. The supporters and followers help establish the ideological cohesion that is necessary by attending rallies and marching in demonstrations. They work with enthusiasm on large-scale efforts to build dams and factories or develop agriculture. They sit in bureaucracies and formulate new rules and regulations, or teach the young in schools. They help enforce conformity by denouncing neighbors who appear hostile or indifferent and by working as the guards and soldiers of the revolution. And ultimately, they participate, or at least become complicit, in mass killings.

In the process of mobilization, revolutions create new relations of authority that profoundly alter the nature of daily life. Segments of the population are drawn into the new system or adopt an outer face of conformity with the new order, even though they may be hostile to it. The borders between inner and outer behavior are never fixed, nor are the two realms ever completely separate. The exercise of power is never solely a matter of command. It is an ongoing process of negotiation, one that is marked by conformity, compliance, distance, and withdrawal, a process of fluid movement between inner and outer faces.[28] But the element of naked power, of

---

27 The term is Tim Mason's, and he applied it to fascist states in particular. But it certainly is relevant to communist states as well. See Jane Caplan (ed.), *Nazism, Fascism and the Working Class: Essays by Tim Mason* (Cambridge, 1995). See also Charles Maier, *Dissolution: The Crisis of Communism and the End of East Germany* (Princeton, 1997), 53, 57.

28 I am drawing here especially from Alf Lüdtke, "Einleitung: Herrschaft als soziale Praxis," in *Herrschaft als soziale Praxis: Historische und sozial-anthropologische Studien* (Göttingen, 1991), 9–63, and Thomas Lindenberger, "Die Diktatur der Grenzen. Zur Einleitung," in *Herrschaft und Eigen-Sinn in der Diktatur: Studien zur Gesellschaftsgeschichte der DDR* (Cologne, 1999), 13–44.

violence, is always present. As Alf Lüdtke writes:

Violence does not only mean physical injury or the threat of physical injury, which at the specific moment can be felt as pain. In the foreground is *memory*, which is formed into *experience* – of further suffering, the symbolically transmitted presence of "older" suffering, and the fear bound up with it of the possibility of renewed suffering. Pain and fear, caused by the thorns that lie buried within the inner being, are at least as hard and durable in causing torment and, above all, degradation as the means of compulsion and violence that are felt at the moment the blows rain down upon the body.[29]

In the actions of population purges, the new relations of authority and the centrality of mobilization become especially clear. The outer face of authority relations entails now the wide-ranging participation of the population in expulsions and mass killings. Large numbers of people denounce others to the authorities and serve as the brigade leaders, social workers, and pioneers, but also the jailkeepers, guards, torturers, and killers, of the revolution.[30] As Lüdtke also writes, specifically about the Third Reich but with words that can be generalized to the other cases: "The gruesome attraction of complicity [*Mitmachens*] operates in relation to exclusions and suppressions – and ultimately to murder actions. Participation [*Mit-Täterschaft*] in tormenting other human beings became an integral part of the 'work of domination,' such that the boundary between the guilt of a few and the innocence of many blended away."[31]

RITUALS OF MASS KILLING

In this drive for purity, rituals play a central role. All social systems include sets of rituals that convey the values of the political and social order – the kiss of a papal ring, the kneel before a king, the rise as the judge enters the courtroom.[32] Rituals are *performances* that bind people together, both the active participants and the spectators. Rituals "create and maintain a particular set of assumptions by which experience is controlled.... [They] work upon the body politic through the symbolic medium of the physical body."[33] Rituals "structure and present particular interpretations of social

---

29 Lüdtke, "Einleitung: Herrschaft als soziale Praxis," 49.
30 On denunciation as a social practice, see the *Journal of Modern History* 68, 4 (1997), edited by Sheila Fitzpatrick and Robert Gellately.
31 Lüdtke, "Einleitung: Herrschaft als soziale Praxis," 44.
32 Ibid., 15–18, 27–29, and the classic studies of Victor Turner, *The Forest of Symbols: Aspects of Ndembu Ritual* (Ithaca, 1973), and his *Dramas, Fields, and Metaphors: Symbolic Action in Human Society* (Ithaca, 1974), and of Douglas, *Purity and Danger*.
33 Douglas, *Purity and Danger*, 129.

reality in a way that endows them with legitimacy.... [They also] structure the way people *think* about social life."[34] Rituals are not necessarily static; even in traditional societies, rituals evolve and are not only reflective of existing conditions. "Ritual may do much more than mirror existing social arrangements and existing modes of thought. It can act to reorganize them or even help to create them."[35]

Revolutionary regimes act in just this fashion. They go to great lengths to *create* rituals as a means of binding the population to the new order and thereby securing legitimacy. But two critical developments also alter the character of rituals in the twentieth century. First, the elaboration of rituals is designed to incorporate vast elements of the population not just in the symbolic representation of power but also in its implementation. More and more people become active agents, helping to formulate and execute policies, even, perhaps especially so, in dictatorial systems. The scale of politics becomes greatly enhanced in the twentieth century.[36] Second, the technical means emerge to reach ever larger segments of the population through print, radio, and film and the rapid movement of people and ideas via rail, road, and air. The technology of twentieth-century communications, from the rapidly reproducible leaflet to radio and smuggled cassette recordings, draws ever more numbers into the world of active politics, if as passively complicit as much as actively participant.[37] To be involved in revolutionary ritual, one no longer had to be in the physical space in which the performance was carried out.

Killing is a brute, physical act. It entails, most obviously, the exercise of complete domination, of ultimate power, over the victim. But the way people are killed is a ritual that carries layers of symbolic meaning, just as human sacrifice does in premodern societies. Killing, like other acts of violence and like rituals in general, is a performative act.[38] In genocides, the

---

34 Sally F. Moore and Barbara G. Myerhoff, "Secular Ritual: Forms and Meanings," in *Secular Ritual* (Amsterdam, 1977), 3–24, quotation from 4.

35 Ibid., 5.

36 On the importance of scale, see John Agnew, "Representing Space: Space, Scale and Culture in Social Science," in J. Duncan and D. Ley (eds.), *Place/Culture/Representation* (London, 1993), 251–79.

37 Here I am drawing from, and somewhat revising, the classic formulation of the "aestheticization of politics," developed in scattered, numerous writings by Siegfried Kracauer, Walter Benjamin, and many others. See also the classic essays of Kracauer, "The Mass Ornament," in *The Mass Ornament: Weimar Essays*, trans. Thomas Y. Levin (Cambridge, Mass., 1995), 75–86, and of Benjamin, "The Work of Art in the Age of Mechanical Reproduction," in *Illuminations*, trans. Harry Zohn (New York, 1968), 243–44. However, by placing the emphasis so heavily on the ornament and manipulation, Kracauer and Benjamin undervalued the participatory nature of fascism, turning the masses into mere spectators and the essence of the entire movement into spectacle.

38 See David Riches, "The Phenomenon of Violence," in *The Anthropology of Violence* (Oxford, 1986), 1–27, and Allen Feldman, *Formations of Violence: The Narrative of the Body and Political Terror in Northern Ireland* (Chicago, 1991).

meanings of the act are conveyed to the thousands, even millions, of people involved, the perpetrators, bystanders, victims, and survivors, through the treatment of the body. As two scholars have written about the mass killings in Indonesia in 1965, when paramilitary gangs killed people by hacking them apart, dumping most of the body parts somewhere else, but leaving the organs in front of the victims' houses, "the body becomes not simply the means of death but a vehicle for effecting more traumatic symbolic and ritual violence."[39]

With a few exceptions, the phenomena associated with ethnic cleansings and genocide under revolutionary states – roundups, deportations, killings – are notably similar across particular cases.[40] Mass execution in gas chambers was a Nazi specialty, and torture as a part of ritual confession was perfected by communists. But Nazis drove people out in deportations and death marches and probably 40 percent of Jews were not killed at Auschwitz and the other death camps but in mass shootings and by the deprivations of transport and confinement.[41] Nazis too at times extracted confessions as acts of public humiliation from their Jewish victims, and routinely tortured all sorts of other people.[42]

In the practice of violence, the perpetrators sometimes followed direct orders from above. But they were also enormously inventive in the exercise of brutalities. They created their own rituals of violence, a sign of the centrality of popular participation in genocides.

Deportation

At 2:00 AM in the morning of May 17, 1944, Tatar homes were suddenly broken into by NKVD agents and NKVD troops armed with automatics. They dragged

---

39 Leslie Dwyer and Degung Santikarma, " 'When the World Turned to Chaos': 1965 and Its Aftermath in Bali, Indonesia," paper presented at the Comparative Genocides Conference, Barcelona, December 2000, and Chapter 13 in this volume.

40 Amid a substantial literature, I draw here especially from Wolfgang Sofsky, *The Order of Terror: The Concentration Camp* (Princeton, 1997); *Traktat über die Gewalt* (Frankfurt am Main, 1996); and "Gesetz des Gemetzels," *Die Zeit* 15 (April 2, 1998): 53. See also Norman M. Naimark, *Fires of Hatred: Ethnic Cleansing in Twentieth-Century Europe* (Cambridge, Mass., 2001), for a careful discussion of similarities and differences in various ethnic cleansings.

41 See Herbert, *Vernichtungspolitik*, and Christopher R. Browning, *Ordinary Men: Reserve Police Battalion 101 and the Final Solution in Poland* (New York, 1992). The classic work about the anonymous, bureaucratic nature of the killings is, of course, Hannah Arendt, *Eichmann in Jerusalem: A Report on the Banality of Evil*, rev. ed. (New York, 1964), who based much of her evaluation on Raul Hilberg, *The Destruction of the European Jews* (Chicago, 1961). The "neatness" of Nazi exterminations, a supposedly anonymous, bureaucratic process, has been hugely exaggerated.

42 Heinrich Himmler issued an order in 1942 that officially sanctioned torture to gain "useful information," but these kinds of activities had been going on since the moment the Nazis seized power in 1933. See also Edward Peters, *Torture*, expanded ed. (Philadelphia, 1996), 105, 124–25.

sleeping women, children, and old people from their beds and, shoving automatics in their ribs, ordered them to be out of their homes within ten minutes. Without giving them a chance to collect themselves, they forced these residents out into the street, where trucks picked them up and drove them to railroad stations. They were loaded into cattle cars and shipped off to remote regions of Siberia, the Urals, and Central Asia. . . .

These people left their homes naked and hungry and traveled that way for a month; in the locked, stifling freight cars, people began to die from hunger and illness. The NKVD troops would seize the corpses and throw them out of the freight car windows.[43]

Random Shootings

[I]n the middle of the night we were asleep in a room. In our room there were about fifteen persons. In the middle of the night we hear . . . shooting. . . . When we came [into the other rooms] there lay shot all who were living in those rooms. Two children with a father . . . everything was shot. A man lay with his stomach completely torn open.[44]

Mass Shootings

[On November 3 at Majdanek] they . . . called out all . . . twenty-three thousand people. . . . Just the Jews. . . . Two days before, eighty men had been taken out. And they were told to dig very large pits. And nobody knew what these pits were for. . . . Ultimately, it turned out that those pits were for the people who had dug them. . . . They went up in rows of fives, children, mothers, old, young, all went up. . . . They told them all to undress. Young women flung themselves at the sentries and began to plead that he should shoot them with good aim so that they should not suffer. . . . And the sentries laughed at that and said, "Yes, yes. For you such a death is too good. You have to suffer a little."[45]

Concentration Camps

The SS took no great pains with many of the Gypsies. . . . During the first three months of arrest, many of the younger children died of starvation and disease. . . . Once I observed that several 8–12 year old children were compelled to lie on the ground while booted SS men marched over their bodies. . . . I lost eight brothers and sisters as well as my parents under the Nazis.[46]

43 From the testimony of Shamil Aliadin, a Crimean Tatar, before the Central Committee of the CPSU in 1957, in Aleksandr Nekrich, *Punished Peoples* (New York, 1978), 111.
44 Testimony of Nechama Epstein, in Donald L. Niewyk, "Holocaust: The Genocide of the Jews," in Samuel Totten, William S. Parsons, and Israel W. Charney (eds.), *Genocide in the Twentieth Century: Critical Essays and Eyewitness Accounts* (New York, 1995), 192.
45 Ibid., 199–200.
46 Testimony of Lani Rosenberg, in Sybil Milton, "Holocaust: The Gypsies," in Totten, Parsons, and Charney, *Genocide in the Twentieth Century*, 246–47.

Beatings

July 13, 1995: The Serbian guards took a few [Muslims] to the gate, pushed them through a gauntlet and beat them to death with crowbars. A few had specialized in delivering blows with an ax to the backs of the prisoners, others in cutting their throats with a knife. In the evening 296 of the approximately 400 men were still alive. At night they were driven to the execution place.[47]

Selections

Friends and comrades, it gives me pleasure to introduce myself as the leader of this region. Welcome. As you all know, during the Lon Nol regime the Chinese were parasites on our nation. They cheated the government. They made money out of Cambodian farmers.... Now the High Revolutionary Committee wants to separate Chinese infiltrators from Cambodians, to watch the kind of tricks they get up to. The population of each village will be divided into a Chinese, a Vietnamese and a Cambodian section. So, if you are not Cambodian, stand up and leave the group. Remember that Chinese and Vietnamese look completely different from Cambodians.[48]

Killing Fields

"If you ask me," said another, "we should take him to the field beyond the village." ...

The field was about three kilometres away, a patch of open ground with a small wood at one end. When we went to work, we passed it and we could see from a distance three large open pits from which came the most horrific smell. We could have gone there if we'd wanted to, since they were intended to keep us in terror. But nobody I knew ever went. There was always a flock of crows around.[49]

Extermination Camps

The horde of people ... were driven outside with hard blows and forced ... to go the few hundred metres to the "Shower Room." ... Then panic broke out.... But blows with rifle butts and revolver shots soon restored order and finally they all entered the death chamber. The doors were shut and, ten minutes later, the temperature was high enough to facilitate the condensation of the hydrogen cyanide ... the so-called "Zyklon B." ... Twenty to twenty-five minutes later, the doors and windows were opened to ventilate the rooms and the corpses were thrown at once into pits to be burnt. But, beforehand the dentists had searched every mouth to pull out the gold teeth. The women were also searched to see if they had not

---

47 The event is related in Sofsky, "Das Gesetz des Gemetzels," 53.
48 Quoted in *Cambodian Witness: The Autobiography of Someth May*, ed. James Fenton (London, 1986), 117.
49 Ibid., 201.

hidden jewellery in the intimate parts of their bodies, and their hair was cut off and methodically placed in sacks for industrial purposes.[50]

Torture and Confession

After weeks of torture Phat gave Duch [the head of Tuol Seng] a handwritten confession of his "activities of betrayal" that was more than eight pages long. Later . . . he admitted to moral crimes as well. . . . In March he wrote by hand a sixty-four-page document which he signed at the bottom of each page, confessing to an elaborate but simple-minded spy network operated at times by the CIA, at other times by the Vietnamese. . . .

After completing the sixty-four-page confession, Phat's mission for the party was over. His file was closed. His body was disposed of.[51]

The Disposal of Bodies

[In the Soviet Gulag, a bulldozer clears the way for the men to log a new area of the forest.] The bulldozer scraped up the frozen bodies, thousands of bodies of thousands of skeleton-like corpses. Nothing had decayed: the twisted fingers, the pus-filled toes which were reduced to mere stumps after frostbite, the dry skin scratched bloody and eyes burning with a hungry gleam. . . .

Grinka Lebedev, parricide, was a good tractor driver, and he controlled the well-oiled foreign tractor with ease. Grinka Lebedev carefully carried out his job, scooping the corpses toward the grave with the gleaming bulldozer knife shield, pushing them into the pit and returning to drag up more.[52]

The immense brutalities depicted here are made possible by the complete powers granted to the perpetrators by the regimes they serve. The killers come as agents of a state or a state-in-the-making. They carry the epaulets of power on their bodies – uniforms, fearsome insignias, jackboots, weapons of various kinds, as had the NKVD troops who deported the Crimean Tatars and the Nazi concentration camp guards. They arrive rapidly, often in screeching trucks or running in marched time, with weapons displayed. Or they stand guard over their victims, beating or shooting them at will, or even trampling over their bodies, as was the case of the Roma and Sinti (Gypsy) children. They spread fear, deliberately, by their display of power and by the knowledge, which becomes quickly apparent to the victims, that the perpetrators can take life at any moment.

50 Testimony of André Littich about Auschwitz, in Jeremy Noakes and Geoffrey Pridham (eds.), *Nazism, 1919–1945*, vol. 3: *Foreign Policy, War and Racial Extermination* (Exeter, 1988), 1180.
51 From Elizabeth Becker, *When the War Was Over: The Voices of Cambodia's Revolution and Its People* (New York, 1986), 291–94.
52 Varlam Shalamov, "Lend-Lease," in *Kolyma Tales*, trans. John Glad (New York, 1980), 178–80.

The killers take control of a defined space, whether it be a building, camp, neighborhood, train car, or field. They ring the area with security forces, making escape nearly impossible. In guard towers or on the hills above an area, they attain visual domination over the victims. While individuals may be rendered inhuman by the blank look on a guard's face, the complete lack of recognition, as a mass the victims are subject to sweeping visual control.[53] The total power over space is fear-inspiring because it means control over the individual body, where it can move, where it cannot. This is the meaning of the concentration camp, pioneered by the Americans in the Philippines and the British in the Boer War, which then became one of the key features of the twentieth century. It is also the meaning of the places of roundup and selection, often the market square in a village or the meeting in open air or in a large hall, as when the Khmer Rouge separated out ethnic Chinese. The concentration camp, the marketplace, and the meeting hall, secured by troops, mark the ultimate control over humans in space. In the confined space of the camps, the guards are given complete license to brutalize and kill, and death becomes a normal by-product of existence.[54] In these confined spaces, they are even free to shoot randomly, killing and maiming at will.

The killers also take control of that other dimension of human existence, time. They do not kill everyone immediately, not even at Auschwitz. They drag out the process, for hours, days, months on end. Sometimes they know that they will kill their victims, sometimes they just demonstrate a complete disregard for human life that, over time, leads to death from deliberate deprivation and brutality. In face-to-face killings, they change the rhythm of the process – going for long breaks, for example, while the victims wait in fear. They take their time, make a sport out of the terror they inspire. Such was the fate of many Jews and Roma and Sinti confined to concentration camps, and also of the victims in Tuol Sleng, the infamous Khmer Rouge prison.[55] Torture was a drawn out affair, meant to extract ever lengthier and more complicated confessions from the prisoners.

It is particularly difficult to make sense of the matter of confession when both the torturer and victim know that the victim will in any case be killed. Clearly, torture is a form of total domination in which some people revel at the complete physical and psychological destruction they deliver to the

53 Compare Omer Bartov, *Mirrors of Destruction: War, Genocide, and Modern Identity* (New York, 2000), 3–4 and 232, n. 1, with Allen Feldman, "Violence and Vision: The Prosthetics and Aesthetics of Terror," in Veena Das et al. (eds.), *Violence and Subjectivity* (Berkeley, 2000), 46–78.

54 Note the guidelines given to SS concentration camp guards at Dachau in the early 1930s, which demanded an extreme level of brutality. See the text in Noakes and Pridham, *Nazism, 1919–1945*, 2: 502–4.

55 See David Chandler, *Voices from S-21: Terror and History in Pol Pot's Secret Prison* (Berkeley, 2000).

individual. As with killings, the torturers are given license to pursue their actions by the murderous policies of the regimes they serve. The revolutionary regimes of the twentieth century all revived and expanded the practice of torture, which had begun to wane from the Enlightenment and especially in the course of the nineteenth century.[56] Ironically, the immensely powerful revolutionary state of the twentieth century imagined enemies everywhere. Those who seek total power and are completely convinced of the rightness of their cause can only explain failures by treachery and sabotage, leading to a continual, paranoiac search for enemies. Rule by terror has a way of folding in on itself, becoming an endless cycle that ultimately consumes its very perpetrators.[57]

Yet this pattern of "devouring" the children of the revolution, of extracting ritualized confessions, seems a pattern not just of any police state, but of communist ones in particular. Perhaps here we see a perverse transformation of the communist ideal of a harmonious society. The Nazis and Serb nationalists defined their enemies in overtly racialist or nationalist terms, by descent. Communist ideology, rooted in Enlightenment universalism, presumed that all human beings, regardless of descent, would come to see the light of communism. Hence the enemies had to be forced to confess their sins to find the path to the cause, even while their transgressions were so great that they had also to be killed. Torture demonstrated the power of the regime on the body of the victims; it is a "spectacle of absolute power."[58] On a more basic level, the torturers seem also to have enjoyed their complete domination, their ability to reduce the victim to a body in pain, closed in on itself so that all it knows is the hurt.[59] At Tuol Sleng their final power lay in the arbitrary decision of when finally to kill the individual whose fate had been sealed the moment he or she was arrested.

In the end, even the corpses of victims are denied dignity, thrown from freight cars, shoved around by bulldozers, left to rot for animals. As Mary Douglas writes, the "body as a symbol of society . . . the powers and dangers credited to social structure reproduced in small on the human body" relates

---

56 Peters, *Torture*, 74–140.

57 Hannah Arendt, *On Violence* (New York, 1969), 55.

58 Sofsky, *Traktat über die Gewalt*, 83–100, quotation from 88. Allen Feldman goes further: "The performance of torture does not apply power; rather, it manufactures it from the 'raw' ingredient of the captive's body. The surface of the body is the stage where the state is made to appear as an effective material force." *Formations of Violence*, 115.

59 "[Beauty] opens out to the world, inviting further sighs, objects, and interpretants to partake of its bounty, of its essence. Pain, by contrast, when embodied, closes in on itself. Where beauty extends itself, pain finds affirmation in its intensification. Beauty repressed can be painful; pain expressed is susceptible to incredulity." E. Valentine Daniel, *Charred Lullabies: Chapters in an Anthropography of Violence* (Princeton, 1996), 139.

even to the dead body of those considered beyond the pale.[60] Like the body of a Crimean Tatar thrown from a train taking its passenger-load to the place of exile, the bodies of the Kolyma laborers are the final mark, real and symbolic, of the violent population politics of modern states. The corpses of the ensnared individuals – thrown, deposed, shoved, slashed – are denied the barest shred of respect, like the bodies of Jews burned in crematoria or those of Cambodians left to rot in the killing fields. The dead bodies are, indeed, like the logs the great Soviet author and Gulag prisoner Varlam Shalamov first thought them to be. Violated in life, the bodies are degraded in death. And the degradation does not occur anonymously, but at the hands of a guard on a transport leading a population into exile or a fellow inmate who wields the controls of a tractor.

Like other, less brutal forms, rituals of genocidal killings create emotional bonds among the perpetrators, joining them together in a structure of feeling and a community of action.[61] Ritual, Victor Turner argues, "is . . . a mechanism that periodically converts the obligatory into the desirable. . . . [T]he dominant symbol brings the ethical and jural norms of society into close contact with strong emotional stimuli."[62] So it is with rituals of violence in modern societies. The brutalities visited upon targeted populations were always social acts, carried out by groups of perpetrators acting in concert and witnessed by many others, victims, bystanders, and other or future perpetrators. Indeed, the SS commandant of Dachau, Theodor Eicke, issued explicit regulations that beatings of prisoners were never to be carried out by an individual guard, but always with others and with witnesses. Similarly, the Nazi guards who ran over children's bodies or inserted Zyklon B gas at Auschwitz, the Khmer Rouge cadres who selected ethnic Chinese or "new people" and tortured prisoners, the NKVD troops who deported Tatars, and the Serbs who beat Muslims at Srebenica all acted together in a social group.

The brutalities were initiated and carried through under the immense pressure of conformity and often under the formal command structure of an army or security force. The mass killers of Srebenica and elsewhere unleashed their deeds against civilians as part of revolutionary projects, carried out in the context of war or military-like mobilizations. The killings were not anarchic eruptions of age-old hatreds, or the result of individuals and groups acting solely of their own accord. The killings took place within the larger frame of revolutionary politics centered on the reshaping of the

---

60 The quotation is from Douglas, *Purity and Danger*, 116. See also Feldman, *Formations of Violence*.
61 "Structure of feeling" comes from Raymond Williams. See also Sofsky, *Traktat über die Gewalt*.
62 Turner, *Forest of Symbols*, 30.

social body. However random the killings, however arbitrary the fate of an individual as victim or survivor, these actions always involve some level of planning. The murder actions unfold within a larger, regime context of domination and exclusion.

Among the perpetrators there were, no doubt, a range of reactions, from inner revulsion to begrudging compliance to intense enthusiasm – the ever shifting boundaries of the inner and outer face of authority relations.[63] Small, everyday gestures – common laughter, a slap on the shoulder, shared drinks – bound the perpetrators together in the enterprise of mass killings. And they were bound together by gender. Few were the women involved in such actions, even in Cambodia where the regime went to great lengths to mobilize them for the revolution. Genocide and ethnic cleansing and all the additional acts of violence associated with them are overwhelmingly the work of men. They are sometimes worn down by the killing; many times they kill simply because they are following orders. But many also derive thrills from the common devotion to a higher cause, from their immense power over other human beings, from the freedom to transgress wildly the normal boundaries of human interaction. They revel in the killing, in the display of power and brutality.[64]

Genocide is, then, a dual process. The perpetrators never act solely on their own; they operate in a structure of action defined by regime goals. But they also create rituals of their own – running over children's bodies, delivering blows to particular body parts, shooting wildly into rooms, throwing corpses from trains – that give meaning, chilling meaning, to the killings.

CONCLUSION

In the twentieth century genocides became more frequent, more extensive, and more systematic. The reasons lay not only in advanced technologies that permitted the rapid eradication of large numbers of people. The cluster of explanations has to begin with World War I and the new mass, industrial-style killing it introduced. The war created a culture of violence that the postwar fascist movements and renowned authors like Ernst Jünger and Gabriele D'Annunzio warmly celebrated. The war did not end for them in 1918; they transferred the culture of the battlefield to politics, advocating brutality and violence – including mass population purges – as the path to a higher order of existence. The Great War created not only a culture of death

---

63 See Browning, *Ordinary Men*, for the range of reactions at the outset of the killing operation.
64 See Sofsky, *Traktat über die Gewalt*, 56–57.

but also a culture of killing, and one that was often tied to the ideology of race. It is no accident that the very first modern campaign of genocide, the Turkish slaughter of Armenians, occurred in the context of World War I.

The culture of killing was easily transferable to the huge political projects of the revolutionary regimes that emerged first out of the Great War. These revolutions were about far more than the structures of polities and societies, the factors invariably emphasized in the massive scholarly literature on the nature of revolution. Twentieth-century revolutions were very centrally about the very basic composition of society, those who could be honored members of the new order, those who had to be extirpated. In their drive to create a new society that would overcome the flaws of the old, that would put an end to internal divisiveness and open up pathways of prosperity and happiness, revolutionary regimes had a fundamental, homogenizing impulse. Even as they created new hierarchies of power, their vision of the future was of a society bereft of difference.

Revolutionary movements and regimes worked very hard to mobilize their populations. Popular participation, whether achieved voluntarily or by compulsion or (most often) by some combination of the two, is a defining feature of twentieth-century revolutions and distinguishes them from more traditional tyrannies. Ethnic cleansings and genocides on a twentieth-century scale would simply not be possible without the actions of tens and hundreds of thousands of men under arms and the thousands of "small acts" like denunciations, looting, and cheering on the killers that vastly broadened the scope of participation.[65] In these actions, people created rituals of violence that brutalized the victims and bound the perpetrators ever more closely to the genocidal regimes under which they lived. Genocides, then, are deadly to the victims; they are also events whose corrupting character travels deep into society. The successors to the societies that have been consumed by mass violence cannot escape the legacy; they remain overburdened by the past, precisely because of the participatory nature of genocides in the modern era.[66]

Modernity is polyvalent; no single practice or system marks its "ultimate" fulfillment, and certainly not the Third Reich, as Horkheimer and Adorno and, more recently, Detlev Peukert argued. One might well wonder why Switzerland or Denmark does not signify some kind of "ultimate" stage of development. But certainly one aspect of modernity has been the deep, massive intensification of violence directed at defined population groups.

---

65 "Perpetrators and witnesses stimulate one another." Ibid., 116.

66 I have adapted this point from Daniel's comment that "the Sri Lankan experience is overburdened with the present, a present 'under (traumatic) erasure.'" See *Charred Lullabies*, 107.

Numerous cases of genocide occurred prior to the twentieth century. Sometimes they were carried out by armies of the state, as in the Roman destruction of Carthage, sometimes, as in many colonial settings, by settlers acting with the tacit acceptance of the authorities. But these events lacked the systematic, total character of twentieth-century genocides, which involved states with enormously enhanced capacities and populations that were made complicit in the brutal purges of targeted populations. When the powers of modern states were hinged to the revolutionary impulse and an ideology of purity, the results could be deadly.

4

Seeking the Roots of Modern Genocide

On the Macro- and Microhistory of Mass Murder

OMER BARTOV

I

The idea and practice of genocide are most probably as ancient as the idea and practice of war. Indeed, war and genocide have always been closely related, just as both are predicated on the existence of a certain level of human culture and civilization. The biblical concept of a war of annihilation (המרוח תמחלמ) or the destruction of Carthage by the Romans, are two familiar instances of the manner in which the eradication of another culture in war or in its immediate aftermath serves as an important instrument in the assertion of group or national identity. Indicatively, in both cases – as in many others – destruction is not only justified but also lauded as a noble act sanctioned by God (for the Jews) or glorifying the republic (for the Romans). In some instances, the intention to perpetrate genocide may not be implemented, or may be implemented only in part; conversely, genocide can also be the unintended consequence of a policy or a set of actions whose initial goal was different. The mass death of Native Americans can probably serve as an example for both models: on the one hand, the intention to destroy the indigenous populations of the Americas did not wholly succeed, especially in Latin America, where most states still contain large numbers of Indians or people of mixed race (with the notable exception of Argentina); on the other hand, more Native Americans probably died from exposure to European diseases than from intentional killing.[1] What seems to be indisputable is that because it is both the product of civilization and the instrument of asserting identity, the wholesale murder of entire categories of human beings can be found in numerous cultures at some point of their history.

1 David E. Stannard, *American Holocaust: The Conquest of the New World* (New York, 1992).

75

The simplest definition of *modern* genocide is that it is mass murder conceived and perpetrated by modern states and organizations. This in turn
depends on our definition of the modern period and of modern states and
organizations. Conversely, the nature of genocidal actions is also a measure
of the modernity of the perpetrator organization. In this sense, bureaucratic,
industrial, systematic genocide may actually serve as a signifier of modernity,
even if we would like to label it barbarism. However, the victims of genocide
need not be at the same point of development as their murderers; indeed, in
numerous modern genocides they were not, which greatly facilitated both
the organization of killing and its legitimization. Hence the mass murder
of the Herero of South West Africa by the German Imperial Army in the
early years of the twentieth century had many of the attributes of a modern
genocidal undertaking, despite, or perhaps precisely because of, the fact that
the Herero were a premodern society.[2] The mass murder of the Armenians
by the Ottoman Empire, for its part, while it contained elements of premodern genocidal ideologies and practices, can also be seen as an important
harbinger of state-organized mass killing of domestic populations in time of
war, nation building, and ethnic conflict.[3]

The first legal definition of genocide, however, was accepted by the
international community only many decades after the practice had already
been tried and implemented, in some cases on an extraordinarily large scale.
Yet this definition, which also introduced the very term "genocide" to
describe the phenomenon, has helped much neither in defining what is
genocide nor in limiting its scope and prevalence. Indeed, the growing
attention to genocide in the popular media, among scholars, and even in
some political circles is itself an indication of the failure of the United
Nations to enforce its own policy of mobilizing the international community
against mass murder.[4] Between Cambodia and Rwanda, the past few decades

2 Tilman Dedering, " 'A Certain Rigorous Treatment of All Parts of the Nation': The Annihilation
  of the Herero in German South West Africa, 1904," in Mark Levene and Penny Roberts (eds.),
  The Massacre in History (New York, 1999), 205–22; Helmut Walser Smith, "The Talk of Genocide,
  the Rhetoric of Miscegenation: Notes on Debates in the German Reichstag concerning Southwest
  Africa, 1904–14," in Sara Friedrichsmeyer, Sara Lennox, and Susanne Zantop (eds.), *The Imperialist
  Imagination: German Colonialism and Its Legacy* (Ann Arbor, 1998), 107–23; Jan-Bart Gewald, *Herero
  Heroes: A Socio-Political History of the Herero of Namibia, 1890–1923* (Oxford, 1999).
3 Vahakn N. Dadrian, *The History of the Armenian Genocide: Ethnic Conflict from the Balkans to Anatolia to
  the Caucasus*, 3rd rev. ed. (Providence, 1997); Richard G. Hovannisian (ed.), *The Armenian Genocide in
  Perspective* (New Brunswick, N.J., 1991); Ronald Grigor Suny, "Religion, Ethnicity, and Nationalism:
  Armenians, Turks, and the End of the Ottoman Empire," and Ara Sarafian, "The Absorption of
  Armenian Women and Children into Muslim Households as a Structural Component of the Armenian
  Genocide," both in Omer Bartov and Phyllis Mack (eds.), *In God's Name: Genocide and Religion in the
  Twentieth Century* (New York, 2001), 23–61 and 209–21, respectively.
4 On the merits and limitations of the newly established International Criminal Tribunal for the Former
  Yugoslavia (ICTY) in The Hague, see Maria Ivkovic, "Obfuscating Responsibility: The Implications

have witnessed a tremendous expansion of this practice.[5] Simultaneously, the emergence of the term "ethnic cleansing" in the course of the war in Bosnia came to denote a phenomenon that dates, in its modern guise, at least as far back as the late nineteenth century (in the same region of Southeastern Europe and Anatolia).[6] Again, it should be noted, both modern genocide and modern ethnic cleansing have usually taken place during time of war under circumstances closely related to war conditions.

On December 9, 1948, the United Nations adopted the Genocide Convention, in which genocide was defined as "any of the following acts committed with intent to destroy, in whole or in part, a national, ethnical, racial or religious group, as such." These acts include "killing members of the group"; "causing serious bodily or mental harm to members of the group"; "deliberately inflicting on the group conditions of life calculated to bring about its physical destruction in whole or in part"; "imposing measures intended to prevent births within the group"; and "forcibly transferring children of the group to another group."[7] This has long been recognized as a problematic definition both because it is too open-ended and vague, in that it does not distinguish between outright killing and other forms of violence and persecution, and because it fails to mention the targeting of political groups and social classes, thereby excluding a vast portion of the victims of state-organized violence in the twentieth century. Quite apart from the general ineffectiveness of the UN in enforcing decisions not supported by the major powers, and the fact that states are highly reluctant to intervene in

---

of Courtroom Rhetoric at The Hague," B.A. Honors thesis, Brown University, 2001; Payam Akhavan, "Justice in The Hague, Peace in the Former Yugoslavia? A Commentary on the United Nations War Crimes Tribunal," *Human Rights Quarterly* 20, 4 (1998): 737–816; Michael P. Scharf, *Balkan Justice: The Story behind the First International War Crimes Trial since Nuremberg* (Durham, N.C., 1997). More generally, see Gary Jonathan Bass, *Stay the Hand of Vengeance: The Politics of War Crimes Tribunals* (Princeton, 2000); Howard Ball, *Prosecuting War Crimes and Genocide: The Twentieth-Century Experience* (Lawrence, Kans., 1999); Carla Hesse and Robert Post (eds.), *Human Rights in Political Transitions: Gettysburg to Bosnia* (New York, 1999); Aryeh Neier, *War Crimes: Brutality, Genocide, Terror, and the Struggle for Justice* (New York, 1998); Martha Minow, *Between Vengeance and Forgiveness: Facing History after Genocide and Mass Violence* (Boston, 1998). For recent work on war crimes, see Omer Bartov, Atina Grossmann, and Mary Nolan (eds.), *The Crimes of War: Guilt and Denial in the Twentieth Century* (New York, 2002); István Deák, Jan T. Gross, and Tony Judt (eds.), *The Politics of Retribution in Europe: World War II and Its Aftermath* (Princeton, 2000); Roy Gutman and David Rieff (eds.), *Crimes of War: What the Public Should Know* (New York, 1999).

5 R. J. Rummel, *Death by Government* (New Brunswick, N.J., 1996); Samuel Totten, William S. Parsons, and Israel Charny (eds.), *Century of Genocide: Eyewitness Accounts and Critical Views* (New York, 1997).

6 Norman M. Naimark, *Fires of Hatred: Ethnic Cleansing in Twentieth-Century Europe* (Cambridge, Mass., 2001), 17–56; Dan Diner, *Das Jahrhundert verstehen: Eine Universalhistorische Deutung* (Munich, 1999), 195–201.

7 Frank Chalk and Kurt Jonassohn, *The History and Sociology of Genocide: Analyses and Case Studies* (New Haven, 1990), 10, and for a general discussion of definitions and the relevant literature, 8–27. See also the study by Leo Kuper, *Genocide: Its Political Use in the Twentieth Century* (New Haven, 1981).

the domestic affairs of other states lest their own sovereignty be challenged, it is clear that the definition of genocide depends to a large extent on the political context within which it is discussed.[8] This would be the case even if we accepted a much narrower definition that would limit genocide to the organized attempt by a state entirely to annihilate the physical existence of another ethnic or racial group. For one thing, while preventing genocide before it occurs is hindered by the fact that the intention to perpetrate it is exceedingly difficult to prove, waiting for clear signs of implementation often means that the response would come too late. This, for instance, was the case of the Nazi genocide of the Jews and the Hutu genocide of the Tutsis, as well as much of the Serbian "ethnic cleansing" of Bosnia.[9] But it should also be stressed that while we are used to thinking of genocide in negative terms, it has not infrequently been seen as a legitimate or even glorious action, normally presented as a preventive undertaking in anticipation of genocide by the very group targeted for murder. This was, of course, Heinrich Himmler's view of the "final solution."[10] Positive descriptions by the perpetrators of "ethnic cleansing" are even more common, as for instance in the cases of the population transfers of Greeks and Turks after World War I, the mass deportations of whole ethnic groups by the Soviet Union after World War II, the expulsion of millions of Germans from Eastern Europe, the expulsion of hundreds of thousands of Palestinians from Israel in 1948–49, and the continuing efforts to create ethnically homogeneous areas in the former Yugoslavia by Croats, Serbs, and ethnic Albanians.[11]

8 On April 17, 2001, a Belgian court began the trial of four Rwandans accused of taking part in the genocide of the Tutsi in 1994. This is the first case in which a jury will judge people accused of war crimes in another country. A partial precedent was the arrest of General Augusto Pinochet of Chile in Britain. Belgium, of course, is the former colonial power in Rwanda and was directly involved in the events leading to the genocide there. It has also ratified rights conventions that allow it to try people for international crimes. The United States has up to now strongly objected to this practice. Meanwhile, the International Criminal Tribunal for Rwanda, set up by the UN in Arusha, Tanzania, has convicted only 8 people out of 44 detainees. In Rwanda itself 4,500 have been tried, some 100 executed, and over 100,000 await trial. Some 800,000 Tutsis were murdered in the space of a few months during the 1994 genocide. See Marlise Simons, "An Awful Task: Assessing Four Roles in Death of Thousands," New York Times, April 30, 2001, A3. See further in Gérard Prunier, The Rwanda Crisis: History of a Genocide (New York, 1997).

9 David S. Wyman, The Abandonment of the Jews: America and the Holocaust, 1941–1945 (New York, 1998); Philip Gourevitch, We Wish to Inform You That Tomorrow We Will Be Killed with Our Families: Stories from Rwanda (New York, 1998); David Rieff, Slaughterhouse: Bosnia and the Failure of the West (New York, 1996).

10 See more in Omer Bartov, Mirrors of Destruction: War, Genocide, and Modern Identity (New York, 2000), 25–30.

11 Mark Mazower, Dark Continent: Europe's Twentieth Century (New York, 1999), 61–63; Misha Glenny, The Balkans: Nationalism, War and the Great Powers, 1804–1999 (New York, 1999); Terry Martin, "The Origins of Soviet Ethnic Cleansing," Journal of Modern History 70, 4 (December 1998): 813–61; Naimark, Fires of Hatred; Amir Weiner (ed.), Modernity, Revolution, and Population Management in the Twentieth Century (Stanford, forthcoming); Benny Morris, The Birth of the Palestinian Refugee Problem,

The open-ended definition of genocide can also be used to blur the distinction between perpetrators and victims and to legitimize one kind of violence in the name of preventing another. Thus, for instance, both in left-wing and right-wing West European intellectual circles it is not uncommon to hear the argument that there is no essential difference between the American genocide of the Indians, the enslavement and cultural genocide of Africans, the mass killing of the Vietnamese in the war with the United States, the expulsion and maltreatment of the Palestinians by the Israelis, and the Nazi genocide of the Jews. The unspoken assertion here is, of course, that the United States has no right to present itself as the upholder of world justice, and the Jews have no right to claim any special status by dint of their not-so-unique victimhood.[12] It thus seems to me that while the growing literature devoted to defining and categorizing genocide may add to its obviously crucial juridical conceptualization (even if much of it is written by sociologists and political scientists), a deeper historical understanding of the roots and reality of genocide requires a different approach.

II

As is the case with most historical events, genocide has been conventionally investigated on its own terms, mostly at a degree of generalization that allows a good understanding of its organization and perpetration on a national or local level. For understandable reasons of sources and methodology, this approach has been biased in favor of studying the perpetrators. The victims and bystanders have usually been examined separately and less systematically. The two types of historiography have rarely been integrated.[13] Conversely, the phenomenon of modern genocide as such has hardly been integrated into the general historiography of the modern era, and satisfactory comparative

---

1947–1949 (Cambridge, 1989); Misha Glenny, *The Fall of Yugoslavia: The Third Balkan War*, 3rd rev. ed. (New York, 1996); Marcus Tanner, *Croatia: A Nation Forged in War* (New Haven, 1997), 221–98; Tim Judah, *The Serbs: History, Myth and the Destruction of Yugoslavia* (New Haven, 1997), 168–310; Michael A. Sells, *The Bridge Betrayed: Religion and Genocide in Bosnia* (Berkeley, 1998); Julie A. Mertus, *Kosovo: How Myths and Truths Started a War* (Berkeley, 1999); Michael Ignatieff, *Virtual War: Kosovo and Beyond* (New York, 2000).

12 See, e.g., Alain Brossat, *L'épreuve du désastre: Le xxe siècle et les camps* (Paris, 1996), 20, 23. A more complex view in Catherine Coquio (ed.), *Parler des camps, penser les génocides* (Paris, 1999). For an allegation of Jewish instrumentalization of the Holocaust, see Norman G. Finkelstein, *The Holocaust Industry: Reflections on the Exploitation of Jewish Suffering* (New York, 2000); and a more balanced view in Peter Novick, *The Holocaust in American Life* (Boston, 1999).

13 One important recent exception is Saul Friedländer, *Nazi Germany and the Jews*, vol. 1: *The Years of Persecution, 1933–1939* (New York, 1997). But this volume is concerned only with the prewar years.

studies of genocide are hard to come by.[14] It is for this reason that the rest of this chapter is devoted to some thoughts on the need to develop two very different and yet related approaches to the study of modern genocide. First, because, just like any other historical event, genocide cannot be understood on its own terms, I propose employing a comparative framework that may facilitate making distinctions between the unique and common features of modern outbreaks of mass murder. Second, taking precisely the opposite perspective, I argue for the need to focus on the local level so as to grasp the sociocultural dynamic that makes for outbreaks of violence within communities that have often existed in mutual interdependence for centuries.

In studying state–directed mass crimes it seems obvious to employ a comparative method. And yet, precisely because we are speaking here of crimes committed by states, both comparison between degrees of state criminality, and investigations of the relationship between the individual citizen and the criminal state, contain within them a variety of political and moral quandaries whose primary source is in the issue of legalized criminality.[15] Thus, for instance, on the face of it the Ottoman genocide of the Armenians served as a blueprint and precedent for subsequent cases of genocide, of which the clearest immediate example is the Holocaust.[16] And yet, a variety of interests have made a close comparison of these two events, and an investigation of the possible links between them, extremely difficult.[17] This is all the more remarkable since the novel that made the single most important contribution to bringing the genocide of the Armenians to public attention was Franz Werfel's *The Forty Days of Musa Dagh*, which was in fact written with an eye to the growing persecution of the Jews in the 1930s and was eventually widely read by young Jewish rebels in the ghettos and subsequent generations of Israeli youngsters as a symbol of resistance to slaughter.[18] The reasons for the resistance to comparison are not hard to find.

14 For some attempts in this direction, see Yves Ternon, *L'état criminel: Les génocides au xxᵉ siècle* (Paris, 1995); Mihran Dabag and Kristin Platt (eds.), *Genozid und Moderne*, vol. 1: *Strukturen kollektiver Gewalt im 20. Jahrhundert* (Opladen, 1998); Zygmunt Bauman, *Modernity and the Holocaust* (Ithaca, 1991); Hans Maier (ed.), *Wege in die Gewalt: Die modernen politischen Religionen* (Frankfurt am Main, 2000).

15 Ingo Müller, *Hitler's Justice: The Courts of the Third Reich*, trans. Deborah Lucas Schneider (Cambridge, Mass., 1991); Michael Stolleis, *The Law under the Swastika: Studies on Legal History in Nazi Germany*, trans. T. Dunlap (Chicago, 1998); Michael R. Marrus, *The Nuremberg War Crimes, Trial 1945–46: A Documentary History* (Boston, 1997).

16 Vahakn N. Dadrian, *German Responsibility in the Armenian Genocide: A Review of the Historical Evidence of German Complicity* (Watertown, Mass., 1996).

17 Roger W. Smith et al., "Professional Ethics and the Denial of the Armenian Genocide," *Holocaust and Genocide Studies* 9 (Spring 1995): 1–22.

18 Franz Werfel, *The Forty Days of Musa Dagh*, trans. G. Dunlop (New York, 1934); Yair Auron, "Zionist and Israeli Attitudes toward the Armenian Genocide," in Bartov and Mack, *In God's Name*, 267–88; Yair Auron, *The Banality of Indifference: Zionism and the Armenian Genocide* (New Brunswick, N.J., 2000).

The Turkish government has always denied that an Armenian genocide had taken place. Many other states, including Israel, most Western countries, and the United States, have been wary of antagonizing Turkish authorities and have therefore consistently played down this episode in the waning days of the Ottoman Empire in favor of furthering their economic and strategic interests in the region. Conversely, many survivors of the Holocaust have been reluctant to compare their fate with the disasters that befell others, lest the genocide of the Jews be marginalized or contextualized in a manner that would belittle their suffering. Considering that the Armenians were persecuted in part also for their Christian faith, as well as for their national identity, it was difficult for Jews who perceived their own persecution as rooted in Christian antisemitism to feel sympathy for Christian victims of Moslems.[19]

Another instance of the difficulty of comparison can be gleaned from the changing interpretations of the links, similarities, and distinctions between Nazism and communism. As the debate over the recent publication of the *Black Book of Communism* has shown once more, and as had already become clear during the totalitarianism debate in the 1950s, comparisons between Nazi Germany and Stalinist Russia can and do carry a heavy ideological burden.[20] Without going into the well-known details of this debate, it must be conceded that it clearly demonstrates the extent to which comparison of state-organized murder is never, and can never be, entirely innocent. In this context the case of Cambodia is especially telling. The rampage of the Khmer Rouge has been compared with the Holocaust (as for instance during the *Historikerstreit*, the German historians' controversy in the mid-1980s over the uniqueness of the Holocaust); it

---

19 For a comparison of the reconstruction of collective identity after genocide, see Maud Mandel, "Faith, Religious Practice, and Genocide: Armenians and Jews in France Following World War I and II," in Bartov and Mack, *In God's Name*, 289–315. On Armenian memories of genocide, see Donald E. Miller and Lorna Touryan Miller, *Survivors: An Oral History of the Armenian Genocide* (Berkeley, 1999).

20 Stéphane Courtois et al., *The Black Book of Communism: Crimes, Terror, Repression*, trans. J. Murphy and M. Kramer (Cambridge, Mass., 1999). See also François Furet, *The Passing of an Illusion: The Idea of Communism in the Twentieth Century*, trans. D. Furet (Chicago, 1999); Abbott Gleason, *Totalitarianism: The Inner History of the Cold War* (New York, 1995). A recent history of Nazi Germany that makes a case for similarity with the Soviet system is Michael Burleigh, *The Third Reich: A New History* (New York, 2000). A comparison of personalities is Alan Bullock, *Hitler and Stalin: Parallel Lives* (New York, 1992); and of systems, Ian Kershaw and Moshe Lewin (eds.), *Stalinism and Nazism: Dictatorships in Comparison* (Cambridge, 1997). Different opinions on the usefulness of the concept of totalitarianism can be found in Krzytof Pomian, "Totalitarisme," *Vigntième Siècle* 47 (July–September 1995): 4–23; Klaus-Dietmar Henke, "Die Verführungskraft des Totalitären," Hannah-Arendt-Institut für Totalitarismusforschung, *Berichte und Studien* 12 (Dresden, 1997); Ian Kershaw, "Nazisme et stalinisme: Limites d'une comparaison," *Le Débat* 89 (March–April 1996): 177–89; Henry Rousso (ed.), *Stalinisme et nazisme: Histoire et mémoire comparées* (Brussels, 1999).

was used as an example of communist criminality (in Western Cold War rhetoric); it was said to be another consequence of American imperialism (in communist Cold War rhetoric); and, most recently, it was also linked to ethnic prejudice and racial persecution.[21] Hence we must be aware that comparative methods bring with them a significant liability that can often prejudice one's conclusions or the reactions and understanding of the public.

Nevertheless, it would be unwise to reject comparative methods simply because of their potential for obfuscation and abuse. Indeed, this very susceptibility to political mobilization indicates the extent to which this approach can reveal the close intellectual, ideological, organizational, and historical links between discrete instances of genocide, which is, of course, why comparisons were so vehemently resisted in the first place. Uncovering the common denominators of modern genocide will, moreover, not only teach us more about the roots of specific instances but also about the continuing presence of this threat in the modern psyche just as much as in modern politics, whether as actual policy or as memory and imaginary.

One of the most crucial questions that a comparative study of genocide can address is the relationship between what might be seen as immanent predilections in human society or individual human beings, and the emergence of an idea and a practice at a given time and place and its migration from one society to another. A great deal has been said, and some written, on the potential of everyone to become a serial killer under certain circumstances, as well as the potential of all human societies to develop genocidal trends. In the debate between Daniel Goldhagen and Christopher Browning, both scholars invoked a variety of authorities and offered a radically different reading of essentially the same historical documentation in order to support their polar interpretations. For Browning, the German killers were "ordinary men," in the sense that anyone might have acted similarly under similar circumstances; for Goldhagen, they were "normal Germans," in the sense that all Germans, but only Germans, would have been willing

---

21 Ben Kiernan (ed.), *Genocide and Democracy in Cambodia: The Khmer Rouge, the United Nations and the International Community* (New Haven, 1993); Kiernan, "Genocidal Targeting: The Two Groups of Victims in Pol Pot's Cambodia," in P. Timothy Bushnell, Vladimir Shlapentokh, Christopher K. Vanderpool, and Jeyaratnam Sundram (eds.), *State Organized Violence: The Case of Violent Internal Repression* (Boulder, 1991), 207–26; Eyal Press, "Unforgiven: The Director of the Cambodian Genocide Program Rekindles Cold War Animosities," *Lingua Franca* (April–May 1997): 67–75. Kiernan presented a paper on the Cambodian genocide as ethnic persecution at the conference on Lessons and Legacies: Laws, Evidence, and Context, the Holocaust Educational Foundation, Florida Atlantic University, Boca Roton, November 1998. Further in Jean-Louis Margolin, "Cambodia: The Country of Disconcerting Crimes," in Courtois et al., *The Black Book of Communism*, 577–644.

and able to step into their shoes.[22] The point to be made here is that this debate is unlikely to progress much further as long as it focuses on only one case of genocide or, indeed, on just a few killing squads. The assumption of similarity to or distinction from other societies must ultimately be based on comparison, and neither scholar offered a truly comparative perspective. There are echoes here of the *Sonderweg* (special path) debate, in which for a long time a certain model of normality was assumed against which German uniqueness was opposed, all without any detailed comparison between the alleged "normality" of Britain and France, and the consequently "peculiar" historical development of Germany. Once such scholars as Geoff Eley and David Blackbourn actually proposed this comparison, much of what had been seen as "unique" about the German case melted away.[23]

There have also been proposals in the past to trace the ways in which the idea of genocide, or "ethnic cleansing," migrated over time and space. Probably the most original sustained attempt to uncover the deep historical and cultural roots of twentieth century state-organized violence can be found in Hanna Arendt's *The Origins of Totalitarianism*.[24] Arendt argued that European imperialism, along with Christian antisemitism, were at the core of a set of ideas and practices that made European states increasingly susceptible to resort to mass violence legitimized and propelled by ideologies of expansion and superiority, unity and purity, civilization and barbarism. But Arendt's insights into the links between imperialism and antisemitism took half a century to be disseminated within the larger scholarly community. For long, totalitarianism as a concept was seen primarily as a key to comparing Nazism and Bolshevism. Only the resurgence in the study of colonialism, on the one hand, and of antisemitism and the Holocaust, on the other,

---

22 Christopher R. Browning, *Ordinary Men: Reserve Police Battalion 101 and the Final Solution in Poland* (New York, 1993); Daniel Jonah Goldhagen, *Hitler's Willing Executioners: Ordinary Germans and the Holocaust* (New York, 1996). For the debate, see Geoff Eley (ed.), *The "Goldhagen Effect": History, Memory, Nazism – Facing the German Past* (Ann Arbor, 2000); Robert R. Shandley (ed.), *Unwilling Germans? The Goldhagen Debate* (Minneapolis, 1998); Norman G. Finkelstein and Ruth Bettina Birn, *A Nation on Trial: The Goldhagen Thesis and Historical Truth* (New York, 1998); Julius H. Schoeps (ed.), *Ein Volk von Mördern? Die Dokumentation zur Goldhagen-Kontroverse um die Rolle der Deutschen im Holocaust* (Hamburg, 1996). The most important psychological study on which Browning relies is Stanley Milgram, *Obedience to Authority* (New York, 1975).

23 The classical example of the *Sonderwegtheorie* is Hans-Ulrich Wehler, *The German Empire, 1871–1918*, trans. K. Traynor (1973; Leamington Spa, 1985); the refutation, David Blackbourn and Geoff Eley, *The Peculiarities of German History: Bourgeois Society and Politics in Nineteenth-Century Germany* (Oxford, 1984).

24 Hannah Arendt, *The Origins of Totalitarianism* (1951; London, 1968). See also Carl J. Friedrich (ed.), *Totalitarianism* (1954; New York, 1964). See further in Steven E. Aschheim, "Nazism, Culture and *The Origins of Totalitarianism*: Hannah Arendt and the Discourse of Evil," *New German Critique* 70 (Winter 1997): 117–39.

finally facilitated the return to Arendt's original thesis. Thus, for instance, recent research has been focusing on the links between the German genocidal policies against the Herero of South West Africa, German involvement in the Ottoman genocide of the Armenians, and Nazi policies against the Jews in the 1930s and 1940s.[25]

Recent work on the links between German colonial policies and definitions of citizenship has also begun to revise earlier conventions about the origins of the idea of German nationalism and how it differed from the French concept.[26] Indeed, a closer look at the French case through the prism of France's interaction with its colonial holdings also demonstrates that while the colonizers obviously had an impact on the identity of the colonized, this was anything but a one-sided process. It is now being argued, for instance, that in the wake of the Algerian War and the arrival of the *pieds noirs* on French soil conceptualizations of citizenship in France underwent a profound, albeit incomplete transformation.[27] Most relevant to the present discussion is new research currently under way on the links between German concepts of race in Africa and of Jews in Europe. Preliminary findings indicate that there was a complex relationship between the dehumanization and fear of Africans and the antisemitic discourse in late nineteenth-century and early twentieth-century Germany. Indeed, many of the terms we usually associate with the Holocaust originated in German debates over the colonies in Africa.[28]

Hence, despite the difficulties and perils of a comparative approach, among which we must also include the threat of superficiality and glibness, there is little doubt that it can reveal much about modern genocide that had eluded earlier scholars who focused on discrete cases. Most clearly, comparative studies indicate that modern genocide – narrowly defined as

25 See Chapter 7 in this volume by Isabel Hull. See also note 2.
26 Laura Wildenthal, " 'She Is the Victor': Bourgeois Women, Nationalist Identities, and the Ideal of the Independent Woman Farmer in German Southwest Africa," in Geoff Eley (ed.), *Society, Culture, and the State in Germany, 1870–1930* (Ann Arbor, 1997), 371–95; Rogers Brubaker, *Citizenship and Nationhood in France and Germany* (Cambridge, Mass., 1992). Such research has also had interesting repercussions on our understanding of gender and the impact of colonialism on the evolution of its conceptualization in Europe. For the range of influences on German society, see Friedrichsmeyer et al., *The Imperialist Imagination*.
27 Todd Shepard, "Decolonizing France: Reimagining the Nation and Redefining the Republic at the End of Empire," Ph.D. dissertation, Rutgers University, 2001.
28 Christian Davis is writing a Ph.D. dissertation at Rutgers University tentatively titled "Colonialism, Antisemitism, and the German-Jewish Consciousness," which addresses this issue. See further in Cornelia Essner, "Zwischen Vernunft und Gefühl: Die Reichstagsdebatten von 1912 um koloniale 'Rassenmischehe' und 'Sexualität,' " *Vierteljahrshefte für Zeitgeschichte* 6 (1997): 503–19; Smith, "The Talk of Genocide." For the origins of the German *imaginaire* of race and gender in connection with the colonies, see Susanne Zantop, *Colonial Fantasies: Conquest, Family, and Nation in Precolonial Germany, 1770–1870* (Durham, N.C., 1997).

the eradication of an entire ethnic or racial group – is closely linked to the emergence of the nation-state in Europe and the spread of European empires across the world. Here the appearance of modern antisemitism and the rhetoric of the "nationalization of the masses" also played a crucial role.[29] From this perspective, studying the origins of genocide in a comparative mode is akin to analyzing some of the most crucial and pervasive aspects of modern society, political organizations, and ideologies.

III

This being said, some fundamental questions tend to elude comparative studies on the scale outlined here, just as they defy analyses of genocidal systems on the national level.[30] The categories of difference and similarity, origins and mutual influences that preoccupy comparative studies rarely tell us much about social dynamics of individual communities subjected to or complicit in genocide. And yet, notwithstanding the modernization of the killing process and the bureaucratic and technological capacities available to the modern state in organizing violence, much of the reality of genocide always occurs on the local level, in the interaction between friends and neighbors, as well as the encounter with and reception of forces arriving from outside the community. Moreover, the conduct of the community is often crucial to the success or failure of state-organized genocide in a given area, as was clearly seen in the Holocaust. To be sure, when speaking of the local level or, indeed, of individual or collective psychology, we are bound to identify elements that have remained unchanged over time and across cultures. But other factors will often be radically transformed under changing circumstances, leading in turn to radical changes in outlook and conduct. This is the point at which a community based on interaction and cooperation may be metamorphosed into a community of genocide.[31]

---

29 George L. Mosse, *The Nationalization of the Masses: Political Symbolism and Mass Movements in Germany from the Napoleonic Wars through the Third Reich* (1975; Ithaca, 1991); Peter Pulzer, *The Rise of Political Anti-Semitism in Germany and Austria*, rev. ed. (Cambridge, Mass., 1988); Bartov, *Mirrors of Destruction*, 91–142.

30 The classic model for this approach is Raul Hilberg, *The Destruction of the European Jews*, rev. ed., 3 vols. (New York, 1985).

31 The most striking examples of massacres on the local level within the framework of a much larger genocidal undertaking to have received recent scholarly or journalistic attention concern the Holocaust, Bosnia, and Rwanda. See Jan T. Gross, *Neighbors: The Destruction of the Jewish Community in Jedwabne, Poland* (Princeton, 2001); Nick Ceh and Jeff Harder (eds.), *The Golden Apple: War and Democracy in Croatia and Bosnia* (New York, 1996); Roy Gutman, *A Witness to Genocide* (New York, 1993); Florence Hartmann, "Bosnia," in Gutman and Rieff, *Crimes of War*; Gourevitch, *We Wish to Inform You*.

My main argument here is that we cannot understand certain central aspects of modern genocide without closely examining the local circumstances in which it occurs. These circumstances can be understood only by taking into account all groups of which a given community is composed, and by considering the evolution of relationships between the groups and of their self-perceptions and views of each other over a relatively long span of time. For what is inherent to genocide on the local level is that it frequently involves a moment in which neighbors and friends, even family members (especially where intermarriage had become common), turn on each other often with almost unimaginable savagery and cruelty. This was the case, for instance, in many mixed communities in Eastern Europe, where Poles, Ukrainians, Belorussians, Lithuanians, Russians, Germans, Latvians, Estonians, and so forth, lived in close proximity with each other and with their Jewish neighbors, and had done so for centuries. While violence was never far from the surface and erupted every once in a while, it was only with the German invasion that endemic hostility and aggression were transformed into a genocidal explosion of unprecedented ferocity. This was also the case in Rwanda and Burundi, in Bosnia, in Cambodia, and, with some qualifications attributable to local and international constraints, also in Palestine and Israel, Indonesia, Maoist China and Stalinist Russia, and quite a few other spots across the globe. In other words, what needs to be investigated is the link between (physical and social) proximity and (economic, cultural, and political) interdependence on the one hand, and the outbreak of violence that seeks entirely to eradicate one or more of the groups that make up the community, often accompanied by acts of brutality, humiliation, and dehumanization that seem to defy generations of shared living, not necessary in perfect harmony, but in an equilibrium that in many ways had – until that point – constituted the core of the community's material and spiritual existence.

Studies of this kind require rather different skills from comparative work. Ethnographic and sociological training or at least sensibilities, as well as a certain literary ability, would be of much use. Indeed, both comparative and what I would call here community studies are based on the assumption that historical understanding can be greatly enriched by making use of other disciplinary methods and perspectives. This is at least partly related to the sense of frustration among historians with the limits of their conventional methods in explaining genocide. A community study of the type envisioned here will also normally require significant linguistic skills or professional assistance, because the community would be composed of groups speaking different languages or dialects, as well as claiming different cultural traditions and often belonging to different religious faiths. The student of such a community would need to make use of as much personal material as can be found (the existence of such sources is crucial to the success of an undertaking of this nature) and might need to conduct interviews and employ methods of oral history. In other words, while limited to a small geographical area and a restricted number of protagonists, such a community study is a rather complex undertaking. It might thus be argued that the difficulties involved outweigh the anticipated benefits, considering that all we might ultimately come up with would be a more or less reliable reconstruction of the life and death (of part) of a community. Obviously, I do not share this view. Rather, I feel that much of what we have been unable to grasp when looking at the "big picture" can be much better understood when seen at the local level where the personal interaction between people, their prejudices, needs, and urges, as well as their memories, traditions, and perceptions, would all have to be taken into account. The devil, I would say in this context, is in the local.[32]

To clarify why I perceive this approach to be of particular importance to our understanding of the mechanics of mass violence on the local level, and how this links to the issue of genocide – that is, state-directed mass murder – rather than being subsumed merely under the category of local massacres, I now turn to a single case which is the focus of a new research project in which I am currently engaged.

The town of Buczacz sits astride the Strypa River, some thirteen miles north of the Dniester, thirty-five miles south of the provincial capital Tarnopil (Tarnopol in Polish), and about eighty miles southeast of L'viv (Lwów in Polish, Lvov in Yiddish, Lemberg in German), which was the capital of Galicia under Austrian rule and of Polish Red Ruthenia before

---

32 The debate surrounding the publication of Gross's *Neighbors*, in Poland and elsewhere, is a good indication of the potentially explosive nature of such studies, despite the fact that Gross does not attempt to reconstruct the social and cultural fabric of life in Jedwabne before the war. See, e.g., "Polish Face Truth of Jedwabne," *New York Times*, March 12, 2001; Peter Finn, "Painful Truth in Poland's Mirror: Book on 1941 Massacre of Jews Shifts Blame from Nazis to Neighbors," *Washington Post*, March 14, 2001; Adam Michnik, "Poles and the Jews: How Deep the Guilt?" *New York Times*, March 17, 2001, A15, A17; Steven Erlanger, "Soul-Searching at Another Polish Massacre Site," *New York Times*, April 19, 2001, A3. See the debate in the pages of the *Times Literary Supplement*: Abraham Brumberg, "Murder Most Foul: Polish Responsibility for the Massacre at Jedwabne," March 2, 2001, 8–9; and letters to the editor by Jan Nowak and Czeslaw Karkowski, March 16, 2001, 17; by Abraham Brumberg, March 23, 2001, 17; by Norman Davis and Werner Cohn, March 30, 2001, 21; by Vaiva Pukite, Tony Judt, and Abraham Brumberg, April 6, 2001, 17; by Norman Davis, April 13, 2001, 17. In the Israeli press, see Sever Plotzki, "1,600 Jews Locked in a Barn and Burned Alive" (in Hebrew), interview with Jan Gross, *Yediot Aharonot*, January 19, 2001, 20–21; "Poles Accept Blame for 1941 Massacre of Jews," *Jerusalem Post*, March 15, 2001. On an early postwar massacre of Jews in Poland, see Krystyna Kersten, "The Pogrom of Jews in Kielce on July 4, 1946," *Acta Poloniae Historica* 76 (1997): 197–222.

the first partition of Poland in 1772. Between the world wars Buczacz was less than forty miles from the Soviet border. Founded in the fourteenth century by the noble Polish Buczaczki family, the city developed into an important trade center between Poland and the Ottoman Empire in the sixteenth century. In the seventeenth century Buczacz passed into the hands of the Potockis, one of the most powerful noble families in Poland.

Jews are known to have resided in Buczacz since the fifteenth century. During the Cossack siege of 1648 and the Turkish attacks and partial conquest in 1672 and 1675 the Jews participated in the fighting. The community absorbed many refugees from the massacres of Hetman Bogdan Chmielnicki's Cossacks. But following these devastating wars the Jews of Buczacz recovered, seceded from the religious jurisdiction of the Lvov community, built an impressive synagogue, and obtained permission to reside in all parts of the city and pursue all occupations, as well as gaining jurisdictional autonomy.

For much of the next two centuries the Jews constituted the single largest ethnic and religious group in Buczacz, alongside the Poles and Ruthenians, who later came to be called Ukrainians. The Jews worked as agents for the Polish nobility, managing or renting their estates. By 1915 about a fifth of the large estates in the Buczacz district were owned by Jews, who were also the first to learn German following the partition of Poland. After the severe occupational and residential restrictions imposed by the Austrians in 1772 were lifted in 1848, the community began to grow and flourish, reaching close to 8,000 people, or just over half of the total population of Buczacz, by 1910. Engaging in commerce and, from the late nineteenth century, in petty industry, Jewish tailors, furriers, smiths, bookmakers, and wagon drivers practically dominated these trades. By the early twentieth century they were also entering the professions in increasing numbers. Relations between the majority of Mitnagdim (traditionalists), and the smaller groups of Hassidim (pietists) and Maskilim (secular-minded supporters of the Enlightenment) were largely cordial, as were relations with the gentile Polish and Ukrainian population. Thus the first elected municipal government of Buczacz established in 1874 comprised twelve Jews, nine Poles, and nine Ukrainians. Indeed, in 1879 the Jew Bernard Shtern was elected mayor, a position he held until 1921, while also serving as head of the community after 1890 and being elected as representative to the Austrian parliament in 1911.

Although the community established the only modern hospital in Buczacz in 1891, modernized the school system, and promoted a variety of cultural institutions, the early years of the twentieth century also witnessed a rise in antisemitism that led to increased emigration of Jews to North America. With the outbreak of World War I most of the Jews fled to the western parts of the Austro-Hungarian Empire, and those who stayed behind were subjected to brutalities by Cossacks serving in the Russian army. Between 1918 and 1919 Buczacz came under the rule of the short-lived Ukrainian republic and was then briefly occupied by the Red Army in the course of the Russo-Polish War. The retreat of Soviet forces was followed by a spate of murder, pillage, and rape of the Jews by bands of Petliura's Ukrainian nationalists. By 1921 there were only 3,858 Jews out of a total population of 7,517 in Buczacz, and even after the partial recovery of the town, ten years later the Jewish population stood at a mere 4,439 people. Once at the heart of one of the largest and most vibrant concentrations of Jews in Eastern Europe, the Jews of Buczacz, as those of numerous other neighboring towns, were undergoing a process of pauperization and demoralization. Discriminatory policies by the Polish government, which ruled Galicia throughout the interwar period, excluded Jews from a variety of trades and industries and ensured that Eastern Galicia remained economically underdeveloped and depressed. Following the death of Poland's military ruler, Marshal Pilsudski, in 1935, official Polish antisemitism increased. Thus by the late 1930s the municipal high school imposed a quota on Jews, and the teachers seminary admitted no Jews at all. These political and economic conditions must have contributed to the growing influence of the Zionists in Buczacz, who ruled the community in coalition with other Jewish political parties. During those years of precipitous decline, the Jews of Buczacz could at least boast of having produced some of Eastern Europe's most renowned figures, among whom the historian Emanuel Ringelblum and the future Nobel Prize–winning author Shmuel Yosef (Shai) Agnon are best remembered. (Buczacz was also the birthplace of Sigmund Freud's father.)

In accordance with the Ribbentrop-Molotov Pact that divided Poland between Nazi Germany and the USSR, Buczacz came under Soviet rule in September 1939. Jewish institutions were now largely suppressed, and many Jewish refugees fleeing the Germans and seeking shelter in Buczacz were deported into the interior of the Soviet Union. With the German attack on June 22, 1941, hundreds of young male Jews were conscripted into the Red Army. As the Soviets withdrew, and even before German forces marched in on July 7, Ukrainian nationalists began brutalizing the Jews, accusing them of collaboration with the Soviets. On July 28, 1941, helped by local collaborators, units of Einsatzgruppe (SS and SD murder squad) D executed about 350 mostly educated Jewish males. At that time the Germans also ordered the creation of a Jewish council supported by a

Jewish police force. Throughout the fall of 1941 Jews were conscripted to forced labor, robbed of their property, and deprived of food and medical care. Then, on October 17, 1942, a German unit assisted by Ukrainian police sent 1,600 Jews to the Belzec extermination camp and killed on the spot a further 200 Jews who tried to escape. Another "Aktion" took place on November 27, 1942, in which a further 2,500 people were sent to Belzec, while some 250 were shot for trying to hide or escape. In late 1942 the Jews were enclosed in a walled ghetto, into which Jews from other communities were also brought. Many died from epidemics produced by the unsanitary conditions. On February 1–2, 1943, 2,000 were taken out and executed. The killings went on unabated, costing the lives of some 3,000 people in April and May 1943. In mid-June 1943 the last survivors of the ghetto were murdered by mass shootings in the vicinity. The small Jewish resistance group failed in its attempt to prevent the "Aktion" of April 1943 and dispersed. Other Jewish partisans still operating in the woods after the liquidation of the ghetto were wiped out by retreating German army units in February 1944. When the Red Army marched into Buczacz on March 23, some 800 surviving Jews came out of hiding in the area, only to be murdered when the Germans temporarily recaptured the city. When Buczacz was finally liberated on July 21, less than 100 Jews were left. The remaining 400 former Jewish residents of Buczacz who spent the war in the USSR returned to their hometown only briefly and went on to live in Israel or North America. Today there are no Jews in Buczacz, or any memorial to the fate of its Jewish community.[33]

IV

The main outlines of the genocide of the Jews in East Galicia, in which almost the entire Jewish population, numbering some 500,000 people, was murdered, have recently been reconstructed by two young German scholars.[34] Until their studies were published, we knew relatively little about

33 This account is based on the following sources: Danuta Dombrovska, Avraham Wein, and Aharon Weiss (eds.), *Pinkas Hakehilot: Polin. Encyclopedia of Jewish Communities from Their Establishment to the Aftermath of the Shoah of World War II*, vol. 2: *Eastern Galicia* (in Hebrew) (Jerusalem, 1980), 83–89; Yisrael Cohen (ed.), *The Book of Buczacz* (in Hebrew) (Tel Aviv, 1956), 39–74 (chronicles), 233–302 (testimonies); Yad Vashem, section 0.3 (testimonies [in Hebrew]): Simcha Tischler, file 10229, recorded June 26, 1997; Yisrael Muncher, file 5878, recorded April 27, 1990; Esther Paul, file 6723, recorded October 23, 1992; Halfon Eliyahu, file 8553, recorded October 21, 1947.

34 Dieter Pohl, *Nationalsozialistische Judenvernichtung in Ostgalizien, 1941–1944. Organisation und Durchführung eines staatlichen Massenverbrechens* (Munich, 1996); Thomas Sandkühler, *"Endlösung" in Galizien. Der Judenmord in Ostpolen und die Rettungsinitiativen von Berthold Beitz, 1941–1944* (Bonn, 1996).

the manner in which the Holocaust unfolded in this region from the perspective of the Nazi administration, although both personal accounts and yizkor bicher (Jewish community memorial books) provided insights into the manner in which these events were experienced by the victims. Based on a wide range of German, Polish, and Ukrainian sources, this new scholarship offers an accurate depiction and analysis of the sequence of events, the agencies involved, and to some extent the motivation of the local German organizers of the genocide. Other recent studies have also added greatly to our knowledge of the collaboration by local Polish and especially Ukrainian elements in the persecution of the Jews.[35] However, with the partial exception of Martin Dean's work, while this scholarship makes limited use of Jewish sources, it refrains from providing the Jewish and, for that matter, the local gentile perspective of these events. Thus the picture created in these studies is one of a German invasion that brings in its wake a genocidal policy against the Jews that is in part aided and abetted by the non-Jewish population for a variety of reasons ranging from prejudice and opportunism to nationalist aspirations. Reading such studies is, of course, a very depressing experience. And yet, the reader gains very little understanding of how genocide actually unfolded on the ground, and what was the nature of the social fabric upon which these policies were enacted and to which it reacted. Compared with the yizkor bicher of precisely the same towns mentioned in German accounts, one gains the disturbing impression that these were two entirely distinct events.

The recent controversy over the Wehrmacht Exhibition in Germany, and subsequent publications relevant to that debate,[36] have begun to attract more attention to the importance of uncovering the social reality of East Galicia prior to the arrival of the Germans in order to understand the manner in which genocide actually took place.[37] The critics of the exhibition were mainly concerned with the two preceding years of Soviet occupation in East Galicia, because these supposedly created or at least greatly exacerbated gentile hostility toward the Jews who were seen as collaborators with the

---

35 Martin Dean, *Collaboration in the Holocaust: Crimes of the Local Police in Belorussia and Ukraine, 1941–44* (New York, 2000). On Belorussia, see now Bernhard Chiari, *Alltag hinter der Front. Besatzung, Kollaboration und Widerstand in Weißrußland 1941–1944* (Dusseldorf, 1998); Christian Gerlach, *Kalkulierte Morde. Die deutsche Wirtschafts- und Vernichtungspolitik in Weißrußland 1941 bis 1944* (Hamburg, 1999).

36 See, esp., Bogdan Musial, *"Konterrevolutionäre Elemente sind zu erschießen." Die Brutalisierung des deutsch-sowjetischen Krieges im Sommer 1941* (Berlin, 2000). See also Jan T. Gross, *Revolution from Abroad: Soviet Conquest of Poland's Western Ukraine and Western Belorussia* (Princeton, 1988).

37 On the exhibition itself, see now esp. Hamburg Institute for Social Research (ed.), *The German Army and Genocide: Crimes against War Prisoners, Jews, and Other Civilians, 1939–1944* (New York, 1999); Hannes Heer and Klaus Naumann (eds.), *War of Extermination: The German Military in World War II, 1941–1944* (New York, 2000). On the controversy, see Bartov et al., *The Crimes of War.*

Bolsheviks. Hence the crucial collaboration with the Nazis in murdering the Jews is traced back to alleged Jewish collaboration with the Soviets against their neighbors. This view remained current in local accounts long after the end of the war.[38] Complicating matters even further was the Soviet policy vis-à-vis the local nationalists who collaborated with the Nazis with the hope of gaining independence from Soviet rule, on the one hand, and the Soviet reluctance to recognize the specificity of Jewish victimhood under Nazi rule, on the other.[39] Conversely, Jewish memories of this period tend to stress the brutality of local collaborators (and, in some cases, of Jewish Kapos or policemen) even more than that of the Nazis not least because they were often known by name, had been neighbors for generations, and now not only helped the Nazis but often took action on their own initiative and hunted down Jews who escaped to the countryside with greater efficiency and perseverance than many German units.[40]

Yet, merely reconstructing the two years of Soviet occupation that preceded the German invasion is hardly sufficient as a context for the events of 1941–44. In order to understand the specific manner in which the genocide unfolded, and to take in the different contemporary perspectives as well as the differing perceptions of subsequent historiography, memory, and representation, one must go much farther back. Indeed, what I would argue is that while genocide has very distinct immediate causes, it also must have far deeper local social and cultural roots that largely determine the manner in which it ultimately occurs. In this sense, the narrative of genocide must begin at the end – the moment at which everything comes together and breaks apart in one explosive release of violence – and then slowly move back, carefully peeling away the layers of different memories and histories, searching for the stitches that bound that society together and for the tears and wounds that festered underneath.

---

38 See a brief summary of Ukrainian literature in Pohl, *Nationalsozialistische Judenvernichtung*, 397–98. See further in Jan T. Gross, "A Tangled Web: Confronting Stereotypes concerning Relations between Poles, Germans, Jews, and Communists," in Deák et al., *The Politics of Retribution*, 74–129; Timothy Snyder, " 'To Remove the Ukrainian Problem Once and for All': The Ethnic Cleansing of Ukrainians in Poland, 1943–1947," *Journal of Cold War Studies* 1–2 (1999): 86–120; Peter J. Potichnyi and Howard Aster (eds.), *Ukrainian-Jewish Relations in Historical Perspective* (Edmonton, 1988); Zvi Gitelman et al. (eds.), *Cultures and Nations of Central Eastern Europe: Essays in Honor of Roman Szporluk* (Cambridge, Mass., 2000); Peter J. Potichnyi (ed.), *Poland and Ukraine, Past and Present* (Edmonton, 1980); Ivan L. Rudnytsky (ed.), *Rethinking Ukrainian History* (Edmonton, 1981).

39 Amir Weiner, *Making Sense of War: The Second World War and the Fate of the Bolshevik Revolution* (Princeton, 2000).

40 See, as just one example, Irene Horowitz and Carl Horowitz, *Of Human Agony* (New York, 1992), 86–93.

What occurred in Buczacz between 1941 and 1944 might not have happened at all, or at least not in the same manner, had the Germans not marched in. And yet genocide would have been much harder to accomplish, and its success much less complete, had the Germans not found so many collaborators willing, even eager, to do the killing, the hunting down, the brutalizing and plunder for the occupiers. Nor would more than a few of the handful of Jews who did survive live to tell the tale had it not been for those Ukrainians and Poles who gave them food, shelter, and a hiding place, even if at times they charged them for the service. After all, such people risked their lives and those of their families for hiding Jews. Only a meticulous reconstruction of life in towns such as Buczacz, whose mix of populations, division of economic roles, social stratification, and religious distinctions were typical of these regions in Eastern Europe, will provide clues to why hundreds of thousands of Jews were butchered by their neighbors or at least right next to them without even token opposition and with a great deal of glee and relief. It may also help us understand why some people, often simple, illiterate peasants, saw the humanity of the persecuted and protected them from the killers.[41]

Eastern Galicia was a society that for many generations had formed links of economic interdependence. To be sure, resentment was never far from the surface, and was marked by periodic outbreaks of violence. In part this can be traced to the fact that the Ukrainians were even poorer than the Jews and associated the latter with their Polish landlords. In part it had to do with religious differences, especially anti-Jewish sentiments, but also tensions between Unitarian Ukrainians and Catholic Poles. Finally, increasing friction was related to the budding nationalism among all three groups. Still, the socioeconomy of Eastern Galicia, just as much as its culture, was a conglomerate of all religions, ethnicities, languages, and traditions. To this must be added the fact that many middle-class Jews were moving away from the traditional way of life as they moved out of the shtetlach (small and predominantly Jewish towns) and began providing their children with a secular education, often associated with German letters, learning, and schooling. Thus, quite apart from Polish, Ukrainian, and Yiddish, especially the rising Jewish bourgeoisie took up the German language and along with it other attributes of German culture. And then, of course, there was the growing

---

41 For three moving accounts of life in an East European shtetl, see David Zagier, *Botchki: When Doomsday Was Still Tomorrow* (London, 2000); Theo Richmond, *Konin: A Quest* (New York, 1995); Eva Hoffman, *Shtetl: The Life and Death of a Small Town and the World of Polish Jews* (London, 1998).

impact of Zionism and the spread of the Hebrew language as a secular tongue rather than as the language of prayer and religious study.[42]

Clearly, the determination of the Nazi regime to murder the Jews is key in explaining the Holocaust. But it is also crucial to realize that while in much of Eastern Europe the Germans had no trouble in unleashing an astonishing surge of local violence against the Jews, this was hardly the case in many other parts of Western Europe; hence the need to focus on local dynamics even when striving to understand the whole. For while such specificity may appear to tell us a great deal about one place and very little about the phenomenon as a whole, I would argue that the event of genocide as such must also be reconstructed from the bottom up, from such specific cases of internecine conflict and violence to the larger context that transforms them from isolated incidents of massacre to full-scale mass murder. If we move from Buczacz to Sarajevo, or from East Galicia to Rwanda, we discover the same complexity of relationships on the local level, and similar links between the local and the national sphere. As scholars writing on Rwanda have pointed out, our very understanding of the alleged differences between the Tutsis and the Hutus is based on a conceptualization of Rwandan society that was superimposed on it by colonial rule and the Catholic Church, and was only subsequently internalized by the local population.[43] Similarly, our easy, not to say facile distinctions between victims, perpetrators, and bystanders, between collaborators and resisters, Jews and Gentiles, occupiers and occupied, must be subjected to a much more careful historical examination on the local level. What was happening in Buczacz between 1941 and 1944? How did old loyalties and allegiances, friendships and ideological affiliations, old prejudices and fresh memories of persecution and victimhood work themselves out under the impact of German occupation, between one Soviet occupation and another?

In some respects, we cannot speak of genocide on the local level. Massacre and mass killing become genocide only when an entire ethnic group is targeted by the state. By the same token, however, our understanding of genocide remains highly limited as long as we do not go beyond the level of state organization and mass victimhood. As I have tried to argue, only by raising our eyes over the horizon of a specific genocide, and by lowering

---

42 For background, see Deborah Dash Moore (ed.), *East European Jews in Two World Wars: Studies from the YIVO Annual* (Evanston, 1990); Ezra Mendelsohn, *The Jews of East Central Europe between the World Wars* (Bloomington, 1983); Yisrael Gutman, Ezra Mendelsohn, Jehuda Reinharz, and Chone Shmeruk (eds.), *The Jews of Poland between Two World Wars* (Hanover, 1989).

43 Timothy Longman, "Christian Churches and Genocide in Rwanda," and Charles de Lespinay, "The Churches and the Genocide in the East African Great Lakes Region," both in Bartov and Mack, *In God's Name*, 139–60, 161–79, respectively.

them to a specific locality in which genocide was implemented – even if those subjected to it did not know that their fate was part of a much larger event – will we be able to advance our understanding of this phenomenon. In both cases, this is a difficult exercise. An informed comparison of different genocidal systems calls for a great deal of learning and synthesizing of data, and requires the construction of a usable analytical framework that would make sense of the comparison. Investigating local communities requires a combination of detective work in seeking out evidence and literary ability to write the story of a community in a manner that will bring it back to life.

In the case of such a site as Buczacz, we are blessed with the works of the great writer Agnon, many of whose stories are suffused with the sights, smells, and characters of his birth town Buczacz and its surroundings. Moreover, quite apart from the impressive yizkor bich of Buczacz, which collects much historical data on the town along with photographs, personal recollections, testimonies, and documents, as well as the important encyclopedia of Jewish communities in Eastern Europe, the archives of Yad Vashem in Jerusalem contain a wealth of information about the town culled especially from accounts by survivors of the Holocaust.[44] In the last few years agents of the United States Holocaust Memorial Museum in Washington, D.C., have been microfilming documents in these parts of the Ukraine that will be of much help in reconstructing the official history of the town and the lives of its Polish, and Ukrainian inhabitants. Many other documents are held at the Austrian National Archive in Vienna, since Buczacz was for long under Austrian rule, and may also be found in Ukrainian, Polish, and Russian archives. Some accounts by local non-Jews of events under Soviet and German occupation have already been published, while others await recovery from the archives or other collections. These will serve in reconstructing the view of those often erroneously described as bystanders but who in fact were active participants in the events.[45] Finally, the records of German units that descended on Buczacz in July 1941 and of its subsequent German occupiers will need to be examined. Here it would be especially important to reconstruct the profile of the units involved and, where possible, of individual soldiers, SS and Gestapo officials, and other agents of the Nazi regime. Existing research indicates that there is sufficient information to put together a good picture of the German occupiers and perpetrators and to analyze the relationship between them and the various groups under their control. One other invaluable source is the archive in Ludwigsburg,

---

44 See note 33.
45 See, e.g., Waldemar Lotnik, *Nine Lives: Ethnic Conflict in the Polish-Ukrainian Borderlands* (London, 1999).

which collected the interrogation records of suspected Nazi criminals investigated by the West German police. It is from such sources that one may be able to construct a more intimate profile of the killers.[46] Conversely, documentation of higher Nazi officials will establish the links between events in Buczacz and the larger context of the genocide in East Galicia and, beyond that, the Holocaust as a whole.

To conclude, I have tried to argue that part of the project of understanding modern genocide is to investigate discrete cases of mass murder within a larger historical context, on the one hand, and to examine closely individual occurrence of mass killing that formed part of an entire genocidal undertaking, on the other. For instance, Raul Hilberg's *The Destruction of the European Jews* is rightly seen as a model for reconstructing a single case of state-organized mass murder. Yet this approach can be tremendously enriched, and its explanatory potential can be greatly enhanced, by situating it in the context of twentieth-century mass murders, and by zooming in on the manner in which policies dictated at the top took shape at the point of contact between perpetrators, victims, and a variety of bystanders, collaborators, and resisters. This is the moment that interests me most: for genocide is, ultimately, also about the encounter between the killer and the killed, usually with a fair number of spectators standing by. How do we get to this point, and why do people play the roles they do when it arrives? This is what I hope to understand a little better through my future study of Buczacz.

46 It is from this archive that much of the information used in Browning, *Ordinary Men*, and Goldhagen, *Hitler's Willing Executioners*, is taken.

5

Genocide and the Body Politic in the Time of Modernity

MARIE FLEMING

The term "genocide" derives from the Greek word *genos* ("race") and *cide* (from the Latin *occidere*, meaning "to kill"). It was introduced in 1944 by the jurist Raphael Lemkin and refers to a type of mass killing widely regarded as the most egregious of crimes. Lemkin identified the phenomenon itself decades earlier, in the massacre of the Armenians in Turkey. In 1921 he insisted that the doctrine of state sovereignty was not a license to kill millions of innocent people, and he agitated in the 1930s for international support from criminal lawyers to address the question of what to do about murderous regimes. Finally, in the 1940s, in the aftermath of war and Nazi atrocities, he and other jurists successfully pressed to get genocide recognized as a crime in international law. The definition provided by the 1948 Genocide Convention registered the considerable anxiety Lemkin felt about planned and systematic state persecution and destruction of racial and religious groups. Although he had also voiced concerns about criminal mistreatment of "social" groups, the General Assembly of the United Nations, under pressure from the Soviet Union, retreated from what looked like a possibility of including "political and other groups" in the list of potential victims.[1]

Some researchers are now convinced that genocide is not really a new crime at all and that genocidal acts against helpless populations have been going on for many centuries, perhaps even thousands of years. Certainly, there have been plenty of mass crimes throughout history and too much slaughter of innocent civilians, especially under war conditions. If we adopt a broad view, however, genocide can become a synonym for mass killings. This approach might make it possible, as Frank Chalk says, to identify "any

---

1 See Raphael Lemkin, *Axis Rule in Occupied Europe* (Washington, D.C., 1944); Frank Chalk, "Redefining Genocide," in George J. Andreopoulos (ed.), *Genocide: Conceptual and Historical Dimensions* (Philadelphia, 1994), 47ff.

underlying patterns and common elements that may reveal the processes at work."[2] However, many social scientists will not want to risk losing the historical specificity of individual cases by understanding them as having happened since the beginning of time. Moreover, it does seem to be intuitively correct that there is something historically unprecedented about state-planned and state-sponsored mass killings of civilian populations. Also new is the nature and involvement of the people in these crimes. In the twentieth century ordinary citizens have been routinely mobilized in support of genocidal regimes, and they have participated in various, often critical ways. Unlike the people who might have played some role from time to time in earlier massacres, the citizens who rallied around their leaders in the modern regimes were also speaking in the name of a sovereignty they identified with themselves. The systematic need of modern regimes for popular mobilization and the sovereign status of the participating body politic establish crucial differences between the more recent cases of genocides and what took place in earlier times. Is there something, then, about the nature of sovereignty and law that can help us understand the genocides in the time of modernity?

The idea for this chapter comes from Theodor Adorno's suggestion that our experiences should now include the feeling that "Auschwitz" can "repeat itself." As we reflect on the twentieth century, Adorno's claim seems sadly warranted. The Nazi genocide against the Jews was "repeated" in the latter part of the century, in places as culturally and politically diverse as Cambodia, Yugoslavia, and Rwanda. Nor, since September 11, 2001, can we afford to disregard the genocidal rhetoric of Al Qaeda and other such networks that cry "Death to America." I believe it is an urgent task facing all of us to try to figure out just what this repeatability of genocide turns on, and my chapter is a contribution to that task.

I discuss the work of several theorists who have tried to understand how unthinkable acts of genocide became possible in modernity, but I owe a special debt to Michel Foucault, who is also the recipient of my harshest criticism.

GENOCIDE AND THE IDEALS OF MODERNITY

The postwar period of German historiography was dominated for decades by the question "how could it happen" in the land of Goethe and Beethoven, as if Nazism was essentially a horrible mistake, an aberration from the normality of historical developments, a throwback to barbaric times. This approach

2 Chalk, "Redefining Genocide," 50.

characterizes genocide as bloody and murderous acts committed by those claiming the power of death and understands the acts as totally out of sync with a modernity that stands for enlightenment, progress, and life. The first important representative of this approach was sociologist Ralf Dahrendorf who published a widely acclaimed account of Germany as a "faulted nation." In his book Dahrendorf took an idealized Great Britain as the model of a progressive nation, and on any number of significant measures, from social mobility, to independence of thought, political culture, and the structure of academic institutions, Germany was shown to have fallen ominously behind.[3]

The view that Germany's troubles could be traced to a faulted historical development has been adopted by influential scholars. For example, philosopher Jürgen Habermas contends that Nazism was a consequence of Germany's not having been able to follow Britain and France in maintaining the ever precarious balance between the universalist and particularist elements of a national identity. Habermas asserts that particularism was heavily imprinted on German nationalism from the beginning and that Germans did not easily free themselves of a passionate attachment to the notion of cultural and ethnic uniqueness. He claims that this overvaluing of particularism, together with the consciousness of having taken a special path, insulated Germany, kept it from becoming a modern nation-state, and ultimately led to Auschwitz. Habermas believes that to prevent "another" Auschwitz, we have to become ever more modern, practice cosmopolitanism, embrace "constitutional patriotism," and support extraterritorial entities such as the European Community.[4]

Dahrendorf and Habermas express great confidence in the ideals of modernity. For them, genocide is not essentially related to modernity but rather is a hangover from the past, a barbarism that erupts in the midst of an admittedly difficult and complex period of historical development.[5] This type of explanation runs up against Adorno and Max Horkheimer's claim that genocide is a potentially regressive feature of the civilization process and related in an essential way to the rationality of modern capitalist exchange and bureaucratic administration. This more negative assessment of modernity was provided by Adorno and Horkheimer in 1944.

3 Ralf Dahrendorf, *Society and Democracy in Germany* (London, 1968).
4 Jürgen Habermas, "Historical Consciousness and Post-Traditional Identity: The Federal Republic's Orientation to the West," in *The New Conservatism: Cultural Criticism and the Historians' Debate* (Cambridge, Mass., 1989), 249ff.
5 Cf. Jean-François Lyotard, *The Differend: Phrases in Dispute* (Minneapolis, 1988), 106: "Nazism... attacks the time of all of modernity.... one does not dare think out Nazism because it has been beaten down like a mad dog, by a police action.... It has not been [and cannot be] refuted."

Their book, *Dialectic of Enlightenment*, written while they were in exile in the United States and as they listened to news from Germany about the final stages of the Third Reich, was situated at a crossroads of twentieth-century thought.[6] It reflected older "decline of the West" themes, which were widespread on both left and right (Oswald Spengler, Ernst Jünger, Walter Benjamin, Marc Bloch, earlier Horkheimer and Adorno, also Martin Heidegger, Hans Sedlmayr), and it provided a basis for what became known as the "instrumental rationality" thesis in the closing decades of the twentieth century.

For Horkheimer and Adorno, the Enlightenment did not begin in the eighteenth century, as the textbooks state. Rather, the historical Enlightenment was actually preceded by a process of enlightenment, which began centuries before recorded history. The myth of Odysseus, they argue, was already an enlightenment. It anticipated the Enlightenment of the eighteenth century, and it recorded and celebrated the triumph of calculative thinking at the center of modern science and capitalism. They claim that Odysseus, the hero of Homer's *Odyssey*, was a protobourgeois figure who was already familiar with calculative reasoning.[7] On his long voyage homeward, Odysseus had to make his way through treacherous waters, and he used guile and cunning to secure his life against both the evil demons and the seductive natural deities. But Horkheimer and Adorno also maintain that the modern period ushered in a new and more dangerous stage of human life. In their view, the Enlightenment was not just a continuation of the civilization process but rather a more sophisticated and vastly more destructive form of older human attempts to dominate nature for the sake of self-preservation. Following Marx, they write that, whereas earlier societies produced both for use and for exchange, the capitalist mode of production is increasingly dominated by exchange. They suggest that this development also increases the probability of regression. According to their analysis, National Socialism, which is a crisis of this sort, signifies a pathological longing to escape the trials of civilization and to regress to the mimetic, or imitative, practices of early humans. In Nazism, opportunities for mimetic

---

6 Max Horkheimer and Theodor W. Adorno, *Dialectic of Enlightenment* (1944 [in German]; New York, 1972).

7 As understood by Horkheimer and Adorno, calculative reasoning is the type of abstract mental activity we engage in when we want to figure out how best to reach our goals, and it includes thinking about strategies and means for making nonhuman nature yield to human needs. For Horkheimer and Adorno, this logical process is essentially the same throughout a range of concrete activities: hunting animals for food or clothing, clearing land to plant crops, navigating the seas, building machinery, working on an assembly line in a factory, executing an order on the floor of the stock exchange, or working in a bureaucracy in the modern welfare state.

behavior are stealthily provided through rituals, uniforms, the "skulls and disguises, the barbaric drum beats, the monotonous repetition of words and gestures." This "organized imitation of magic practices" cannot operate without an Other, and it singles out the Jews as representing civilization and thus as discouraging all mimetic activity that does not contribute to the advance of science and instrumental rationality.[8]

Adorno and Horkheimer characterize the place occupied by the Other in the Nazi psyche as contradictory and unstable. The Nazis both despise the Jews and are fascinated by them. The Nazi "machinery needs the Jews." According to *Dialectic of Enlightenment*, the very scorn heaped upon the Jews is an "embittered imitation" of them. In this view, the Nazi accusation that the Jews participate in "forbidden magic and bloody ritual" is actually a sort of fulfillment, at a conscious level, of a deep-seated fascist desire to regress to archaic practices of sacrifice. One projects one's own impulses – to engage in the forbidden mimetic activity – onto the other, the "prospective victim." They maintain that victims are "interchangeable according to circumstances – gypsies, Jews, Protestants, Catholics, and so on." They also claim that the Nazis "imitate" their "mental picture" of the Jews, so that it is of no consequence whether the Jews are actually like what the Nazis imagine them to be.[9]

Dialectic of Enlightenment has won a lasting place in history and theory. What presents a problem for many twenty-first-century readers, however, is the flaw at the core of the analysis: everything flows toward a totalizing construction of reality. As Lyotard suggests in reference to Adorno, their thesis of the "dialectic of enlightenment" is still dominated by an Other that has to be overcome. That Other is Capital.[10] Despite the complexity of their analyses and their still important insights, Horkheimer and Adorno believe that the world will be put right if only we could find a way to rid ourselves of the Evil of Capital. As I see it, we should resist understanding fascism as having an essence and we should develop more differentiated analyses to

---

8 Horkheimer and Adorno, *Dialectic of Enlightenment*, 3ff., 168ff. They use the concept of mimesis to refer to persistent traces, in the human psyche, of archaic experiences: yearning for union with nature, for Paradise, but also terror in the face of the Absolute, the unknown. To appease the terror and find favor with Providence, humans in archaic times resorted to blood offerings. As civilization advanced, such mimetic practices were forbidden. However, the mimetic impulse, which cannot be eliminated, managed to get expressed in other ways, in magic and rituals, also in the "imitative" arts like painting and poetry.

9 Ibid., 171ff. In their book, Horkheimer and Adorno do not identify Odysseus in racial or ethnic terms. Cf. Anson Rabinbach, *In the Shadow of Catastrophe: German Intellectuals between Apocalypse and Enlightenment* (Berkeley, 1997), 166ff., who maintains that they understand Odysseus as a Jewish figure.

10 Jean-François Lyotard, "Adorno as the Devil," *Telos* 19 (spring 1974), 127ff.

account for Nazi and other genocides. At the same time, we need to be attentive to Adorno's message that we have "to arrange [our] thoughts and actions so that Auschwitz will not repeat itself, so that nothing similar will happen."[11]

The two approaches to genocide that I have been discussing link up to modernity in different ways. The Dahrendorf-Habermas thesis interprets the Nazi genocide against the Jews as resulting from Germany's failure to develop liberal-democratic social and political structures. Horkheimer and Adorno see the disaster more broadly, as something that is located in German history, but that should be understood as a crisis of civilization. But neither approach appreciates the significance of the societal and cultural bases of popular support for, and participation in, twentieth-century dictatorships and genocidal regimes. In fact, there has been a tendency in the specialized literature to write off the importance of such support by suggesting that the people who cheered on their leaders were really subjects of terror or indoctrination, at best willing dupes. Postmodern and poststructuralist thinking does not allow for such easy dismissals of active popular engagement with dictatorial regimes.

Before I critically examine Foucault's poststructuralist understanding of modernity and its relation to genocide, I want to refer to the "instrumental rationality" thesis that is often associated with the "dialectic of enlightenment."

GENOCIDE AND INSTRUMENTAL RATIONALITY

The "instrumental rationality" thesis shifts attention to methods employed in the persecution and destruction of victims and to the state of mind of individuals and groups involved in the perpetration of the crimes. An influential version of that thesis was put forward by Zygmunt Bauman, who is persuaded by the findings of the Milgram experiment that a great number of "normal" people anywhere can inflict pain on others under conditions of authority and relative anonymity. Bauman also suggests, drawing on Hannah Arendt's analysis of totalitarianism, that bureaucratic distancing and instrumental thinking not only allowed Germans to become indifferent to the fate of the Jews under Nazism, but also led Jewish leaders in the camps to cooperate with their captors in the destruction of less well connected Jews. He claims that Germans who had personal experience with Jews might go along with racist thinking in the abstract, but that when it came to

---

11 Theodor W. Adorno, *Negative Dialectics* (New York, 1983), 365.

individual Jews, they could come up with an infinite number of reasons for why a Jewish person they knew should be exempted from some ruling or other.[12] Bauman's thesis has since been undermined by research that portrays ordinary Germans as actively engaged in the construction of Nazi myths and willing participants in Jewish and other persecutions.[13] But what about the point that recurs, here and in the literature generally, that genocide seems to be connected in some significant way to instrumental rationality and bureaucratic procedures?

One question that arises out of this discussion regards the process itself. Should we conclude that "Auschwitz" and other twentieth-century genocides were modern phenomena because of the methods used in the killings? Administrative murders are systematic and detailed, coldly efficient, totalizing and globalizing in their intended and/or logical reach. Related questions concern the supposed need for technical means to murder large numbers of people and the desensitizing effects of bureaucratic distancing on the perpetrators. We should wonder, first of all, how true it was, even for Germany, that the killings were carried out in an overwhelmingly bureaucratic and technological fashion. We should not underestimate the significance of the coldly brutal "administrative murder" that Adorno spoke about[14] and the horrific stories of the gas chambers. But we need to keep in mind that millions of people, as many as half the number who perished, were killed by the Nazis in un-bureaucratic ways, on marches, in mass shootings, planned starvations, and in various sorts of confinement. Let us also remember that in Rwanda, where hundreds of thousands, perhaps close to a million, people were hacked to death within a few months by means of crude instruments like machetes and farm tools, the genocide was planned by those in power and in the near absence of modern technology. As for the supposedly desensitizing effects of bureaucratic distancing, the brutal face-to-face murder of the Tutsis by tens of thousands of ordinary Hutus, many of them poor farmers, utterly disproves that thesis. We also have plenty of other evidence that discounts the bureaucratic distancing thesis, recently from the genocidal events in the former Yugoslavia.

All this is still not to deny that there are no significant links between genocide and instrumental rationality, but whatever they are, we need to do more work to specify them. One might also look at factors such as modern communications systems, the role played by the print media, radio, film, and

---

12 Zygmunt Bauman, *Modernity and the Holocaust* (Ithaca, 1989).
13 For an analysis of the "productive" aspects of the interaction between Nazi leadership and ordinary Germans, see Robert Gellately, *Backing Hitler: Consent and Coercion in Nazi Germany* (Oxford, 2001).
14 Adorno, *Negative Dialectics*, 362.

television, all of which surely had important implications for many aspects of public involvement.

The theorists I have discussed so far all seek, in various ways, to understand genocide as a murderous act by a perpetrator (or perpetrators) claiming the power of death. As I now discuss, Foucault, one of the most influential theorists to emerge in the latter part of the twentieth century, maintains that genocide should rather be seen in terms of the modern discourse of life and sexuality.

In the opening pages of Foucault's *Discipline and Punish*, we get a graphic description of the torture and death in 1757 of Damiens, the regicide, followed by a timetable for a prison house eighty years later. Foucault's aim is to chart the disappearance of the public spectacle of punishment and its replacement at the end of the eighteenth century with a modern penal system in which punishment is hidden behind prison walls. As in his other works, the year 1750 (or thereabouts) becomes the dividing line between the "classical age" and the modern period.[15] The classical age, he explains in the introductory volume of his *History of Sexuality*, was still marked by central features of the ancient idea of sovereignty. Although the sovereign's power over life and death was no longer viewed as absolute, the power he exercised was, as in ancient times, connected to death rather than life. His right of life was a right to kill, or to decide not to kill: he could "take life or let live."[16]

Foucault claims that we are gravely mistaken to see Thomas Hobbes's classical account of sovereignty as having anything to tell us about the power mechanisms of the modern period. In fact, Foucault believes that focus on the spirit of sovereignty, understood as a singular will distilled from a multiplicity of individual wills, only causes us to turn away from those signs all around us of a new power of life that has been steadily and stealthily insinuating itself into ever more crevices of reality. His own project, which he views as the "exact opposite" of Hobbes's *Leviathan*, is not only not directed at the central spirit of sovereignty, but turns away from the idea of sovereignty altogether.[17] It also has no truck with any substantive view of power. According to Foucault, to speak of modern power is to claim

---

15 Michel Foucault, *Discipline and Punish: The Birth of the Prison* (New York, 1979), 3ff.
16 Michel Foucault, *History of Sexuality*, vol. 1 (New York, 1990), 135–36.
17 Michel Foucault, *Power/Knowledge: Selected Interviews and Other Writings, 1972–1977* (New York, 1980), 97–98.

that power ("le" pouvoir) does not exist. "In reality power means relations, a more-or-less organized, hierarchical, co-ordinated cluster of relations."[18] What we have to understand, he claims, is that the procedures of power that developed in conjunction with the emergence and spread of capitalism fundamentally transformed the power mechanisms of the classical age. The old power of death now gives way to the "administration of bodies and the calculated management of life."[19]

This transformation to the regime of "biopower" develops around two poles. One centers on the "body as machine: its disciplining, the optimization of its capabilities, the extortion of its forces, the parallel increase of its usefulness," while a second pole works on the "species body, the body imbued with the mechanics of life and serving as the basis of the biological processes: propagation, births and mortality, the level of health, life expectancy and longevity." Foucault aims to show that "life," and consequently "sex," enters into history at the juncture of the "body" and the "population." "Sex was a means of access both to the life of the body and the life of the species." In the normalization processes of modernity, individuals get a sex and they are made visible. However, for Foucault, individuals are never made visible in their normality, but only in their abnormality, in their deviance from the norm. Hence, in a discourse of sexuality organized around the Malthusian couple, we get the hysterical woman, the masturbating child, and the perverse adult seeking his pleasure in homosexual and pederastic unions. Foucault views this coming into existence of "sex" as fundamental for the modern type of power. Whereas at one time certain sexual acts had once been condemned – by the church, for example – as bad deeds, now the individual who commits these acts is himself branded. One is turned into a homosexual; one does not just commit homosexual acts. We have moved, according to Foucault, from a society of blood to a society of "sex." We are a society "with a sexuality."[20]

Foucault's pattern of arguing is quite different from Horkheimer and Adorno's. Whereas the latter see Nazi antisemitism and other racial projects as crises of civilization, Foucault understands the great processes of modernity as a (homo)sexual event. But if, as he argues, the discourse of sexuality replaces the discourse of blood, how does he account for modern racism and twentieth-century genocides? He addressed this question infrequently, but it is clear that he thought hard about it and that he concluded that race and genocide, like everything else in modernity, should be fitted into the

18 Foucault, *Power/Knowledge*, 198.   19 Foucault, *History of Sexuality*, 1:140.
20 Ibid., 139–47, also 100ff.

discourse of sexuality. This is pretty explicit from the last chapter of *History of Sexuality*, which he himself saw as the "fundamental part of the book."[21] There Foucault maintains that, for the classical age, blood was a "reality with a symbolic function." "Power spoke through blood: the honor of war, the fear of famine, the triumph of death, the sovereign with his sword." In the modern period, blood is no longer a reality, though it can be a symbol of something else. By contrast, sex always refers to itself; it can never be a symbol, and is always an "object and a target" of power. He apparently believes that when anyone calls on blood to justify a course of action, the reality that they are trying to justify is always the reality of sex. In the second half of the nineteenth century, he explains, there came into existence a "whole politics of settlement, family, marriage, education, social hierarchization, and property, accompanied by a long series of permanent interventions at the level of the body, conduct, health, and everyday life." It is Foucault's contention that this politics was based on sexuality and biopower and only "received their color and their justification from the mythical concern with protecting the purity of the blood and ensuring the triumph of the race."[22]

Foucault observes that wars have never been bloodier than those in the twentieth century and that regimes have never before been involved in such slaughter of their own populations. However, he claims that this "formidable power of death ... now presents itself as the counterpart of a power that exerts a positive influence on life." This development is decisive, according to Foucault. "The principle underlying the tactics of battle – that one has to be capable of killing in order to go on living – has become the principle that defines the strategy of states. But the existence in question is no longer the juridical existence of sovereignty; at stake is the biological existence of a population." Genocide, he concedes, might well be the "dream" of modern states, but the reason for this has nothing to do with blood. Rather "it is because power is situated and exercised at the level of life, the species, the race, and the large-scale phenomena of population."[23] In Foucault's account, Nazism remains unexplained and inexplicable. "It is an irony of history that the Hitlerite politics of sex remained an insignificant practice while the blood myth was transformed into the greatest blood bath in recent memory."[24]

Foucault's intelligence and passion seeped into every page he wrote. Even his somewhat arid, explicitly calculating style, which mimetically reproduces the "law" of which it is a critique, and his notoriously stubborn refusal to

21 Foucault, *Power/Knowledge*, 222.   22 Foucault, *History of Sexuality*, 1:147–49.
23 Ibid., 137.   24 Ibid., 150.

say where he stood on normative questions, cannot conceal his utopian wish for a liberation of "bodies and pleasures"[25] from *every* sort of law. This wish he generalized into a rejection of any attempt to understand power in terms of sovereignty. The law, he claims, "always refers to the sword."[26]

It is usually overlooked that Foucault's claims about power and sexuality are curiously dependent on a top-down model of the state. "To pose the problem in terms of the State means to continue posing it in terms of sovereign and sovereignty, that is to say in terms of law. If one describes all these phenomena of power as dependent on the State apparatus, this means grasping them as essentially repressive: the Army as a power of death, police and justice as punitive instances, etc."[27] His complaint that political theorists and others have misrepresented modern power because they have not "cut off the King's head"[28] may reveal something about his own misperceptions of power and modernity. Clearly, there is much to learn from what he says about the power of life and the discourse of sexuality. Nonetheless, we have to reject his attempt to define the world around (homo)sexuality, and we should take a closer look at the place of the body in modernity. In the discussion that follows, I defy Foucault's ban on talking about sovereignty and law.

THE BODY POLITIC: SITE OF THE POWERS OF LIFE AND DEATH

Genocide as a crime in modernity reflects the status of the "body" of the people. As such, it stands in contrast to, yet extracts from, the traditional crime of regicide in which the body of the king was sacrosanct. A king might be murdered in our own day, but the crime would be viewed as an assassination, hence a different meaning would be produced.

This idea of a people's body and its actual or potential violation is indicated in the way contemporaries sometimes use derivatives of "genocide" to represent particular wrongs. Terms such as ethnocide, linguicide, omnicide, politicide, gynocide, gendercide, or femicide, are almost always pleas for public recognition of whatever charge is being made, and often it is meant as a serious proposal for redescribing what is felt to be a past or present injustice. Israel Charny suggests that we need a "generic definition of genocide that does not exclude or commit to indifference any case of mass murder of any human beings, of whatever racial, national, ethnic, biological, cultural, religious, and political definitions, or of totally mixed groupings of any or all the above." Charny ends his long (but not exhaustive) list of types of

---

25 Ibid., 157.
27 Foucault, *Power/Knowledge*, 122.

26 Ibid., 144.
28 Ibid., 121.

genocide by criticizing "definitionalism."[29] Indeed, one might suggest that his own categorization, which aims to find a place for every conceivable form of genocide, ends up as an argument for not having a definition at all. It is not difficult to see why some might feel it is insensitive, if not immoral, to expand the list of "cides." But, even if one should sometimes exercise restraint in linking a particular group's suffering to the most horrendous of crimes, the practice of suggesting this linkage indicates a certain logic related to the modern idea of the "body politic" that underlies the public discourse of modernity. I would now like to make some observations on what we can gain by examining texts in modern political and legal theory.

Hobbes, writing in 1651, imagines each individual human being (male or female) as an independent power, moved by self-interest, equally vulnerable, and basically equal in physical and intellectual capacities. To resolve the problem of the "war of all against all" that "naturally" develops from competing individual interests, he constructs a model of society in which the ruler is a body that incorporates all the other bodies into himself.[30] In this amazing image, the Leviathan is both ruler and ruled, a "Commonwealth," an "Artificial Man," a "Body Politique." The sovereign's power itself is derived from each individual's natural right of self-defense, which the individual never gives up, not even under the lawful or repressive rule of the sovereign.[31] Hobbes's proposed resolution to the "war" problem is usually taken to be an argument for absolute rule, but as the supporters of monarchy in the seventeenth century saw all too clearly, the Leviathan was far removed from their vision of a kingship deriving its legitimacy by "divine right." The relationship between above and below is now internal rather than external, as in the older models. The very identities of ruler and ruled merge and become inseparable.

The trope of the body, so striking in Hobbes, continues in the work of Locke and Rousseau. Whereas the former ambiguously introduces the authority of the people as the final arbiter,[32] the latter explicitly states that the "people" are the sovereign, one and indivisible. Rousseau writes about the "public person," or "body politic," with its own "will," and claims that it is inconceivable that the moral and collective body of the "people" would ever want to harm any of its constituent parts. Harming oneself would

---

29 Israel W. Charny, "Toward a Generic Definition of Genocide," in Andreopoulos, *Genocide*, 74ff.
30 I use the masculine pronoun here, even though I believe that the gender of the Leviathan is not clear-cut; at most it is ambivalently masculine.
31 Thomas Hobbes, *Leviathan*, ed. C. B. Macpherson (Harmondsworth, 1968).
32 John Locke, "An Essay concerning the True Original, Extent and End of Civil Government," in *Social Contract*, introd. Ernest Barker (Oxford, 1960), 1ff.

mean causing one's blood to flow, and it does not require a huge leap of imagination to suggest that the body politic, if it had its own will, also had its own blood. One suspects that the seventeenth-century idea of the body politic sets in motion a distinctive dynamic: the king has/is one body, so the people have/are one body. How can a people be multiple? There is also a new concern that informs Rousseau's thought. In the logic of the dominant trope, he raises the question of the inevitable decline and decay of the body politic, along with what appeared to him to be a constitutive inability to represent the perfect body. The system of capitalist inequality, he said, was constantly pressing people into conformity, making them other-dependent, preventing them from being authentically who they were.[33] He yearned, even though he believed it was useless, for a time in the distant past, the "golden age" of the patriarchal nuclear family, rural and self-sufficient, with its upright men and nurturing women. This was the age, he declared, "at which you would want your species to have stopped." It was the "veritable youth of the world."[34]

The idea of the body politic is structurally built into all modern polities. Certainly, the dream of a people, one and indivisible, can be read off the surface of almost all the many liberal and democratic constitutions constructed in Europe and America since the French Revolution. But genocidal states in the twentieth century seem especially concerned with the cleansing and purification of the body politic. This emphasis on purity is not as such new and can be traced to Plato, but it takes on new meaning in the modern nation-state. The cleansing operation is now directed at, and within, the body of the people rather than part of society (the philosopher-ruler, as in Plato, or later the aristocracy). Moreover, whereas the ruler is traditionally conceived of as external to the ruled, in the modern period the interactive relationship of people and state (as "one" body) generates the cooperation and the participation of the people in that cleansing operation. Hitler said that establishing the "real community of the people" required the "moral purification of the body politic," and throughout the regime, public discourse was replete with references to ridding the communal body of "degenerative elements," "destructive cells," "sickness," and especially the "parasites."[35] In Nazi Germany, "enemies" of the people were called "vermin" and "lice," and under the Khmer Rouge in Cambodia, they were referred to as "microbes" and "pests buried within." Ben Kiernan draws our attention to

---

33 John-Jacques Rousseau, *On the Social Contract; Discourse on the Origin of Inequality; Discourse on Political Economy* (Indianapolis, 1983).
34 Rousseau, "Discourse on the Origin of Inequality," in *Social Contract*, 119, 145.
35 See Gellately, *Backing Hitler.*

these troubling parallels. He also notes that in these cases, but also in others, there is an idealization of cultivation and a celebration of the peasantry.[36]

As indicated earlier, the peasant body makes its appearance in Rousseau, who uses it to indicate his vision of what an authentic life would be like without the greed of the capitalists. Whereas Rousseau thought we had no choice but to try as best we might to adapt an ideally perfect nature to an inevitably imperfect world, the Pol Pot regime mercilessly tried to reshape the world to bring it into line with the peasant ideal. "The possibility of preserving a healthy peasant class as a foundation for a whole nation can never be valued highly enough," said Hitler in 1925.[37]

There is a strong tendency, as we can see from discussions of the Martin Heidegger case, for example, to equate *völkisch* thinking with racism and antisemitism. However, I am not persuaded that holding peasant values necessarily involves racism or antisemitism, and they do not seem to make people any more prone to commit various types of mass crime. Nor should we overlook the evidence that, despite similarities in the discourse of peasantry, the ideal it espoused could take on very different meanings in different cultural contexts and even within a particular culture. In Nazi Germany, for example, there were highly competing views, ranging from a conservative *völkisch* tradition expressing nostalgia for a pretechnological and rural utopia, to the radical mix of technological advance, statism, and *Volk* favored by Hitler. As well, we should keep in mind that modern atrocities are not always linked to peasant values. The Soviet Union under Stalin sided with the proletariat, but, as it prepared the way for industrialization and communist internationalism, it perpetrated the most brutal acts of terrorism against its own population, particularly the peasants.

Moreover, the discourse of degeneracy is not peculiar to genocidal regimes in the twentieth century and certainly was not invented by them. At the time of the great French Revolution those claiming to represent the "people" routinely condemned aristocrats as decadent and good-for-nothings. In the nineteenth century the socialists were the first to be drawn to visions of a healthy population and getting rid of degenerates, the heartless pimps who preyed on destitute women compelled by misfortune to sell their bodies, no less than the mean-spirited capitalists who drained the lifeblood from honest, hardworking folk. The Italian anarchist and peasant supporter, Cesare Lombroso, developed theories of poverty and criminality that won attention from socialists of all colors. He tried to distinguish

36 Ben Kiernan, "Twentieth Century Genocides: Underlying Ideological Themes from Armenia to East Timor," Chapter 2 in this volume.
37 Adolf Hitler, *Mein Kampf* (Boston, 1943), 138.

"born" criminals from the political (revolutionary) ones who fought the rich on behalf of the people, and he theorized that it was possible to identify the physical features of naturally criminal elements. Only a healthy populace rid of the filthy rich and protected from the corrupting influence of the degenerates could ever hope to take its true place in the nation and in history.[38] These words sound awfully close to what might be the rhetoric of some genocidal demagogue, but at the time it was the supposedly sound advice of a man of science who was also viewed as a progressive.

SPACE AND THE BODY POLITIC

Genocidal regimes have been preoccupied with securing space for the body politic. Hitler announced his foreign policy and expansionist intentions in 1925[39] and was actively planning for war the day he took power.[40] Several chapters in this volume identify significant connections between war, revolution, and genocide throughout the twentieth century. The power of death is not supplanted by the power of life, as Foucault argues. Rather, the sword passes to the body politic, which is rooted as much in blood and death as in sex and life.

The passing of the sword to the body politic is also related to the more general process of European expansion and the destruction of cultures that accompanied that expansion. No sooner had Hobbes fired the imagination of his contemporaries with his idea of a "Common-wealth" and an "Artificial Man" than the missionary John Eliot, a contemporary of Hobbes, dreamed of a "Christian Commonwealth" (the title of one of his many books) that potentially included the whole world. Migrating to America in 1631, Eliot was devoted to "saving" the natives of New England and relentless in his efforts. He learned the Indian dialects, preached to Indians in their own languages, trained some of them to be teachers and helpers, and spent enormous energy writing handbooks and instructional manuals, including a "logic primer" to "instruct Indians in the use of reason."[41]

Some have used the term cultural genocide to indicate a systematic, largely intentional, pattern of destroying an existing culture, although, from Eliot's example, it would probably be more correct to say that under colonial rule, missionaries serving the cause of Europe do not so much set out to

---

38 See Cesare Lombroso, *Crime, Its Causes and Remedies* (Boston, 1911).
39 Hitler, *Mein Kampf*, 131ff.   40 Gellately, *Backing Hitler*.
41 John Eliot, *The logick primer: Some logical notions to initiate the Indians in the knowledge of the rule of reason and to know how to make use thereof: especially for the instruction of such as are teachers among them* (Cambridge, Mass., 1672), available on microfilm.

destroy a culture as they do not even recognize that there is one. That is why people like Eliot could apparently feel so high-minded in supposing that they were giving something to the natives as opposed to taking something away. (From their perspective, what was there to take?) For Eliot, Indian languages were a barrier to God's message, and he had to cross or dismantle that barrier if the Indians were ever to get access to the Holy Scriptures. True, Eliot's attitudes were to some extent transformed by his contact with the Indians and he became one of the "good" missionaries, as a recent study energetically argues.[42] However, I am saying (in a deconstructionist sort of move) that, precisely because of his "goodness," Eliot is all the more interesting and powerful as an example of the intersubjective violence connected with Europeanization. How is it that missionaries who simply meant to do good works, those who even cherished the humanity of the natives, worked so single-mindedly to try to transform them into "our" image?

Certain aspects of the assimilationism associated with European expansionism can also be found in twentieth-century genocides. In Nazi Germany the early camp system explicitly aimed at reeducating political "enemies," the socialists and the communists, to "save" them for the Fatherland. This contrasts with Nazi policies toward the Jews. Whereas crude and disrespectful measures could at times be used to determine whether certain individuals from some groups could be candidates for Germanization, it could never be conceded that a Jewish person might be remade into a German. For Nazis, with their (admittedly) multidimensional, yet peasant-inspired image of the *Volk*, it became unthinkable that the Jewish people, so closely identified with internationalism, both capitalist and Bolshevist, could ever be transformed into *völkisch* Germans. If there is anything to this, Germans would have been following a line of thinking that stems from Rousseau. So too would the Rwandan Hutus whose state-racist and peasant-inspired policies led to exterminationist actions against the Tutsis, all of whom as a group had been identified as privileged representatives of the former colonial master.

CONCLUDING REMARKS

In genocidal regimes in modernity, leaders and "people" joined forces to shape a "body politic," and the participation and involvement of the population was central to the mission of cleansing, from that sovereign body,

---

42 Richard W. Cogley, *John Eliot's Mission to the Indians before King Philip's War* (Cambridge, Mass., 1999).

those elements deemed "unfit" to belong. In Nazi Germany, for example, the "body politic," understood as leader and people united in a common will and common blood, was claiming the right of death, in a modern tradition still bearing traces of older models of sovereignty. They were not just claiming the right of life, as Foucault suggests, with the discourse of blood mixed in for "color." The scandal of the Foucaultian discourse of sexuality is that the victims of the Nazi and other genocides become unintended consequences of a politics that issues from nowhere in particular and whose target and object is always sex, never race and ethnicity, not even in the case of the Jews murdered in the name of "Aryan" blood. Foucault's emphasis on life is crucial to an understanding of the microphysics of power in modernity, but we have to protest his arrogant prohibition of all discussion of sovereignty and law. He mistakenly calls on us to "cut off the King's head" and does not see that the power of the sword has long since passed to the body politic.

Genocides and genocidal acts, like ethnic cleansing, are always historically and culturally specific, individually complex, and highly unpredictable. The "modernity" of genocides would appear to be a repeatability tied to the very idea of the "body politic," which is always oriented to its health and growth and to a persistent need to stave off decline and decay. In other words, the "body politic," the sign of sovereignty and law in modernity, is the axis on which the possibility of genocide, hence its repeatability, turns. This does not mean that genocides are inevitable but that they are all too likely and can happen anywhere. Given the contingent and historical nature of genocides, it is virtually impossible to predict them, and we are a long way off from establishing any sound basis for intervention into genocidal regimes. What we can do, however, is to try to ascertain how to reevaluate, and revalue, the idea of the body politic that underlies modern culture and politics. Understanding our own situation may assist us in trying to devise national and international institutions that seek to weaken the repeatability of genocides everywhere. To learn from Adorno, we have "to arrange [our] thoughts and actions so that Auschwitz [and Cambodia and Yugoslavia and Rwanda] will not repeat [themselves], so that nothing similar will happen."

PART II

Indigenous Peoples and Colonial Issues

6

Genocides of Indigenous Peoples

Rhetoric of Human Rights

ELAZAR BARKAN

> Perhaps in time the whites will suffer in the knowledge of what they have done. But
> they cannot expect forgiveness.
>
> Peter Read, *A Rape of the Soul So Profound*

Indigenous peoples the world over have suffered various forms of extermination ever since they were "discovered" by Europeans. This is particularly true with regard to the "New World" and the Pacific Islands. Africans too have suffered, if in different ways. The extensive calamities of colonialism and imperialism have been second to no other calamities. In many places populations have been totally and purposefully exterminated, in others they have "died out" and disappeared, and in still other sites only a few remain as a memory, an exhibit, of a lost world. Many of the victims, such as the Caribs or the Arawak of the Caribbean Islands have not only been exterminated but have also largely been erased from memory. When Hitler reputedly dismissed the Armenian genocide, he did not even mention the Herero of South West Africa who were the victims of Germany's first genocide of the century. These are the victims that few even remember. The actual horrors of the colonial wars are too often overlooked. Indigenous peoples have only recently become candidates to be considered victims of genocide, rather than merely vanishing peoples. Perhaps one of the most recent cases to capture Western attention was of the Yanomami, whose destruction began in the 1960s and 1970s.[1]

The magnitude of colonial and imperial destruction, with its multiple manifestations, poses special difficulties in understanding or even studying these historical and, in different ways, ongoing contemporary events. Far

---

1 The extensive destruction of native peoples in the Americas outside the United States unfortunately could not be dealt with here. While there is substantial discussion about Brazil and many other Latin American countries, Argentina for one is hardly ever featured. The demography of the country

from being unspeakable or indescribable, the actions of the perpetrators were at least partially documented since the earlier days. Mutilation and death of indigenous peoples were almost a continuous component of imperialism and colonialism over the centuries. Few have ever matched the Spanish brutality as described by Bartolome de Las Casas, who recounted incidents in which men bet on whether they could slice their victim in two with a single stroke of an ax, babies' heads were smashed open against rocks, and dogs were trained to disembowel humans and were reared on the flesh of their victims.[2] From Las Casas to the North American colonialists and around the globe, many encounters had their own chroniclers, but many others have been forgotten. Las Casas is noteworthy as an exception: he had no parallels among English colonialists. The most favorable statements about the Native Americans in the English context came from those who did not leave England to witness them firsthand.[3]

How should historians approach the destruction of indigenous peoples? This question is anything but new. In the mid-nineteenth century, W. H. Prescott's widely read history of Spain described the conquest of America. He celebrated progress, even if it meant the destruction of the great civilizations of the Aztec and the Inca. Prescott's contemporary, Theodore Parker, was enraged and took him to task because at every point in his narrative Prescott "excused, palliated, and condoned until, in the end, one was forced to conclude that his moral sensibilities were as calloused as his judgment was warped." Who was Mr. Prescott, asked Parker, "that he should suspend judgment over the hideous cruelties and iniquities of the conquistadors?" Indeed, it is one thing to explain but another thing to condone the crimes of the past.[4] I think this is the central admonition historians have to address, especially historians of genocides. Parker's demand 150 years ago should be even clearer today.

Changing standards and the emerging expansive application of human rights to all people, including indigenous peoples, mean that colonization

may suggest it ought to. See, e.g., The Center For World Indigenous Studies <www.cwis.org>. For the controversy, see Patrick Tierney, *Darkness in El Dorado: How Scientists and Journalists Devastated the Amazon* (New York, 2001). Clifford Geertz, "Life among the Anthros," *New York Review of Books*, February 8, 2001. Judith Shulevitz, "The Close Reader: Academic Warfare," *New York Times*, February 11, 2001. David L. Chandler, "Looking into the Heart of Darkness," *Boston Globe*, January 23, 2001.

2 Mark Cocker, *Rivers of Gold, Rivers of Blood: Europe's Conquest of Indigenous Peoples* (New York, 2001), 49.

3 Kirkpatrick Sale, *The Conquest of Paradise: Christopher Columbus and the Columbian Legacy* (New York, 1991), 280.

4 As quoted by Henry Steele Commager, "Should the Historian Make Moral Judgments," *American Heritage* 17, 2 (1966): 27, 87–93.

and imperialism, which were described in earlier times as "civilizing," are now seen as human rights violations. This reformulation opens the possibility that the devastation should be classified as the worst of historical crimes: genocide. The language of genocide is important, both because of the claims it allows for victims and because of the UN Genocide Convention, whose signatories have agreed to certain obligations. The purpose of the following discussion is to highlight the diverse phenomena, not to exclude possibilities. This entails a replacement of the "uniqueness of the Holocaust" question with a more nondeterministic approach that explores the issue of genocide within a context and not against a universal yardstick.

THE TROPE OF VANISHING

The devastation of indigenous peoples was always evident to colonialists. Europeans on the frontier developed the trope of the vanishing natives, which remains a fundamental frame for our understanding of the relationship between progress and the old. "Vanishing" is a romantic notion. From animals to peoples and from plants to cultures, our evolutionary world view is built upon change. Yet, while evolution may have no direction as a principle, culturally we view it as progress. Western society did so long before Darwin. Over the past five centuries progress has largely been seen in positive terms, while counterforces have been viewed critically, as degeneration. The classification into progress or degeneration has clearly been culturally subjective. To this framework also belongs the contradictory notion of vanishing as one of loss. In the colonial world there was also a middle ground between those who wanted to stamp out actively the "degenerate forces" and those who were sorry to see the simplicity of "noble savage" or "paradise" disappear but, alas, thought they could do nothing to prevent that disappearance. This middle ground included officials, missionaries, and others who displayed "benign neglect" toward the native and who viewed the disappearance with neither celebration nor regret. These various attitudes should not be effaced when we examine the colonial legacy. This spectrum of attitudes created the trope of the "last of the . . ." – Mohicans, Tasmanians, Ishi, or any other number of vanishing peoples. Some were "noble savages" and others wretchedly poor and "inferior," but all vanished before our very eyes.[5]

5 "Yet, there are still a number of tribal enclaves where men, women and children are living much the same way as their forbears have through the centuries. Before these, too, vanish forever, it is the mission of the tribal photographer to focus his/her camera on these individual clans, to make a permanent record of their unique lifestyles. In accomplishing this, the photographer becomes both historian and conservator of tribal customs." Edward Mendell, "Photographing Vanishing Cultures," *Petersen's Photographic* (Magazine), July 2000.

Vanishing peoples is usually a passive discourse. It has no agents as such. The dominant forces are progress and evolution. This is the discourse and paradigm that anthropology usually adopts and its foremost challenge has been to survey and record as many tribes as possible before their final disappearance. This remains the contemporary modernizing discourse, underscoring with more or less alarm the continued cultural and physical disappearances, including various predictions of rates of extinction of languages. "About half the known languages of the world have vanished in the last five hundred years. . . . A brief look around the world today reveals that the trickle of extinction of the last few centuries is now turning into a flood."[6]

Elsewhere, it might be interesting to explore the relationship between the trope of "vanishing" and the politics of anthropology. But obviously, the disappearance of peoples and cultures is a reality, not a theoretical construct or a paradigm. The question that faces us concerns the causes of, and the stakes made apparent in the language of describing, the disappearance. Are there, and if so, who are, the responsible agents? Was it merely an evolutionary structural change for which no individuals were responsible, or should we view the extinction of peoples as crime and assign guilt? And not least, how would the possible answers to the previous questions affect how we view ourselves and how we respond?

THE DESTRUCTION OF AMERICA

The representation of the destruction of tribal societies as a result of European expansion is a subject of intense controversy, at least within certain discourses. Over the past decade or so demonstrations and counterdemonstrations have become a seasonal tradition, reshaping the image of Columbus Day. The controversy is over the legacy of colonialism in America. It is generally accepted that over time the indigenous population declined by more than 95, even 98 percent at its lowest point. The meaning of that statement in reference to long chronologies is problematic but is outside the scope of this chapter. The questions here are whether the vast majority died and the society shrank or were the people eliminated? And how do the distinct descriptions matter?

From the colonial perspective there was ample reason to imagine the impending vanishing of the indigenous peoples as simply a matter of natural course. In contrast, commentators who look at it from the indigenous

---

6 Daniel Nettle and Suzanne Romaine, *Vanishing Voices: The Extinction of the World's Languages* (New York, 2000), 2. They argue for the use of "extinction and murder" to describe the phenomenon.

perspective claim it to be genocide. The language of genocide, however, is fairly recent and controversial. From the European perspective, the language and the specificities advanced by advocates of applying the term "genocide" to the indigenous context seem misplaced, exaggerated. Its use is an emotional subject. It carries a sacred quality that both sides want to preserve. Thus, the controversy is how to employ it.

David Stannard's *American Holocaust* is one of the controversial depictions of genocide in the Americas. What constitutes, in Stannard's eyes, the holocaust in the title of the book? There may not be a simple answer to this question. Stannard would like us to differentiate between inadvertent death and intentional killing. He distinguishes his analysis from other scholars who "analyzed the early impact of the Old World on the New" and, through a "novel array [of] research techniques," identified "disease as the primary cause of the Indians' great population decline."[7] His rationale for demarcating and distinguishing his work from those historians who focus on disease is that theirs displaces "responsibility for the mass killing onto an army of invading microbes," thereby creating the impression "that the eradication of those tens of millions of people was inadvertent," inevitable, and an "unintended consequence" of human migration and progress. Stannard wants to show us otherwise. He argues that while "microbial pestilence and purposeful genocide" operated independently at times, disease and genocide were usually interdependent forces. He acknowledges that disease and genocide are two separate issues, yet they are intertwined, and we are never really sure where the distinction falls.

Stannard's language grabs attention, but he also makes the mistake of conflating the past and present in the Native American case. While prejudice continues to erode Native American culture, mystifying past and present by claiming that extermination-as-genocide remains a policy is, at the very least, offensive to previous generations of Native Americans and the adversarial situation they faced. Moreover, Stannard's dissonance between headlines and content is most apparent in his use of the term "holocaust."

When Stannard speaks of the Jewish Holocaust, he largely discusses the term in reference to the concise, time-specific extermination of Jews during World War II. Both in his, and in common, usage "Jewish Holocaust" does not refer to the much more varied and longer-standing European histories of discrimination against Jewish populations. It is these varied, longer-standing antagonistic and, at times, devastating atrocities that might be considered analogous to the Native American case, although there are major

---

7 David E. Stannard, *American Holocaust: The Conquest of the New World* (New York, 1992), xii.

distinctions. But Stannard talks about Native American devastation as a continuous undifferentiated genocide. Further, the construct "American Holocaust" is ambivalent. It is not elaborated in the text. It clearly refers neither to the victims nor to the perpetrators. While Stannard describes a real record of atrocities he creates a moral dissonance by effacing distinctions between diverse historical records. Presumably his aim is to claim the total numbers of deaths, regardless of causes, as the evil of colonialism. Yet lumping everything together increases the number of the claimed victims, but diminishes the moral poignancy of the claim.

Does Stannard successfully make the case for intentional genocide? Consider his discussion of the role of disease in skewing pre-Columbian population estimates. Stannard endorses the higher figures accepted among scholars, as well as the explanation that previous estimates are too low because of the "likelihood that European diseases once introduced ... often raced ahead of their foreign carriers and spread disastrously into native population centers long before the European explorers and settlers themselves arrived."[8] He then goes through the sources and describes the destruction in detail. Yet neither his statement nor his description corresponds to the thesis of the book, which assigns guilt for intentional action. Stannard overstates his case. Traditional notions of guilt or responsibility can hardly apply to the diseases that raced ahead of the Europeans, at least not in the same way that conveys guilt to intentional killing. Instead, maintaining the distinction between intentional and "collateral" responsibility will reduce the number of victims in the first category but would allow Stannard to sustain his thesis.

Elizabeth Fenn has thoroughly analyzed recently the case of biological warfare in the eighteenth century and the question of responsibility. She describes a "continuum in which accusations and discussions of biological warfare were common, and actual incidents may have occurred more frequently than scholars have previously acknowledged," but she is careful to note that no certainty can be established as to the results. Her investigation focuses on Jeffrey Amherst's role. He advocated infecting the Indians, as did other British officials who carried out such a plan even before receiving his orders to do so. British officers therefore demonstrated a documented intent to infect the enemy (other Indians seem to have been implicated in a much

---

8 Ibid., 268. Also Henry F. Dobyns, *Their Number Became Thinned: Native American Population Dynamics in Eastern North America* (Knoxville, Tenn., 1983), 25. Dobyns argues that precontact life ended after the smallpox pandemic of 1520–24. The impact spread geographically beyond any European presence. Russell Thornton, *American Indian Holocaust and Survival: A Population History since 1492* (Norman, Okla., 1987). Ann F. Ramesofsky, *Vectors of Death: The Archaeology of European Contact* (Albuquerque, 1987). Daniel T. Reff, *Disease, Depopulation and Cultural Change in Northwestern New Spain, 1518–1764* (Salt Lake City, 1991).

earlier case) and can be proved to have taken deliberate measures to spread smallpox among Indians, but we have no certainty that the significant numbers of subsequent deaths were caused by resultant infection. The historical record points to widespread intention to infect the enemy, but no concrete implemented policy by Amherst, despite his support for the infection.[9]

What about cases of rumored infections? How extensive was the smallpox devastation? The scope seemed to have been substantial but not overwhelming. It caused fatalities that impacted the local situation, but not demographic devastation. Fenn's evidence suggests fatalities range between scores to perhaps a few hundreds in exceptional circumstances. This creates a dissonance between the notion of genocide and the evidence of a few hundred deaths in cases of rumored (even if fairly likely true) infections. The designation of genocide in terms of numbers, however, may be more pertinent to the invasion two centuries earlier, where many more perished from diseases. But there is lack of concrete information regarding the question of intentionality that led to genocidal behavior.

In his claim, Stannard is very close to Dobyns who presents the devastation of the indigenous population in a similarly polarized way. In Dobyns's work the mild titles are in direct tension to the harsh reality. "Their number became thinned"[10] is perhaps one of the more structurally "passive" descriptions one could imagine to describe the consequences of the colonial operation. "Native American depopulation during the sixteenth century far exceeded that of later times. Yet the number of Native Americans who did survive into the latter portion of that demographically disastrous century was great enough to prompt some Europeans to advocate measures for further thinning."[11] This is very much a description of genocide. That he uses passive language does not suggest that Dobyns is uncritical of the anti-Indian policies and actions. On the contrary, this criticism is the purpose of his book. Yet, precisely because of this, his choice of Diego de Escalante Fontaneda's words, "their number became thinned," produces a numbing effect. Dobyns "explicitly apologizes" that the book may be controversial. Although he does not shy from an academic controversy, the anesthetic language he uses to describe genocide almost forces him to maintain the question of genocide as, at most, an implicit theoretical question – implicit, and not named. "Much has been written about Colonial mistreatment of Native Americans, and some exploitation did occur. Still abuse killed comparatively few Native Americans compared with the destruction wrought by germs

9 Elizabeth A. Fenn, "Biological Warfare in Eighteenth-Century North America: Beyond Jeffery Amherst," *Journal of American History* (March 2000): 1552–80.
10 Dobyns, *Their Number*, 19.   11 Ibid., 8.

and viruses."[12] The untold number of those "comparatively few" killed by abuse, which may well run into the millions, is not the focus of his scholarship. Instead, his focus is on the structural devastation for which assigning responsibility is highly problematic. We are left wondering what exactly constituted the genocide? Previous writers have described the genocide as murders and atrocities committed by perpetrators, in this case, Europeans. Although Dobyns correctly states that "colonial mistreatment of natives killed fewer by far than did Old World diseases," the atrocities were horrific and devastating on their own terms. Because, as Dobyns describes it, structural devastation and not colonial mistreatment had greater impact, how then does such structural analysis impact the use of the term genocide?

Stannard suggests to us that racism was foundational for genocide. While the precise demarcation of racism and the individuals' culpability in social norms is a perplexing question, there is little doubt that social and political racism toward Native Americans (and other indigenous peoples) was extensive and devastating in its consequences. But how do we make the leap from general racism to responsibility for genocide? Stannard does not help us. Employing the Genocide Convention as a guide, Stannard ends the book with a rhetorical statement: "[I]t is impossible to know what transpired in the Americas during the sixteenth, seventeenth, eighteenth, and nineteenth centuries and not conclude that it was genocide."[13] This is hardly satisfactory. Destruction, devastation, and atrocities were no doubt the results of the colonial conquest. This is hardly news and is not the book's novelty, though the details are compelling. Yet we are left to our own imagination to demarcate and understand the extent of the genocide that Stannard says was and is intentional. In order to employ the term productively, however, we have to determine what ought to be included under "genocide": should we divide the devastation between genocidal (intentional) and nongenocidal factors?

In *Missionary Conquest* George Tinker both highlights the urgency of incorporating the term genocide into the study of the history of Native Americans and argues for a broader definition of genocide that would include the notion of cultural genocide and the interrelated subcategories of political, economic, social, and religious genocide. In contrast to Stannard, Tinker does not limit the infliction of genocide to intentional actions but argues that even positive intentions can lead to genocide. Consequences, not intentionality, are the dominating factor. Viewed from this perspective, the fact that Native American peoples were subjected to genocide should be self-evident, although it was rarely articulated as policy.

---

12 Ibid., 24.   13 Stannard, *American Holocaust*, 281.

Tinker argues that although there is certainly no evidence that European missionaries ever engaged in the systematic killing of Indian people, they actively participated in the cultural genocide of Native Americans. These missionaries subverted their own ideology of Christian salvation in order to advance "civilization," which has meant "continued bondage to a culture that is both alien and alienating and even genocidal against American Indian peoples."[14]

The text is particularly germane to the present analysis by its attribution of guilt and responsibility. Tinker claims that all nonnatives were accomplices in the cultural genocide of Native Americans, regardless of their personal intent or direct participation. Ultimately that means that all missionaries and even Christianity (as a white authority structure) were invariably guilty. Indeed the consideration of sainthood for any of the missionaries is "the canonization of genocide," a claim, we should add, that would presumably find sympathy among those who objected to the canonization or beatification of Popes Pius XI and XII. "Christian missionaries – of all denominations working among American Indian nations – were partners in genocide." Yet none of the missionaries Tinker discusses explicitly attempted to inflict cultural genocide. Instead the guilt is deduced from the genocidal results that Tinker claims are patently obvious in retrospect, namely the demographic decline of the native peoples.[15]

Tinker's position creates a difficulty because it proclaims every individual member of a society guilty of genocide independent of his or her participation. This has several effects. It blurs the distinction between such members and actual perpetrators so that the agency and responsibility of particular perpetrators is lessened. It further lessens particular perpetrators' responsibility by attributing guilt based on later structural developments. Yet it goes beyond a condemnation of the society, to attributing individual guilt to all members. This may spread guilt too widely and too thinly.

Further, neither intentions nor actions are brought to bear on the question of guilt. Tinker explicitly says that cultural genocide quite often is not the overt intention but "results from the pursuit of some other goal" such as economic or political gain. And in the particular case of the missionaries, the gain was neither institutional nor personal. This unwitting responsibility, despite "the best of intentions," determines the missionaries' guilt "of complicity in the destruction of Indian cultures and tribal social structures – complicity in the destruction . . . and in the death of the

---

14 George E. Tinker, *Missionary Conquest: The Gospel and Native American Cultural Genocide* (Boston, 1993), 5.
15 Ibid., 67, 4, 112.

people to whom they preached."[16] Tinker sees in this perhaps one of the most "fearful aspect[s] of the missionary history of conquest and genocide," namely "the extent to which it is a history of 'good intentions.' "[17] Naiveté disappears according to Tinker, when missionaries accepted government money. I think the issues raised are grave and complicated, but this focus on money is simplistic. The challenge of responsibility for unintended consequences, which Tinker underscores, remains.

THE NOBLE SAVAGE

In evaluating the colonial violent encounter, the lack of documentation of preencounter indigenous peoples or, in other cases, merely ignoring available data facilitates and even seduces the projection of cultural characteristics on the indigenous peoples.[18] The traditional colonial description of savages as violent, depraved, or in desperate need of civilizing left much to be desired in terms of realism. On the other side are those who ignore the violence, the atrocities, and the warfare of the Aboriginal society, constructing an image of "civilized life purged of its vices."[19] This constructs a mirror image of the colonialist propaganda that was prevalent ever since the Spaniards made sure that those in Europe were aware of the indigenous cruelty. The descriptions of savagery were less a testimony of one's shock at the violence and more a way to facilitate the conquest and justify morally and politically any and all policies. It established support back in Europe and facilitated a justification of the conquest as eradicating cannibalism. In this, the sixteenth-century conquistadores had close affinity to the British who conquered Benin, "the City of Blood," four hundred years later.

How violent were indigenous peoples in the precontact period? Recognizing that we do not have the data for many societies means we do not know: neither the savage nor the noble savage is a valid historical generalization. The little evidence we possess came mostly from the colonial sources,

---

16 Ibid., 4.
17 Tinker names a subchapter "Good Intentions, Naiveté and Genocide" and says missionaries "surely did not intend any harm to Indian people" (ibid., 15). Instead, "culpability was prescribed," it was "impossible to avoid individual complicity," and "the missionaries facilitated the exploitation, but did not benefit from it" (ibid., 16–17).
18 For a strong statement about the dramatic transformation of the indigenous people between precontact and postcontact primordial society or the fragility of oral tradition, see Dobyns, *Their Number*, 24–26, 338–43, and on the noble savage, 333–34.
19 E. Panofsky, *Meaning in the Visual Arts* (New York, 1957), 297. Cocker, *Rivers of Gold*, points to Dee Brown's *Bury My Heart at Wounded Knee* as one of the most popular revisionist histories of the American Indian Wars, who, even as he attempts sympathetically to present the defeated Indians from "their own" perspective, persists with the trope of the noble savage.

the enemies of the indigenous peoples. Yet, when we talk about evaluating responsibility and guilt, we rely on one-sided testimony. The improbable contrast of a "savage" with a "noble savage" remains a contentious issue.

The tone of Stannard's work is an example of the portrayal of the noble savage as a trope that underscores the colonial genocide. Occasionally he makes explicit claims regarding those good old times, as when he claims that the life expectancy and health of the Indians surpassed those of the Europeans, as did their culture in earlier days.[20] Perhaps, but how would we know? One writer who underscores the tension between "savage" and "noble savage" is Mark Cocker. He tries to redress the romantic view by emphasizing the violence within the Native American cultures and by assigning some level of responsibility (shortcomings?) to the Indians for various aspects of the collusion with colonialism. Yet, he does not shift the blame. For example, while describing the help Indians gave to the Mexican conquistadores in conquering their own people, he does not diminish the colonialist responsibility for the atrocities.[21]

Similar destruction was repeated across the globe and the centuries. But the use of the term "genocide" is not limited to outright killing. It is being employed to describe wide-ranging policies, including assimilation and education.

THE LOST GENERATIONS OF CHILDREN

In the latest controversy over genocide, we move from the atrocities of killing to abuse and efforts to destroy indigenous culture. Policies toward indigenous peoples in some of the former British colonies in the first half of the twentieth century have become the substance of political debate.[22]

Australia's Stolen Generation

Consider the controversy that erupted in April 2000 in Australia when, in a statement to Parliament, Conservative Minister for Aboriginal and Torres Strait Islander Affairs John Herron declared that the number of Aboriginal

20 See Russell Thornton, review of Stannard, *American Holocaust*, in *Journal of American History* (1994): 1428, and Stannard, *American Holocaust*, 11, for prehistoric cultural superiority.
21 After discussing the various indigenous peoples' contribution to Cortes's conquest, Cocker, *Rivers of Gold*, 84–85, concludes: "An infinite capacity for disunity (illustrated by the tens of thousands of Americans fighting for the Cortesian army) is almost a defining element of tribal society. Indigenous communities were invariably guilty of a type of collective myopia, a deep failure to see the European threat as anything but a local context."
22 Colin Tatz (1999), Genocide in Australia, AIATSIS Research Discussion Papers No. 8, Canberra <http://www.aiatsis.gov.au/rsrch/rsrch_dp/genocide.htm>; Henry Reynolds, *Aboriginal Sovereignty: Reflections on Race, State and Nation* (London, 1996).

children taken by authorities from their mothers and placed with white families or put into orphanages was overblown by Aboriginal activists. The consequence of these abductions has become known as the "Lost" or "Stolen Generation."

The practice existed between the 1910s and 1970s. Most of the children who were kidnapped were "mixed" Aborigines, the outcome of "cohabitation" between white men who often exploited Aborigine women. The children were taken from their mothers in order to become part of the white society. Pure Aborigines in their remote desert settlements were expected to die out over time. Expressing the conventional view of the time, in 1906 a white man with the title protector of Aborigines, James Isdell, was quoted by the commission as saying: "The half-caste is intellectually above the Aborigine and it is the duty of the state that they be given a chance to lead a better life than their mothers."[23] Consequently, among the kidnapped children there was a "hierarchy," with lighter-skinned Aboriginal children being adopted by white families and those with darker skin usually going to orphanages. Those with much darker skin were exempted from this practice. In order to avoid the kidnappings, mothers were reported to have rubbed their babies with charcoal and animal fat. The testimonies of the forced separation and of physical abuse are horrific. The number of removed children is estimated at up to 100,000, though it is impossible to ascertain definitely. This is partially because, in the "best interests" of the children, authorities destroyed many of the records of these children that detailed who their real parents were.

"No," stated Herron. *Only* 10 percent were kidnapped that way, and "we're arguing it's not a generation if it was 10 percent. If it was a generation it means the whole generation so we think it's a misnomer." Senator Aden Ridgeway, the only Aborigine to serve in Australia's Parliament, and who sees the issue as an attempt at cultural genocide, compared Herron's comments to "denying the Holocaust."[24]

This was one more salvo in the controversy over the "Stolen Generation." In April 1997 the Human Rights and Equal Opportunity Commission investigated the policy of removing Aboriginal children from their families and placing them in institutional settings or white foster homes. Its 1997

---

23 Ronald Wilson, *Bringing Them Home: Report of the National Inquiry into the Separation of Aboriginal and Torres Strait Islander Children from Their Families*, Human Rights and Equal Opportunity Commission (Sydney, 1997). Also, "I would not hesitate for one moment to separate any half-caste from its Aboriginal mother, no matter how frantic her momentary grief might be at the time. They soon forget their offspring." James Isdell, Western Australian traveling protector, 1909.

24 Shawn Donnan, "Furor over Scale of Aboriginal Assimilation," *Christian Science Monitor*, April 4, 2000.

published report, *Bringing Them Home*, instantly became a best seller and directed national focus on the human tragedy that it termed "genocide."[25] Although the government pretended that the adoptions were benevolent acts of providing the children with a "good home," the commission described a policy to eliminate the Aborigines from Australia. Furthermore, because Australia adopted the United Nations Convention against Genocide in 1949, which defines genocide as including, among others things, "forcibly transferring children of the group to another group,"[26] the commission concluded that the removal fit the legal definition of genocide, because the foremost purpose of the policies was the elimination of Aboriginal life and cultures. The commission concluded that Australia was responsible for restitution to the victims, to individuals, and also to families and communities. Because it was believed that it was neither possible nor desirable to prosecute those responsible, the recommendations did not include retribution.

The result of the inquiry was that the perpetrators admitted it happened, the victims learned that their families grieved for them, government officials at the state level apologized, as did church leaders, and there evolved a whole routine of public apology through the "Sorry Days." The culture of apology has taken root, and the "Lost Generation" has become a formidable aspect of Australia's efforts to come to terms with its own past.

Bringing Them Home estimated the number of kidnapped children to be between 10 and 33 percent of all Aboriginal children. Herron's attempt to claim the lower estimate and deny wrongdoing created an uproar, and for the past few years this has been the most contentious and divisive racial issue in Australia. Nobody disputed the suffering or the violence that the policies inflicted on the Aborigines, and indeed the report included testimonies that could not help but move the reader. Yet the Conservative government works diligently to minimize its extent, as though thereby eliminating the intentions or the criminal aspects as understood by the commission.

Attempts to shift the demands to the courts have not yet succeeded. The High Court also rejected an Aborigine demand for compensation (July 1997). The court accepted that laws in place in 1918 in the Northern Territory had authorized the removal of "Aboriginal and half-caste children from their parents" if the authorities considered it in the children's interest. In addition, judges rejected the genocide designation. Instead, the court

25 Michael Perry, "Aborigines Tell Horror Tales of Whippings, Rapes," Reuters North American Wire, May 26, 1997. Wilson, *Bringing Them Home* <http://www.austlii.edu.au/au/special/rsjproject/rsjlibrary/hreoc/stolen_summary/index.html>.
26 See UN Convention on the Prevention and Punishment of the Crime of Genocide <http://www.unhchr.ch/html/menu3/b/p_genoci.htm>.

viewed this action as "misplaced" and "an attempt to exceed powers." These words can apply to both genocide or misplaced policies. The commission's report, however, suggests that the historical judgment would view the "Lost Generation" as more than a misplaced bureaucratic action. Aborigines continue to bring cases to trial and to appeal the decisions of lower courts.

In 2000, in an attempt to rebut the earlier commission, the government claimed the numbers in the report were higher than they should have been, because they included categories of children who should have been removed for welfare reasons and those who were put up for adoption. Because the numbers cannot be conclusively adjudicated (because of destroyed documents), the dispute over numbers is meant only to obfuscate the matter. Subject to public criticism (April 2000), both Prime Minister John Howard and Minister Herron apologized for offending certain Aborigines, but not to the "Stolen Generation," the existence of which they continue to deny.[27]

CANADA'S INDIGENOUS CHILDREN

Canada has its own abused indigenous children, a case comparable to the "Stolen Generation," if on a smaller scale. In 1996 the Canadian Royal Commission concluded that thousands of students died in horrible conditions at residential schools and thousands more were physically and sexually abused in the effort to "elevate the savages." The investigation followed years of rumors about the church schools where indigenous children were taken, often forcibly, in a purported effort to "civilize" them. More than 100,000 Aborigine children went through Canada's system of 125 residential schools since the mid-nineteenth century. These schools were run by the Roman Catholic, United, Anglican, and Presbyterian churches. The stories spurred a full-blown national self-examination. The government has been involved in steps toward restitution, but the main focus has been on the churches, which have been the subject of lawsuits brought by tribes whose children were wrongfully imprisoned and were physically, emotionally, and sexually abused at church schools.

The reports in the press are of children who were taken away from their families, sometimes for as long as eight years, and were brought up in an atmosphere that was, in the best of cases, "emotionally sterile." More often they were subject to direct abuse, resulting in what may become known as

27 See *Age* reports: Brendan Nicholson, "Canberra Attacked over Human Rights Report," April 2, 2000; Rod Mcguirk, "PM, Herron Say Sorry," April 7, 2000; Kerry Taylor, "Stolen Children Turn Backs on PM," April 14, 2000; Louise Dodson, "Herron Uses Court Case for Support," August 19, 2000; Kerry Taylor, "Hayden Draws Fire over 'Sorry' Speech," October 13, 2000.

a "post colonial syndrome," producing dysfunctional families and leading to myriad tragedies: crime, child abuse, suicide, drug abuse, and alcoholism.[28] For the plaintiffs it was institutionalized child labor, sadism, and pedophilia. Perhaps one of the most perplexing aspects is that the practice continued into the 1970s. The separation of indigenous peoples from their families and culture remained informed by an ideology of "civilizing." The system was finally closed down in 1996. The number of lawsuits could reach as many as twenty thousand in the next decade.[29]

The United States had its own long-standing boarding schools for Native American children with a similar extent of abuse. However, the term *Education for Extinction* is yet to capture public attention as a human rights issue.[30] The American indigenous dilemma is far less central to U.S. mainstream politics than in any of the other ex-British colonies. The notion of genocide, while warranted as much or more than in those other countries, is still confined to radical writers. It is intriguing, indeed, that no mainstream American historians have written about the fate of the Native Americans as genocide.

NEW ZEALAND'S GENOCIDE

In New Zealand, the rhetoric of genocide recently took center stage. It erupted when Associate Maori Affairs Minister Tariana Turia decried the holocaust inflicted on the Maori. Turia described to a conference of psychologists what she called a "post colonial traumatic stress disorder,"[31] bundling together the consequences of colonialism to describe causes of problems in Maoridom, what others call the dysfunctional life of Maori. While the context of her claim was rather temperate, she made the headlines by referring to colonization as holocaust.

This was not the first time the concept was used in New Zealand. The Waitangi Tribunal also came under fire in 1996 for describing the nineteenth

---

28 DeNeen L. Brown, "The Sins of the Fathers: Newfoundland Wrestles with Legacy of Church School Abuse," *Washington Post*, October 15, 2000.

29 Colin Nickerson, "Indian Lawsuits over Schools Shake Churches in Canada," *Boston Globe*, September 12, 2000. "Churches Reaping Harvest," *Toronto Star*, August 26, 2000. "Churches Could Face Ruin," *Gazette* (Montreal), August 20, 2000. "'Stolen' Native Wants Family, Culture Back," *Ottawa Citizen*, October 10, 2000.

30 David Adams, *Education for Extinction: American Indians and the Boarding School Experience, 1875–1928*, (Lawrence, Kans., 1995.)

31 An analogous concept is advanced by Alvin Poussaint and Amy Alexander in *Lay My Burden Down* (Boston, 2000), which talks about "post-traumatic slavery syndrome," though here the success of one part of the community seems to be at fault as much as the deprivation of another, and the focus is on the health care crisis since 1980.

century's Taranaki land confiscation as the "holocaust of Taranaki history," in its interim report on the Taranaki claim. Their history is a good example of how the conflicting images of the noble savage wrap the debate. Was the Taranaki society peaceful, or was it part of the larger Maori culture of warfare? Did the Maori support signing the Treaty of Waitangi because they saw it as a means of halting Maori violence against Maori, or were the Maori victims of the unprovoked colonial war?[32]

In August 2000 New Zealand politics was ripe for such a dispute. Politicians pandered in all directions, and for a short period it seems the debate consumed the national energy. The emotional dispute led to exaggerations. In order to reject the comparison of the Maori experience to the Holocaust, politically moderate people felt they were seemingly pushed to excuse New Zealand's colonial oppression and exploitation, as well as imperialism. To argue that the colonialists who exploited the Maori were "angels by comparison with Hitler and his henchmen"[33] may be true, but the excessive apologetics in the debate displayed deep insensitivity to the victims.

Prime Minster Helen Clark formally reprimanded Turia and insisted that she never again use "holocaust" in relation to New Zealand colonization. Clark asserted that this was not censorship, merely government policy. The specific argument was that her position as a minister prevents her from using a specific terminology that contradicts government policy, in this case, "holocaust." Beyond the formal rebuke, however, the debate introduced the concept of genocide to the New Zealand discourse. In the short run, the government suffered despite the rebuke and was viewed as too pro-Maori.

Despite the national aspect of these cases – as Australian, Canadian, or New Zealander – it is noteworthy that there was nothing specifically national about it. There was great similarity between these ex-British colonies. Indeed the commitment to take the "Indian out of his primitive state, raising him up and making of him ... an honest citizen" was shared throughout the colonial world for centuries.[34] This uniformity of abuse throughout the colonial system constituted the very method of extinguishing indigenous culture. That it included physical and sexual abuse, not merely neglect, is instructive in evaluating the way a "discourse" turns individuals into criminals, even under the rhetoric of a lofty civilizing mission.

---

32 Jonathan Milne, "War Never Ended in Taranaki. What Turia Really Said," *Dominion* (Wellington), September 2, 2000, reports on the opinion among the current Taranaki.
33 Editorial, *Nelson Mail*, August 31, 2000.
34 Statement of the Canadian minister of Indian affairs, made in 1908, as quoted in "Churches Could Face Ruin," *Gazette* (Montreal), August 20, 2000.

VARIETIES OF GENOCIDE

The Holocaust is the nonparadigmatic genocide par excellence. The intentions, actions, and means of the perpetrators combined to annihilate most of the targeted victims. In contrast, other genocides and candidate genocides, perpetrated against indigenous peoples over the last five centuries, did not continuously share intentions, means, and policies. Despite the changing configurations that caused the undeniable horrors, the consequences and the destruction were widespread. Judged in isolation, each case is a testimony for unimaginable suffering and cannot be ranked on any human scale. But what are we to name these endless cases of horrific destruction?

The claims of uniqueness for the Jewish Holocaust obviously raised the stakes of naming, establishing an aura of sacredness for particular victimization over others. Supporters of the uniqueness thesis fear that a wide application of the term genocide will lead to its "secularization," making it applicable in numerous and very different circumstances. As a horrific but nonunique destruction, genocide would be viewed as a term like "war," a concept that demands much glossing and articulation before anyone can glean the contours of a particular genocide or its substance. A more encompassing demarcation will validate the victims' perspectives and would delegitimize the claim of uniqueness. Thus the Holocaust becomes in hindsight a singular, extreme case of genocide, neither privileged nor unique. Whatever else its characteristics, as a historical phenomenon the Holocaust will likely maintain its role as an event that instigated the Genocide Convention and the Human Rights Convention. But this is a historical specificity and cannot translate into a hierarchy of importance, suffering, or victimization.

When it comes to the question of genocide, the complexity of colonial history is reduced to a polarization of the tropes of "noble savage" and "genocidal colonialist." This antithetic history creates a resistance in an audience and becomes an obstacle for accepting the usage of the term genocide to describe the indigenous destruction. We would do well in this context to remember that in the pre-twentieth-century world, the criticism of violence, atrocities, and killing was an exception. Ideology was often more important than violence, and the end justified the means. This has been changing in the twentieth century, mostly under the fear of global annihilation. As the ability to destroy has accelerated ever faster, so has the growing skepticism that any ideology merits violence, let alone atrocities. In contrast, earlier savagery, whether displayed by the colonial invaders or by the local population, was rarely criticized. Critics of violence were the exceptions, not the representatives of their time.

The myopia of colonial histories about genocides has led to an "overview" that has failed to take account of the infinite diverse colonial experiences. Indigenous peoples were (and are) inordinately diverse; their homogeneity existed only from the Western perspective. Colonialism caused genocide on numerous occasions but not always. The attempt to conflate five hundred years of global history into a single characterization is bound to be wrong. Not all colonialism and colonialists were genocidal, but certainly many were. When historians hedge their bets, they emphasize the various factors that contributed to the devastation of indigenous people: in addition to biological factors and disease, there were internal warfare among indigenous peoples (along with the support for the Spanish) and, yes, colonialism. There were so many reasons for the destruction that we rarely focus on the genocide. One reviewer of Stannard writes: "The Spanish merely put the finishing touches on the disintegration of the Maya civilization, and the Aztec empire may very well have been destroyed by a rival group instead of the Spaniards."[35] Should not such a claim be understood under the dreaded "denial" category? Similar to the naming of genocide, denial presumably should also be context-sensitive. Only wide recognition of indigenous destruction as genocide will acknowledge such opinion as denial. At present, these are more likely uninformed opinions. This suggests that the significance of the definition is in giving full acknowledgment to the horror, while at present such speculation can exist without a whiff. (A thought experiment: try and read the sentence by replacing Spanish with Nazi, and Maya with Jews. For the rival group, read another fascist or communist regime. Take your pick. It is clear such a statement could not be uttered.)

On the other hand, M. Annette Jaimes raises the stakes by rejecting a comparison of the Indian calamities to merely any genocide, such as those suffered by Armenians, or in Paraguay, or even East Timor. In her estimation, none of these were terrible enough, none convey the enormity of the genocide against Native Americans. Only the policies of the Nazi destruction of the Jews can be compared with the United States policies against the Indians.[36] This is a clear example of genocide pageantry. Not only does she minimize the suffering of many around the world and buy into a rigid hierarchy of genocides, but by comparing the United States to the Third Reich, she also excludes the destruction of the Indians before U.S. independence, or the Spaniards' role. Instead, she is interested in denouncing the current United States, even at the cost of ignoring the lives of the very victims she is purportedly defending. Thus, by continuously evoking Hitler, her attempt is to establish similarity with, and hence reify, the Holocaust as the generally admitted single (unique?) worst event.

Describing both mass systematic slaughter and forcing children into an assimilated boarding school under the category of genocide may justifiably be perplexing, even though this is precisely what the UN Genocide Convention specifies in its five categories. Are we to talk about the events, the intentions, or the consequences? Could we think about such diverse phenomena, which include unexpected and misunderstood epidemics, in a similar language and category with violent imperial policies aimed at killing, destroying, and exiling whole populations? What about misplaced efforts, such as attempts to save or improve the fortunes of indigenous peoples, which end up, at times, contributing to the suffering of individuals and to the extinction of the specific group?

When we break up the colonial experience, the various events of destruction and victimization become candidates to be viewed as genocidal. Most are terrible enough that, if we reject the concept of "genocide," it would seem to deny the victims the proper acknowledgment, in their own view, for their suffering. It thus would seem sensible, perhaps obvious, to grant such recognition. Yet, a historical determination still has to take place.

In the case of naming the destruction of indigenous peoples as genocidal, the historical perspectives and rhetorical stands are profoundly in conflict, partly because the debate is still held captive by the world view that informed European expansionism. The rejection of the use of the term genocide is about exclusion, about segregating the suffering of indigenous peoples as somewhat different than other "more terrible" genocides. Instead, once we acknowledge the equality of indigenous people, we can recognize that atrocities committed against them also constitute genocide. Then we can also begin to differentiate between the types of acts committed against indigenous peoples to determine which were genocidal, or what aspects of genocide took place under different circumstances.

The importance of writing about genocide, and not merely about a host of factors and passively vanishing tribes, is to shift the conversation so as to be able to recognize the colonial process as one actively committed to exploit and settle the newly found lands through the destruction of the local population. In the colonialists' views the continents were both empty and wasted away by indolent inhabitants. There was no room for the savages in a civilized world, and they had to disappear. The diseases were convenient for the colonists because these diminished the resistance. But the diseases did not have to have been inflicted intentionally for the conquest to be genocidal.

Unintended spread of the disease entailed a different type of responsibility. What type of responsibility?

This is a highly complex issue. There is little doubt that the colonialists intended for the "savages" to disappear, to die. The intent to kill was certainly there. The known cases of actively infecting the population were relatively small compared with the results of the natural epidemic and the destruction. There was intent, there was result, but there was relatively little action. A formalist reading would presumably have to exonerate most colonialists who were not actively seeking to infect the indigenous population. It seems to me too much of a technicality. This calls for a rethinking of the notion of genocide, rather than a formalist designation. The colonial invaders meant to inherit the earth, and they were eager to bring about the extinction of the natives. To what extent would they have gone? I think we have to see this as a form of genocide, different than others, but not lower on any hierarchy of suffering or racism.

One of the counterfactuals that has been raised less frequently (as opposed to the claim that the Aztec empire would have been destroyed anyhow) is the question, What would have happened had the Native Americans not died of disease? The outcome would have most likely looked more like Central America, or perhaps Africa and Asia. In all of these, European colonialism did not kill off comparable percentages of the inhabitants, even as it inflicted horrific atrocities. Informed by similar racism and expansionist ideology, but faced with different local conditions, colonialism led to dramatically different outcomes in each continent. If the question is what most determined the outcome of colonialism, I think there could be little doubt that biology ranked as chief agent. Or, put differently, there were nonhuman agents that framed the outcome. But that does not mean that the conquest in South Africa or of the Herero was less genocidal, and by extension there is no reason to assume that the colonialist in the New World would have hesitated to destroy much of the indigenous peoples had they not died of disease.

Much of the conversation is too generalized. It is important to emphasize that the "colonial project" in singular is a misleading lens through which to view the relation between Europe, its emigrants, and the rest of the world. The phenomena are just too diverse. In some cases when we talk about genocide, we explore the actions of a particular regime within a short period of time against a specific group(s). It can be viewed as a unified action. Nazism or Rwanda easily fit in this category. Colonialism is different. It encompasses so many distinct components that an attempt to compose it all under one category will necessarily lead to either uninformed abstractions or inaccuracies, which will undermine any conclusion. One such generalization, which has received only segmented endorsement, is the attempt to portray Columbus as the agent responsible for all the suffering that chronologically followed him. No doubt he had his own shortcomings, and his actions are rightfully criticized to some degree. But it hardly makes sense to impose the kind of allegations piled on him and still maintain historical credibility. For example, the anti-Columbus literature not only makes him responsible for all the destruction that follows; the critics also see the greedy motives of the early Spaniards as more influential in the drive to dominate the new territories than the monotheistic imperialism of saving the natives' souls and assume that such motivation conveys more guilt. Not everyone would subscribe to either the demarcation or this ideological hierarchy.

The lack of a single a priori source of evil (e.g., greed) does not mean that there were no responsible agents for the colonial atrocities. There is little doubt that multiple genocides were inflicted upon indigenous populations in numerous cases. But not the whole colonial project can be regarded as genocidal. During five hundred years many millions died from extermination, domination, and natural causes but there is no way to classify the numbers who died. Although the decline of the population was not merely a passive "decline," it was also not an orchestrated homogenous extermination. There is no doubt that in the multifaceted description of the "encounter" there is a crucial need to underscore the genocides that did take place. But the general indiscriminate use of the term and the difficulty of the research have largely left us still in the dark. It has remained a space where radical writers are more prominent; however, their overenthusiasm and moral outrage often undermine the scholarly persuasion. It also has a counterproductive impact on the public. It seems to me that concrete descriptions of genocide are more effective in generating sympathy for the survivors than a blank indictment that is counterintuitive.

The predicament is how to maintain the specificities of various events and the distinctions among forms of ethnic destruction, while not giving the appearance of minimizing the suffering of some and privileging others?

The replacement of a global colonial genocide with multiple cases of local genocides is a shift in scale, not in severity. Victims are attracted by the concept genocide to describe their suffering because by becoming part of the penultimate form of catastrophe they receive recognition for their suffering. Only the Holocaust may be viewed as worse, and indeed the two are often intertwined in their usage. However, genocide has a special appeal because of the Genocide Convention. As an international agreement, the convention carries obligations for signatories. This is a tall order, and nations are justifiably reluctant to define a conflict and a war as genocide, because it requires them to act. The convention, however, leaves room for widely divergent claims.

The hesitation to use the concept of genocide leads writers to distinguish between genocide and ethnic cleansing or, as it used to be called, ethnocide. This approach sees the various categories as conveying specific meaning: ethnocide is cultural genocide, which is distinct from ethnic cleansing that is not quite genocide but only diminishes some victims. If ethnic cleansing is perceived as somewhat less terrible than "full genocide," the term appears to diminish those whose destruction falls in that category. Naturally, victims strive not to see their suffering as less than that of other groups; all aspire to the highest "rating." But should we view these distinctions as "real" differences in history, despite the victims' wishes? The urge to classify the cases, even without hierarchy, raises the issue of organization. But according to what principles? One stumbling block is the language of the Genocide Convention. The parameters of the Genocide Convention are broad enough to include ethnic cleansing and cultural genocide and the international responsibilities that go along with it. While intuitively some might attempt to demarcate and limit genocide to intentional consistent extermination of a nation or group while designating other horrendous acts of cultural extermination, mass exile, or even widespread death from disease by another name, the moral persuasion of such a distinction is diminishing. Genocide is becoming a family name to a host of horrendous crimes carried out in the name of politics and ideological xenophobia.

As the histories of indigenous peoples are taken more seriously, and human rights are extended to indigenous peoples, their historical mistreatment is examined carefully and evaluated by the same yardstick as other atrocities. As the focus shifts to the human experiences of the natives, events are revisited and revised. The more attention paid to the victims and their suffering, the less possible it is to merely focus on the heroic components of the encounter. Instead the focus of historical research should underscore more the genocidal component of colonialism. Such histories would challenge the complicity of the bystanders, as well as the responsibility of our generation, for the historical injustices.

Thus, the European guilt was at least a collective myopia, a deep failure to acknowledge the equality of indigenous people and the vast number and varied array of atrocities and genocides inflicted upon them. More likely this has been a willful denial of responsibility and guilt, hiding behind the structural explanation of biological agents. It is time to reverse course and acknowledge the responsibility and extent of the destruction purposefully inflicted by colonialism, although not upon all indigenous peoples, and not in similar fashion. The recognition would lead to a differentiation between structural changes in power relations, which carry more limited agency and responsibility, and active perpetration of crimes, for which amends ought perhaps to be made in some form. And, yes, we must also recognize human equality by engaging the category of genocide to describe some of the indigenous destruction, though not others.

Let us paraphrase Parker: who are we that we should suspend judgment over the hideous cruelties and iniquities of colonialism?

7

Military Culture and the Production of "Final Solutions" in the Colonies

The Example of Wilhelminian Germany

ISABEL V. HULL

It has been almost fifty years since Hannah Arendt made her bold statement, in *Origins of Totalitarianism*, that imperialism was one of the chief factors leading to totalitarianism and to its "final solutions."[1] She argued that imperialism was basically the idea and practice of limitless expansion for its own sake. Originally an economic notion akin to capitalism, imperialism in practice kicked itself loose from the limits imposed by profit and apotheosized violence as a conscious aim in itself. "Violence administered for power's (and not for law's) sake turns into a destructive principle that will not stop until there is nothing left to violate."[2] In the colonies, vague, insubstantial race thinking mutated into racism, the justification for the horrors perpetrated by whites against nonwhites in the situation of limitless violence.[3]

Arendt's hypothesis is most obviously convincing on the level of ideology.[4] It is no accident that the most radical proponents of imperialism were also the first to cement into a single world view modern racism, antisemitism, ruthless Social Darwinism, the dream of total domination, the militarization of society, and the worship of war as the best means (even goal) of politics. In Germany the Pan-Germans, who began institutional life in 1890 as one of several procolonial agitation groups, brought the destructive principles of imperialism home to Europe, to be applied to Europeans in a future

---

1 Hannah Arendt, *The Origins of Totalitarianism* (New York, 1951).
2 Ibid., 137.   3 Ibid., 183–86.
4 Woodruff Smith's account is functionalist and somewhat bloodless, but nonetheless valuable: Woodruff D. Smith, *The Ideological Origins of Nazi Imperialism* (New York, 1986). Sven Lindqvist's recent book is livelier, more imaginative, and makes many excellent connections, but it does not provide an analysis of the movement from brutal punishment, to massacre, to mass extermination. It ignores the central role of the military in exterminatory practices, and its account of South West Africa is inaccurate. Sven Lindqvist, *"Exterminate All the Brutes": One Man's Odyssey into the Heart of Darkness and the Origins of European Genocide*, trans. Joan Tate (New York, 1996).

German continental imperium. When Arendt wrote, the Pan-Germans were thought to have been the insignificant lunatic fringe of German politics. Later research has shown they were in fact important to German domestic politics, because after 1908 they not only provided institutional links among a panoply of right-wing organizations, but also captured nationalist discourse, displacing the government as the spokesmen and arbiters of nationalist-security policy.[5] The simultaneous failure of Germany's official imperial policy and the desire, expressed in countless, nationalist agitation groups, to retain all of imperialism's most destructive qualities, permanently radicalized and transformed the German right wing from government loyalists to vehement critics.[6] Chancellor Bernhard von Bülow's attempts to tame this process by rushing ahead of it in the so-called Hottentott elections of 1907 (banking on nationalist sentiment aroused during the revolt in South West Africa) failed utterly.[7] In short, Germany's imperial experience transformed both right-wing ideology, laying solid foundations for later National Socialism, and the domestic political spectrum.

Nevertheless, many historians of imperialism have been reluctant to accept Arendt's hypothesis when it comes to practice.[8] The major hindrance seems to be the (correct) observation that all imperial powers behaved despicably in the colonies, but only Germany went on during World War II to pursue complete extermination as national policy.

In order to identify the historical processes that culminated in the National Socialist "final solution," one must distinguish atrocity and massacre, on the one hand, from final solutions, on the other.[9] Atrocities committed against indigenous rebels and civilians and administrative massacres were, if not ubiquitous, certainly so common in imperialist practice that they must be regarded as standard operating procedures. They indicate the existence of three precipitating or enabling factors for final solutions: the sheer ability to kill large numbers of people (technological and organizational superiority),

5 Roger Chickering, *"We Men Who Feel Most German": A Cultural Study of the Pan-German League, 1886–1914* (Boston, 1984).
6 Geoff Eley, *Reshaping the German Right: Radical Nationalism and Political Change after Bismarck* (New Haven, 1983); Marilyn Shevin Coetzee, *The German Army League: Popular Nationalism in Wilhelmine Germany* (Oxford, 1990); Roger Chickering, "Der 'Deutsche Wehrverein' und die Reform der deutschen Armee 1912–1914," *Militärgeschichtliche Mitteilungen* 25 (1979): 7–35.
7 George Dunlap Crothers, *The German Elections of 1907* (New York, 1941); Katherine Lerman, *The Chancellor as Courtier: Bernhard von Bülow and the Governance of Germany, 1900–1909* (Cambridge, 1990), 167–209.
8 E.g., David K. Fieldhouse, *Die Kolonialreiche seit dem 18. Jahrhundert* (Frankfurt, 1965), 220–21, 357–39.
9 Helen Fein makes this same point in "Genocide, Terror, Life Integrity, and War Crimes: The Case for Discrimination," in George J. Andreopoulos (ed.), *Genocide: Conceptual and Historical Dimensions*, (Philadelphia, 1992), 95–107, at 99, 105.

the identification of the civilian population as the "enemy," and the dehumanization of this enemy.[10] Imperialism therefore unintentionally cleared the path for more radical developments.

In most cases, colonial atrocities and massacres remained particular events. In contrast, a final solution is a conscious, universal goal: it seeks a total, permanent end to a "problem." It is preemptive, for it seeks to eliminate even the possibility or potential of the "problem" arising or recurring. Final solutions are therefore utopian and ideal. Their vastness makes it unlikely they will be pursued by any organization less powerful than a government. Applied to human society, final solutions dictate the disappearance of the problem population, which may occur via cultural assimilation, deportation, or physical annihilation (genocide). Genocide is therefore the most radical but not the only form of a final solution.[11] I believe that understanding how genocide develops is easier if one focuses not on the killing but on the final, or total, aspect of the goal. The question then becomes, Under what conditions does a government or its agents arrive at such a destructively utopian policy?

For years, I taught that Hannah Arendt was intuitively right in her surmise that imperialism was the main factor conveying Europe toward final solutions, but I could not locate the link between the two, except in ideology. I now believe that link is the military, whose practices in the imperial situation followed an internal dynamic that favored final solutions. Without being anchored in actual practice and perpetuated in institutions, ideology would scarcely have endured long enough to capture a state. Citing the military will not surprise many scholars who have observed how often militaries are involved in genocide.[12] However, few have attempted to analyze why late nineteenth- and early twentieth-century militaries should have been so primed to follow this developmental logic, or why the German military might have been especially likely to have done so. In a brief chapter it is not possible to explore all the ramifications of these questions, but it is possible

---

10 On predisposing factors: Herbert C. Kelman, "Violence without Moral Restraint: Reflections on the Dehumanization of Victims and Victimizers," *Journal of Social Issues* 29, 4 (1973): 25–61; Neil J. Smelser, "Some Determinants of Destructive Behavior," in Sanford Levitt and Craig Comstock (eds.), *Sanctions for Evil: Sources of Social Destructiveness* (San Francisco, 1971), 15–24; and Troy Duster, "Conditions for Guilt-Free Massacre," in ibid., 25–36.

11 On the definition of genocide and its various types, see Frank Chalk and Kurt Jonassohn, "The Conceptual Framework," in Chalk and Jonassohn (eds.), *The History and Sociology of Genocide: Analyses and Case Studies* (New Haven, 1990), 3–43; Israel W. Charny, "The Study of Genocide," in *Genocide: A Critical Bibliographical Review* (London, 1988), 1–19; Vahakn N. Dadrian, "A Topology of Genocide," *International Review of Modern Sociology* 5 (Fall 1975): 201–12.

12 Erin Staub, *The Roots of Evil: The Origins of Genocide and Other Group Violence* (Cambridge, 1989), 67, 78.

to dissect in detail one such occurrence, the most famous one, in German South West Africa. This example reveals a pattern of (German) military culture that played a critical role in predisposing later decision makers and institutions beyond the military to conceive of, tolerate, and/or attempt final solutions to political problems.

THE REVOLT IN SOUTH WEST AFRICA, 1904–1907

In the twenty years since Germany had established a protectorate over South West Africa (SWA) in 1883, about 2,000 mostly male settlers had come to the arid, sparsely populated colony. A combination of factors, not least white pressure on native lands, caused the dominant tribe in the colony's center, the cattle-herding Herero, to rise in revolt in January 1904. They were followed in rebellion by the much less numerous Nama to the south, in October 1904. Crushing these uprisings took over three years, cost almost 600 million marks, and involved 14,000 soldiers transferred from the German army. The Germans found the fighting extremely difficult, unused as they were to desert conditions in which no infrastructure of roads, telegraphs, or waterlines eased their movements. The military effort was Germany's largest before 1914; 1,500 men died, half of them from illness.[13] But the Herero and Nama lost infinitely more. A handful of writers cite poor statistics to justify their denial of the vast demographic catastrophe.[14] But well-informed contemporary observers and postwar demographic data agree on the immensity of the human destruction suffered by Africans. Most historians accept a death rate of between 75 and 80 percent for the Herero (out of an original population of 60,000–80,000 people), and of about 45–50 percent for the Nama (whose prewar numbers were around 20,000).[15] Official German military statistics admitted that the internment camps, which contained not just surrendering male rebels but also women and children, had compiled a death rate of 45 percent.[16] In addition to

13 Kommando der Schutztruppe im Reichs-Kolonialamt, *Sanitäts-Bericht über die Kaiserliche Schutztruppe für Südwestafrika während des Herero- und Hottentottenaufstandes für die Zeit vom 1. Januar 1904 bis 31. März 1907*, 2 vols. (Berlin, 1909), 2:405.
14 Gert Sudholt, *Die deutsche Eingeborenenpolitik in Südwestafrika; von den Anfängen bis 1904* (Hildesheim, 1975), 40–44; Brigitte Lau, "Uncertain Certainties: The Herero-German War of 1904," *Migabus* 2 (1989): 4–5, 8; Günter Spraul, "Der 'Volkermord' an den Herero; Untersuchungen zu einer neuen Kontinuitätsthese," *Geschichte in Wissenschaft and Unterricht* 39, 12 (1988): 713–39.
15 Horst Drechsler, *"Let Us Die Fighting": The Struggle of the Herero and the Nama against German Imperialism (1884–1915)*, trans. Bernd Zollner (London, 1980), 214; Helmut Bley, *South-West Africa under German Rule* (Evanston, 1971), 151–52; Horst Grunder, *Geschichte der deutschen Kolonien*, 3rd ed. (Paderborn, 1995), 121.
16 Schutztruppe Kommando, "Sterblichkeit in den Kriegsgefangenenlagern in Südwest-Afrika," Nr. KA II. 1181, undated, Bundesarchiv-Berlin, R 1001, Nr. 2140, pp. 161–62.

the sheer numbers, the commander who set this military policy, Lieutenant General Lothar von Trotha (June 1904–November 1905), announced in October 1904 his intention to achieve a final solution in SWA, in which mass death to the point of extermination was an acceptable outcome.

Neither the genocide nor, more generally, the final solution in SWA was ordered in Berlin. If Trotha had received such an order, even a verbal one, he would surely have said so when he later defended his extremism in private correspondence with his superior, Chief of Staff Alfred von Schlieffen, with Chancellor Bülow, and with SWA governor Colonel Theodor Leutwein.[17] As it was, he explained that "I received no instructions or directives from His Majesty upon my appointment to commander in SWA. His Majesty simply said that he expected me to crush the uprising by all means and explain to him later why it had begun."[18] The phrase "by all means" was a standard expression routinely used in connection with colonial revolts.[19]

Not only was no order given, Trotha's *Vernichtungspolitik* (policy of destruction) was opposed by Governor Leutwein; Chancellor Bülow; the Social Democrats and Left Liberals in the Reichstag; missionaries; even ruthless Social Darwinists like Paul Rohrbach, who was in SWA when the revolt broke out; and, finally and belatedly, also by the white settlers there, who did not want their labor supply eliminated. The settler's inflammatory rhetoric at the beginning of the revolt, however, certainly contributed to an atmosphere conducive of annihilation.

In the absence of an order and in the face of much opposition, the "final solution" in SWA developed out of military practices. The institutional prerequisite for this "final solution" was therefore total military control over military policy and over the colony. This occurred in two stages. The first was the immediate transfer of authority from the governor, himself a soldier experienced in putting down revolts, to the General Staff. Although Governor Leutwein still prosecuted the initial campaigns (from January to June 1904), he took his orders from the General Staff, rather than from the chancellor via the Foreign Office, which was the normal chain of command in the colonies. Unseating the "civilians" in favor of military experts happened because it was in the kaiser's constitutional power (his *Kommandogewalt*) to do so, and because the revolt was immediately identified as a

---

17 This correspondence is in BA-Berlin, R 1001, Nr. 2089. August Bebel, the Social Democratic leader, surmised in the Reichstag that Trotha probably received a verbal order, *Stenographische Berichte über die Verhandlungen des Reichstags*, XI Legislaturperiode, II Session 1905/06, vol. 218, 131st Sitzung, December 1, 1906, 4060.

18 Trotha to Leutwein, Windhuk, (copy) November 5, 1904, BA-Berlin, R 1001, Nr. 2089, pp. 101–3.

19 Isabel V. Hull, "Military Culture and 'Final Solutions' in Wilhelminian Germany," ch. 1, unpublished manuscript.

national security issue. The deaths of 158 white settlers (98 percent of them male) at the revolt's start impressed even colonial skeptics in the Reichstag with the metropolitan's duty to protect German settlers. Even more threatening was the rebels' challenge to German state authority and prestige. The director of the Colonial Office, Dr. Oscar W. Stuebel, declared in the Reichstag to general approval that "Germany's honor demands the repression of the uprising by all means."[20] If the rebellion were not decisively crushed, Germany's ability to be a colonial power would seem doubtful and therefore its status as a great power after the British model would be diminished. *Weltpolitik* (world policy) and Great Power politics made a mere colonial revolt into a major national security threat.

The second stage in the consolidation of military power occurred because of strictly military judgments. A difficult military victory achieved by Governor Leutwein at Oviumbo, in which the Herero were driven permanently into a defensive position at Waterberg, but in which Leutwein momentarily retreated for strategic reasons, was judged by the General Staff to be a defeat. This misjudgment rested upon a series of basic assumptions embedded in German military culture. The first involved heightened expectations of easy victory by superior Europeans over inferior Africans (a type of generalized race thinking ubiquitous in the imperial situation and common to all colonial armies). A second assumption, however, was a peculiar German military investment in cheap, quick, symbolically decisive victories in order to circumvent the civilian oversight that came with extra Reichstag military appropriations, but especially in order to demonstrate absolute German military superiority, because the military, thanks to assiduous efforts by itself, the monarch, Conservatives, and latterly ultranationalist agitators, had become synonymous with monarchical stability, social discipline, and Germany's future as a prosperous Great Power. In short, the German military bore tremendous symbolic-political weight; its defeat, indeed even momentary strategic retreat, was unbearable and unthinkable.

Consequently, the chiefs of the General Staff and the Military Cabinet successfully convinced the kaiser to remove Leutwein for Trotha, who had earlier distinguished himself as a ruthless suppressor of native revolts in German East Africa. When Trotha arrived in SWA in June 1904, he declared martial law, and in November, when he and Leutwein clashed over *Vernichtungspolitik*, Trotha replaced Leutwein as governor. SWA remained under total military control until Trotha's own removal and return to Berlin in November 1905.

---

20 *Stenographische Berichte*, vol. 199, March 17, 1904, pp. 1896, rest of debate, 1889–1906.

Putting the military in charge was thus the result of a complex of large factors: Germany's constitutional setup (which gave the kaiser and his military advisers sweeping power), national policy (*Weltpolitik*), national identification heightened by acceptance of the doctrine of national security (even on the part of former opponents of colonialism in the Catholic Center and Left Liberal parties), and central tenets of military doctrine (which themselves were formed in interaction with important characteristics of Germany's political culture).

With Trotha's arrival in SWA there began the logical unfolding of German military standard operating procedures on both the level of doctrine and of practice (i.e., on both the conscious and on the habitual and unselfreflexive levels). The resulting pattern can be analyzed into six moments.

THE MILITARY PATTERN OF DEVELOPMENT TOWARD FINAL SOLUTIONS

Destruction (Vernichtung)

Late nineteenth-century German military doctrine held that the destruction of the enemy was the goal of warfare. When Carl von Clausewitz originally enunciated this principle, he meant "destruction of the enemy's military forces." Wilhelminians meant the same thing, but in an age when industrialism and technological growth threatened to expand military targets to include civilians and the economy, it is perhaps significant that the phrase had become reduced simply to "destruction of the enemy."[21] Nevertheless, military men believed their foe to be primarily soldiers.

By the 1890s *Vernichtung* had developed into a specific dogma that called for swift, offensive movement, if at all possible culminating in a single, concentric battle of annihilation. Whereas the "cult of the offensive" was characteristic of most European military cultures at this time, the single battle of annihilation was peculiarly German.[22] It is most evident in Schlieffen's famous plan, but it was also the basis for naval strategy. In both cases, the dogma was a response to perceived German weakness: on land, in response

---

21 (General) Julius von Hartmann, "Militärische Nothwendigkeit and Humanität. Ein kritischer Versuch," *Deutsche Rundschau* 13 (1877): 111–28, 450–71; 14 (1878): 71–91; at 13 (1877): 455, 461.

22 Stephen van Evera, "The Cult of the Offensive and the Origins of the First World War," *International Security* 9, 1 (Summer 1984): 58–107; Jack Snyder, *The Ideology of the Offensive: Military Decision Making and the Disasters of 1914* (Ithaca, 1984); Jehuda L. Wallach, *The Dogma of the Battle of Annihilation: The Theories of Clausewitz and Schlieffen and Their Impact on the German Conduct of Two World Wars* (Westport, Conn., 1986).

to "encirclement" by France and Russia; at sea, in the face of the world's greatest naval power, Britain. Extreme offense, the simultaneous concentration of all one's forces, the hope that one's technological and technical prowess might overcome numerical weakness, the daring (even foolhardy) risking of one's entire effort at a single stroke, the demand of extreme self-sacrifice from one's troops and sailors, and the discounting of logistical limits and of the enemy's possible responses – all these features of the dogma were required to transcend Germany's inferiority and to permit it to behave like a world power, a paramount power, instead of merely one of the five European "Great Powers." The dogma of the single battle of annihilation was thus the military reflection of that curious mix of ambition and desperation characteristic of Wilhelminian politics.[23]

This dogma was the default program, the "prescription for victory," in which all German officers were trained.[24] Although it was developed for European circumstances, the dogma was applied willy-nilly in the colonies, where it was almost impossible to achieve. Lack of infrastructure made the movement of supplies and the concentration of men extremely difficult; worse, huge trains prevented mobility and flexibility, precisely what guerrilla wars required.

Not surprisingly, therefore, the single battle of annihilation is just what Trotha attempted in SWA. He spent June and July inching his forces forward, until they virtually surrounded the Waterberg, the last main water source before the Omaheke desert, where an estimated 60,000 Herero, the entire people, were holed up. The terrain was so difficult that the German forces, new arrivals from the metropole, were exhausted and had used up their fodder and water, by the time the attack began. Trotha deployed his forces unevenly, blocking a breakthrough west back into the center of the colony, while leaving the eastern route into the desert more sparsely defended. One historian has concluded from this that Trotha wanted the Herero to escape into the desert where they would die.[25] This is surely wrong, for Trotha not only informed Berlin just before the battle that "I will attack the enemy simultaneously with all units, in order to destroy him," as the dogma required, but he also had built a stockade for the 8,000 prisoners (the maximum official estimate of Herero warriors) he expected to take,

---

23 Summed up in Kurt Riezler's marvelous phrase, "the necessity of the impossible": Riezler, *Die Erforderlichkeit des Unmöglichen* (Munich, 1913); Hartmut Pogge von Strandmann and Imanuel Geiss, *Die Erforderlichkeit des Unmöglichen* (Frankfurt am Main, 1965).
24 Schlieffen's phrase: Jehuda Wallach, *Das Dogma der Vernichtungsschlacht; die Lehren von Clausewitz and Schlieffen and ihre Wirkungen in zwei Weltkriegen* (Munich, 1970), 124.
25 Horst Drechsler, "The Hereros of South-West Africa," in Chalk and Jonassohn, *The History and Sociology of Genocide*, 230–48, at 241–42.

and even had ordered 1,000 chains for them.[26] Everybody expected a great German victory; civilian administrators, missionaries, and businessmen were already meeting to divide the prisoners among themselves.[27] Instead, due partly to two errors by unit commanders, the Herero suffered only light casualties and escaped into the desert.

Trotha had now (August 11, 1904) achieved a victory somewhat akin to Governor Leutwein's at Oviumbo. He had in fact defeated the Herero, whose leaders concluded they could not win, who now sent out peace feelers, and who never again posed a serious military risk or engaged in regular battle. But this was not enough to qualify as a victory according to the inflated German military standards of the day: it was not a total victory of force, where the enemy was either dead, captured, or submitted unconditionally. It had not demonstrated German military invincibility and therefore had not convincingly reestablished German authority and order.

Rejection of Negotiations

If the object of German military intervention had been to defeat the Herero, then Trotha should now have negotiated the Hereros' surrender, as Leutwein urged him to do. But negotiations were unthinkable. Trotha later (1909) explained why: if the breakthrough had not happened, then the possibility of negotiation would have existed, and a regular court would have brought the murderers and ringleaders to the gallows, the weapons and cows would have gone to the government, and the rest of the tribes would have returned to the sunshine of the all-highest (i.e., His Majesty's) mercy. As the situation was, however, there could be no question of negotiations on August 12 and 13, if one did not want to testify to one's own weakness and embarrassment. This would have been immediately clear to the enemy and would have meant a renewal of the war as soon as the band had recovered from the first shock.[28]

26 Lothar v. Trotha, "Directive for the Attack against the Herero," August 4, 1904, cited in General Staff, *Kämpfe der deutschen Truppen in Südwestafrika; Auf Grund amtlichen Materials*, 2 vols. (Berlin, 1906–7), 1:153; Paul Rohrbach, diary entry, August 10, 1904, in Rohrbach, *Aus Südwestafrikas schweren Tagen: Blätter von Arbeit and Abschied* (Berlin, 1909), 167; and August Franke's diary entry, August 5, 1904, Bundesarchiv-Koblenz, Nachlaß Franke, Nr. 3, p. 85. For further corroborating statements from contemporaries of Trotha's intentions, see Hull, "Military Culture," ch. 1.
27 Missionaries Dannert, Lang, Hanefeld, Elger, Brockmann, and Wandres to Rohrbach, August 1, 1904, Vereinigte Evangelische Mission-Wuppertal, C/o, 5; Rohrbach, *Aus Südwestafrikas schweren Tagen*, 167; District Administrator Burgsdorff to Governor, Nr. 1364, Gibeon, August 18, 1904, BA-Berlin, Kaiserliches Gouvernement Deutsche-Südwest-Afrika, Zentralbureau Windhoek (R 151 F), D.IV.L.E., vol. 1, p. 1.
28 Lothar v. Trotha, "Politik und Kriegsführung," *Berliner Neueste Nachrichten*, no. 60 (February 3, 1909): 1.

For Trotha and for many of his fellow officers, anything short of a total victory of military force signaled weakness and constituted a security threat. Again we see the exceedingly high standards of victory the German military had manufactured for itself. Trotha's intransigence, however, was encouraged by several other factors. Both the kaiser and widespread public opinion, as it was reflected in the bourgeois press at the beginning of the revolt, rejected negotiations until the rebels had been "punished."[29] This trope of colonial warfare, eternalized in the phrase "punitive expedition," construed rebels as outlaws and understood punishment in the old-fashioned way as physical suffering, rather than as the incarceration appropriate to (one's own) citizens. Infliction of physical suffering was what one did to one's inferiors, and the military instrument was singularly apt, because it was one of the last spheres in Europe where flogging and degradation were still permitted (though increasingly controversial).

Thus a number of separate cultural strands combined to make negotiation a questionable activity, especially because it carried the suggestion of some equality between the negotiating parties and recognized the political existence of native groups, which German colonialism, at any rate, was out to erase.[30]

Pursuit

If the single battle of annihilation was the first default program of German military doctrine, pursuit was the second. As all commanders knew, if the first did not succeed, then one pursued the enemy ruthlessly, until one had either forced "him" (as the books always put it) to fight, thus recreating the conditions of the battle of annihilation, or one had ground his forces into oblivion. Not surprisingly, Trotha immediately ordered such a pursuit and, until the end of September, chased the chimera of a final, decisive "battle" with the Herero.[31]

In fact, the parlous state of the German troops and their mounts dictated that most soldiers remain behind at water holes, forming a kind of cordon

---

29 The liberal *Berliner Zeitung*, for example, called for "punishment [*Bestrafung*]," but when alleged atrocities by German troops had been reported, hastened to add that while "a certain strictness is necessary [in handling the revolt], this must not degenerate into brutality." v. Gadke, "Die militärische Lage in Deutsche-Südwestafrika," *Berliner Zeitung*, no. 63 (February 4, 1904): 1, and titleless article of no. 141 (March 17, 1904): 1. Kaiser Wilhelm had forbidden negotiations without his prior consent.

30 Colonial Director Stuebel had set the goal of suppressing the revolt as: "to end the quasi-independence the natives still enjoyed in politics." *Stenographische Berichte*, vol. 197, January 19, 1904, p. 364.

31 Trotha, tel., August 12, 1904, Hamakari, reprinted in Conrad Rust, *Krieg und Frieden im Hererolande; Aufzeichnungen aus dem Kriegsjahre 1904* (Leipzig, 1905), 376–77; Trotha to Bülow, tel. Okahandja, September 25, 1904, BA-Berlin, R 1001, Nr. 2116, p. 25.

against Herero reinfiltration into the colony, while the two most resilient units pursued the fleeing Herero deeper into the waterless desert. Only the very first skirmish resembled a battle. The rest, although listed as "battles" or "fights" in the official history and reported in the telegrams to Berlin as such, were rather encounters in which German troops fired on fleeing Africans. A very small number of Herero, perhaps 2,000, made it through the desert and into Bechuanaland on the other side. Some managed to slip through the cordon back into SWA, where they tried to eke out an existence in the veld. But the great majority of the Herero people died of thirst during the "pursuit," as the surviving daughter of the chief Zacharia graphically described to Trotha at the beginning of October, as the skeletons beside the dried river beds attested, and as the official history concluded, describing the "shocking fate that the mass of the people had met in the desert": "The punishment had come to an end. The Hereros had ceased to be an independent tribe."[32]

The mass death of the Herero people was therefore the result of a standard military procedure, described (and perhaps experienced) by most of the German participants in terms of conventional combat. Mass death came from the practices of waging war, not (yet) from an announced policy aiming at genocide. Perhaps this is one reason why the participants, even Trotha himself, doubted the magnitude of the dying, even as they had daily proof of it. For many, it seemed the Herero had simply vanished, and German officers were seized by the fear that they would return to continue the war. This fear contributed to Trotha's decision to make total clearance of all Herero the actual goal of military policy. Before turning to this decision, however, we ought to examine more closely the practices that made mass killing easy or likely by encouraging or habituating soldiers to indiscriminate slaughter. For a great many Herero died not of thirst but by shooting. These practices can be located in institutional habits, deep-seated expectations on the part of troops, and specific orders concerning war conduct.

Practices Conducive to Mass Killing

Many scholars have noted that suffering, frustrated troops are more apt to engage in retaliatory atrocities than are others.[33] Part of the reason Germany's

---

32 Trotha to Bülow, tel., Northeast Epata, October 1, 1904, BA-Berlin, R 1001, Nr. 2116, pp. 35–36; General Staff, *Die Kämpfe der deutschen Truppen*, 1:214.
33 E.g., Robert Jay Lifton, "Existential Evil," in Levitt and Comstock, *Sanctions for Evil*, 37–48, at 38; C. Fourniau, "Colonial Wars before 1914: The Case of France in Indochina," in J. A. de Moor and H. L. Wesseling (eds.), *Imperialism and War: Essays on Colonial Wars in Asia and Africa* (Leiden, 1989), 72–86, at 83.

troops in SWA suffered and became frustrated were circumstantial, but there were also structural-institutional reasons that made unnecessary suffering likely. One of the main reasons lay in inadequate provisions; field troops received two-thirds rations and suffered widespread malnutrition and scurvy. Medical treatment was wholly inadequate, as the official postwar report acknowledged.[34]

Provisioning (logistics) was the stepchild of the German military. No ambitious officer chose to specialize in it, for German military culture stressed fighting above any and all ancillary activities. Even the Schlieffen Plan's minute choreography left critical aspects of provisioning to the chance of finding food and fodder near the battlefield.[35] Aside from the premium placed on combat, the traditional Prussian aversion to those arch-civilian concerns of economics and management played a strong role in relegating logistics to the sidelines, despite the advancing "professionalization" of the officer corps before 1914.[36] The gap between Germany's military and colonial ambitions and its actual power to achieve them (evident in the vagueness of *Weltpolitik* and in all of Germany's war planning) would only have encouraged the general staff to overlook realistic planning, which threatened to expose the unreality of world power dreams.

In the colonies, haphazard provisioning was fatal. Colonies typically lacked a developed infrastructure and reserves of familiar food and potable water, yet the dogma of the battle of annihilation required masses of men and matériel, the very stuff of European superiority. In short, logistical failure was virtually preprogrammed in the colonies.

This problem might have been made good by training small units of colonial-warfare specialists, who, acclimated to overseas conditions, could have moved lightly and swiftly as the native peoples did. But Germany was both a new imperial power and one dedicated to the principle of colonialism on the cheap. The suggestion to form an expensive colonial force was repeatedly rejected. The alternative, relying on native allies, worked in German East Africa, but not in SWA, where the influx of metropolitan soldiers brought with it the conviction that natives were unreliable and

---

34 "Überblick über die bei der Entsendung von Verstärkungen für die Schutztruppe in Südwest-Afrika gesammelten Erfahrungen und die in der Kommissionsberatungen zu erörternden Fragen, 1. Nov. 1908," Bundesarchiv-Militärarchiv Freiburg, RW 51, vol. 18, 74–81; Kommando der Schutztruppe, *Sanitäts-Bericht*, vol. 1.

35 Martin van Crefeld, *Supplying War: Logistics from Wallerstein to Patton* (Cambridge, 1977), ch. 4.

36 Michael Geyer, "The Past as Future: The German Officer Corps as Profession," in Geoffrey Cocks and Konrad H. Jarausch (eds.), *German Professions, 1800–1950* (Oxford, 1990), 183–212; Morris Janowitz, "Professionalization of Military Elites," in *On Social Organization and Social Control* (Chicago, 1991), 99–112.

that Germans, superior by nature and by training, should do everything themselves.

The failures of logistics and preparation, which were deeply institutionalized defects, were all the more shocking because of the high expectations they disappointed. The general racial hybris of Europeans in Africa (and elsewhere) combined with the specific military hybris of the Prusso-German military meant that troops expected a quick and easy victory. One gets the sense that they were almost offended when that sort of victory eluded them. And frustrated hybris is surely one of the most dangerous kinds.

But German troops had another expectation that at first glance seems incompatible with colonial combat. They had been trained for a conventional European war. They were therefore prepared to fight uniformed soldiers, clearly demarcated from civilians, equipped with standard weapons, and behaving according to European standards (e.g., attacking openly and surrendering when wounded). Instead, they met a foe who might be wearing a German *Schutztruppe* uniform (stolen from a fallen soldier) or be indistinguishable except by sex from noncombatants; who fought stealthily; who often had to resort to homemade weapons, which left dirty, ragged wounds; who fought until death; who killed wounded German troops; and who engaged in ritual mutilation of dead soldiers.

The expectations of conventional European warfare were, of course, the foundation of international law, which had been codified in a series of recent conferences. That is, conventional behavior and those who abided by it were covered by legal protection; those who contravened it were subject to reprisals. At the international conferences the German delegates, military and civilian, had distinguished themselves by their uniquely high standards of "order" and conventionality.[37] German representatives were far less willing to grant regular combatant status (and thus the protection of the Geneva Convention on prisoners of war) to irregular troops than were the representatives of France or of smaller European nations. And the Germans were far readier to sanction severe reprisals against civilians for a whole range of activities that other nations found acceptable, even patriotic. In short, Germany held a much more rigid conception of order and propriety than did other European powers, and it was quick to label the unconventional a violation of international law even in Europe, much less in a colony where most legal experts opined that international law did not apply in the first place. Wherever international law did not apply, whether because of unconventional practices or colonial exclusion, German military officials and

37 Geoffrey Best, *Humanity in Warfare* (New York, 1980), 172–79, 180–89, 195–99, 226.

many jurists argued that there were no limits at all to sheer force. This condition of the unlimited is what Arendt, following Joseph Conrad, identified as the most lethal and dangerous aspect of imperialism. The spiral toward the unlimited was built into the dynamic among Germany's institutionalized practices, which came close to guaranteeing failure; the high expectations its troops (and officers, kaiser, and public opinion) held of the military; and the unrealistic expectations they all held of their foes' conduct.

If these general circumstances increased the chances that troops would use too much force, there is evidence that in SWA soldiers received official encouragement to kill beyond the normal bounds of war. This matter is controversial, and I have elsewhere discussed at length the complicated evidentiary basis for the judgments I offer here.[38] Circumstantial evidence, but no surviving written order or direct acknowledgment by participants, suggests that when Trotha assumed command in SWA in June 1904, he ordered troops to kill all adult Herero males when they commenced the battle of Waterberg. Such an order would have meant killing the male wounded and prisoners but sparing women and children. Whether the motivation for such an order was the assumption that in colonial warfare all adult (non-aged) males were ipso facto warriors, or that this policy would wipe out all further military and especially political resistance, or that revenge was necessary for the Herero's affront to German authority or to the conventions of European warfare, is impossible to reconstruct with certainty. Even if in fact such an order was never given, which is possible, Trotha nevertheless made public statements upon his arrival that "no war may be conducted humanely against nonhumans," indicating his approval of "sharp" or extreme conduct on the part of his soldiers.[39] Even in the absence of a direct order, then, German soldiers will have received the impression before the battle that excessive force was expected or certainly condoned by their commanding officer.

The massacre that accompanied the battle of Waterberg was therefore prepared for, if perhaps not entirely intentionally. The indiscriminate killing of the wounded, male prisoners, women, and children has also been a subject of controversy, but eyewitness reports on both sides confirm that it occurred at Waterberg and probably continued during the "pursuit."[40] Trotha himself tried to regain control of his troops and to focus their excessive force on adult males only in an order issued immediately after Waterberg that forbade

---

38 See Hull, "Military Culture," ch. 2.
39 Otto Dannhauer (military correspondent), "Brief aus Deutsch Südwestafrika," *Berliner Lokalanzeiger*, no. 358 (August 2, 1904): 1–2, written June 26, 1904.
40 Hull, "Military Culture," ch. 2.

the killing of women and children but expressly permitted the shooting of "all armed men who were captured."[41] Trotha thus attempted to widen the bounds of the usually permissible while imposing limits against wholesale slaughter. This balancing act was probably not successful. Evidence of various kinds indicates that troops released from one major taboo found it hard to observe others. The "pursuit" consisted largely of German soldiers shooting after fleeing natives, regardless of their status or condition. I do not wish to suggest that all units shot everyone they encountered; prisoners (male and female) were taken and some, especially adult women, survived the war. The very lopsided postwar demographic ratio of women to men shows that there was a tendency to spare women, as Trotha had ordered. Nevertheless, the general pattern of conduct during the "pursuit" was widespread shooting, including of male prisoners. Relentless shooting, in addition to the direct deaths it caused, pushed dehydrated, desperate people back into the desert, where they died en masse. There was little to choose between these two techniques of mass death. The "pursuit," which was both a standard operating procedure and a set of practices developing from the circumstances of SWA, effectively destroyed most of the Herero people by the end of September 1904.

Trotha's October Proclamation: Annihilation as Explicit Goal

On October 2, 1904, Lieutenant General von Trotha issued a proclamation to the Herero people. After alluding to their crimes, he concluded, "The Herero people must leave this land. If it does not, I will force it to do so by using the great gun [artillery]. Within the German border every male Herero, armed or unarmed, with or without cattle, will be shot to death. I will no longer receive women or children, but will drive them back to their people or have them shot at. These are my words to the Herero people."[42] To the German troops he explained what he meant: "I assume absolutely that this proclamation will result in taking no more male prisoners, but will not degenerate into atrocities against women and children. The latter will

---

41 Schlieffen to Bülow, Nr. 13297, Berlin, December 16, 1904, BA-Berlin, R 1001, Nr. 2089, p. 107; letter of Trotha's chief of staff, Lt. Col. v. Beaulieu, cited in General Staff, *Kämpfe der deutschen Truppen*, 1:186.

42 Trotha, Proclamation of October 2, 1904, copy, J. Nr. 3737, BA-Berlin, R 1001, Nr. 2089, p. 7; another copy in "Kaiserliche Schutztruppen und sonstige deutsche Landstreitkräfte in Übersee" [RW 51], "Militärgeschichtliches Forschungsamt: Dokumentenzentrale, Schutztruppe Südwestafrika" (vol. 2), BA-MA Freiburg. Reprinted in Rust, *Krieg and Frieden im Hererolande*, 385; *Vorwärts*, Nr. 294 (December 16, 1905); Drechsler, *"Let Us Die,"* 243; Jon M. Bridgman, *The Revolt of the Herero* (Berkeley, 1981), 128.

run away if one shoots at them a couple of times. The troops will remain conscious of the good reputation of the German soldier."

The most puzzling aspect of Trotha's proclamation has always been its timing, coming after the actions and effects it "orders" to occur. The proclamation does three things: it makes explicit and uniform ("no more male prisoners") the already customary tactics employed by German troops, it attempts once again to regain control over troops tempted to commit "atrocities," and it takes the effect of the "pursuit" (the complete disappearance of the Herero) as the explicit aim of military policy. Not surprisingly, surviving documents indicate no change in military conduct in the weeks after October 2.[43]

Trotha's proclamation was his response to the failure of the second default program of German military doctrine: pursuit. Troops had not managed to get the Herero to turn and fight, so that they could be clearly defeated in battle. Exhausted, suffering German troops had arrived at the last known water hole in the colony on September 29, but apart from finding a few Herero, the expected final battle did not occur. As after Waterberg, Trotha now sought to escape pressure to negotiate, the obvious alternative under the circumstances. Knowing his proclamation would be "controversial," as he put it, he explained his decision in a letter to Chief of the General Staff von Schlieffen: "For me, it is merely a question of how to end the war with the Herero. My opinion is completely opposite to that of the governor and some 'old Africans.' They have wanted to negotiate for a long time and describe the Herero nation as a necessary labor force for the future use of the colony. I am of an entirely different opinion. I believe that the nation must be destroyed as such, or since this was not possible using tactical blows, it must be expelled from the land operatively and by means of detailed actions."[44] Farther along in the letter when he explains what will happen to the women and children turned back by German troops, Trotha admits he is talking about mass death, not simply disappearance: "I think it better that the nation perish rather than infect our troops and affect our water and food."[45] Nonetheless, engaging in the doublethink typical of the campaign,

---

43 Hull, "Military Culture," ch. 2.
44 Trotha to Schlieffen, Okatarobaka, October 4, 1904, BA–Berlin, R 1001, Nr. 2089, pp. 5–6. Partly reprinted in Drechsler, "*Let Us Die*," 160–61; Horst Drechsler, *Aufstände in Südwestafrika; Der Kampf der Herero and Nama 1904 bis 1907 gegen die deutsche Kolonialherrschaft* (Berlin, 1984), 86–87; Drechsler, "Hereros," 244–45; Bley, *South-West Africa*, 164.
45 While the food and water situation was indeed serious, this excuse did not motivate the proclamation; it merely justified causing the certain death of harmless civilians. On justification, as opposed to motivation: Martha Finnemore, "Constructing Norms of Humanitarian Intervention," in Peter J. Katzenstein (ed.), *The Culture of National Security: Norms and Identity in World Politics* (New York, 1996), 153–85, at 159; Smelser, "Some Determinants," 23; Edward M. Opton Jr., "It Never

Trotha sums up the possibilities: "They must either die in the desert or try to cross the Bechuanaland border." We know that only about 2,000 Herero made it across the border.

In the course of the campaign, Trotha had thus moved from one sort of finality to a far larger one. The single battle of annihilation was supposed to "destroy" the nation politically, by killing and capturing all its warriors and forcing the people to submit to unconditional surrender. When that failed (even though by different standards of reckoning, Waterberg was a success), the pursuit was supposed to achieve the same thing. The "pursuit," too, was a success insofar as it destroyed the bulk of the people, but it did not unequivocally demonstrate the superiority of German arms in a conventional battle nor consequently restore unquestioned state authority or order, because surviving Herero might stealthily return to the colony. Therefore, the next logical unconditional solution was not surrender but disappearance. This could take two forms: expulsion or death. Trotha did not care which. The point was to achieve a total and final solution: the permanent end of any possibility of further revolt, disorder, or challenge to German authority.

Death by Imprisonment

In order to give the solution by force the greatest chance against the solution by negotiation, Trotha sent notice of his proclamation by slow boat, rather than telegraph, and to the Chief of Staff only, rather than to the chancellor as well. When it finally arrived in Berlin in late November 1904, both Schlieffen and Bulow rejected Trotha's policy, but, significantly, not for the same reasons. Bülow cited humanitarian, economic, political, and diplomatic grounds, whereas Schlieffen merely judged *Vernichtungspolitik* impractical.[46] The military's bias toward accepting final solutions was once again demonstrated.

Nevertheless, together and with the (reluctant) help of the chief of the military cabinet, Bülow and Schlieffen convinced the kaiser to reverse Trotha's policy and offer surrendering, unarmed, and innocent Herero amnesty. In the meanwhile, the Nama clans had revolted, and ultimately civilians and warriors of both peoples were collected into internment camps, which defined the last phase of the war.

Happened and Besides They Deserved It," in Levitt and Comstock, *Sanctions for Evil*, 49–70, at 63–67.

46 Bley, *Southwest-Africa*, 166–67; Schlieffen to Col. Dept., Nr. 12383, Berlin, November 23, 1904, BA-Berlin, R 1001, Nr. 2089, pp. 3–4.

Internment camps, especially when they held primarily or exclusively civilians, were called at the time "concentration camps." They were an imperial-military invention, designed to frustrate guerrilla warfare by removing the civilian population and thus exposing the remaining fighters to easier and clearer conditions of battle. Both Britain and Spain had established concentration camps before the Germans faced the situation in 1905. Death rates in such camps were high because European militaries were not trained in, nor did they attach much priority to, mastering the complex logistics required to maintain women, children, the aged, and the ill in hastily built but quasi-permanent locations.[47]

The German military attached an even lower priority to the needs of the imprisoned for a number of reasons. The higher symbolic value attached to the military in Germany produced, if possible, an exaggerated valuation of actual fighting and therefore relegated all other, noncombat considerations to a zone of indifference, if not disdain. The institutionalized disregard for adequate provisioning and the concomitant expectation of German suffering set a low standard of care, which, of course, was lower still for the "enemy": one could not treat Herero prisoners, whether warrior or civilian, better than one did one's own troops.[48] Racism worsened treatment still more, not simply in the idiosyncratic cases of outright viciousness, but more important in structural ways, whether because of the widespread belief that "natives" required less food than Europeans, or because one simply did not bother to note what food Africans could digest. Administrative incompetence was widespread and made worse by the constant rotation of officers, a practice applied equally, and with equally bad effects, in the field.

The most lethal factor, however, was the desire to punish. This motive is clear in the official rations for African prisoners, set under and approved by Trotha. Prisoners received one-fifth the meat of the most punitive ration Great Britain permitted for civilians interned during the Boer War, and only one-sixth of the two-thirds ration German field troops received, which already caused widespread malnutrition and scurvy among the *Schutztruppe*. No provisions were taken against scurvy and no regular milk portion was provided, although milk in some form was the Herero's principal diet. The

---

47 See the scathing criticisms leveled by the Fawcett Commission at the British military administration in South Africa during the Boer War: Great Britain, Parliament, *Report on the Concentration Camps in South Africa by the Committee of Ladies Appointed by the Secretary of State for War Containing Reports on the Camps in Natal, the Orange River Colony and the Transvaal*, Cd. 893 (London, 1902), 6–7, 16–18.

48 This was a standard principle: General Staff, *Kriegsgebrauch im Landkriege* (Berlin, 1902), 15; C. Lueder, "Das Landkriegsrecht im Besonderen," in Franz v. Holtzendorff (ed.), *Handbuch des Völkerrechts*, vol. 4 (Hamburg, 1889), 371–545, at 435; Christian Meurer, *Die Haager Friedenskonferenz*, vol. 2: *Das Kriegsrecht der Haager Konferenz* (Munich, 1907), 122.

official ration, like the official blanket and clothing allotment, was designed at the very least to produce extreme suffering. Disease and death were clearly acceptable by-products of this treatment. When Trotha left SWA, his successors raised and varied the official ration, but not by much. Their internal correspondence indicates that they did not want African prisoners to die, but the factors listed here set hard limits to the amount of alleviation they dared to introduce.[49]

The picture in SWA is similar to that which Christian Streit found in his study of the mass death of Soviet prisoners of war in Nazi hands: a lethal mixture of conviction and administrative indifference.[50] The German military acknowledged a death rate of about 45 percent in its camps in SWA, as compared with about 25 percent in the British camps in South Africa.[51]

The deaths in the British camps were ultimately stopped by the political intervention of civilians and outraged public opinion, which led to the removal of camp administration from military hands. In Germany, such an outcome was not possible, primarily because of several features of Germany's political culture. First, both the constitution and accepted practice relegated almost complete control over warfare to the military experts. Colonial critics of Trotha's policies of destruction were simply ignored, because they had no business interfering in military matters. High-level bureaucrats in SWA, chiefly Deputy Governor Hans von Tecklenburg and his successor, Deputy Governor Oskar Hintrager, accepted the military's nearly paranoid arguments about security and their punitive schema and consequently agreed with the lethal policies the military pursued; indeed, they even added to these by demanding the deportation to other colonies of surviving rebels and their families.[52] Death rates among the deportees were even higher than in the camps in SWA. Meanwhile, the informed criticism of missionaries concerning both the conduct of the war and the camp conditions was disqualified from the beginning by Chancellor Bülow's misguided but well-established tactic of vilifying the missionaries as disloyal in time of war. Socialist critics had always been labeled as traitors, so their observations in the Reichstag had considerably less effect than similar critical speeches in Parliament, where loyal opposition was a time-honored tradition. Therefore,

---

49 For data and discussion of provisioning the camps, see Hull, "Military Culture," chs. 3 and 7.
50 Christian Streit, *Keine Kameraden: Die Wehrmacht and die sowjetischen Kriegsgefangenen, 1941–1945* (Bonn, 1991).
51 And about 58 percent among Soviet prisoners of war in Germany: S. Burridge Spies, *Methods of Barbarism? Roberts and Kitchener and Civilians in the Boer Republics, January 1900–May 1902* (Cape Town, 1977), 268; Thomas Pakenham, *The Boer War* (London, 1979), 518; Omer Bartov, *The Eastern Front, 1941–1945: German Troops and the Barbarisation of Warfare* (New York, 1986), 153.
52 Hull, "Military Culture," ch. 3.

divide-and-rule, the presumption of military infallibility, and the civilian government's indiscriminate use of nationalist mobilization techniques all combined to insulate military policy from outside intervention.

Therefore, the camps were only stopped from inside, through the intervention of a freethinking commander, Colonel Ludwig von Estorff, whose horror at the conditions he found was only surpassed by his feelings of personal honor: "For such hangmen's services I can neither detail my officers, nor can I accept responsibility...," he notified Berlin.[53] He closed the worst camp on his own orders and cleared it in under two days.

CONCLUSION

What I have argued here is that the tendency for the German military to gravitate toward "final solutions" was built into its military culture, understood as part of its habitual practices and the (largely unexamined) basic assumptions embedded in its doctrines and administration.[54] The imperial situation did nothing to contravene these habits or inclinations and everything to encourage them. The already pernicious assumptions borne of race thinking developed into genuine racism under the shock of imperial practices.[55] Many factors encouraged among European troops the spiral of revenge: the difficulty and frustrations of colonial warfare made worse by structural deficits in planning and administration, the enemy's strange or "exotic" fighting practices, and the difficulties distinguishing civilians from warriors in guerrilla wars. Worse, fewer brakes inhibiting unnecessary violence existed in the colonies: international law was widely thought inapplicable there; in settler colonies the non–economically-minded (which is to say almost all military men) could regard indigenous peoples as expendable; and the restraints provided by identification or by the intervention of observers sympathetic to the "natives" were largely missing.[56]

It is important to underscore that, while German military culture differed somewhat from the cultures of other late nineteenth- and early twentieth-century European armies (chiefly by being even more purely military),

---

53 Estorff to Command of Schutztruppe in Berlin, tel. Nr. 461, Windhuk, April 10, 1907, BA–Berlin, R 1001, Nr. 2140, p. 88.
54 The conception of military culture I use comes from a combination of cultural anthropology and organizational culture theory. Space limitations prevent a discussion of this concept here. Hull, "Military Culture," ch. 5.
55 Here, too, I agree with Arendt, who distinguishes between race thinking and racism and argues that the latter is a result of imperialism more than it is a cause. Arendt, *Origins of Totalitarianism*, 183–86.
56 Militaries are thoroughly uneconomical institutions: Hans Paul Bahrdt, *Die Gesellschaft und ihre Soldaten; zur Soziologie des Militärs* (Munich, 1987).

European military culture in this period was surprisingly uniform and carried within it the tendency to favor final solutions when lesser operations failed, as they often did in the colonies. Thus Germany's military culture and its imperial dilemmas were more alike than different from those of its neighbors. Where Germany differed was in its political culture and institutions. Bismarck's effort to safeguard the conservative Prussian monarchy had yielded a national constitution that intentionally truncated parliamentary power and shielded the military from civilian oversight. The structure of government and the resulting political culture were not surprisingly less capable than, for example, comparative British or French institutions in subsequently curbing the military's tendencies to go to extremes. German political institutions were thus less able to cut short the development toward "final solutions," a failure that therefore encouraged the institutionalization of this tendency inside the military to a degree found nowhere else. This is the much-remarked upon "autism" of the German military, which meant that the propensity to grasp at "final solutions" became reinforced and ever more ingrained, and therefore more likely to be resorted to in future.[57]

What is the relation between the pattern revealed in SWA and the "final solution" the Nazis directed against the Jews and ultimately against other racialized targets? In the little space remaining, I cannot do more than sketch how the argument runs. The National Socialist "final solution" may be analyzed into two parts: the practice of extermination and the ideological identification of the populations to be exterminated. I have argued that the practice of extermination was already operating in the military, not motivated by ideology but developing instead from habits and basic assumptions embedded in military culture. SWA was part of a pattern of developmental possibilities; it was not an aberration. A very similar outcome occurred from 1905 to 1907 in German East Africa, where the tactic of slash and burn used to crush all political resistance during the Maji-Maji revolt ended in the deaths of an estimated 200,000 to 300,000 Africans, completely and permanently depopulating several large districts in the colony.[58] The two events are not identical, but they do clearly illustrate the military's institutional preference for solving political problems with total, unlimited force.

57 On autism in organizations: Dieter Senghaas, *Rüstung- und Militarismus* (Frankfurt am Main, 1972), 46–54; Bernd Schulte, "Die Armee des Kaiserreichs im Spannungsfeld zwischen struktureller Begrenzung und Kriegsrealität, 1871–1914," in *Europäische Krise and Erster Weltkrieg; Beiträge zur Militärpolitik des Kaiserreichs, 1871–1914* (Frankfurt, 1983), 72.
58 The best account is by Detlev Bald, "Afrikanischer Kampf gegen koloniale Herrschaft; Der Maji-Maji-Aufstand in Ostafrika," *Militärgeschichtliche Mitteilungen* 19 (1976): 23–50. On casualties: John Iliffe, *A Modern History of Tanganyika* (Cambridge, 1979), 165, 199–200.

This developmental logic, which during the Wilhelminian period was not enunciated as an a priori goal, continued to operate during World War I. The European theater of war, with its limits imposed by identification with the enemy, international law, and other factors, acted as a brake to the full-blown development of the logic, but its operations are nonetheless visible – for example, in the mobilization for "total war" after October 1916 and the mass deportation (and typically bad treatment) of civilians from Belgium and Poland. But outside of Europe, in Anatolia, which all Europeans still regarded as the "Orient" and hence not subject to limiting European rules, the logic of "final solutions" manifested itself in the extermination of the Armenians by Germany's ally, Turkey. This is a complex story; it was due neither solely to the war nor certainly to Germany, which played a very subsidiary role. Nonetheless, certain high-ranking German military advisers to the Turks recommended the deportations and accepted the resulting genocide, and military-security arguments identical to those in SWA and German East Africa were decisive in preventing the many official (mostly but not entirely civilian) German voices raised against it, from moving the German government to effective resistance against its ally's policy.[59]

In my view, World War I took the Wilhelminians' unintentional ground-work and transformed it into a political juggernaut. The war created the believable, existential, national emergency that brought together the practical military propensity for the total solution of force and the paranoid world view of the Pan-Germans, who had already identified the Jews (and secondarily the Slavs) as the racial enemy. Especially after 1916, the twinning of total military practice with an ideology of racism directed against Europeans seemed to many people a reasonable response to the crises caused by global war. For the first time, practice and ideology came together. The movement most perfectly expressing this conjuncture came to be National Socialism. Of course, many events, which were not inevitable, had to occur for this practical world view to take control of the government and to create the next war in order to realize its own "final solution." But the institutional and organization-cultural foundations unintentionally laid in the Wilhelminian military were necessary before National Socialism could exist in the first place.

---

59 See Vakahn N. Dadrian, *German Responsibility in the Armenian Genocide: A Review of the Historical Evidence of German Complicity* (Watertown, Mass., 1996).

8

"Encirclement and Annihilation"

The Indonesian Occupation of East Timor

JOHN G. TAYLOR

When the Indonesian armed forces launched their invasion of East Timor on December 7, 1975, there was a general consensus that it would be a short-lived affair. The poorly armed East Timorese independence movement would be no match for the Indonesian army. Internationally, Indonesia was seen by the governments of the industrialized states as a crucial regional ally, whereas East Timor had no significant international support and could easily be isolated economically, politically, and diplomatically by Indonesia.

Yet, almost a quarter of a century later, this "short-lived" intervention had not achieved its aim of integrating East Timor into the Indonesian Republic. Indeed, quite the opposite had occurred, with East Timor's people voting overwhelmingly for independence on August 30, 1999. In pursuit of Indonesia's aim, however, at least 200,000 East Timorese, almost one-third of its preinvasion population, had died.[1] Thousands had been detained without trial, tortured, and disappeared. Most had been forcibly resettled, and lived under constant military surveillance. For most of this twenty-four-year

---

1 In an official Portuguese census of 1970, East Timor's population was recorded as 609,477. In a 1974 census undertaken by the Dili diocese, the population was recorded as 688,771. In 1980, an Indonesian census gave a total population of 555,000. A church survey in 1982, published by the United Nations, gave an estimate of 425,000. If we assume a growth rate of 1.7 percent (which was fairly typical of the 1960s), the population in 1980 should have been 713,000. On the basis of the Indonesian census, there is a decline of 158,000. Using such approaches it was estimated by many authors that at least 200,000, or almost one-third of the preinvasion population had died since the invasion. Research in the late 1980s by Amnesty International supported this 200,000 estimate. In the 1990s, most governments agreed with this figure. For example, in 1993, the Foreign Affairs Committee of the Australian Parliament reported that "at least 200,000" had been killed since the 1975 invasion (*Australia's Relations with Indonesia*, Joint Committee on Foreign Affairs, Defence and Trade [Canberra, 1993], 6). As early as April 1977, former Indonesian foreign minister Adam Malik stated that 50,000 to 80,000 had already been killed (*Sydney Morning Herald*, April 5, 1977). His comments followed the visit of a group of Indonesian church workers to East Timor at the end of 1976. Questioning local priests, they gave a figure of 100,000 already killed by that date.

period the leading governments of the industrialized world either ignored these events, or acquiesced in them, accepting Indonesian interpretations they knew were false.

In this chapter I focus on two issues. First, why were such extraordinary levels of brutality directed against the East Timorese population by its occupying army and administration? What led to the genocide? Second, why did the governments of the world acquiesce in these events? Were there important strategic reasons for their tacit support for the Indonesian occupation, or did East Timor suffer because it had little international value? Having excused and supported Indonesia for so many years, why did governments then change their policies so dramatically in 1999, recognizing East Timor's right to self-determination? Following the Indonesian military and government's rejection of East Timor's vote for independence, why did these governments prepare to put pressure on the Indonesian regime to accept this outcome? Why was something so fundamental for a territory's future denied for so many years and then so dramatically accepted by the international community? If – as stated by governments in the late 1990s – East Timor had the right to self-determination, why did these governments actively support policies that effectively denied this for so many years? How can we explain this volte-face?

In order to examine these issues, we need to look briefly at East Timor's contemporary history, focusing in particular on the impact of the Indonesian invasion and occupation of the territory.

COLONIAL RIVALRY AND RESISTANCE

The Portuguese established the first colonial administration on Timor in 1702. They disputed and fought with the Dutch for control over the island for the next three centuries. The two halves of the territory finally were separated in an agreement signed by the two powers in 1913, the Dutch taking the west and the Portuguese the east. Revolts against colonial rule were frequent, with the last of these continuing from the late 1880s to 1912. During the Second World War East Timor was occupied by the Japanese. By the time the Japanese surrendered in 1945, approximately 60,000 East Timorese, or 13 percent of the population had died.

In 1949 West Timor became part of the Indonesian Republic. Portugal retained East Timor, where an embryonic nationalist opposition emerged in the 1960s, based upon young people educated in Catholic schools and the Dili Seminary, or trained in a radicalizing Portuguese army.

On April 25, 1974, the Portuguese Armed Forces Movement overthrew the Caetano regime, and began a process of decolonization in Portugal's African and Asian colonies. In East Timor, political groups were organized.

THE ROAD TO INDEPENDENCE

Several parties emerged, with the Timorese Democratic Union (UDT) and Fretilin (the Front for an Independent East Timor) gaining support from most of the population. Due largely to its literacy, health, and cooperative programs, Fretilin became the most popular party by the end of 1974. In January 1975, UDT and Fretilin entered into a coalition, with both parties agreeing with the Portuguese to move toward independence, which was to be achieved within three years.

In the early months of 1975 the Indonesian army began making border incursions into East Timor. Citing the growing radicalization of younger Fretilin members, the Indonesian military persuaded a group of UDT leaders to break the coalition with Fretilin by organizing a coup in Dili, East Timor's capital, in August. During this coup attempt, the Portuguese governor and administration left Dili for neighboring Atauro Island – never to return. As East Timor's colonial troops deserted en masse to Fretilin, the coup failed. UDT members fled to the border with West Timor, where – as a condition for entering Indonesia – they had to sign documents calling for East Timor's integration. These were used in December to justify Indonesian intervention.

By September 1975 Fretilin controlled most of the territory. Its leaders called repeatedly for the Portuguese to return and complete decolonization. Lisbon refused, and the Fretilin administration became a de facto government. Observers visiting the country during this period agreed that Fretilin had popular support and administered the territory efficiently.

From mid-September onward, Indonesian military pressure intensified. On November 28, in the hope of taking their case to the United Nations, Fretilin declared East Timor independent. On December 7 Indonesia launched a full-scale invasion.

INVASION

An air and sea attack on Dili, using bombers, paratroops, and marines, was followed by brutal treatment of the population, particularly the small Chinese community, who, paradoxically, had been some of the strongest supporters of Indonesian intervention. After three months of conflict, how-ever, the Indonesian army controlled only some of the coastal and border regions, and areas accessible from the country's tiny network of roads, ema-nating from Dili. Many of the East Timorese population left the towns and larger villages to regroup in less accessible, mountainous areas, organized by Fretilin. For the next two years, Fretilin troops, supported by the popula-tion, defended these areas, and engaged Indonesian troops as they tried to advance into the interior. Frustrated by their inability to make significant military headway, Indonesian troops began to terrorize the population living outside Fretilin areas. Villages were destroyed, crops burned, and villagers killed by marauding troops. At this stage, killings were largely spontaneous, unorganized, and reactive.

MILITARY CAMPAIGNS

A qualitatively new phase of the Indonesian campaign began in September 1977. Troop numbers were increased and draconian controls imposed upon the population, isolating the territory from the outside world. In an op-eration named "Encirclement and Annihilation," mountain areas in which people had taken refuge were bombed. Saturation bombing was accompa-nied by defoliation of ground cover.[2] Famine aggravated the effects of injury, disease, and displacement. During 1978 and 1979 tens of thousands of East Timorese came down from the mountains, forced to occupy lower-lying regions. Indonesian troops awaited them. During these years, many mas-sacres were reported from East Timor and, later, by refugees in Portugal and

---

2 A letter sent to a relative in a refugee camp in Lisbon, written on September 17, 1980, described the effects of the bombing on the village of Zumalai, on the south coast: "Many elements of the population were killed under inhuman conditions of bombardment and starvation.... The waters of the river were filled with blood and bodies. Husbands, fathers, brothers all in the same agony survived who knows how." A letter written during the bombardment, published in July 1978, read "Pray for us, that God will quickly send away this scourge of war. The mountains shake with bombardment, the earth talks with the blood of the people who die miserably" ("A Letter from Timor Marked X," *Northern Territory News* [Darwin], July 28, 1978). A refugee testifying *in camera* to an Australian Senate Enquiry on East Timor in 1982–83 gave the following account of the bombing campaign in 1978: "It was necessary to leave the village in the daytime to hide from the aeroplanes that would drop bombs. The land would shake because of the bombs dropping, there was noise all the time and the bombs would make huge holes in the ground. So in the mornings at first light we would move back into the hills leaving behind the old and sick who could run no more.... The bombs dropped every day. Aeroplanes flew from 8 am till midday and then again in the afternoon. Firstly an aeroplane came to check if there was any smoke, a couple of minutes later the bomber would come and drop bombs, wiping out whole villages." Cited in *Hadomi* (Victoria), August 1982. (This special issue of *Hadomi* reproduced anonymously extracts from the evidence of East Timorese who testified to the inquiry. These testimonies were not included in the Senate Inquiry Verbatim Records because they had been submitted *in camera*.)

Australia. One of the fullest documented was on November 23, 1978, when 500 people who had gathered at the foot of the Vadaboro Mountain, in the Matebian range, in the belief that they were surrendering, were executed by Indonesian soldiers.[3]

Following the bombing campaigns, the population was placed in newly created resettlement camps. Inhabitants were prevented from traveling beyond the confines of these camps, and were restricted in their cultivation and harvesting. Dependent on the military for basic medical supplies and foodstuffs, they received little, and starvation became widespread. A letter received from Dili in June 1979 told of people "slowly dying in the villages of Remexio, Turiscai, Maubara, Betano and Suro."[4] When a priest visited Maubisse, a village some forty kilometers south of Dili, in March 1979, he discovered that, according to records contained in a prayer book, 5,021 of a 1976 population of 9,607 had been killed.[5] USAID estimated that 300,000 were living in camps by the end of 1979. Describing conditions in one of the camps, in Remexio, fourteen kilometers south of Dili, a journalist whose visit had been organized by the Indonesian government, wrote: "In Remexio, as in other villages, the people are stunned, sullen and dispirited. Emaciated as a result of deprivation and hardship, they are struggling to make sense of the nightmarish interlude in which as much as half the population was uprooted."[6]

Despite the onslaught of the late 1970s Fretilin groups continued to engage the Indonesian military, supported by the local population. Infuriated, the army devised a new strategy, using noncombatants to flush out resistance groups. Operasi Keamanan (literally, Final Cleansing) took men aged from eight to fifty from the resettlement camps and villages, organized them into small groups, and forced them to walk, in fencelike formation, in front of units searching for Fretilin members. The latter were forced either to surrender or engage in combat by firing on their own people. Fretilin groups were flushed out of their areas and chased until they were surrounded, captured, and killed. One of the largest of these corrals was in the Aitana region, in the central-eastern part of the country. An eyewitness who had been a

---

3 This is just one of many examples recounted by refugees in conversation. Another case, for example, was in Taipo, where approximately 300 were killed – elderly people were reportedly burned alive in their houses, women and men were tied together and shot, and children executed in front of their parents.

4 This quotation, taken from an anonymous eyewitness account, is contained in *Dossier on East Timor*, published by the Australian Council for Overseas Aid (ACFOA) (Canberra, 1982).

5 This quotation is taken from an interview of an anonymous East Timorese by Father Pat Walsh, in Jakarta, on March 15, 1982, and is reproduced in *Dossier on East Timor*, 4.

6 David Jenkins, "Timor's Arithmetic of Despair," *Far Eastern Economic Review*, no. 29 (September 1978).

member of the human chain reported: "It was a ghastly sight. There were a great many bodies, men, women, little children strewn everywhere, unburied along the river banks, on the mountain slopes. I would estimate about ten thousand people had been killed in the operation."[7] Operasi Keamanan lasted almost a year, after which it was used regularly as a tactic against the rapidly dwindling numbers of Fretilin units. In 1983–84, for example, Operasi Persatuan (Operation Unity) combined "clean sweeps" of areas with intensive bombing.

HUMAN RIGHTS ABUSES

Abuses have been widespread since 1975, with disappearances, imprisonment without trial, torture, and the use of arbitrary force the norm. For example, in August 1983 Indonesia troops stationed in Viqueque entered a village called Malim Luro, where, "After plundering the population of all their belongings, they firmly tied up men, women and children, numbering more than sixty people. They made them lie on the ground and then drove a bulldozer over them, and then used it to place a few centimetres of earth on top of the totally crushed corpses."[8]

Many of those detained in the late 1970s and early 1980s, particularly after the "annihilation" and "fence of legs" operations, subsequently disappeared without trace. Indonesian soldiers had their own way of describing disappearances. They called them *mandi laut* (gone for a swim); people who had been captured were been taken by helicopter and dumped into the sea with weights on their feet. During the early years of the occupation, the military focused on Fretilin supporters and the more educated strata – seminarians, nurses, public officials, and teachers. Particular sites were designated as killing grounds, to which people were taken in groups and murdered. In many cases, large numbers were involved. Many refugees have described an incident in

---

7 This quotation is taken from an interview by Carmel Budiardjo with Christiano Costa, who escaped from East Timor in October 1987. Further information on Operasi Keamanan is provided, by an East Timorese who kept a diary during the campaign. He wrote: "One group of the forced patrol has spent the last five days without food and was only able to satisfy its hunger with leaves from the forest and water. Because they were incapable of going any longer, they organised some of their number to meet the commander and demand food. And what did the commander reply? He shot his pistol into the air several times. And so without food and without any source of protection from the cold of the mountains, or sleeping facilities, many people have been suffering from fatal diarrhoea. Those who are sick are left behind. They are left to die by the side of the path. And those who struggle on with great difficulty finally return to Dili or other districts, walking all the way. The population thus return to their villages in a severely debilitated state."

8 From a refugee report contained in a collection published by the Australian Coalition for East Timor, May 1986.

Lacluta, southeast of Dili, in September 1981, in which at least 400 people were killed, mostly women and children.[9]

The military's objective of terrorizing the population into submission was also evidenced in their widespread use of imprisonment and torture.[10] An East Timorese who worked for the Indonesian Red Cross described how "The Indonesians have prisons everywhere. For example where there is a chief of police, he has a prison; where the red berets are, there is a prison; the military police have their prison; an infantry unit will have its prison, artillery units theirs; the District Command one, the Secret Police have theirs."[11] Imprisonment was both arbitrary and indeterminate. Cases were recorded of imprisonment for refusing to give food to Indonesian troops, or for straying too far from a resettlement village. Once in prison there was no means of knowing if the sentence was for a week or for months. No trials were held until 1984, and then only for those detained in Dili. At any time during detention, prisoners could be taken out by troops and killed. Many interrogation sessions in the main towns were held in family houses, whose previous occupants had either fled or been imprisoned. Prisoners provided labor for military projects, and many were forced into personal service for military officers.

The use of torture was officially sanctioned throughout East Timor. Army guidelines published in July 1982 outlined a set of "established procedures": preliminary interrogation; classification of suspects; main interrogation; decision to murder, imprison, or release.[12] The severity of torture appears to have increased as the occupation developed. Beginning with beatings,

---

9 An eyewitness to this massacre related how "Indonesian soldiers took hold of the legs of small children and threw them around in the air a number of times and smashed their heads against a rock. There was a woman who asked that one of the children be given to her after the mother had been killed. At that time, a soldier permitted the woman to take this small child, but a few minutes later he grabbed the child and killed him. The poor woman who asked for the child was not too wise, because she too was then killed. There was one other person who asked for one of the children to be given to her.... The army person did not want to hear her pleadings and in front of everyone destroyed the body of this small child, who had done no wrong. And then this soldier opened his mouth, showing his teeth with a smile, and said ... "When you clean your field, don't you kill all the snakes, the large and small alike?" This quotation is taken from a refugee account published in the *Age* (Melbourne), May 14, 1982.

10 This "terrorising" is illustrated in a letter written from Bobanara in February 1984: "In the month of February alone, more than fifty people were killed. But it is being said that the military plan to kill altogether 167 people in this zone. Only then, they say, will they be able to re-establish peace" (from a letter received in Lisbon in April 1984, in a collection held by Jill Jolliffe).

11 This quotation is taken from the submission of Jose Guterres, an East Timorese who worked for the Indonesian Red Cross, to the UN Human Rights Commission, Geneva, 1987. Kopassus is the special forces unit of the Indonesian army, responsible for intelligence operations in East Timor.

12 See "Established Procedure for Interrogation of Prisoners," *Instruction Manual No. PROTAP/01-B/V11/1982*, published by the Military Region Command XV1 Udayana, Military Resort Command 164 Wira Dharma Dili, July 9, 1982.

burning with cigarettes, and sexual abuse, the army and police progressed rapidly to electric-shock treatment, systematic cutting of the skin and limbs, and, in the mid-1980s, crucifixion with nails.[13]

MILITARY CONTROL

Indonesian policies for controlling the indigenous population were pervasive and systematic. In January 1980 a refugee described Dili as "A world of terror: Police units forcibly break up small groups on the streets, residents are afraid of being arrested for listening to foreign broadcasts, mail is censored, the use of Portuguese is forbidden, and the Timorese live in fear of being denounced as sympathisers for the guerrillas."[14]

Military surveillance operated at all levels of society. Starting at the village level, there were local garrison troops. These were assisted by civil defense units (Rakyat Terlatih, or "Trained People's Force"), most of whom were locally recruited. Alongside them were "village guidance" officials (*badan pembinaan desa*, or *Babinsa*), released from their duties in the Indonesian army to direct local village officials on security issues. In every village, there were also intelligence agents, employed to listen in on conversations and report back to the military, and agents provocateurs (known locally as *bufos*, or "clowns"). A further security level was formed by the mobile police brigade (*Brimob*), a paramilitary force used to deal with local protest. Above *Brimob* were regular Indonesian infantry battalions, rotated every 8 to 12 months. An additional level was formed from the special force *Kopassus* units, responsible for intelligence operations, torture, and interrogation. A final level was formed of armed groups introduced by *Kopassus* in the early 1990s, known as *ninja*. These comprised groups clad in black, masked, and armed with knives, attacking people on the street at night, and organizing the burning of houses and the killing of livestock. Amnesty International in particular reported many cases of abductions by *ninja* gangs in the 1990s. Most of their targets were pro-independence activists and their relatives. From the late 1980s *Kopassus* commanders also recruited what they termed groups of *keman* (thugs). Based in local command posts, they subdued and controlled the surrounding population through terror tactics. In the 1999 pre- and postreferendum period these groups formed the core of many pro-Indonesian paramilitary units.

---

13 Descriptions of crucifixion have been provided by several refugees. This comes from a testimony given to my research student, Rui Gomes, when interviewing an East Timorese refugee in Lisbon, in preparation for a BBC television program.

14 From an interview with an East Timorese resident in Dili, in *Dossier on East Timor*, 226–29.

Many of the violent acts committed by individuals and groups within this system were often spontaneous and unpredictable, features that particularly terrified the local population. For example, in 1988 an East Timorese refugee testifying to the UN Sub-Commission on the Prevention of Discrimination, stated, "When I was 16, I was living in Baucau. I saw a Missionary Sister helping two men from Quelicai who were injured when some soldiers suspected them of being guerrillas. They were stoned to death in front of me and the nuns, by Indonesian soldiers from battalions 315 and 731."[15]

FORCED RESETTLEMENT AND MIGRATION

From 1980 onward, most East Timorese were placed in resettlement camps, in sites created away from their original homes and villages. People were rehoused in zones far from areas of resistance, and any potential reemergence of resistance based on traditional units such as the clan, hamlet, or village was undermined by a deliberate separation of groups from each of these units in the villages of a particular region.

Located close to newly constructed roads or at intersections, the camps comprised groups of huts and houses constructed of grass or palm leaves, with the outer areas occupied by the military, local militia, and camp administrators, living in houses with galvanized iron roofs. During the 1980s, in many areas the grass huts were replaced with simple prefabricated houses, and settlements were developed in lowland areas which traditionally had been avoided by East Timorese, because they were prone to malaria, had poor water supplies, and a much hotter climate than the mountain villages.

Each resettlement village was subjected to a rigorous system of internal control. Alongside the military, there were members of the Indonesian police force and teams of *babinsas* reorienting the village's inhabitants. "The babinsas are everywhere," wrote Monsignor Marthino da Costa Lopes, bishop of East Timor from 1978 to 1983. "They are the ones who have to know about everything happening in the villages and settlements. Everything has to be reported to them."[16]

All movement in and out of resettlement villages was controlled, with people only being allowed to travel if they had been granted a *surat jalan* (travel pass). During the night, groups from the village's population were forced to guard perimeter fences. Because no cultivation took place within the village's confines, inhabitants were allowed to tend gardens at 500 to

---

15 East Timorese refugee, Anselmo Aparicio, in a testimony given to the UN Sub-Commission on Prevention of Discrimination and Protection of Minorities, Geneva, 1988.
16 "Interview with Former Bishop of East Timor," *Tapol Bulletin* (London), no. 59 (1983): 6.

1500 meters distance. Either as a form of sanction or as a security measure, this garden tending was often curtailed by the military, despite the need for food in the villages. Consequently, food shortages were a frequent occurrence. In 1988 a Catholic Relief Services worker wrote: "The main problem in the resettlement camps is shortage of food. The areas where people are allowed to go are very restricted, whether they are growing or harvesting crops. Most families can only have 100–200 square metres of ground, which is insufficient to feed a family throughout the year. They have to fall back on collecting wild fruit, roots and leaves; these are also in insufficient quantities because the army forbids them to go far from the camp."[17]

Restricting the use of labor for domestic cultivation, the army began to direct it into forced work on road building, house construction, logging, and the cultivation of crops for export – sugar, coffee, and even rice. The aim of this exercise was clear; having forcibly altered traditional patterns of settlement, the army used the resettled and controlled population as a basis for a massive economic and social transformation, using labor to cultivate cash crops for export on small farms and plantations, created outside resettlement village boundaries. Many military commanders, members, and associates of President Suharto's family benefited monetarily from the setting up of monopolies, based on crops cultivated on these farms, exporting cloves, coffee, sandalwood, cumin, and copra, as well as traditional goods such as textiles.[18] By 1984 there were 400 resettlement villages in East Timor, and by 1990 almost all East Timorese were living in them.

In addition to providing labor for cash crop cultivation, population movement had a further objective, particularly from the late 1980s onward. In the more fertile regions of East Timor, such as Ermera, Maliana, and Bobonaro, families were transmigrated from Indonesia itself. Transmigrants were given land formerly occupied by East Timorese farmers, who received no compensation. In this way, growth centers were created, attracting spontaneous migrants from West Timor and other islands of Eastern Indonesia. This led to increasing land alienation and economic disadvantage for the indigenous population.

---

17 Interview with Mr. Antonio Tavares, a former Catholic Relief Services employee in East Timor, conducted by Mr. Jean-Pierre Catry, Lisbon, 1988.
18 In chapter 9 of my book, *East Timor: the Price of Freedom* (London, 1999), I examine one of these monopolies, PT Denok, set up by Generals Benny Murdani, Dading Kalbuadi, and Sahala Rajagukguk. It began by controlling coffee cultivation and trading, but rapidly moved into other areas after 1980, to the extent that it almost controlled the entire export economy in 1982. Its lucrative position then began to be challenged by other Indonesian companies in the military hierarchy, notably in the late 1980s by companies owned and controlled by President Suharto and his associates. This process has been examined in some detail by the Indonesian writer and academic, George Aditjondro.

THE SECOND GENERATION

Living under such controlled conditions, and threatened constantly with sanction through a widespread system of intimidation, human rights abuses, and extermination, it is remarkable that the armed opposition to the occupation survived twenty-four years. This was due not only to support from the population but also to the remarkable emergence of opposition in the towns and villages of what Indonesia called the "second generation" – youth and students raised during the occupation, whom the Indonesian government had hoped to "resocialize" as integrated Indonesian citizens. These groups supported the armed resistance but also in the 1990s were responsible for bringing East Timor to international attention, particularly in the aftermath of the infamous Santa Cruz massacre.[19] Much to the annoyance of the military, they organized protests during the visits of international dignitaries to East Timor and combined this with brief occupations of and demonstrations outside embassies in Jakarta.

This is an important issue, because the emergence of this opposition was accompanied, first, by a strengthening of the Indonesian military system of control and sanctions and, second, by signs of an awareness within some foreign governments that the East Timor situation was beginning to have an adverse impact on international perceptions of Indonesia.

Turning to the first issue, given the evidence of widespread brutality, human rights abuses, and genocidal actions committed by the Indonesian armed forces, how are we to explain the policies, campaigns, and actions of the Indonesian armed forces in East Timor?

THE AIMS OF THE MILITARY PROJECT

From its inception, the campaign to incorporate East Timor was first and foremost a military project. As early as mid-1974 Bakin, the Indonesian Military Intelligence Coordinating Agency, had finalized the details of its annexation plans. A key player in this was Major General Ali Murtopo, head of Opsus, the special operations unit that had masterminded President Suharto's most successful operations to overthrow former President Sukarno

---

19 On November 12, 1991, the Indonesian army killed 273 unarmed demonstrators in and around the Santa Cruz cemetery, Dili. The demonstration followed a memorial mass for a student, Sebastiao Gomes, killed by Indonesian troops. Events such as this had occurred in East Timor previously, but this time there was a crucial difference – the actions of the military at the cemetery were filmed by a photojournalist who managed to hide his videotapes and smuggle them out of the country. The events of the massacre were shown on television screens worldwide. Public reaction influenced several governments to condemn the violence, and international agencies began to reappraise their policies on East Timor.

and to incorporate West Papua (West Irian). He was assisted by Admiral Sudomo, head of Kopkamtib, the army's security command and interrogation unit; Major General Benny Murdani, head of the intelligence operations of Kopkamtib; and by Suharto's close friend, Lieutenant General Yoga Sugama, a leading figure in both Opsus and Kopkamtib. In essence, these men formed Suharto's inner circle in the mid-1970s. They were the godfathers of Indonesia's Orde Baru (New Order), with Suharto at their head. From the early border incursions to the UDT coup attempt, from the post–August 1975 destabilization to the full-scale invasion, they directed events locally, devised the final strategies for the invasion and early occupation years, and organized international support for Indonesian actions. Despite the Cold War rhetoric through which they justified the invasion, as they saw it the aim of the occupation was essentially threefold.

First, from both the military and state viewpoint, they were concerned that an independent East Timor might set a "negative example" for other areas of Indonesia. The military has always lived with a stereotypical nightmare, in which one area of Indonesia after another decides that it can run its own affairs and begins to argue for greater autonomy, even independence. If East Timor could achieve this, why not resource-rich West Papua, Aceh, Riau, or even Kalimantan? Under Suharto, the Javanese elite thrived economically from its exploitation of Indonesia's "outer provinces," maintained by a highly centralized, Java-based rule. Second, both the Indonesian government and military were impressed by the potential of the newly discovered offshore oil deposits in the Timor Sea, south of the island, which it considered could boost Indonesia's growth, with its focus on oil exports in the early OPEC years.[20] Third, the armed forces wished to display their military skills and prowess, demonstrating that Indonesia could be the reliable regional military ally that the United States was seeking in Asia, after its loss of Vietnam. Indonesia had established its military intelligence credentials during 1965–66 and in the 1969 West Irian campaign, but it needed

20 In the 1960s and early 1970s, exploration indicated that there were rich oil and natural gas deposits in the Timor Sea, south of East Timor. They were particularly rich in an area known as the "Timor Gap," a zone lying between the Indonesian and Australian maritime borders, formally controlled by the colonial power, Portugal. Early estimates suggested that the Timor Gap potentially could be one of the largest deposits in the world, generating as much as 5 billion barrels of oil and 50,000 billion cubic feet of natural gas. These estimates have since been scaled down drastically, as it became recognized that drilling would be much more difficult than initially envisaged, and the deposits were smaller than originally thought. This did not prevent both the Australian and Indonesian governments trying every means possible to enter the Timor Gap and start drilling. A treaty between them was signed on December 11, 1989, with drilling beginning in the Gap on February 9, 1991. Eleven exploration contracts were subsequently awarded, but following the referendum decision of August 30, 1999, new negotiations have been opened between East Timorese representatives and the Australian government, because the Indonesian-Australian agreement of 1988 can no longer hold.

to display its more professional side by conducting a successful military campaign.

Politically, the armed forces were supported by nationalist politicians who wished to "complete" Indonesia's maritime borders by removing what they saw as a colonial anachronism, and by small, isolated radical Islamic groups, directing their propaganda against East Timorese Catholicism. Military strategists also cited a "strategic" issue, which they considered had some importance to the United States – that nuclear submarines passing through the archipelago had to go through the Ombai-Wetar straits, to the north of East Timor. The only alternative was to go south of Australia, adding days to the journey from the Indian to Pacific Oceans. Such, however, were not the main factors. The key issues were the unity of the state, oil potential, and the need for a successful military campaign.

MILITARY CONTROL

In the early years of the occupation of East Timor, the armed forces were embarrassed and frustrated by their inability to defeat and eradicate Fretilin. The bombing campaigns of 1978–79 were an attempt to deal with this situation. The operations conducted in their aftermath became increasingly brutal, as Indonesian troops vented their frustrations on a local population that supported and protected Fretilin units. To these abuses was added the sanction of direct control of the population through location in resettlement camps, marking the beginning of the military campaign to systematically restructure the territory economically and to "resocialize" its people, inculcating the norms and traditions of Indonesian rule. In this, the military received what it considered tacit support from the governments of industrialized countries. In international forums, Indonesian versions of events were accepted, and East Timorese versions either ignored or derided. The key factor in the switch from reliance on ground to antipersonnel aerial attack in 1979 was strengthened by the use of newly acquired ground-attack aircraft from the United States and, later, from other governments, such as the United Kingdom.

The terrorizing of the local population was intensified during the "fence of legs" operations in the early 1980s, particularly through the use of indiscriminate violence, combined with systematic slaughter on the completion of fence operations. As these military campaigns continued, commanders of their operations gained rapid promotion through army ranks as a result of their "battle experience" – which in the 1980s could only be gained in East Timor. Consequently, many of the leading Indonesian generals of the late

1980s and 1990s had served in East Timor and portrayed it internally as a successful military occupation, essential for the security of the nation. This portrayal required both a rigorous control of information on East Timor to the outside world and a determination to quash any criticism, in whatever form, of the occupation in both East Timor and Indonesia.

During the 1980s the military also began to use the territory as a counterinsurgency training ground for its troops, in which new techniques were tried against the indigenous population. More important for Indonesia, this area was also used as a testing ground for intelligence operations that were later used against opponents of President Suharto. In East Timor, these operations were directed primarily against the younger leaders of the "second generation" and their families, particularly in the aftermath of the Santa Cruz massacre in November 1991. Key in this process was the passing of control over military operations to Kopassus, led by commanders who had been influential in directing the Santa Cruz massacre. Kopassus Group 3, responsible for East Timor operations, was commanded by Major General Prabowo, Suharto's son-in-law, who began to establish the territory as his personal fiefdom in the 1990s. Group 3 became the nerve center of the campaign to crush the independence movement, deploying the irregular troops of the *ninja* gangs. These operated in the towns and larger villages, and were supported by locally recruited paramilitary units. The activities of these groups led to a marked increase in human rights abuses, notably in the years 1991–95. As the deputy rector of East Timor University described it in November 1995, "the situation in the territory is one of terror, tension and persecution" – typified in the title of the armed forces' 1997 campaign: Operasi Tuntas (Operation Eradicate).

THE CAUSES OF BRUTALITY

Throughout the years of the Indonesian occupation, brutal tactics were used to terrorize and intimidate the population – systematic killings of groups and targeted individuals, arbitrary use of detention and beatings, and widespread torture. These occurred in a society restructured economically and socially to facilitate the use of such tactics. As the occupation developed, these were used more thoroughly and extensively. As we have seen the reasons for this seem to have been:

- An increasing frustration by troops at their inability to defeat armed opposition.
- A widespread resentment within the armed forces at the emergence of opposition within the second generation, and their determination to remove it by directed terror and intimidation.

- A perception within the armed forces that outside governments – notably those of the industrialized states – were supporting Indonesian actions, underwritten by a continuing supply of weaponry.
- The use of East Timor as a training ground for troops and for the testing of military intelligence tactics.
- The importance of the East Timor campaign for military promotion, and the subsequent refusal by leading generals to admit that the campaign had been mistaken in conception and implementation.
- The prevalence within the military of the stereotyped view that any concessions on East Timor's status would have a "knock-on" effect for regions in Indonesia, such as West Papua and Aceh.
- The economic value of the territory, not only for its oil resources but also for the wealth gained from monopolies controlled by leading generals, members and associates of the family of President Suharto.
- The fact that, on a more general level, the East Timor occupation was a project devised and implemented at the highest levels of the armed forces and political system, so closely interrelated with the culture and workings of this system that, particularly in the 1990s, it became clear that fundamental changes in this system were a precondition of any change in East Timor.

COMPLICITY AND ACQUIESCENCE

Focusing on this issue of political change within Indonesia leads into our second question, Why did the governments of the industrialized states acquiesce in the occupation and its subsequent events? Raising this question also entails asking why this policy, maintained well after the fall of President Suharto, was abruptly changed in 1999, with an internationally agreed acceptance of the right to self-determination, a right that most governments had denied overtly or covertly through their acceptance of the Indonesian position.

In the period leading up to the December 1975 invasion, and in the early years of the occupation of East Timor, governments such as those of the United States went to extraordinary lengths to justify Indonesian intervention. As early as September 1974, Australian Prime Minister Whitlam urged Suharto to integrate East Timor, stating that "An independent East Timor would be an unviable state, and a potential threat to the area."[21] In August 1975 the American ambassador to Indonesia, John Newsom, hoped that if Indonesia invaded East Timor it would do so "effectively, quickly,

---

21 Quotation taken from *The Future of Portuguese Timor*, Document BP/60, Department of Foreign Affairs, Canberra, September 11, 1974.

and not use our equipment."[22] Speaking at a seminar on December 12, 1975, he stated that the U.S. government had "not disapproved" of the invasion.[23] Following the killing of Australian, British, and New Zealand journalists by Indonesian troops in Balibo, in East Timor's western region, on October 16, details of the event, monitored by the Australian government's Defence Signals Division, were passed to the U.K. and U.S. governments. The contrast between these governments' knowledge of these events and their public utterances was neatly expressed in a cable sent to Canberra by the Australian ambassador shortly after the murders: "Although we know it is not true, the formal position of the Indonesian Government is still that there is no military intervention in East Timor." Questioning this "formal position," he concluded, "would invite a hurt and angry reaction."[24] Concerned that the removal of Whitlam might lead to a policy change, the U.S. government stressed to the new prime minister, Malcolm Fraser, that American "security interests" required the continuing "good will" of the Suharto government.[25] Fraser then traveled to Jakarta for a four-day visit, where, in a press conference, he concluded that "Australia now acknowledged the merger, for purely humanitarian reasons."[26]

Despite their detailed knowledge of events in East Timor, governments continued to give support, and – for some – public justification to Indonesian actions throughout the occupation. In January 1978, as the Indonesian air force was refining its saturation bombing of East Timor's interior, Australia gave de facto recognition of integration, shortly followed by de jure. The switch in tactics from ground to air attack in the 1978–79 "encirclement and annihilation" campaigns was given added impetus by the supply of ground attack aircraft from the United States and the United Kingdom. These supplies continued throughout the 1980s, supplemented with helicopters, missiles, frigates, battlefield communication systems, armored vehicles, and military training.

INTERNATIONAL PORTRAYAL

Throughout the late 1970s and 1980s, governments continually minimized the adverse publicity generated by the horrifying accounts of annexation

---

22 Newsom's comment is cited in a cable from Richard Woolcott, Australian Ambassador to Indonesia, to Prime Minster Gough Whitlam's secretary, Alan Renouf, August 17. Cited in G. J. Munster and R. Walsh (eds.), *Documents on Australian Defence and Foreign Policy, 1968–75* (Sydney, 1980), 200.
23 Newsom later became under secretary for political affairs in the Carter administration.
24 This cable is cited in Bruce Juddery, *Canberra Times*, May 31, 1976.
25 Quotation taken from Michael Richardson, "Don't Anger Jakarta," *Age*, August 3, 1976.
26 "Canberra Accepts Jakarta Takeover of East Timor," *Times*, October 12, 1976.

provided from refugees and internally, notably from church sources. At the height of the "encirclement and annihilation" campaign, in 1978, the U.S. State Department claimed that "most of the human losses in East Timor appeared to have occurred prior to Indonesia's intervention."[27] Earlier, in March 1977, the State Department's country officer for Indonesia had testified that the people of East Timor were "happy" with integration: "They have decided that their best interest lies, at this time, in incorporation with Indonesia."[28] At the height of the 1978 bombing campaign in which the only recourse for East Timorese was to hide in mountain caves, the U.K.'s minister for overseas development wrote: "I had a talk with the Foreign Minister of Indonesia two weeks ago. Amongst other points which arose was one which startled me. He said that GNP per head was only sixty dollars, and that the living conditions (in East Timor) were appalling: he said that many people still actually live in cave dwellings."[29]

Similar statements were made by governments in relation to many events in the 1980s; elections in which no East Timorese parties could field candidates were offered as acts of self-determination, starvation was portrayed as a result of seasonal food shortages, and so on. The statements of some ministers were openly, and outrageously, dismissive. In an interview on arms supplies, Alan Clarke, minister for defence in the Thatcher government, interviewed in 1993, was asked the following question: "In East Timor, the Indonesian regime ... by all credible accounts has killed one third of the population. Isn't that ever a consideration for the British Government?" He replied "It's not something that often enters my thinking, I must admit."[30]

In a similar vein, in February 1991, the year of the Santa Cruz massacre, Australian Foreign Minister Gareth Evans, stated, "The truth of the matter is that the human rights situation in East Timor has, in our judgement, conspicuously improved, particularly under the present military arrangements." Nine months later, he described the massacre as "an aberration, not an act of state policy."

Through their support for Indonesia, governments including those of the United States, Australia, and the United Kingdom created an international climate in which Indonesian actions could be condoned. Other governments fell into line, either aggressively supporting Indonesian annexation,

27 United States State Department, *Human Rights Report on Indonesia* (Washington, D.C., 1978).

28 *Human Rights in East Timor and the Question of the Use of US Equipment by the Indonesian Armed Forces*, Hearing before the subcommittees on International Organizations and Asian and Pacific Affairs of the Committee on International Relations of the House of Representatives, March 23, 1977.

29 Quotation taken from a letter from Judith Hart, minister for overseas development, to Geoffrey Edge, MP, December 27, 1978. A copy of the letter is in the possession of John Taylor.

30 John Pilger, *Distant Voices* (New York, 1994), 309.

in the case of Japan, or quietly abstaining, in the case of most European governments. International forums became arenas in which, as a result of interventions by such governments, the central issues of illegal occupation, human rights abuses, and self-determination were never seriously discussed. During the UN Fourth Committee debate on East Timor in 1982, for example, the Vanuatu representative was quietly informed by the Australian delegate that his government might curtail its aid to Vanuatu unless its prime minister took a less supportive stance on self-determination for East Timor.[31]

Whether it was a question of strategic interests, arms supplies, or access to potential oil wealth, the world's leading governments acquiesced in, condoned, and at times supported Indonesia's occupation. This was crucial to the military, both for the maintenance of this occupation and for its portrayal of East Timor in Indonesia.

REFERENDUM

The events of 1999, and particularly those in the days and weeks prior to and after the referendum on autonomy within Indonesia, on August 30, are by now well known. In a sudden policy change, on January 27, the Indonesian government stated that if the people of East Timor wished to leave the Indonesian Republic, then Indonesia was prepared to "let East Timor go." This was followed by an agreement signed on March 11 by Indonesia and Portugal (still formally the colonial power), under UN auspices, for a "direct ballot" to be held, to decide whether the East Timorese people wanted autonomy within the Indonesian Republic or independence. A further agreement, signed on May 5, established a UN Assistance Mission (UNAMET) to oversee the ballot, with the Indonesian armed forces responsible for security in East Timor in the period up to and including the referendum.

Following the January statement, sections of the Indonesian armed forces, notably the Koppassus batallion, began a campaign in East Timor, with the aim of intimidating the population into voting for autonomy. They used targeted killings, disappearances, attacks on villages, and forced movement of the population into western, border areas. Several examples can be cited from the many occurrences.[32] On March 8 villagers in Sare, near Haitola,

31 This incident, which occurred during the 1982 debate on East Timor in the UN Fourth Committee, was related to me by two sources, both of whom attended, and both of whom reported it independently of the other.
32 Most of these accounts come from local church sources, from members of nongovernmental organizations, local administrators, UN workers, and visiting journalists.

Ermera district, reported that 1,600 refugees had fled into the mountains after attacks by pro-autonomy paramilitary groups on the town of Guiso, near Maubara. On April 6 a large pro-autonomy paramilitary force launched an assault on Liquica Church, where 2,000 people had been sheltered since April 4. During this attack, 57 people were killed and 35 wounded. Following a rally outside the Indonesian governor's house in Dili, paramilitary groups toured Dili, attacking houses of known independence supporters. During the day, 17 people were killed by paramilitaries. On July 12 UNAMET estimated that 60,000 people had already been displaced from their homes as a result of pro-autonomy paramilitary action. The Catholic Church estimated on August 6 that, in the preceding six months, militia attacks had claimed 3,000 to 5,000 lives, and that 80,000 had already been displaced.

Despite these terror tactics, by the beginning of August, it became apparent to both Indonesian and local paramilitary commanders that the majority would vote for independence. Addressing a pro-integration rally in Dili on August 26, the leader of a paramilitary group Aitarak (Thorn), Eurico Guterres, stated that East Timor "will become a sea of fire" if there is a vote in favor of independence. On August 30, in a 98 percent turnout, 78 percent of the population voted for independence, 21 percent for autonomy. Indonesian troops and local paramilitaries then unleashed a campaign of total destruction – killings, selective destruction of property, and looting of anything movable across the border into East Timor. An estimated 300,000 people fled to the mountains, and 150,000 were taken into camps in West Timor. Militia leader Herminio da Silva Costa vowed, "We will burn East Timor and start all over again." Following the evacuation of the UN mission, the orgy of destruction was halted only by the entry of an Australian-led peace-keeping force.

VOLTE-FACE

In the events of 1999, there is a total volte-face on East Timor policy, both within Indonesia and internationally. The Indonesian government accepts that there should be a referendum on East Timor's future. In reaching this position, the Indonesian president says that he has been influenced by a letter from the prime minister of Australia, stating that East Timor has the right to self-determination. The United States government becomes a strong supporter both of the referendum and the UN role in supervising it. Its representatives warn the Indonesian president that if the referendum is not held properly and on time, it will adversely affect U.S.-Indonesian relations. The governments of the European Union agree. How are we to explain this?

Undoubtedly, popular opinion, notably in Australia, played a part. The award of the Nobel Peace Prize to Bishop Belo and East Timor's leading external representative, José Ramos-Horta, together with the ensuing press coverage of events in East Timor, marked a high point in the lobbying campaign by civil-society organizations to bring East Timor to international attention. From this point onward, it became a newsworthy item, with press and television increasingly reporting human rights abuses. Yet, similar events have been reported in the media, but very few have resulted in international intervention of the kind experienced in East Timor.

INDONESIA IN TRANSITION

In a book published on East Timor in 1991,[33] I concluded that there was little likelihood of any change in East Timor unless there were fundamental political changes in Indonesia. With the removal of President Suharto in May 1998, such changes appeared to be under way. Indonesian society momentarily became more open, political parties were created, elections promised, and the role of the military questioned. These political changes were accompanied by a pervasive economic crisis, which could only be dealt with by a fundamental restructuring, aided by international institutions such as the World Bank and the International Monetary Fund and by interventions from the governments of industrialized states, notably the United States.

Anxious to distance himself from the economic mismanagement and corruption of the later Suharto years, Indonesia's new president, B. J. Habibie, searched for policies that could win international support and portray him as a reformer capable of guiding Indonesia away from the corrupt authoritarianism of recent years. If these policies could be accepted without too much opposition in Indonesia, then so much the better. East Timor seemed a suitable case, particularly after the receipt of the Howard letter. "I will prove to the world that I can make a contribution to world peace as mandated by our constitution. It will roll like a snowball, and no-one can stop it," Habibie concluded in a February interview. Thus a space was opened in Indonesian politics, during a period critically assessing Suharto's authoritarian rule, in which the military was somewhat discredited and there was an enforced economic dependence on overseas governments and international

33 John G. Taylor, *Indonesia's Forgotten War: The Hidden History of East Timor* (London, 1991).

financial institutions. This enabled the East Timor issue to be reassessed – momentarily.

The governments of the United States and Australia then took this further. For the Australian government it was a popular move internally, achieved at little cost in the prereferendum period. It felt that it was assisting the move in Indonesia away from the corruption and mismanagement of the Suharto regime, which had become increasingly inefficient, economically, in relation to Australian interests. Most of what it needed in relation to oil exploration could be negotiated with a government in East Timor, particularly if the latter favored Australia as a result of its role in assisting the holding of a referendum. Finally, Indonesia no longer had the strategic importance accorded it in the 1970s and 1980s.

The declining strategic importance of Indonesia also played a part in policy changes by the U.S. government. Suharto's Indonesia had become economically counterproductive and sections of its military forces had become inefficient and corrupt. There seemed nothing to be gained by continuing to support its East Timor venture. As scenes of paramilitary brutality were increasingly displayed on television screens worldwide, the case for supporting the referendum and its outcome became increasingly positive.

The results of the policy switch were remarkable to behold. With the paramilitary campaign raging in East Timor, on September 8 Indonesian Foreign Minister Ali Alatas scoffed at the very idea of an international peace-keeping force, saying that it would have to "shoot its way into East Timor." He warned the world, "Don't pressure us, don't give us ultimatums ... because it doesn't help and it is not realistic."[34] Four days later, however, Habibie announced in a televised address that the Indonesian government had agreed to the entry of a peace-keeping force. In New York, Alatas conceded that Indonesia was accepting the entry of a peace-keeping force, with no conditions attached.

Between September 8 and 12, two other statements had been made. On September 10, the president of the World Bank, James Wolfensohn, informed Habibie: "For the international community to be able to continue its full support, it is critical that you act to restore order and that your government carry through on its public commitment to honour the referendum

---

34 John Gittings, "Humiliation as Jakarta Talks Tough," *Guardian* (London), September 7, 1999.

outcome."[35] He followed this by deciding to hold back a $600 million loan negotiated earlier in the year. The International Monetary Fund also stated that it was suspending a planned mission to Indonesia that was a prerequisite for approval of the next tranche of $450 million. At the same time, President Clinton informed a White House Conference, that, "If Indonesia does not end the violence, it must invite the international community to assist in restoring security." Most importantly, however, he continued, "It would be a pity if the Indonesian recovery were crashed by this, but one way or another it will be crashed if they don't fix it, because there will be overwhelming public sentiment to stop the international economic cooperation."[36] The U.S. ambassador to Indonesia was just as direct: "If the Indonesian military aid and abet the so-called militia – which, in my view, are really an extension of the military of Indonesia and an outrageous group of thugs doing outrageous things – if they get involved in some nasty stuff and do not co-operate, they are certainly asking for major problems."[37] On the day before Habibie agreed to the entry of the peace-keeping force, Clinton reiterated his points during an Asia Pacific Economic Cooperation (APEC) conference in New Zealand, emphasizing once more that East Timor "would have" the independence it had chosen.

For Indonesia's military, political, and economic elites, the threat of sanctions now seemed very real. The Indonesian economy required a gigantic injection of capital to restructure its banking system. Some of this had been forthcoming from the International Monetary Fund and other institutions, combined in the Consultative Group on Indonesia, but it was not yet sufficient. Any threat to its being delayed or withdrawn would be disastrous, because successful bank restructuring was a condition for the continuing investment so crucial for Indonesia's recovery. It was a combination of this threat, together with an earlier move to suspend arms sales, that seems ultimately to have persuaded Habibie, his cabinet, and most leading military figures to accept the entry of the peace-keeping force.

ACCEPTANCE AND INCOMPREHENSION

The Indonesian government and armed forces were stunned by the widespread scale and strength of the international denunciations of their

---

35 Ian Black, "West Threatens a Tougher Stance," *Guardian*, September 11, 1999.
36 David Usbourne, Andrew Marshall, and Richard Lloyd-Parry, "West Warns Indonesia: Stop the Killing or Become a Pariah," *Independent* (London), September 10, 1999.
37 Michael Richardson, "With a Warning to Jakarta, UN Force Prepares to Land in East Timor," *International Herald Tribune*, September 18–19, 1999.

actions in East Timor. Were they not simply implementing policies that had been practiced for years, condoned by the very governments that were now condemning them? Why were these governments undermining both tacit and public agreements on the status of East Timor as a part of Indonesia, which had been in place for a quarter of a century? Why were governments so intent on promoting a referendum on self-determination, which they had resolutely refused for so many years?

It seemed that a unique set of events, within Indonesia and internationally, had combined to produce a brief period in which self-determination could be exercised. In much the same way that Indonesia's elites could not comprehend this, its military forces could not understand why they had to be restrained. If the governments supporting and training them believed strongly in the need for self-determination in East Timor, they argued, why had they not stated this in 1974 or, indeed, at any time during the occupation?

THE PRICE OF FREEDOM

The increasingly brutal nature of Indonesia's military occupation, which had its own dynamic, was condoned for years by the world's leading governments. By giving tacit support to the military occupation, they bear some responsibility for the actions of the Indonesian and paramilitary commanders who so viciously tried to overturn the referendum result. In the short term, as a consequence of the changing policies of these governments, East Timor was able to exercise a choice for which its people had fought for so many years. Yet, due to the longer-term strategies of these governments, the price of its freedom has been unbearably, unnecessarily, and intolerably high.

PART III

The Era of the Two World Wars

9

Under Cover of War

The Armenian Genocide in the Context of Total War

JAY WINTER

One of the signal challenges of the historical profession is to provide a guide to understanding the century that has just passed while recognizing that the language historians use is in significant ways inadequate to the task. In that historical narrative, to talk of genocide is unavoidable, but the grammar of historical analysis withers when used to encapsulate the history of genocide.

Some have called this problem a crisis of representation, formulated famously by Adorno in the rhetorical statement that after Auschwitz there can be no poetry. His injunction was to try to write poetry nonetheless. It may be useful to recast Adorno and to say that after Auschwitz there can be no linear history, and yet we must try to write it nonetheless. My claim is that this insight was true long before Auschwitz, and that the need to recognize it and reflect on it was evident well before the Second World War.

Here is the predicament we face. Dietrich Bonhoeffer wrote that only those who cried for the Jews had the right to sing Gregorian chants. I want to suggest that only by confronting the horror of the Armenian genocide of 1915 can we begin to locate the Holocaust of the Second World War within the history of the twentieth century. For both crimes occurred under the cover of world wars; and both disclosed the devastating logic and power of a new kind of war, "total war."

This contextual issue matters crucially, in part because it is essential to a reading of the evidence, but also because it provides us with a way out of the absurdity of measuring genocidal acts against each other. Both were unique; both require comparison to enable us even to begin to talk about them. The framework for such comparison must remain tentative and incomplete, but at least part of it must be located in the phenomenon of total war.

189

TOTAL WAR AND GENOCIDE IN THE TWENTIETH CENTURY

Let me try to summarize my argument.[1] I believe that the Great War was total war, and the first of its kind. When industrialized nations, supported by imperial dominions, took the decision to go to war, and stayed at war over an extended period, they opened a Pandora's box. What they let free was a kind of war unlike any the world had ever seen before. Our search to understand the historical setting of both the Armenian genocide of 1915 and the Holocaust of the Second World War brings us abruptly to this new framework of violence and international conflict, which I call "total war."

The notion of total war is at the heart of this interpretive essay, and it is a term notoriously difficult to specify. In its constituent parts, total war resembled other conflicts. The elements out of which it was forged were not at all new. There were anticipations and precursors; the American Civil War, as we shall see, is one of them. But taken together, the concatenation of the elements of the mass mobilization of industrialized societies produced a new kind of war. Its constitutive parts had existed separately before 1914 but had never been fused together. In addition, the sum of the vectors of international violence was greater in 1914–18 than in any previous war. Here a difference in degree – an exponential increase in the lethality and reach of warfare – turned into a difference in kind.

In elaborating some of the unique features of this phenomenon, I want to reiterate that it is in their multiplicative character, their tendency to amplify each other, that the true nature of total war must be sought. In this case, the whole is much more terrible than the sum of its parts.

The best way of using the term total war is less as a description than as a metaphor, suggesting rather than defining a decided turn for the worse in international conflict. And total war is never literally total. It is "totalizing" in the sense that the longer it lasts, the more human and material resources are drawn inexorably into its vortex. The spiral toward total war, begun in 1914, was a process resembling the approach of an asymptote to a mathematical limit; as in Zeno's paradox, it never gets there. A Weberian view is that the notion of total war is an ideal type, a heuristic rather than a descriptive tool.[2] I believe the term has more bite than that, though it needs to be handled with care. When the war of 1914 failed to produce a rapid outcome, when it turned into a form of siege warfare among industrial powers whose

---

1 I am grateful for critical comments and suggestions generously offered by Khachig Tololyan.
2 Roger Chickering, "Total War: The Use and Abuse of a Concept," in Manfred F. Boemeke, Roger Chickering, and Stig Förster (eds.), *Anticipating Total War: The German and American Experiences, 1871–1914* (Cambridge, 1999), 23.

dominions stretched across the world, it mutated into another kind of war, bigger, more lethal, and more corrosive than any previous conflict. It is to that new kind of war that the word "total" appropriately applies.

Some have viewed the Peloponnesian Wars as total; others cite the Thirty Years' War of the seventeenth century, and eighteenth-century warfare among empires truly spanned the globe. From a number of viewpoints, there is force in these arguments. But on balance, I cannot accept them as extending the category of total war prior to the twentieth century. The birth of industrial warfare on the world scale after 1914 was, in my view, a revolutionary event. The intersection of that event with genocidal acts is the critical point I want to explore.

That transformation occurred precisely in the period when the Armenian genocide took place. The fact that Turkey was not among the leading industrial nations is neither here nor there; the war Turkey joined on the side of the Central Powers soon became a new kind of war, to whose radical character Turkey contributed through carrying out the Armenian genocide. In effect, total war did not produce genocide; it created the military, political, and cultural space in which it could occur, and occur again. Another way of putting the central point is to see total war as both the context and the outcome of genocide. My claim is that genocide is part of the landscape of total war. Indeed, genocide helped create total war. No one can deny that the Armenian genocide took place under the eyes of the German army and that the killers operated with impunity until after the war was over. And even then, such justice as was administered under Turkish military law barely touched the surface of the crimes – crimes the very existence of which are still denied by the authorities of the present-day Turkish state. The killers got away with the crime. This is what Hitler meant when, in a controversial and still disputed set of remarks, he asked "Who, after all, speaks today about the annihilation of the Armenians?"[3] Whatever his precise words, the meaning was clear. Racial war, biological warfare, ethnic cleansing were on the map in 1918 in a way that went beyond the experience of earlier conflicts. And when war visited Europe again in 1939, and when it turned into a world war, Hitler returned to this phenomenon – the phenomenon of genocide in the context of total war. In effect, without the Great War and its precedents, Auschwitz was unthinkable.

That is my argument. These remarks are preliminary attempts to set elements of the history of genocide in the context of the two massive industrial

---

3 See the remarks and discussion in Norman M. Naimark, *Fires of Hatred: Ethnic Cleansing in Twentieth Century Europe* (Cambridge, Mass., 2001), 57.

wars of what Charles Maier has called the age of territoriality.[4] Other pathways to genocide existed before 1914 and after 1918. My argument is about a subset of the category, genocide, the one located indelibly in the cultural history of the Great War.

One reason why the category "total war" is the right one to use in this period is that it is imbedded in contemporary usage. This is hardly surprising. That something radical had happened in the nature of warfare became apparent within months of the outbreak of hostilities in August 1914. The worldwide reach of the war was evident in the April 1915 landing at Gallipoli by a combined force of British, French, Australian, and New Zealand troops. This landing, clearly aimed to knock Turkey out of the war, precipitated elements of the genocide, clearly planned before the assault on the peninsula. But the globalization of the conflict describes only one facet of this new kind of war. At virtually the same time, other features of total war emerged. In April 1915 the German army first discharged canisters of poison gas on the battlefields of Ypres in Belgium. Soon the Allies responded in kind. In Brussels Edith Cavell was arrested for helping wounded British servicemen to evade capture. She freely admitted her actions and was shot in Brussels in October. In May 1915 the *Lusitania* went down, sunk by a German torpedo off the Irish coast; 1,200 civilians perished, including 190 Americans. Whether or not the ship was carrying munitions, it was certainly entering a combat zone. Zeppelin attacks reached London, causing civilian casualties. Among them were children in a Hackney elementary school. Paris too was bombed by long-range artillery. Investigations of German atrocities against civilians in Belgium were published; we now know that such crimes were not the product of propaganda. They occurred and were known and tolerated by the German general staff.[5] Such is the *Schrecklichkeit*, the frightfulness of this new kind of war. On the eastern front, massacres of civilians occurred in Serbia and in what is now Poland. For Eastern European Jews, 1915 was a catastrophic year; Russian soldiers in retreat brought pogroms to many towns and villages, whose residents were suspected of helping the German or Austrian armies. Perhaps 250,000 Jews were either expelled or fled from Galicia.[6]

Once again, there was much here that Europe and the world had seen before. Civilians had always been trampled on by invading armies. What

---

4 Charles Maier, "Consigning the Twentieth Century to History: Alternative Narratives for the Modern Era," *American Historical Reveiw* 105 (June 2000): 807–31.
5 See John Horne and Alan Kramer, *German Atrocities: A History of Denial* (New Haven, 2001).
6 Mark Levene, "Jews in Poland and Russia," in P. Panayi (ed.), *Minorities in Wartime* (Leamington Spa, 1995), 22–33.

was more disturbing now was not only the scale of the disaster but the implication visible for all to see that such acts were not unfortunate by-products of war but were built in to the nature of the conflict itself. The boundaries between civilian and military targets were fading fast.

Industrial power exponentially increased the lethality of battle. This is why the bloodbath of the first year of the war was so unprecedented. By the end of 1915, when (according to some estimates) 1 million Armenians had been killed or perished at the hands of Turks and their subordinates in Western Asia, more than 2 million soldiers had already been killed on the war's disparate battlefields. Perhaps twice that dizzying number had been wounded. And this was just the beginning: by 1918, 9 million men had died in uniform.[7]

The first year of the conflict, when the war of movement produced stalemate and when the Armenian genocide was perpetrated, was its most costly phase. The brutalizing character of total war starts here, in 1914–15, with massive casualties, and crimes against civilians on both the western and the eastern fronts, both of which left a legacy of bitterness and hatred in their wake.

The scale of the carnage was such as to persuade many contemporaries that the first year of the war was the time when the rules of engagement of warfare clearly changed, and changed forever. Those who waged war in 1914 saw it as a limited conflict, consistent with a nineteenth-century model of belligerency. Some, like the younger Moltke, chief of staff of the imperial German army, wondered whether it would be a long war, but most believed that there would be a clash of arms, followed by a decisive outcome.[8] They were wrong. A year later, that model was shattered, and not only by the level of violence employed. The conflict was then termed "the Great War" – a phrase first used repeatedly in April 1915 – not only because of its scale but because of its unlimited, revolutionary character.

To reiterate my position. Elements of total war existed before 1914; and genocide happened under other circumstances. The interpretation I offer applies to genocide under the cover of industrial warfare between 1914 and 1945. Other paths to genocide have appeared – in Rwanda, Cambodia, as earlier in the North American plains. The term "genocide," is of relatively recent coinage, and cannot be taken as a unity but as a general class of crimes of different origins and different character. The systematic killing of the subjects of a nation by agents of their own state is certainly genocide;

7 Jay Winter, *The Great War and the British People* (London, 1985), ch. 3.
8 Stig Förster, "Dreams and Nightmares: German Military Leadership and the Images of Future Warfare, 1871–1914," in Boemeke et al., *Anticipating Total War*, 343–76.

but so is the extermination of others deemed outside "civilization." I believe such definitional questions ought to be treated cautiously and, if possible, the boundaries surrounding genocide ought to be drawn liberally and not exclusively.

My argument applies only to genocide in the two world wars. Locating them in their time and place may help us avoid universalizing the quest for some underlying cause of all genocides, as well as avoiding the untenable argument that any particular genocidal campaign is outside history. These crimes may – indeed do – challenge our historical imagination, but they must never be allowed to defeat it.

FACETS OF TOTAL WAR

Because the term total war is a contested one, I would like to take some time, before turning to its relevance to the history of genocide, to elaborate further five of its features:

1. Crossing the military participation threshold.
2. Direct and ongoing linkages between front and home front.
3. The redefinition of the military as the cutting edge of the nation at war.
4. The mobilization of the imagination.
5. The cultural preparation of hatred, atrocity, and genocide.

Military Participation Threshold

The Great War was total war in part because between 1914 and 1918 the proportion of the male population aged eighteen to forty-nine in uniform passed an arbitrary threshold: about 50 percent of the cohort. Once passed, that participation ratio stayed there or above for an extended period.

Among combatants in the 1914–18 war, France and Germany mobilized the highest proportion of the relevant male cohorts: about 80 percent of men aged fifteen to forty-nine on the eve of the war were conscripted. Austria-Hungary mobilized 75 percent of its adult male population in the relevant age groups; Britain, Serbia, and Turkey called up between 50 and 60 percent. The Russian case is on the lower edge of what I call total mobilization, which is of course never literally total: approximately 16 million men or 40 percent of the male population aged fifteen to forty-nine served during the war.

But even in this case, it is easy to see that total war meant a transformation of the age composition and sex ratio of large parts of the home population. Not so in the United States, where in the brief space of eighteen months, about 4 million men or only 16 percent of the relevant cohort served in uniform in the Great War.

Second, total casualties and losses as a proportion of those who served passed a threshold beyond previous experience: wherever the threshold is, the total of roughly 9 million dead soldiers (according to varying estimates) is beyond it: this constitutes roughly one in eight of the men who served. Adding statistics on other casualties, it is apparent that roughly 50 percent of the men who served were either prisoners of war, wounded, or killed. Another way of putting the point is to say that while one in eight was killed, three in eight became casualties of war.

Here again national variations must be noted: the most murderous theater of operations was the eastern front, where disease and enemy action described the course of a nineteenth-century war waged with twentieth-century weapons. Of all Serbs who served in the war, 37 percent were killed; roughly one in four Romanians, Turks, and Bulgarians also perished. On the western front, where the war was won and lost, combat was about half as lethal: German and French losses were about one in six of those who served; British losses were one in eight. Still, families suffered the loss of individuals, not of statistics, and whatever the ratios, the lists of the fallen grew to a point that only metaphor or poetry could suggest the universal horror of the war.

Another feature of total war may be more surprising. Initially casualties among social elites were higher than among the rest of the population. The longer the war lasted, the greater was the democratization of loss. The reason is that officer casualties were higher than those in the ranks, and the social selection of the officer corps mirrored inequalities in prewar life. Consequently in its initial phases, the higher up in the social scale was a man, the greater were his chances of becoming a casualty of war. By 1917 elites were sufficiently decimated to require the armies to draw junior officers from wider social groups, which in their turn suffered disproportionately higher casualties in the last two years of the war.

Among the poor and the underprivileged, the story is different. Prewar deprivation saved the lives of millions of working-class men and poor peasants, whose stunted stature and diseases made it impossible for them to pass even the rudimentary standards of medical fitness for military service during the war. In the British case, roughly 35 percent of the men examined for military service were either unfit for combat or unfit to wear a uniform at all. They were the lucky ones.[9]

9 For a fuller discussion, see Winter, *The Great War and the British People*, ch. 3.

Linkage

Casualties on this scale tied front and home front together in new and complex ways. There is an abundant literature on the mobilization of labor in war economies[10] and on the ambiguous effects of the war on women's work and welfare.[11] It is clear that total war went into high gear when all the combatants were either industrialized or part of a system of world trade based on industrialization.

But there is another level on which linkage was more than a metaphor; it was a palpable reality. In 1914–18, despite what many soldiers and journalists wrote, civilians knew how bad war was, even if they didn't see the landscape in which the fighting took place. From 1914 they saw millions of refugees streaming away from the fighting in Belgium, France, Serbia, eastern Germany, Russia; soon enough they saw the mutilated; they mourned the dead; they knew the pain of loss which by 1918 in one way or another hit most households in combatant Europe. It is simply not true to say that civilians did not know how murderous the war was. They knew, they mourned, though the newspapers almost never acknowledged the omnipresence of grief.

The Cutting Edge

War efforts of this scale and duration required the recognition that armies were the cutting edge of the nation at war: well-being at home vitally affected the capacity of armies to go on, and thereby well-being at home directly affected the outcome of the war. This was true not only because armies of workers had to supply armies of soldiers but also because war on this scale entailed hardship and sacrifice for the families of soldiers, an issue fundamental to *their* will to fight.

In this respect, the outcome of war became a function of a joint operation. Defining morale as the determination of both soldiers and civilians to go on with the war, a cease-fire came when one side imposed its will on the morale of the other, by demonstrating that further sacrifice was pointless because the war could not be won.

This is hardly a revolutionary finding, although it has led to massive misunderstanding about why the Allies won and the Central Powers lost the

---

10 See the references in P. Fridenson (ed.), *The French Home Front* (Oxford, 1992).
11 See the references in R. Wall and J. Winter (eds.), *The Upheaval of War: Family, Work and Welfare in Europe, 1914–1918* (Cambridge, 1988), and more recently Susan Pedersen, *Family, Dependence, and the Origins of the Welfare State: Britain and France, 1914–1945* (Cambridge, 1993).

war. The war came to an end when the morale of *both* the German army and the German home front crumbled in 1918; both front and home front came to see that the war could not be won.[12] The fact that they crumbled together is hardly surprising, though the linkage has been obscured by Hitler's claim that the reason the front soldiers had to surrender was because they were betrayed by cowards at home – the stab-in-the-back legend.[13]

What Hitler said was almost exactly the reverse of the truth: there was a stab in the back, but the knife was wielded by the military leaders of Germany who led their country into a war they could not win and then brilliantly shifted responsibility for the disaster onto all shoulders other than those who really bore the blame. But Hitler's statement about linkage between front and home front did disclose a feature of total war of great importance, not only to the 1914–18 struggle but to later conflicts. Among the lessons the Nazis took from the Great War was that to undermine the material well-being of the civilian population was to endanger the war effort as a whole. That is one reason why the Nazis kept living standards relatively high for "Aryans" during the 1939–45 war and why they displaced the deprivation suffered by their elders in 1914–18 at home onto the backs of *Untermenschen*: Slavs, political prisoners, Gypsies, and Jews.[14]

For the Nazis, Aryans were entitled to a minimum standard of living, better than that provided in the 1914–18 war, when the official ration could not keep anyone alive. In the Great War, to avoid starvation, all Germans had to break the law: that meant recourse to the black market, and all the social tensions it entailed.[15]

Democracies were much better at waging war because they took seriously the consent of the governed. Thus, although the Allies had a major advantage in aggregate supplies of essential goods and services, distribution mattered at least as much as supply. And distribution is a political issue, one that always entails the question "to whom."

In important ways the nature of citizenship helped determine the military efficiency of the war effort of the Allies and severely limited the war effort of Germany. This contrast, I argue, was visible on the home front and operated through the prior existence of what the economist Amartya Sen has called a system of "entitlements," a legal and moral framework upon which distributive networks rest.[16] In Paris and London the entitlements

12 See W. Deist, *Militär Staat und Gesellschaft* (Munich, 1991).
13 Adolf Hitler, *Mein Kampf* (New York, 1939).
14 L. Borchardt, "The Impact of the War Economy on the Civilian Population," in W. Deist (ed.), *The German Military in the Age of Total War* (Oxford, 1984).
15 See A. Offer, *The First World War: An Agrarian Interpretation* (Oxford, 1990).
16 Amartya Sen, *Poverty and Famines* (Oxford, 1976).

of citizenship – located in the right to a minimum level of subsistence – helped preserve communities at war by *enforcing* a balance of distribution of necessary goods and services between civilian and military claimants. In Berlin, a different order of priorities existed. The military came first, and the economy created to service it completely distorted the delicate economic system at home. My claim is that Allied adaptation and well-being reflected a more equitable and efficient distributive system than existed on the other side of the lines. In both Britain and France civilians got more, both because they had more and because their share of the national income was preserved, despite spiraling claims for men and resources from the generals. The Germans disregarded the need for such a balance and created the first military–industrial complex in history, and its record in waging war was an unmitigated disaster.

The argument that follows is a simple one. With respect to work, to wages, and to consumption patterns, the rudimentary structure of everyday life was compromised more in wartime Berlin than in Paris and London. This contrast was primarily an outcome of different sets of social relations and different meanings of citizenship leading to a different order of priorities about the relative importance of civilian capabilities and functionings when measured against military needs. That contrast came into focus in the latter half of the war, with the arrival of Hindenburg and Ludendorff to commanding positions both within the armed forces and within German society as a whole in 1916, and at a time when new economic structures were introduced both domestically and internationally by the Allies.

Ultimately, the contrasts between entitlements in Paris and London, on the one hand, and Berlin, on the other, provide in miniature, a glimpse of the wider political and economic tests of the war. Those tests exposed different approaches to citizenship, as understood in terms of the entitlements of people to a set of capabilities and functionings necessary for them to go about their daily lives. The Wilhelmine regime failed that test; the Allies on balance passed it.

Why was this so? Two approaches to this problem may be distinguished. The first emphasizes aggregate wealth and command of imperial supplies. From this point of view, the greater the shortages, the greater the pressure on an already overextended administrative system. After 1915 the Allies only occasionally faced critical material constraints. When they did, as in the case of coal, administrators on national and interallied levels reacted, and the national and international reserves of the Allies were brought into the equation. In this framework, we can see what *imperial* abundance meant for the well-being of civilians in London and in Paris, and what the absence of such reserves meant for Berliners.

The second approach follows Sen in positing alternatively that it is better to evaluate such crises by defining living standards not through an additive exercise of weights assigned to a basket of consumables, but through an estimation of the way social and political systems provide a cluster of capabilities and functionings that enable people to go about their daily lives.[17] The German system differed radically from that in place in Britain and France in 1914 and, even more so, after 1916, with the ascendancy of Hindenburg and Ludendorff to power. Different approaches to the distribution of goods and resources as between military and civilian claimants produced different material outcomes for the population as a whole. The Allies achieved a balance; the Central Powers, and Germany in particular, patently did not.

Questions of fairness and inequality were also important in the maintenance of morale.[18] In Paris and London local and national leaders were able to provide a more equitable distribution of available goods and services than was the case in Berlin and thereby to avoid for much of the war the damaging atmosphere of suspicion and rancor that poisoned social life in Germany in the last phase of the conflict. Justice mattered, and in their failure to ensure at least the appearance of fair shares for all, civil authorities in Germany lost the trust of the urban population.

It is true that the myth of the invincibility of the German army silenced grumbles and dissent during the great offensive surge begun in March 1918. But by the summer, when it became clear that the war could not be won, dissent returned and amplified. By then Berlin society had fractured into a thousand parts, each trying to find enough food or fuel to survive, each anxiously awaiting news from the front. When the bad news sank in that hopes of victory had vanished, there was nothing left to prop up the regime. It had lost its legitimacy by its failure *both* to deliver victory *and* literally to deliver the goods.

The Mobilization of the Imagination

So far I have emphasized structural features of total war. But this phenomenon is incomprehensible without attending to its cultural history, its capacity to tap the loyalties and prejudices of the home population.[19]

---

17 Amartya Sen, "The Standard of Living: Lecture I, Concepts and Critiques," in G. Hawthorn (ed.), *The Standard of Living* (Cambridge, 1987), 2–3.
18 See Barrington Moore, *Injustice: The Social Bases of Obedience and Revolt* (London, 1978).
19 See J. J. Becker et al. (eds.), *Guerres et cultures* (Paris, 1994).

Slaughter on a grand scale needed justification. To keep intact the domestic commitment to the war effort, an elaborate cultural campaign was organized in each combatant country. Of even greater importance than the proliferation of government agencies was the tendency for civil society itself to foster a cultural campaign with two objectives: steeling the will of civilians to go on; and stifling dissent and thereby making it impossible to think of any alternative other than total victory and total defeat. By and large this campaign worked. Antiwar sentiment grew as the conflict dragged on, but, with the notable exception of Russia, antiwar activists were unable to shorten the war by one day or one hour.

State-directed propaganda had only a minor role to play in this successful effort at cultural mobilization. It succeed only when it locked into messages coming from below, that is from within civil society, about the need to go on with the war. Big Brother did not create consent during the 1914–18 war. The truth is more frightening: the Great War provided much evidence of the propensity for populations to generate internally a commitment to carry on a war of unprecedented carnage.

Political and social elites tried to manipulate opinion, to be sure. Censorship and imprisonment operated, but neither had much force in formulating public opinion in wartime. The effort to mobilize the imagination in wartime came from below[20] and was multifaceted and decentralized. As the conflict dragged on into 1916–17, a remobilization of the popular will to go on took place. Much of this effort to fortify determination was not government inspired or organized. Especially after the great battles of Verdun and the Somme in 1916, the private sector took the lead. Here kitsch, "thrillers," and popular entertainments broadcast direct messages with mass appeal about the virtues of one side and the villainy of the other.[21] Music halls and the gramophone industry expanded rapidly in the war, presenting anodyne or uplifting images to an increasingly tired and irritable population.[22]

In this effort to express the will to victory, avant-garde artists played their part. This is somewhat surprising, given the cosmopolitan character of the arts before the war, and the tendency of avant-garde artists to defy polite conventions and bourgeois sensibilities. But the Great War nationalized artistic movements, dividing across the battle lines artists who before 1914 were engaged in similar explorations of form, color, tonality, and imagery.

---

20 On this theme, see Stéphane Audoin-Rouzeau, *La guerre des enfants, 1914–1918* (Paris, 1993).
21 On thrillers, see Milan Voykovic, "The Culture of Thriller Fiction in Britain, 1898–1945: Authors, Publishers and the First World War," Ph.D. diss., University of New South Wales, 1996.
22 On the gramophone industry, see Peter Martland, "The Development of the Gramophone Industry in Britain, 1880–1935," Ph.D. diss., University of Cambridge, 1990.

Two unusual instances of the mobilization of the imagination may help to show both the efflorescence of avant-garde patriotism in wartime and the problems it confronted. The first is the Ballet *Parade*, the collective effort of Cocteau, Picasso, Satie, Massine, and Diaghelev. The second is Abel Gance's film, *J'accuse*. Both affirmed the cause; in different ways both got somewhat out of hand.

The guiding spirit behind *Parade* was that of Jean Cocteau, aged twenty-five in 1914 and the editor with Paul Iribe from November of that year of *Le Mot*, a journal aimed at defending "pure French tradition" from the "shoddy goods from Munich" and Berlin, and at establishing "common sense, equilibrium, and intellectual order." When Italy joined the war, the cover of *Le Mot* showed Dante's familiar profile, with the simple caption: *Dante avec nous*. In short, patriotic conservatism in the war of cultures was the order of the day. Gone was the sense of avant-garde art as international, critical, detached, disruptive. Instead its function was to promote the cultural war against vulgar German taste.

Two years later, Cocteau found another way to broadcast the cultural supremacy of the Allies. He wrote the scenario of a ballet, in the tradition of the *forain*, or traveling fair, with its hawkers, its temporary stages, on which the company would present a *parade* or a light entertainment to draw in the crowds. The staging of this *parade* was the opportunity of a lifetime: a chance to marry Picasso's cubism to the art of the Ballet Russe, accompanied by the music of Erik Satie.[23]

Cocteau provided the essential element of mediation between highly temperamental artists needed to realize it. Leon Bakst designed the costumes; Léonide Massine provided the choreography. Satie agreed to provide a score, with hints of ragtime and satire, but in a style "typiquement français sans être debussyste."[24] Picasso agreed to provide sets, costumes, and the theater curtain.

The curtain he designed reflected Picasso's period with the Ballet Russe in Italy in 1916. There is a distant view of Vesuvius and unmistakably human figures on the right: two Harlequins, entirely familiar from the *commedia dell'arte* tradition; country folk in "rustic" dress; an Italian sailor; a Spanish guitarist; a blackamoor; and a dog. On the left is a circus scene, with an equestrienne reaching for a monkey, and a Pegasus feeding her foal.

When the curtain rose for the first time on May 18, 1917, at the Théâtre des Champs Elysées, the audience saw an entirely unfamiliar world: a cubist cityscape, with odd perspectives and characteristic gray and green colors. The dancers were a Chinese magician (Léonide Massine), a Little American Girl (Maria Shabelska), and two acrobats (Lopukhova and Zverev) flanked by managers wearing eight-feet-high, head-to-toe cubist relief constructions. The French manager was in formal dress; the American manager, wearing a stovepipe hat, had Manhattan skyscrapers on his shoulders, like an advertising placard. There was originally a third equestrian manager, but he was removed during rehearsals, leaving a two-man horse prancing on the stage.

The audience's reaction was uproar. The noise was so great, Diaghilev recalled, that he thought the chandelier had fallen. As soon as the dancers appeared, the cultural unity of the nation collapsed. The jarring appearance of what were in effect, "ambulant pieces of cubist art," brought back with a vengeance the old divide between avant-garde and conventional tastes. The reviews were tepid or negative. Cocteau had gone too far; a celebration of the Allied cause had become instead a "cause célèbre," full of heated comments, responses, and insults. After a negative notice of his music, Satie replied:

> Monsieur et cher amie,
> Vous êtes un cul, mais un cul sans musique.
> Erik Satie.[25]

The conservative thrust of wartime culture had little room for experimentation, especially in a form that departed so radically from the romantic conventions of ballet.

In a sense, *Parade* was a perfect metaphor for wartime propaganda: the hawker, trying to draw the crowds into his show, illustrates the mix of the commercial and the substantive in propaganda. The message of support for the war and for the way of life of your side had to be sold, and to do so, there emerged the most elaborate and widely disseminated advertising campaign in history. Cocteau's play and Picasso's theater curtain for it drew upon popular culture, the tradition of the *commedia dell'arte*, and used its imagery and assocations to represent the virtues of the Allied cause. Even the United States, which just entered the war, got into the act. Where England (or Russia) fitted into this Latinate conceit is hard to see, but if we make space for artistic license, we can see how *Parade* captured the sense of war as theater, as bloody carnival, as a cultural event as much as a military one.

Film created similar images of the war of competing cultures. Here too the commercial element in propaganda from below was important, though

---

25 Kenneth Silver, *Esprit de Corps: The Art of the Parisian Avant-Garde and the First World War, 1914–1925* (London, 1989), 45, 47, 123, 165.

censorship had a hand in restricting the range of images shown to the public. The problem was that at times films took on a life of their own, and wound up presenting images as shocking to some audiences as *Parade* had been. One such film is a case in point. *J'accuse* by Abel Gance, was filmed in 1918 and released after the Armistice. It started on the plane of patriotic assertion and then took off to explore the mythical realm of the "Lost Generation."

Gance was born in 1889 in Paris, and began to make a name for himself in the theater world of prewar Paris. A play, *The Victory of Samothrace*, interested Sarah Bernhardt until the war intervened. Rejected by the army on grounds of ill health, Gance sold film scripts to the major French companies, Gaumont and Pathé, and started to work as an actor and director in 1914–16. He was fascinated by distorting mirrors and lenses, which produced images he later called "subjective vision." The film *J'accuse* was financed partly by Pathé and received the blessing of the French army's cinematographic service, where Gance worked from 1917. The title *J'accuse* itself – applied first to German atrocities and overall responsibility for the war – suggests its aim at helping to revive flagging spirits.

The film was completed and shown for the first time a few days after the Armistice to an inter-Allied audience at the Hotel Dufayel on the Champs Elysées. Its public opening was at the Gaumont Palace in March 1919. The London premiere was in May 1920; the New York premiere was a year later in May 1921, where Gance dedicated the film to President Harding. He made the acquaintance of D. W. Griffith, through whom the film was acquired by United Artists. Its commercial success surpassed all expectations.

It is easy to see why it succeeded. The structure of *J'accuse* is conventional. It is set in a village in the Midi and presents a familiar love triangle. The film opens to a "farandole," a village dance, and then turns to the circle around Edith Laurin (played by Maryse Dauvray), the unhappy wife of François (played by Romauld Joubé), a brute with a taste for dogs, hunting, and blood. The far more refined Jean Diaz, a poet (played by Severin Mars) is drawn to Edith. She finds consolation in Diaz's company and in the grandiloquent lyric poetry he writes. One of his works is entitled "Les pacifiques" and paints in heavy brushstrokes the idyllic sentiments stirred in him by nature and by Edith. While reading her these poems, Jean and Edith are spied by François, who carefully aims his gun at a nearby sparrow and kills it. The same brutality is shown by Gance in a highly unusual scene of marital rape and despairing sexual submission.

Then war breaks out, and François is immediately mobilized. Not Diaz, who has a few weeks to go before joining his unit. To protect his honor, François sends his wife away to family in the east. Terrible news then follows.

The Germans occupy the village in which Edith is living, and a German soldier rapes her. On hearing of this crime, Jean Diaz hurls at the Germans the epithet "J'accuse" and immediately joins up. After officer training, Diaz is posted to the unit in which his rival François is a soldier in the ranks. The two are reconciled, though, after Jean Diaz takes upon himself a suicidal mission meant for François. Their bond grows strong, as they admit to each other their love for Edith.

So far we are in the world of sentimental melodrama. But what made *J'accuse* into an entirely different film was its ending. In the final sequence, Diaz, the hero, begins to lose his mind. He escapes from hospital and reaches his village. There he summons the villagers and tells them of a dream. The dream as we see it starts in a battlefield graveyard with wooden crosses all askew. A huge black cloud rises behind it, and, magically, ghostlike figures emerge from the ground. They are wrapped in tattered bandages, some limping, some blind walking with upraised arms, some stumbling like Frankenstein's monster. They leave the battlefield and walk down the rural lanes of France to their villages. Their aim is to see if their sacrifices had been in vain. What they find is the pettiness of civilian life, the advantage being taken of soldiers' businesses, the infidelity of their wives. The sight of the fallen so terrifies the townspeople that they immediately mend their ways, and the dead return to their graves, their mission fulfilled. After recounting this dream, the poet, now totally mad, accuses the sun above of standing idly by and watching the war go on. Then he dies.

This sequence of the dead rising from their graves is one of the great scenes of the early cinema. Its force is made even more poignant when we realize that most of the men we see on the screen were French soldiers lent to Gance by the French army to play in this film. Gance's assistant was Blaise Cendrars, who had lost his right arm fighting with the Moroccan Division in Champagne in September 1915. Cendrars survived, but many of those who played the dead in Gance's film returned to the front in the last months of the war and were killed. Some of those we see playing the dead soon became the dead.

In the "return of the dead," Gance found a visionary surrealism, a romantic language of nightmarish quality. *J'accuse* started out as a standard and unremarkable propaganda film about the nobility of the French war effort and German barbarity. But with the assistance of Blaise Cendrars, a man who had seen war in all its ugliness, Gance's film ascends to another level of art. It rises from conventional pieties to transcendental ones.

The Christology of the end of *J'accuse* is unsubtle but compelling. It bears the romantic signature of Gance, a man who, according to one critic, wanted to be Victor Hugo, Henri Barbusse, and D. W. Griffith rolled up into one.[26] Add a touch of the New Testament, and it is clear from whence Gance derived the imagery that lifted his message from melodrama to the mythical realm.

Gance was not against the war, only against the tendency – all too visible among some journalists and politicians – to forget what soldiers had suffered to win it. This is a dangerous message to spread, because it raised the disturbing subject of the exploitation of the war by unscrupulous people on your side of the line. This was a theme found in abundance in soldiers' newspapers and letters.[27] When put in filmic form, this accusation raised a terrible doubt: perhaps the sacrifices at the front were in vain, not because they did not lead to victory, but because of the immorality of the people for whom that victory was sought. Gance's vision captured the sense of an unpaid and unpayable debt the living owed to the dead.[28] This is what gives the end of his film its profound character, so remote from its maudlin initial passages. Gance had started in one enterprise, well within the range of wartime propaganda, and had wandered into another: the evocation of the presence of the dead in the wartime and postwar landscape. His romanticism had simply gotten out of hand.

It is important to note that only occasionally did Gance's vision overpower his pomposity. But that may have been his hidden strength. His message reached its audience through a combination of the very old and the very new. Cocteau did not get the balance right, and given the form in which he worked, perhaps no one could have done so. Gance experimented in cinema to express both pedestrian stories of love and patriotism and transcendental images of dreams, resurrection, and redemption. *J'accuse* has vanished, it is true, while *Parade* has not. But Gance's achievement should not be underestimated. He drew his audience into one familiar world, and then led it to another, the magical world of the trenches and the mythical world of the dead.

In both cases, on the stage and on the screen, we can see how the wartime mobilization of the imagination led in unanticipated directions. No military or political authorities told Cocteau or Gance what to do. They created art forms that fitted a war of unparalleled modernity. Cocteau and Picasso used cubism to convey messages expressed firmly within nineteenth-century

---

26 Georges Sadoul, *Histoire du cinéma mondial. Des origines à nos jours* (Paris, 1949), 167.
27 Stéphane Audoin-Rouzeau, *Men at War: Trench Journalism and National Sentiment in France, 1914–1918*, trans. H. McPhail (Oxford, 1992).
28 On this theme, see Antoine Prost, *In the Wake of War: Anciens Combattants and French Society, 1914–1940*, trans. H. MacPhail (Oxford, 1992).

cultural forms, in particular, the form of the *commedia dell'arte*. Gance used the "high-tech" medium of the day – the cinema – to convey ancient messages about love, sacrifice, redemption. Here we can see the tendency in the cultural history of the war for a revitalization of the old in a conflict of astonishing novelty. Far from initiating a cultural revolution, the Great War was a counterrevolutionary moment in cultural history, the time when the old flared up to make sense of a kind of war the world had never seen before.[29]

The Cultivation of Hatred

In the effort of cultural mobilization, total war entailed the demonization of the enemy. Some of this story is old – witness the wars of religion or the propaganda of the Reformation and Counter Reformation – but aligned with the other elements of this matrix, the cultural history of warfare entered a new and strikingly original landscape. It is a space in which what Peter Gay has called the cultivation of hatred took place, an effort that provided the context in which war crimes of a revolutionary scale and character took place.[30] I refer to genocide as a feature of total war.

It is important to note the contingent nature of this argument. Not all nations engaged in total war committed genocide, but total war created the conditions that made it possible. It entailed the brutalization of millions and thereby raised radically the tolerance of violence in some societies caught up in armed conflict.

Total war is like an infection; it has the capacity to infect many populations, but most – through their legal systems, education, religious beliefs, military traditions, or other convictions and practices – are inoculated against it.[31] Those not so fortunate, those (so to speak) without the antibodies, succumb to the infection, and then the innocent suffer. Under these conditions, and in the context of total war, genocide can occur. It did during the First World War.

This framework is essential to an understanding of the unfolding of the Armenian genocide of 1915. Despite decades of Turkish denials, the outline of this set of staggering war crimes is relatively well known. Its revolutionary character is not.[32] In the hours before dawn on April 24, 1915, Allied

---

29 For a fuller exposition of this argument, see Jay Winter, *Sites of Memory, Sites of Mourning: The Place of the Great War in European Cultural History* (Cambridge, 1995).
30 P. Gay, *The Cultivation of Hatred* (New York, 1993).
31 I owe this image to George Mosse. For a comparison that emphasizes choice and contingency, see Jonathan Steinberg, *All or Nothing: The Axis and the Holocaust* (London, 1990).
32 On the Armenian genocide, see Johannes Lepsius, *Rapport secret sur les massacres d'Arménie (1915–1916)* (Paris, 1987); Tribunal permanent des peuples, *Le crime de silence. Le génocide des Arméniens*

troops landed at Gallipoli, in an audacious and doomed attempt to knock Turkey out of the war. The very same night, the Turkish authorities began a process of repression of internal enemies – the Armenian communities, numbering perhaps 2 million people, concentrated in Anatolia in the northeast, straddling the border with Russia, but also scattered throughout the Ottoman Empire. Under cover of darkness, on April 25, several hundred Armenian men – intellectuals, journalists, professionals, businessmen, clergymen – were taken from their homes and shot. Much of the leadership of the Armenian community had been eliminated. Over the next two years the Armenian population of Ottoman Turkey was forcibly uprooted and expelled to the desert regions of Mesopotamia. In the process between 500,000 and 1 million defenseless Armenians were killed or died of exposure or disease in camps or in the Syrian desert. Statistics on atrocities are never precise or easily verified, but even a conservative estimate of the scale and dimensions of the deportation places loss of life at about 50 percent of the pre-1914 population. In the midst of war, a substantial part of a long-established and prosperous civilian community with identifiable religious and cultural characteristics had been wiped out; these people were sentenced to death *because of* who they were and where they were – in effect, because of their ethnicity. Their fate was indisputably a war crime, which constituted a clear precedent for the Nazi extermination of the Jews. How did this massacre come about?

Tension between Christian Armenians and Muslim Turks long antedated the Turkish revolution of 1908. Armenian separatism had been suppressed with widespread loss of life in 1894 and 1896. After the revolution of 1908, Turkish nationalism under the "Young Turks" changed the nature of the antagonism by projecting an even more adversary and threatening character onto the Armenians living in their midst. The outbreak of war in 1914 seemed to justify Turkish fears: Armenian soldiers served alongside Russian forces in the Caucasus region and threatened fifth-column activity behind Turkish lines. On April 20, 1915, after a period of sporadic intercommunal violence, an armed attack by Turks on Armenians in the eastern city of Van was repulsed by armed Armenians; eighteen Turks were killed in the encounter. This "uprising" provided the excuse for the nocturnal arrest and murder of prominent Armenians four days later, precisely when Turkey faced invasion from the west.

(Paris, 1984); Gerard Chaliand and Yves Ternon, *Le génocide des Arméniens 1915–1917* (Paris, 1981); Richard G. Hovannisian (ed.), *The Armenian Genocide: History, Politics, Ethics* (London, 1992); Richard G. Hovannisian (ed.), *The Armenian Genocide in Perspective* (New Brunswick, N.J., 1986).

The failure of the Allied landing at Gallipoli was the proximate cause of the succession of repressive measures taken in the subsequent months against Armenian civilians. Had the Allied landing succeeded, leading to a rapid advance to Constantinople, the Armenian tragedy would not have occurred. But the failure of the Allies to break out of their beachheads doomed the Armenians to exile and indescribable suffering. Once the Gallipoli landing had occurred, the Turkish regime was indeed besieged on all sides. The decision to expel the Armenians from their homes was taken in this environment of wartime invasion and heavy loss of life among Turkish forces, with Turkish forces engaged both at Gallipoli in the west and against Russian and Armenian troops in the Caucasus.

It is unlikely that a precise written order to exterminate the Armenian people came down from the ruling Turkish triumvirate of Talaat Bey, minister of the interior; Enver Pasha, minister of war; and Djemal Pasha, minister of the navy. The responsibility of these men for collective deportation is clear; but deportation – a time-honored strategy in nineteenth-century Turkey – while tantamount to death for the old, the weak, and the infirm, was not genocide. What turned a war crime into a genocidal act was the context of total war, a context that translated deportation swiftly into the mass slaughter, abuse, and starvation of an entire ethnic group potentially troublesome to an authoritarian regime at war.

Subversion was a universal strategy in the First World War. The imperial character of all the major combatants ensured that this would be so. The Germans stirred up trouble in Ireland and Russia, as well as in Mexico; the British and French dabbled in the Austrian Empire; the Russians were active among Armenians on their common border with Turkey. But only in Turkey did the threat of subversion lead to the extermination of "subversives" – men, women, and children by the hundreds of thousands.

This suggests that the specter of the subversion of a multinational empire in time of war was not in itself the root cause of genocide. This meant more than probing the weak links in an imperial chain. Genocide came out of total war. Total war entailed the obliteration of the distinction between military and civilian targets and the ruthless use of terror in the suppression of domestic groups suspected of offering the enemy tacit or active support.

The notion of "total war" came not out of Turkey but out of the West. Napoleonic warfare in Spain and Russia entailed war against civilians and irregular forces. Fifty years later, American civil warfare added another dimension to the cruelty of armed conflict. It was not a Turk but the American General Philip Sheridan who on September 8, 1870, told the future German chancellor Otto von Bismarck that the "proper strategy" in wartime "consists in the first place in inflicting as telling blows as possible upon the enemy's army, and then causing the inhabitants so much suffering that they must long for peace, and force their Government to demand it. The people must be left nothing but their eyes to weep with over the war."[33] The "people" in question were secessionists, it is true, but they shared the same language, many the same religion, and often came from the same families. What would wartime brutality look like when not tempered by such cultural bonds?

When Turkey entered the war on the side of the Central Powers in 1914, old ethnic quarrels were fused with the new and murderous dynamics of total war. The Armenian massacres arose out of the waging of total war against an internal enemy by a corrupt and incompetent army. Over decades steps had been taken to modernize Turkey's armed forces. As early as the 1830s, Helmuth von Moltke, later chief of staff of the Prussian army and architect of the defeat of the French army in 1870, was dispatched to Constantinople to help reform the Turkish army. The problem remained, though, that however wise his advice, the Turkish army was bound to reflect the corruption of the society it served. In 1915, as much as in the time von Moltke had served with the Turkish army in Armenia and Egypt, poorly paid soldiers and irregulars had to forage for their food. Their supplies made a grand circular tour on the black market back to the government offices that had issued them in the first place. Just to survive, Turkish units engaged in armed skirmishes or raids, which were endemic in the rough terrain of the Turkish-Russian border region.

From mid-1915 these raiding parties destroyed Armenian villages and towns; bandits in Turkish uniform and underpaid and undernourished soldiers killed with impunity, harassed the deportees, and herded them south, toward concentration camps or unprotected confinement in the wilds of the Mesopotamian desert.

The massacre mixed the worst of the old and the new. By 1915 the Turkish empire was fighting for its existence, but more venal motives were also at work in the genesis of the Armenian deportations. Limited though persistent armed resistance by Armenians provided the Turkish leaders with a specious justification for getting their hands on Armenian property, land, and assets. The crime they set in motion initially was theft and brutality on a grand scale, akin to the campaign of "ethnic cleansing" waged by the Bosnian Serbs against Muslims and Croats and the genocide perpetrated by the Rwandan Hutus against Tutsis in the early 1990s. In effect, the Turks

33 Moritz Busch, *Bismarck: Some Secret Page of His History*, 2 vols. (New York, 1898), 1:128.

wanted the Armenians out of the way; they also wanted Armenian wealth and were prepared to kill, torture, and maim to get it. Their motives were old; the means to achieve them were new and chilling. They identified an entire nation as an internal enemy and simply decided to eliminate it.

This crime was not done in the dark. There were numerous witnesses to the deportation and massacre of the Armenian people. One man who saw what was happening was a German missionary in Turkey, Johannes Lepsius, president of the Deutsche Orient-Mission and the Germano-Armenian Society. He prepared a detailed report to his mission, meant for private circulation among influential people in Berlin, who he hoped would be in a position to stop the killings. Censorship precluded public discussion of a matter so potentially embarrassing to Germany's ally. Lepsius's words are unequivocal. He reported that three-quarters of the Armenian people had been stripped of their possessions, chased from their homes, and – if not prepared to convert to Islam – killed or deported to the desert. One-seventh alone has escaped the deportation. Lepsius pointed to political circles around the "Union and Progress Committee" as being responsible for the deportations, validated though they were by government decree. Young Turk "Clubs" in different towns recruited groups of thugs and brigands to "convey" the deportees out of their towns, and to rob, rape, and kill them when convenient.

Testimony by Armenian survivors corroborated Lepsius's account. The city of Baibourt was home to about 17,000 Armenians. In the first two weeks of June 1915, about 70 prominent Armenian men were imprisoned or taken into the hills, presumably to be shot. The Armenian bishop and seven other notables were hanged. Other men who refused to leave the town were killed outright. Then the rest of the population of the town and surrounding villages were deported in three batches.

One widow provided a graphic description of the horror of this journey. She and her daughter were deported with 500 other people on June 14, 1915. Chillingly, the Turkish prefect of the town wished them "a happy journey." The convoy was accompanied by fifteen gendarmes. Two hours after their departure, they were set upon by armed brigands who, in league with their "guards" stole all their possessions. Over the following week, all males over age fifteen were bludgeoned to death. Young women and children were seized and taken away. As the refugees marched on, they saw the bodies of previous deportees. Stripped of any possessions, sleeping without cover, they were soon reduced to near starvation. On the road, they were passed by a convoy of cars carrying about thirty Turkish war widows, en route from Erzéroum to Constantinople. One widow singled out an Armenian and killed him herself with a gendarme's revolver. Then the Armenian widow and her daughter were given the choice: stay with the column or join the Turkish convoy; the price of their salvation was their agreement to convert to Islam. When they reached the plain of Erzéroum, on the banks of the Euphrates River, they saw corpses everywhere. They saw children thrown into the river and to their certain death. Armenian men tried to hide by "taking the veil" and by pretending to be Muslim women; any caught in this guise were summarily shot. After thirty-two days, the widow and her daughter reached Constantinople. What became of them, we do not know.

To form a sense of the enormity of the Armenian deportations, we need to multiply this story thousands of times. The coloration of the persecution varied; its ultimate character and aim did not. These deportations were intended to rid eastern Turkey of an old and prosperous community, whose riches inspired envy and whose separate ethnic identity made them appear as potential enemies in time of war.

The criminal nature of the Armenian deportations was established at postwar Turkish courts-martial held in 1919. In one such investigation, concerning massacres committed in the Yozgat region, three men were indicted. The charges included the premeditated murder of Armenians deported from Yozgat, the pillage of the victims' property, and the abduction and rape of Armenian women. Of an Armenian population of 1,800 in Yozgat in 1915, 88 had survived the war. Abundant proof about these murders existed in the form of cables, coded instructions, and orders signed by the defendants themselves. The court-martial established that there was no provocation or organized resistance to Turkish authority on the part of the Armenians of Yozgat. The men were separated from their families, who were forcibly deported. Instructions for their murder were given to the guards conveying them into exile. Then the property of the victims was seized and distributed. Here is the same story as reported by Lepsius in his 1916 "secret report," validated by Turkish judges themselves. Under articles 45 and 170 of the Ottoman Penal Code and Article 171 of the Military Penal Code, the most senior defendant, Mehmed Kemal, aged thirty-five, was sentenced to death and executed on April 10, 1919, four years after his minor part in this bloody period of Armenian history had begun.

That these crimes constituted genocide has been vigorously contested by Turks and their supporters for generations.[34] The argument is a barren

---

34 Witness the campaign of criticism by Turkish groups and individuals of an account of the Armenian genocide in the third episode of the Public Broadcasting System series I wrote entitled *The Great War and the Shaping of the Twentieth Century* in November 1996.

one; the term "genocide" is necessary to characterize these crimes, because they entailed the systematic deportation, degradation, and murder of an entire people. That children were massacred alongside their elders shows that the crime was intended to wipe out the future as much as the present Armenian population. But it is important to note that however sickening is this chapter of the history of the Great War, it is still not identical to Auschwitz and Treblinka. It is inconceivable to weigh the suffering of one catastrophe against another. That is not my aim. It is simply to place this catastrophe in a very particular time and place.

The Armenian genocide was nonindustrial extermination, with echoes of the earlier massacres both in the Balkans and of Indians in nineteenth-century America. The ideological preparation for it was relatively superficial, and the streams of refugees in other war sectors from East Prussia to Belgium and France in 1914 showed that massive population movements and cruelties were accepted as inevitable in time of war.

In and of itself, deportation was not genocide. Deportation and indiscriminate murder were war crimes that became genocidal in the context of total war. What the Turks did to the Armenians in 1915 and after was not racially motivated. As we have noted, some Armenian women could avoid death by conversion to Islam. The Jews under Nazi occupation were not so fortunate: their fate was sealed by their blood, not by their religious or political convictions.

In sum, the array of war crimes committed by Turkish forces against Armenian civilians constituted a genocidal campaign. Whatever its similarity to nineteenth-century deportations, the slaughter of the Armenian population in 1915 became, under conditions of total war, a genocidal act.

This set of crimes disclosed a facet of total war that has a history of its own. The Armenian massacres were a critical event in the history of twentieth-century warfare. The massacre of the Armenians was not the same as, but constituted a step on the way to, the industrialized murder of European Jewry by the Nazis. As Primo Levi put it, the nature of the offense, in Armenia as well as in Europe, needs to be specified, to be located in time and place.[35] The massacre of Armenians was an attempt at genocide. Following Levi, though, I share the view of Martin Amis (paraphrasing Levi) that the Nazis' plan was "unique, not in its cruelty, nor in its cowardice, but in its style – in its combination of the atavistic and modern. It was at once reptilian and 'logistical.'" The Nazis "found the core of the reptile brain, and built an autobahn that went there."[36]

---

35 Primo Levi, *If This Is a Man*, trans. S. Woolf (New York, 1959).
36 Martin Amis, *Time's Arrow* (London, 1991), 176.

In sum, the Armenian genocide bridged the nineteenth and twentieth centuries, in describing what could happen when motives of ethnic greed and hatred were mobilized by unscrupulous elites in the context of total war. Genocide helped form total war, and total war helped launch genocide. These crimes have been followed by others; each bears its own distinguishing features, and yet since 1914 they seem to share some family resemblance. That is what is meant by the term "genocide."

At this point we confront the challenge stated earlier in this essay. When we begin to explore the history of genocide, we approach some of the limits of the language we use in historical study. But I believe, nonetheless, that we must confront the nature of the beast and call it by its name, in order to locate it within the history of the twentieth century.

In 1919 the Russian poet Akhmatova reflected on the nature of the upheaval through which she was living. Her poem was entitled "Why Is This Century Worse?"

> Why is this century worse than those that have gone before?
> In a stupor of sorrow and grief
> it located the blackest wound
> but somehow couldn't heal it.
>
> The earth's sun is still shining in the West
> and the roofs of towns sparkle in its rays,
> while here death marks houses with crosses
> and calls in the crows and the crows fly over.[37]

What they flew over was a landscape disfigured by a new kind of warfare. The "blackest wound that could not be healed" is one way to describe total war. Its scars are with us still.

---

37 Anna Akhmatova, *Selected Poems*, trans. Richard McKane (London, 1989), 96.

10

The Mechanism of a Mass Crime

The Great Terror in the Soviet Union, 1937–1938

NICOLAS WERTH

In the past few years, the access, though limited, to previously inaccessible documents from the Politburo of the Communist Party of the Soviet Union (CPSU) and the State Security Police has thrown new light on the mechanism, the organization, and the implementation of the "Great Terror."[1] This crucial episode of Stalinism had provoked, long before the opening of the Soviet archives, a number of studies and debates about the amplitude, the reasons, and the purpose of the massacre of tens of thousands of communist officials and of a huge number (the evaluations ranged between hundreds of thousands and several millions) of ordinary soviet citizens – a massacre perpetrated by "a state against its people."[2] In the 1950s American scholars proposed a structural explanation of the Great Terror: as a totalitarian system Stalin's regime had to maintain its citizens in a state of fear and uncertainty, and recurrent random purging provided the mechanism.[3] At the end of the 1960s Robert Conquest published the first detailed account, which was to become a classical reference, of the Great Terror. Based primarily on testimonies or memoirs of those who had survived or deserted the "Fatherland of socialism" and on the numerous Soviet publications in the years of the "Khruschev thaw," the work of Robert Conquest emphasized Stalin's paranoia, focused on the Moscow show trials of old Bolsheviks, and analyzed the carefully planned and systematic destruction of the Leninist party leadership as the first step toward terrorizing the entire population.

---

1 The term "Great Terror" was popularized by Robert Conquest's pioneer study, *The Great Terror* (1968; new ed., updated, New York, 1990). In Russia, this episode is known as the Ezhovschina, "the reign of Ezhov," the people's commissar for the interior and chief of the State Security Police from September 1936 to November 1938.
2 See Nicolas Werth, "A State against Its People: Violence, Repression and Terror in the Soviet Union," in S. Courtois et al., *The Black Book of Communism* (Cambridge, Mass., 1999), 33–269.
3 Zbigniew Brzezinski's *The Permanent Purge* (Cambridge, Mass., 1958) is the clearest statement of this hypothesis.

Conquest's work opened a large debate about the extent to which terror had been a centralized phenomenon, about the respective roles of Stalin and Ezhov, about the categories and numbers of victims involved. In the mid-1980s, the American historian of the "revisionist school," John Arch Getty,[4] contested the idea that Stalin had carefully planned the events of 1936–38.[5] Stressing the increasing tension between the center and the local authorities and the leaders' own obsessive fears over their ability to control the situation, as well as facts of excessive zeal from activists in the party and in the People's Commissiariat for Internal Affairs (NKVD), "revisionist" historians suggested that the exceptional scale of the repressions of 1936–38 might be explained by the fact that local authorities, in order to deflect the terror that was being directed at them, had found innumerable scapegoats on which to carry out repressions, demonstrating in this way their vigilance and intransigence in the struggle against the common enemy.[6] Far from being a planned and long-term project revealing the growing paranoia of an all-mighty dictator, the Great Terror turned out to be a flight into chaos.[7] "Revisionist" historians also vigorously challenged Robert Conquest's estimates of the number of victims of the Great Terror – 6 to 7 million people arrested, 2 to 3 million deaths in camps, over a million executions.[8] But given the total inaccessibility of statistical data on the number of victims at the time of this dispute, the topic appeared to be both particularly vulnerable to political passion and not amenable to solution.

In spite of their fundamentally different approach to the Great Terror, historians of both schools focused on party purges across the 1930s; repression of real or imagined "oppositionists"; show trials of old Bolsheviks; elimination and replacement of political, intellectual, economic, or military elites; and struggle between the center and regional leadership cliques.

---

4 Author of *Origins of the Great Purges: The Soviet Communist Party Reconsidered, 1933–1938* (Cambridge, 1985) and coeditor with Roberta T. Manning of *Stalinist Terror: New Perspectives* (Cambridge, 1993) and with Oleg V. Naumov of *The Road to Terror: Stalin and the Self-Destruction of the Bolsheviks, 1932–1939* (New Haven, 1999).

5 "Even in Stalin's office, there were too many twists and turns, too many false starts and subsequently embarrassing backtrackings to support the idea that the terror was the culmination of a well-prepared and long-standing master-design." Getty and Naumov, *The Road to Terror*, xiii.

6 Getty, *Origins*; Gabor Rittersporn, *Stalinist Simplifications and Soviet Complications: Social Tensions and Political Conflicts in the USSR, 1933–1953* (New York, 1991).

7 "The evidence suggests," wrote Getty, in *Origins*, 206, "that the *Ezhovschina* should be redefined. It was not the result of a petrified bureaucracy's stamping out dissent and annihilating old radical revolutionaries.... In fact, it may have been just the opposite.... The *Ezhovschina* was rather a radical, even hysterical, *reaction* to bureaucracy."

8 Getty wrote in *Origins*, 8, not without a touch of provocation, that in the course of Ezhovshina, "thousands were executed."

Neither of them studied, mainly because of the scarcity of information on the subject, the mechanisms, organization, implementation of mass arrests and mass executions; or the sociology of the victims, who represented a much wider group than party elites or the intelligentsia. Thus, the Great Terror of 1937–38 in the Soviet Union solidified in popular and academic memory as Stalin's attack on political and social elites.

Our knowledge and understanding of the Great Terror have recently progressed considerably – in the first place, on the highly debated topic of the numbers of victims. Access to statistical data on arrests and death sentences pronounced by extrajudicial special courts has confirmed the exceptional and paroxysmal nature of *Ezhovshina*: executed during these two years (1937–38) were more than 85 percent of all people sentenced to the "supreme measure of punishment" by extrajudicial organs between the end of the civil war (1921) and Stalin's death (1953) – at least 682,000 out of a total of 800,000.[9] These figures, which come from two top-secret reports prepared in 1954 and 1963 for Nikita Khruschev,[10] have been recently cross-checked and corroborated by several other top-secret documents.[11] These figures reflect the secret police central authorities' accountancy; they do not include, however, either deaths under torture or during preliminary investigation, or what the tchekists called, in their jargon, "non-ratified execution supplements."[12] In the light of newly accessible documents, it is generally

9 The numbers of people executed, after having been sentenced to death by extrajudicial organs, in 1937 (353,000) and 1938 (329,000) are not comparable with the numbers of those executed during the other most repressive years of the Stalinist period: 23,000 in 1942, 20,000 in 1930. See V. P. Popov, "Gosudarstvennyi terror v Sovetskoï Rossii, 1921–1953" (State terror in Soviet Russia, 1921–1953), *Otecestvennye Arkhivy*, no. 2 (1992): 20–31.

10 The first report was prepared in January 1954 by Krouglov, the minister of interior (its figures are known among specialists of Soviet history as "Krouglov figures"); the second report was prepared in 1962–63 by a special commission of the Praesidium of the Central Committee, headed by N. Chvernik. According to these reports, 4,060,000 persons were sentenced by extrajudicial organs between 1921 and 1953, 1,575,000 of whom in 1937–38. During these two years, 681,692 persons were executed. These figures were first published by V. P. Popov ("Gosudarstvennyi terror"). See also J. A. Getty, T. G. Rittersporn, and V. Zemskov, "Victims of the Soviet Penal System in the Pre-Wars Years: A First Approach on the Basis of Archival Evidence," *American Historical Review* 98, 4 (October 1993): 1017–49; Stephen Wheatcroft, "Victims of Stalinism and the Soviet Secret Police: The Comparability and Reliability of the Archival Data – Not the Last Word," *Europe-Asia Studies* 51, 2 (1999): 315–45.

11 See in particular the NKVD operational orders no. 00447 of July 30, 1937, no. 00439 of July 25, 1937, no. 00485 of August 11, 1937, etc., implementing "mass repressive operations."

12 The Russian historian Oleg Khlevniuk has recently analyzed a remarkable example of these "non-ratified execution supplements." An inspection carried out, in Turkmenistan, at the beginning of 1939 by NKVD special envoys from Moscow revealed that the local NKVD had "overfulfilled" the quotas of "individuals to repress in the first category" – that is, to execute – ratified by the Politburo, by 25 percent, in spite of the fact that central authorities in Moscow had already increased threefold the initial quotas. See O. Khlevniuk, "Les mécanismes de la Grande Terreur au Turkmenistan," *Cahiers du Monde Russe* 39, 1–2 (1998): 197–208.

considered that the number of people executed in 1937–38 was around 800,000.

Top-secret Politburo decisions on the repression of such and such category of "enemies" and consequent "operational orders" issued by central NKVD authorities are among the most important newly released sources for the understanding of the mechanisms and implementation of "mass repressive operations" of 1937–38. These documents confirm that mass repression was indeed the result of initiatives taken at the very top level of the party, labeled as "special top-secret resolutions" of the Politburo, and implemented by the immense NKVD apparatus (370,000 agents). Recent research has shown that mass repression was implemented in the course of centrally planned "operations," decided by Stalin and Ezhov, the head of the NKVD.[13] These "operations" (a dozen of them have been identified) targeted two main groups of "enemies." A first group, defined in the top-secret "NKVD Order no. 00447" dated July 30, 1937, was directed against a wide category of previously identified "social outcasts": the innumerable cohort of "formers," directly and purposefully marginalized in the 1930s ("former kulaks," "former members of anti-Soviet parties," "former Whites," "former tsarist bureaucrats"), but also various kinds of "socially harmful elements" (such as "recidivist criminals," "bandits," "hooligans," "speculators," "sectarian activists," "ex-convicts," or "violators of the passport regime"). A second group, defined in a number of "national operations"[14] ("Polish operation," "German operation," "Finnish operation," "Kharbin operation," etc.), targeted all persons having (or having had) some kind of connection or contact, no matter how tenuous it might have been, with foreign countries – either because of their family background, nationality, profession, previous political commitment, or even place of living (living in borderlands made local inhabitants particularly vulnerable to repression). These mass operations, responsible for most of the arrests and executions in 1937–38, were very different in trajectory and scope from party, industry, and military purges of the elite taking place at the same time. Their goal was not just *replacement*

---

13 In 1937–38, as revealed by the lists of visitors in Stalin's office, Ezhov spent more time than any other person in Stalin's office, more than 900 hours between January 1937 and November 1938! See Register of entries, Stalin's private office, *Istoriceskii Arkhiv,* no. 6 (1994), nos. 2–6 (1995).

14 N. V. Petrov, and A. B. Roginskii, "Polskaia operatsia NKVD 1937–1938" (The Polish Operation of the NKVD in 1937–1938), in A. E. Gurianov (ed.), *Repressii protiv Poliakov i polskix grazdan* (Repressions against Poles and Polish citizens) (Moscow, 1997); N. Okhotin and A. Roginskii, "Iz Istorii Nemetskoï Operatsii NKVD 1937–1938" (From the history of the "German Operation" of the NKVD, 1937–1938), in I. L. Scherbakova (ed.), *Repressii protiv Rossiiskix Nemtsev* (Repressions against Soviet Germans) (Moscow, 1999).

(of "old" elites by "new" ones) but *eradication* of all marginal strata of the population.

The "operation against former kulaks, criminals, and other anti-Soviet elements" (known in NKVD circles as the "00447 operation" or the "kulak eradication program") was the outcome of a vast campaign of social engineering initiated with "dekulakization" (i.e., the deportation of about 2,200,000 peasants in 1930–33). It was also "the culmination of a decade-long radicalization of policing practice"[15] against all "social harmful elements" and other social outcasts.

"National operations" were part of a particular context: strong international tensions, war scares, xenophobia, spymania, and resurgence of Russian nationalism. For the Stalinist leadership, these operations aimed at the elimination of potential and mythical "fifth columnists," ready to perpetrate terrorist acts, wrecking, sabotage should war break out and hostile foreign powers such as Poland, Germany, Finland, and Japan invade. Up to a point, these "national operations" continued a policy initiated – on a relatively small scale – in 1935, by the ethnic cleansing of borderlands.[16] However, a close examination of the "national operations" of 1937–38 shows important differences with the specific "ethnic cleansing" policies that flourished in the 1940s.

As Sheila Fitzpatrick wrote recently, "the events that we label 'The Great Purges' may best be understood not as a simple phenomenon but as a number of related but discrete phenomena, each susceptible of specific historical explanation in a way that the universal phenomenon is not."[17] Far from being a unitary process, the Great Terror was the convergence of several repressive lines. The Great Terror had two sides: a public side and a hidden side. The public side was that of the show trials – the famous Moscow trials of the "Old Bolsheviks" and the provincial trials of local officials. All these trials were more or less successfully staged political theater and, in Annie Kriegel's words, "a formidable mechanism of social prophylaxis."[18] Show trials unmasked conspiracies, singled out scapegoats, denounced "new lords whose inhuman attitudes end up encouraging the formation of an army of

---

15 Paul Hagenloh, " 'Socially Harmful Elements' and the Great Terror," in Sheila Fitzpatrick (ed.), *Stalinism: New Directions* (London, 2000), 286.
16 On Soviet ethnic cleansing policies in the 1930s, see Terry Martin, "An Affirmative Action Empire: Ethnicity and the Soviet State, 1923–1938," Ph.D. diss., University of Chicago, 1996, esp. ch. 8; and "The Origins of Soviet Ethnic Cleansing," *Journal of Modern History* 70, 4 (1998): 813–61.
17 Fitzpatrick, *Stalinism: New Directions*, 258.
18 Annie Kriegel, *Les grands procès dans les systèmes communistes* (Paris, 1972), 160.

Trotskyites."[19] The public side of the Great Terror was also the promotion of a new elite, younger, better-educated, and more obedient, brought up in the strict "Stalinist spirit of the 1930's."

The hidden side of the Great Terror was that of the "NKVD operational orders," taken in compliance with top-secret Politburo resolutions. These were completely hidden transcripts not designed for circulation or discussion in the party, state, or society. The mass operations launched in 1937–38 were a prophylactic measure in the case of a future war, intended to rid the country "once and for all" of "the entire gang of anti-Soviet elements,"[20] that is, of all irreparable social by-products of the upheavals generated by forced collectivization and industrialization. This mass crime was planned as an operation of social cleansing, with its targets, its victimized groups, its "execution quotas," its figures of "individuals to repress in the first (or second) category,"[21] and its "non-ratified execution supplements."

In the limited space of this chapter, I focus on the hidden side of the Great Terror, on the implementation of mass operations. First, I mention briefly some of the most recent and important contributions on well-known topics that had been, for decades, the subject of hot debates, such as center-periphery conflicts, the respective roles of Stalin and of the nomenklatura in the unfolding of the process leading to the Terror, and the trajectory and scope of the purges directed at targeted groups and individuals belonging to political, economic, military, and intellectual elites.

Based on previously inaccessible stenograms of Central Committee plena,[22] on private correspondence between top party leaders,[23] and on local party archives, several recent studies have focused on the growing tensions, especially after 1935, between the party leadership and regional party cliques, which tended to engage in self-protective practices to conceal production shortfalls and other problems from Moscow. The central party leaders, permanently frustrated by the inefficency of local bureaucracies, came to believe that local cliques were engaged in a large-scale conspiracy.

19 From Stalin's speech, dated March 3, 1937.
20 In the words of N. Ezhov, in the "Operational NKVD order no. 00447, 30 July 1937" (English translation in Getty and Naumov, *Road to Terror*, 473–80).
21 In the hidden transcripts of the Politburo top-secret resolutions and the NKVD "operational orders," the "first category" meant "death sentence"; the "second category," confinement in a labor camp for ten years (in exceptional cases, for eight years).
22 In particular, Central Committee plena of June 1935, June and December 1936, February–March 1937 (see Getty and Naumov, *Road to Terror*).
23 A large selection of this correspondence is presented in Oleg Khlevniuk and Alexander Kvachonkin (eds.), *Bolshevitskoie Rukovodstvo. Perepiska, 1928–1941* (The Bolshevik leadership. Correspondence, 1928–41) (Moscow, 1999).

The struggle against "bureaucratism" and "cronyism" gradually developed, in 1936, into a "search for enemies."[24]

In the summer of 1936, while the first Moscow show trial of the "Trotskyist-Zinovievist Terrorist Center" was being staged, the Central Committee encouraged party members, in a top-secret letter of July 29 sent to all communist organizations, to denounce suspicious "Trotskyists" and "Zinovievists." This initiative ignited existing tensions; accusations and counteraccusations proliferated in many party organizations, leading to arrests, mainly directed, at that time, against former party members whose connections with past oppositions made their loyalty suspect.[25] Later in the year, other specific categories were targeted: factory managers, industrial specialists, and engineers, suspected of "sabotaging." Despite mounting tensions, the number of people sentenced in 1936 by "extrajudicial" organs remained comparable with the previous year's figures; according to the centralized NKVD statistical data, "only" 1,118 people were sentenced to the "supreme measure of punishment" and shot in 1936.[26] The "campaign of vigilance" launched by the party leaders at the Central Committee plenum of February–March 1937 extended considerably the range of the potential "enemies," as it warned party members in the first hand (and eventually all Soviet citizens) of the presence of traitors, spies, diversionists, and wreckers in their midst, and rallied them to uncover and denounce on the slightest pretext anyone considered as "suspicious," especially higher-ups, because Stalin had explained that "little people, simple party members . . . are often much closer to the truth than great party lords." This overtly populist campaign, which encouraged, within party cells, "self-criticism" and denunciation of "higher-ups," spread out in the months following the February–March 1937 Central Committee plenum. Nevertheless, only the determined intervention of the NKVD and of special envoys

---

24 Several recent studies focused on center-periphery political conflicts and regional aspects of the Great Purges: see Stephen Kotkin, *Magnetic Mountain* (Berkeley, 1995), esp. ch. 8; Robert Weinberg, "Purge and Politics in the Periphery: Birobidzhan in 1937," *Slavic Review* 52, 1 (1993): 13–27; Hiroaki Kuromiya, *Freedom and Terror in the Donbass: A Ukrainian-Russian Borderland, 1870s–1990s* (Cambridge, 1998), ch. 6; James Harris, *The Great Urals: Regionalism and the Evolution of the Soviet System* (Ithaca, 1999), ch. 6.

25 See David L. Hoffman, "The Great Terror on the Local Level: Purges in Moscow Factories, 1936–1938," in J. Arch Getty and Roberta T. Manning (eds.), *Stalinist Terror: New Perspectives* (Cambridge, 1993), 153–70; Harris, *Urals*.

26 In 1936, 274,670 persons were sentenced by extrajudicial organs (267,076 in 1935; 79,000 in 1934; 239,664 in 1933). The number of persons sentenced to death in 1936 was lower than in the previous years (1,229 in 1935; 2,056 in 1934; 2,154 in 1933; 2,728 in 1932; 10,651 in 1931; 20,201 in 1930). Source: "Krouglov figures" (see note 10).

from Moscow succeeded in breaking up the resistance of regional leadership cliques.[27]

The successful May–June 1937 attack against some of the "great party lords" (the "little Stalins," as they were called among the population) launched a vast purge of all political and economic bureaucracies, which lasted until the end of 1938. Widely publicized in the press, this campaign led to dozens of public show trials of local officials accused of having abused "little people." Many of these show trials were staged in rural areas: they had, in the words of Sheila Fitzpatrick, "something of the old 'Dizzy with Success' smell about them: that is, higher authorities responding to problems in the kolkhoz by shifting the blame to local officials."[28] At the same time, Stalin launched a vast purge of high-ranking Red Army officers, which started with the arrest, in May 1937, of Marshal Tukhachevsky and seven army generals. From May 1937 to September 1938, 35,000 officers were arrested or expelled from the Red Army. Around 11,000 were recalled in 1939–41. It is still unclear how many were executed.

Although proportionally less significant than has generally been believed,[29] the purge of the Red Army, notably at the higher levels, had disastrous effects on the Russo-Finnish conflict of 1939–40 and the initial phase of the war with Nazi Germany. Because the purge of party cadres was the first event of the Stalin era to be denounced, by Nikita Khruschev in his "Secret Speech" to the XXth Congress of the CPSU (February 24, 1956), it is one of the best-known aspects of the Great Terror. Recently declassified statistical data confirm the fragmentary information given by Nikita Khruschev on the purge of the nomenklatura between 1934 and 1939: thus, over 70 percent of the 32,900 officials listed on the Central Committee nomenklatura in 1939 had been appointed during the previous two years, in the place of arrested "enemies of the people."[30] As spectacular and politically important as it might appear, the arrest and execution of most

27 This process is described in Conquest's *Great Terror* (esp. ch. 8); on the example of the West Region, see Merle Fainsod, *Smolensk under Stalin's Rule* (Cambridge, 1965). It has been the subject of several monographs.
28 Sheila Fitzpatrick, *Stalin's Peasants: Resistance and Survival in the Russian Village after Collectivization* (Oxford, 1994), 297. According to Oleg Khlevniuk, between August and December 1937, the Politburo sent precise instruction on the holding of more than forty public show trials of local officials. See Oleg Khlevniuk, "The Objectives of the Great Terror, 1937–1938," in Julian Cooper et al. (eds.), *Soviet History, 1917–1953: Essays in Honour of R. W. Davies* (London, 1995), 158–76.
29 See Roger R. Reese, "The Red Army and the Great Purges," in Getty and Manning, *Stalinist Terror,* 199–202; Roger R. Reese, *Stalin's Reluctant Soldiers: A Social History of the Red Army, 1925–1941* (Lawrence, Kans. 1996); A. Cristiani and V. Michaleva (eds.), *Le repressioni degli anni trenta nell' Armata rossa* (Naples, 1999).
30 Rossiiskii Gosudarstvennyi Arkhiv Stolsial' no-Politicheskoi Istorii (RGASPI), Moscow, f.477/1/41/34–63.

of the members of the local nomenklatura represented nevertheless only a negligible proportion of the victims of the "Great Terror" – a few tens of thousands,[31] out of a total of at least 680,000 persons shot.[32]

In fact, the largest group (approximately 320,000) of people sentenced to be shot were those targeted by the "mass repressive operation" launched at the beginning of August 1937, after the direction of the NKVD had issued "Order no. 00447" (July 30, 1937) "concerning the punishment of former kulaks, criminals, and other anti-Soviet elements." The organization and implementation of this mass murder, the knowledge of which is still very fragmentary, throws light on three crucial issues: the part played respectively by the center and by local authorities; the "quota principle" and the dynamics of overfulfillment of quotas; the links between this "mass operation" and policing practices experimented with earlier during the decade against specific categories of the population.

On July 2, 1937, the Politburo issued a strictly secret resolution ordering regional party authorities to present, within five days, estimates of the number of "kulaks" and "criminals" that they wished to be "administratively arrested and executed after consideration of their case by a three-man commission [*troïka*]" specially set up for the purpose, and of the number of "less active but nevertheless hostile elements ... to be exiled."[33] In the following weeks, while *troïki* were established in all regions and territories across the USSR,[34] local officials responded by presenting precise estimates of the numbers of "kulaks" and "criminals" in their region to be shot or

31 In his "Secret Speech" to the delegates of the XXth Congress of the CPSU (February 24, 1956) Nikita Khruschev mentioned the existence of 383 lists of high-ranking officials and officers of the Red Army sentenced to death. Stalin's own signature, approving the sentence, appeared at the bottom of 362 lists, Molotov's signature on 373, Vorochilov's on 195, Kaganovich's on 191, Zhdanov's on 177, and Mikoyan's on 62. These lists totaled 44,000 names (see *Istocnik*, no. 1 [1995]: 117–30). Between January 1937 and November 1938, the Military Collegium of the Supreme Court of the USSR, which usually examined the cases of "important" people – party officials, Red Army officers, NKVD officials, factory managers, etc. – sentenced more than 36,000 people, of whom 30,500 received the death penalty (*Krasnaia Zvezda*, April 8, 1989, 1). Other judicial and party sources suggest a figure ranging between 40,000 and 60,000 victims among officials.

32 This figure reflects centralized NKVD statistics. It does not take into account "nonratified supplementary executions" and deaths during the preliminary instruction, resulting, in a number of cases, from torture, a widely used practice during these years. See note 12.

33 The text of this resolution was first published in *Trud*, no. 88 (June 4, 1992). English translation in Getty and Naumov, *Road to Terror*, 470–71.

34 These three-man commissions, proposed by regional authorities and individually approved by the Politburo, comprised, as a rule, the regional party first secretary, the chief of the regional NKVD, and the regional procurator. *Troïki* meted out an extremely perfunctory form of justice, because their main aim was to comply with resolutions and quotas sent out in advance. *Troïki* had existed during the civil war; they had been revived during collectivization and dekulakization, abolished in 1934. Since May 1935 there existed "ordinary police troïki" (*militseiskie troïki*), which had the right to expel "socially harmful elements" from towns and to sentence these people to five years of forced labor in a camp.

exiled. Produced in a matter of days, these figures roughly matched the figures of "suspect" individuals already under police (and not only NKVD) surveillance.[35] On July 30, N. Ezhov signed the operational order no. 00447 "concerning the punishment of former kulaks, criminals, and other anti-Soviet elements."[36] The operation was to begin between August 5 and August 15 and be completed within a period of four months. The categories subjected to punitive measures were larger than the categories initially set up ("kulaks" and "criminals") and a very wide range of "suspects" could fall into one of the vaguely specified groups of "enemies." These groups included "former kulaks who have returned home . . ., who have escaped from labor settlements . . ., who carry out anti-Soviet activities"; "members of anti-Soviet parties, former Whites, gendarmes, bureaucrats, reémigrés, sectarian activists, church officials and others, who are in hiding from punishment, who have escaped from places of confinement and who continue to carry out active anti-Soviet activities"; "criminals (bandits, robbers, recidivist thieves, professional contraband smugglers, recidivist swindlers, cattle and horse thieves) who are carrying out criminal activities or who are associated with the criminal underworld . . ., or who are at present kept under guard, and whose cases have been fully investigated but not yet considered by the judicial organs"; "criminal elements in camp and labor settlements who are carrying out criminal activities in them." All these "anti-Soviet elements" were to be broken down into two categories. People in the "first category" ("the most active of the above-mentioned elements") were to be "immediately arrested and, after consideration of their case by the *troïki,* shot." An extract of the *troïka's* minutes would be the only "legal" basis for the execution. People ascribed to the "second category" were "subject to arrest and to confinement in camps for a term ranging from 8 to 10 years."

Order no. 00447 then proceeded by establishing, for every region and republic, round-number quotas of persons subject to "punitive measures" in the first and in the second category. These quotas did not correlate with overall population figures; they only partially corresponded to the figures

---

35 Here are a few examples: the party leadership of Western Siberia sent in estimates of 6,600 "kulaks" and 4,200 "criminals" to be shot, with no initial estimate of exiles; the Orenbourg region party leadership sent in estimates of 1,200 "kulaks" and 520 "criminals" to be shot, 2,390 "kulaks" and 760 "criminals" to be exiled; in the Iaroslavl region, 453 "kulaks" and 232 "criminals" were to be shot, 873 "kulaks" and 392 "criminals" to be exiled. See Tsentr Khraneniia Sovremennoi Dokumentatsii (TsKhSD), Moscow, f.89, per.89, d.49 and 50.

36 First published in *Trud,* no. 88 (June 4, 1992). English translation in Getty and Naumov, *Road to Terror,* 473–80. A more complete version of Order no. 00447 (with quotas for regions not mentioned in Getty and Naumov, *Road to Terror*) is in A. I. Kokurin and N. V. Petrov (eds.), *Goulag, 1917–1960* (Moscow, 2000), 96–104.

presented by regional authorities during the previous weeks.[37] They rather seem to have reflected a focus "on sensitive economic areas where the regime believed the concentration of 'enemies' to be the greatest, or where in previous trials and campaigns the greatest number of oppositionists had been unmasked."[38] The highest quotas concerned Moscow and its region (35,000 persons, of whom 5,000 to be shot), western Siberia (17,000, of whom 5,000 to be shot), southern Urals including the Sverdlovsk and Cheliabinsk regions (16,000, of whom 5,500 to be shot), Leningrad and its region (14,000, of whom 4,000 were to be shot), Azov–Black Sea territory (13,000, of whom 5,000 were to be shot). Ukraine had a quota of 28,800 (of whom 8,000 were to be shot). The total figures amounted to 269,100 persons, of whom 75,950 were to be shot. In fact, although initially planned for four months, "operation no. 00447" lasted fourteen months: approximately 650,000 persons were arrested, of whom 320,000 (or 49.3 percent) were shot.[39]

I now briefly examine three important features of this mass crime: the quota principle; the implementation, in the years preceding the Great Terror, of specific policing practices against "socially harmful elements," as a background of the "mass operations" of 1937–38; the dynamic of "overfulfillment" of quotas which led to a fourfold increase of death sentences with regard to the initial targets.

The round-number quotas of Order no. 00447 were characteristic of the "figure mania" which had spread over every sector of the economy, politics, and social life in the 1930s. They reflected the same kind of "social engineering" that produced dekulakization quotas, five-year plans for the complete eradication of malaria, ambitious graphs concerning the "all-Union liquidation of illiteracy." In matters of "social engineering," the round-number quotas of Order no. 00447 were not unprecedented: at the beginning of 1930, the Politburo commission in charge of dekulakization and the State Political Administration (GPU) headquarters had fixed dekulakization quotas.

On January 18, 1930, Genrikh Iagoda, the chief of the GPU, issued, in compliance with a secret decision taken by the Politburo, a directive addressed to all regional GPU heads, ordering them to send him an estimate of the number of kulaks liable to dekulakization in the area within their

---

37 In some regions (as the Uzbek SSR, Orenburg region, Western Siberian territory, Ordjonikidze region, etc.) the precise local numbers proposed to be shot after the Politburo resolution of July 2, 1937, were higher than the round-number quotas of Order no. 00447. In others (Iaroslavl region, Armenian SSR, etc.), they were smaller.
38 Getty and Naumov, *Road to Terror*, 472.
39 Okhotin and Roginskii, "Iz Istori Nemetskoĭ Operatsii NKVD 1937–1938," 60.

jurisdiction.[40] Two weeks later, after having received more or less precise information from local GPU authorities, Genrikh Iagoda issued Order no. 44/21 giving, for each region, territory, and republic of the USSR, round-number quotas of dekulakization. This directive singled out two categories of kulaks. Kulaks "of the first category" – 60,000 individuals – defined as "engaged in counterrevolutionary activities" or "particularly vicious" (!) were to be arrested and transferred to GPU camps or executed if they put up any sign of resistance.[41] Kulaks "of the second category" – 120,000 families, at the initial phase of the operation – defined as "showing less active opposition, but nonetheless arch-exploiters with an innate tendency to destabilize the regime," were to be arrested and deported with their families to remote regions of the country (Siberia, Kazakhstan, Urals, far North).[42] The list of kulaks in the first category was to be drawn up by the GPU, on the basis of information gathered over the years on "anti-Soviet elements" (these included not only "wealthy" peasants but all sorts of "dubious" people, such as village priests, "police officers from the tsarist regime," small traders, and ex-landowners, members of the "village intelligentsia," who might have been, in the past, members of the "White movement," of "bourgeois" or socialist-revolutionary parties, etc.). Lists of kulaks in the second category were made in situ at the recommendation of local party and other village activists. These practices naturally opened the way to innumerable abuses, looting, and settling of old scores, as dekulakization brigades not only fulfilled but overfulfilled the required quotas.

Far from being the planned operation based on firm quotas the GPU headquarters had dreamed of, "dekulakization" developed as a chaotic and largely uncontrolled process. GPU top officials continually complained about local officials arresting "not the right kind of people" – which was hardly surprising, since no one had ever defined who was a "kulak"![43]

---

40 Directive no. 776 of January 18, 1930. See N. Ivnitski, *Kollektivisatsia i Razkulacivanie* (Collectivization and dekulakization) (Moscow, 1994), 102–10.

41 In addition, their families were to be deported and all their property confiscated. See Ivnitski, *Kollektivisatsia i Razkulacivanie*, 112–14.

42 The special commission from the Politburo, presided over by V. Molotov, that was in charge of dekulakization defined, in the course of the events, a third category. Kulaks in the third category classified by local activists as "loyal to the regime" were to be transferred to the peripheral regions of the districts in which they lived, "outside the collectivized zones, on land requiring improvement." The number of kulaks of the third category is estimated at 400,000 families (between 1.5 and 2 million people).

43 Among innumerable examples, see, Iagoda's remarks at the bottom of the report dated February 15, 1930, which detailed the categories of individuals arrested: "The regions of the Northeast and of Leningrad have not understood the orders, or at least are pretending not to have understood them. They must be forced to understand. We are not trying to clear the territory of popes, shopkeepers, and 'others.' If they write 'others,' that means they don't even know who it is they are arresting. There will be plenty of time to dispose of shopkeepers, popes, and religious activists. What we

Deportation operations were characterized by a complete lack of coordination between the place of departure and the destination, which often resulted in an unprecedented phenomenon of "abandonment in deportation," deportees being often "settled" – that is abandoned – without any shelter on the open steppes or in the middle of marshy forests. This provided no economic benefit for the state, although one of the ideas behind dekulakization had been the planned colonization by deportees of regions of the country that were inhospitable but rich in natural resources.[44] It was not until March 1931 that a special commission, directly attached to the Politburo, was established in order to "stop the dreadful mess of the deportation of manpower" and to reorganize all the mechanisms dealing with the deportees. At that time, initial quotas of dekulakization had been overfulfilled threefold, and the authorities had to manage over a million and a half deportees. From this experience, the party leadership and the GPU drew two lessons: it was more efficient to rely on police records than on denunciations coming from "activists" of all sorts; the implementation of mass deportation as a means of "getting rid of" a stigmatized group was a tricky operation: hundreds of thousands of "dekulakized" escaped from the "special settlements" to which they had been assigned. More expedited and radical measures should be enforced in order to eliminate "once and for ever" socially harmful elements.

The radicalization of policing practices against a wide range of "formers" and "socially harmful elements" in the years preceding the Great Terror provides a bridge between dekulakization and the "mass repressive operations" launched during the summer of 1937.[45] From 1932 onward, fear of mass "social disorder," resulting from the upheavals of forced collectivization, famine, and massive and uncontrolled migration of millions of peasants into towns, became the major obsession of party and police authorities. The newly created passport system (1933) for town dwellers was largely used by the police, both the regular one (*militsia*) and the GPU, to gather information, check social backgrounds, and keep records of all people who had been refused a passport. The "passportization campaign" (1933–34) enforced social quarantine on major cities; hundreds of thousands of "former

are trying to do now is to strike at the heart of the problem by weeding out the kulaks and kulak counterrevolutionaries." See V. P. Danilov and A. Berelowich, "Les documents de la VCK-OGPU-NKVD sur les campagnes soviétiques, 1918–1937," *Cahiers du monde russe* 35 (1994): 671.

44 On "abandonment in deportation," see Nicolas Werth, "Déplacés spéciaux et colons de travail dans la société stalinienne," *Vingtième Siècle*, no. 54 (April–June 1997): 34–50.

45 This point has been developed by Hagenloh, "Socially Harmful," and by David Shearer, "Crime and Social Disorder in Stalin's Russia. A Reassessment of the Great Retreat and the Origins of Mass Repression," *Cahiers du monde russe* 39, 1–2 (1998): 119–48.

people," "marginals," and "socially harmful elements" were rounded up, expelled, or deported.[46] In May 1935 special police *troïki*[47] were established to deal, in a swift extrajudicial procedure, with all "socially harmful elements" liable to deportation or confinement (up to five years) in a labor camp.[48] The category "socially harmful elements" included a wide range of people such as persons with previous criminal convictions, persons with no definite place of work, persons caught in urban areas without a proper residence permit (the so-called "passport violators"), persons who had left the "special settlement" they had been assigned to, "professional" beggars, vagrants, ex-kulaks, "speculators," "hooligans," persons "having ties with the criminal world." In just over one and a half years, police *troïki* sentenced over 260,000 people.[49] Thus emerged a permanent strata of social outcasts and expellees. They could not be reintegrated into Soviet society and were perceived not only as "socially harmful elements" but as the major cause of public disorder and as a politically dangerous group, as a potential fifth column in the event of war and invasion of the USSR.[50]

Among these outcasts, ex-kulaks were the largest group. In 1935–36 the ultimate fate of the deported ex-kulaks became a burning issue. Despite the often-repeated ban on their leaving the places to which they had been assigned, a growing number of deportees fled from the "special settlements" (according to police statistics, as many as 600,000 had "vanished" between

---

46 A report of August 13,1934, summing up the main achievements of the "passportization campaign" stated that 27 million passports had been issued to city dwellers; around 385,000 people had been refused passports, "but to this figure should be added all those who preferred to leave the towns, knowing that they would in any case be refused a passport." Also, 630,000 "violators of the passport system" had been seized by the police. Among them, over 175,000 had been expelled from "passportized areas" and over 65,000 had been sentenced to camp or deportation in extrajudicial proceedings as "declassed," "criminal," or "socially harmful elements" (Gosudarstvennyi Arkhiv Rossiiskoi Federatsii [GARF], Moscow, f.1235, op.141, d.1650). This document was first published in N. Werth and G. Moullec, *Rapports secrets soviétiques. La société russe dans les documents confidentiels, 1921–1991* (Paris, 1995), 45–47. Between June 1934 and November 1935 another 265,000 "socially harmful elements" were removed from major urban areas, 75,000 of them from the cities of Moscow and Leningrad (Hagenloh, "Socially Harmful," 293). On the "passportization campaign" and "purges of the cities," see Nicolas Werth, "A State against Its People," in Courtois et al., *Black Book of Communism*, 175–78.

47 *Militseiskie troïki*, who were different from the GPU *troïki*, were established during collectivization, suppressed in July 1934 as the political police was being reorganized, and renewed in July 1937.

48 GARF, f.8131, op.38, d.6.   49 Popov, "Gosudarstvennyi terror."

50 This was clear, for example, from G. Iagoda's speech to regional police chiefs in April 1935: "For us the most honored matter is the battle with counter-revolution.... But in today's situation, a hooligan, a bandit, a robber – isn't this the most genuine counter-revolutionary? ... In our nation – a nation, where the construction of socialism has been victorious, where there is no unemployment, where every citizen of the Soviet Union is presented with the complete possibility to work and live honorably, any criminal act by its nature can be nothing other than a manifestation of class struggle" (quoted in Hagenloh, "Socially Harmful," 299).

1931 and 1936).[51] Many of these runaways, who had no papers and were homeless, joined the gangs of socially marginal elements and petty criminals that roamed on the outskirts of most of the big cities. For the authorities, these marginals were, in the words of Ezhov, "the chief instigators of every kind of anti-Soviet crime and sabotage." In the weeks preceding the promulgation of Order no. 00447, the NKVD "discovered" in several industrial areas of the Urals and western Siberia "counterrevolutionary insurrectionist organizations among exiled kulaks."[52] Significantly, some of the regions particularly targeted by Order no. 00447 – western Siberia, southern Urals, the Far East, the Azov–Black Sea territory – were precisely the ones that had the largest concentration of deportees, expellees, and other social outcasts driven out of "passportized areas" in the previous years. The "mass operations" launched in the summer of 1937 under Order no. 00447 were to be the final and the most radical stage of the campaigns against "socially harmful elements," the last blow against these previously identified social outcasts. In the words of a local police official, Order no. 00447 was carried out as a "cleansing of cities and surrounding areas." "The basic instruction was to produce as many cases as possible, to formulate them as quickly as possible, with maximum simplification of investigation. As regards the quota of cases, the NKVD chief demanded the inclusion of all those sentenced and all those who had been picked up, even if at the moment of their seizure they had not committed any sort of concrete crime."[53] If the list of names on file was not long enough, police organized sweeps and round-ups of markets or railway stations where marginals and other social outcasts were likely to be found. In order to fulfill (or overfulfill) the quotas, the NKVD – and regular police – made a pretext of every incident for arresting the required number of people: in Turkmenia, the local NKVD used the pretext of an industrial fire to arrest everyone who was on the site;[54] in Sverdlovsk, the local authorities alleged as a pretext forest fires, "set up by white-guard kulak groups of wreckers and terrorists," to claim for "a supplementary quota of 3,000, of whom 2,000 [are] in the first category."[55]

The development of a dynamic leading to "overfulfillment of quotas" was certainly one of the most remarkable features of "mass repressive operations"

---

51 Inspections carried out in the autumn of 1936 revealed situations that were intolerable in the eyes of the authorities: in the Arkhangelsk region, for example, of the 89,700 deportees who had been assigned residency there, a mere 37,000 remained.

52 TsKhSD, f.89, op.43, d.48. 53 Quoted in Hagenloh, "Socially Harmful," 301.

54 J. Arch Getty, G. Rittersporn, and V. Zemskov, "Les victimes de la répression pénale dans l'URSS d'avant-guerre," *Revue des études slaves* 65 (1993): 657.

55 TsKhSD, f.89, op.73, d.155 (Telegram from Vakulin, First Secretary of the Sverdlovsk Party Organization, to Stalin, September 27, 1938).

like dekulakization or the eradication campaign launched by Order no. 00447.[56] For the latter operation, recently declassified top-secret correspondence between the Politburo and local authorities reveals, in chilling bureaucratic transcripts, the dynamics and mechanisms of a mass crime.[57] Planned orders from the center plus bureaucratic reflexes naturally spurred local officials, many of whom had just recently been promoted, to anticipate and surpass the desires of superiors further up the hierarchy and the directives that arrived from Moscow. Already by the end of August 1937 the Politburo was assailed with numerous requests for the initial quotas to be raised. From August 28 to December 15, 1937, the Politburo ratified various proposals for increases concerning 22,500 individuals "in the first category" (to be shot) and 16,800 "in the second category" (ten years in camp). The execution of thousands of people were ratified in short Politburo resolutions drafted as follows: "Approve the proposal of the Altaï territory Party Committee for a supplement of 4,000 in the first category and of 4,500 in the second category."[58] On January 31, 1938, the Politburo approved a further large increase of 57,200, 48,000 of whom were to be executed.[59]

All operations related to Order no. 00447 (which originally were planned to last four months) were extended until March 15, 1938; but once again the local authorities, who had generally been purged several times in the previous year and whose new staff were eager to show their zeal, demanded a further increase of the quotas. On February 17 the Politburo took a decision "increasing the quota for the NKVD of the Ukrainian SSR by thirty thousand."[60] During the next seven months, the Politburo ratified supplementary quotas for more than 100,000 people. The proportion of those sentenced "in the first category" by the *troïki,* who would generally see hundreds of cases in a single day, grew significantly from one-quarter (as planned in the initial quotas set up at the end of July 1937) to one-half of those trapped in Order no. 00447. The explanation for this evolution is amply documented in the correspondence between the center and the provinces: prisons were simply overcrowded, and the setting up of new camps too slow, in spite of provisions taken by the central authorities to expand the camp system.[61] On

56 I developed this point in "A State against Its People," esp. 146–58.
57 TsKhSD, f.89, op.73.
58 TsKhSD, f. 89, op.73, d.103 (October 20, 1937).
59 See Getty and Naumov, *Road to Terror,* 518–19.
60 Ibid., 519.
61 See, e.g., Lavrentii Beria's letter to Stalin (November 30, 1937) explaining that of the 12,000 arrested in Georgia, more than 5,000 were "crowding the prisons . . . because of lengthy judicial procedures," and asking for "swift procedures" and "implementation of the first category" to any "counterrevolutionary convicted of terrorism, spying or diversion" (TskhSD, f.89, op.73, d.108).

September, 21, 1937, the Politburo had, for example, allocated 30 million rubles for the organization of seven large timber camps, with a total capacity of 90,000 inmates.[62] In 1938 the camp population increased by 700,000; in spite of the creation of many new camps, overcrowding was such that the mortality rate in the camps jumped by 200 percent, in comparison with that of the previous year.[63] In this situation, the obvious solution, for the NKVD, was to have a certain number of people in prisons or camps shot.

On February 1, 1938, the Politburo took the following measures "to reduce the inmate population of the Far Eastern camps": "An additional twelve thousand prisoners convicted of espionage, terror, subversion, treason, insurgency and banditry, as well as career criminals ... are to receive immediate punishment of the first category."[64] Among many documents revealing practices of the kind, the following telegram sent by Lev Mekhlis, one of the organizers of the purge in the Red Army, to Stalin on October 28, 1938, is another sinister example of the bureaucratic hidden transcripts of that time leading to mass crime: "Left Chita on the 27th. In Ulan-Ude, I met with Ignatiev, the First Secretary of the Party Regional Committee, and with Tkachev, Chief of the local NKVD. They told me that they had already spent all their 00447 allowance, but that there were still over 2,000 elements in prisons, whose time limit has been over long ago. All these elements are counterrevolutionary kulaks, members of bourgeois parties, clerical activists. The instruction of their case is over, prisons are overcrowded.... They asked me a further allowance for 2,500, a demand that I hereby report to you."[65]

Order no. 00447 was only one among a dozen other "mass operations" launched in the summer of 1937. Ten days before Order no. 00447 was issued, Stalin scribbled, during the Politburo meeting of July 20, 1937, a short note: "ALL Germans working on our military, semimilitary and chemical factories, on electric stations and building sites, in ALL regions are ALL to be arrested."[66] Five days later, on July 25, N. Ezhov sent to all regional NKVD headquarters Order no. 00439. In a long preamble, Ezhov explained that "the German Military Head-Quarters and the Gestapo have

---

62 TsKhSD, f.89, op.73, d.28.
63 A total of 90,000 persons died in the labor camps in 1938. In 1937 the death toll in the labor camps was just over 25,000. See V. Zemskov, *Argumenty i Fakty*, no. 45 (1989): 6.
64 TsKhSD, f.89,op.73, d.124.   65 TsKhSD, f.89, op.73, d.157.
66 This note (Arkhiv Presidenta Rossiiskoi Federatsii [APRF], f.3, Moscow, op.58, d.254a, l.82) is in the file of the top-secret Politburo resolutions dated July 20, 1937. See N. Okhotin and A. B. Roginskii, "Iz Istorii 'nemetskoï operatsii' NKVD 1937–1938" (History of the "German Operation" of the NKVD, 1937–1938), in I. L. Scherbakova (ed.), *Nakazannyi Narod* (The punished people) (Moscow, 1999), 35–74. This article, based on previously inaccessible material from the Presidential and State Security Archives is the most complete account, to this day, of the "German operation."

organized a large network of spies and wreckers operating primarily in defense industries, on the railways, and in other strategic sectors of the national economy." The head of the NKVD ordered the immediate arrest of all Germans employed (or having been employed) in defense factories, on the railroads and in "other sectors of the national economy." But "Germans" were not the only target: Order no. 00439 prescribed the arrest of all Soviet citizens "having, or having had, ties," in one way or another, with "German spies, wreckers, and terrorists."[67] This, of course, considerably widened the scope of the operation, since no more than 4,000 German citizens were registered in the Soviet Union in 1937: among them, about 800 (the great majority of whom worked as engineers in different branches of Soviet industry) were arrested, sentenced, and expelled to Germany.[68] But the total number of people arrested in the process of the "German operation," which lasted until November 1938 (though initially planned for only three months), was 56,787. Among them, 55,005 were sentenced by extrajudicial organs: 41,898 (or 76 percent) "in the first category" (to be shot), 13,107 "in the second category" (five to ten years in camp).[69]

On August 11, 1937, following a Politburo top-secret resolution taken two days earlier, N. Ezhov issued another directive, Order no. 00485, aimed at "the complete liquidation of local branches of the Polish Military Organization and its networks of spies, wreckers, and terrorists in industry, transport, and agriculture." This "Polish operation" – by far the largest of all the "national operations" – would lead, in the next fourteen months, to the arrest of 143,810 people. Of this number, 139,885 were sentenced by extrajudicial organs, of whom nearly 80 percent (111,091) were "in the first category."[70]

The third large "national operation," launched by Order no. 00593 of September 20, 1937, targeted another "suspicious" group of people. The so-called Harbintsy were former personnel (engineers, employees, railway workers) of the Chinese Eastern Railway, who, as Soviet citizens, had been resettled in the USSR after the sale of the Chinese Eastern Railway to Japan in 1935. They were accused of "terrorist, diversionary, and spying activities on behalf of the Japanese services."[71] Six other "national operations" – the "Finnish," "Estonian," "Rumanian," "Bulgarian," "Greek," and "Chinese" operations – followed in October 1937, each targeting a "group of spies,

---

67 Okhotin and Roginskii, "Iz Istorii 'nemetskoï operatsii' NKVD 1937–1938," 36–37.
68 Ibid., 49.   69 Ibid., 66.
70 See Petrov and Roginskii, "Pol'skaia operatsia NKVD 1937–1938," 22–43. This article is the most complete account, to this day, of the "Polish operation."
71 See A. Suturin, *Delo kraevogo masstaba* (A case of regional importance) (Khabarovsk, 1991).

wreckers, and diversionists" working for hostile foreign countries.[72] According to centralized NKVD statistics, from July 1937 to November 1938, 335,513 persons were sentenced by extrajudicial organs in the course of the implementation of the so-called national operations. Among them, 247,157 (or 73.6 percent) were shot[73] – a proportion considerably higher than in the 00447 operation, in the process of which 49.3 percent were sentenced "in the first category."

The launching of the "national operations" was, even more directly than in the case of the 00447 operation, related to Stalin's reading of rearguard uprisings against the Republican regime in Spain during the civil war.[74] Stalin was convinced that hostile powers such as Germany, Poland, and Japan would organize, in the ever more probable event of war, the same kind of rearguard uprisings, resorting to anyone who had had some sort of connection with foreign countries, in order to form a "fifth column of diversionists and wreckers."

In their organization, implementation, and targets, "national operations" had several specific characteristics with regard to the 00447 operation. In the following brief outline, I focus on the two most important national operations, the "Polish" and the "German" one, for which the available information, although still very fragmentary, allows a first approach.

Whereas instructions laid out in Order no. 00447 needed no special preamble, according to N. Petrov and A. Roginskii – for NKVD officials, everything was clear, and the instructions they received merely showed that Moscow was launching the "last blow" against a well-known enemy – Order no. 00485 starting the "Polish operation" required a long explanation.[75] The targets were indeed uncommon: the thirty-page "secret letter" attached to Order no. 00485 explained, in full details, how, for the past twenty years, an immense organization set up by the Polish army headquarters, the so-called Polish Military Organization, had infiltrated many crucial spheres in Soviet

72 One should mention here three other "national operations" of a different kind, launched against Koreans living in the Vladivostok area and Kurds and Iranians living along the Persian-Soviet border in September–October 1937. Aimed at "ethnic cleansing" of border regions, these mass operations, which resulted in deportation (as in the case of 172,000 Koreans, deported to Kazakhstan) or expulsion (as in the case of approximately 25,000 Kurds and Iranians), were different from operations resulting in the mass murder of individuals targeted for their supposed "links" with hostile foreign countries.

73 Okhotin and Roginskii, "Iz Istorii 'nemetskoi operatsii' NKVD 1937–1938," 69.

74 This point has been convincingly argued by Oleg Khlevniuk, on the basis of Stalin's correspondence with Soviet diplomats and NKVD officials in Spain in the months preceding the "Great Terror." See O. Khlevniuk, "The Influence of the Foreign Context on the Mechanisms of Terror," paper presented at the International Conference on La Russia nell' eta delle guerre (1914–1945). Verso un nuovo paradigma, Cortona, October 24–27, 1997.

75 Petrov and Roginskii, "Pol'skaia operatsia NKVD 1937–1938," 23.

politics and the economy, starting with the Polish Communist Party and the Polish section of the Komintern, and up to defense industries or large collective farms in the Ukraine. Order no. 00485 (as well as all the other directives concerning "national mass operations") did not fix any quotas of people to sentence "in the first" or "second category" but indicated several categories of people to arrest. In the case of the "Polish operation," these were:

- All Polish ex–prisoners of war, who had remained in the USSR.
- All Polish refugees settled in the USSR.
- All Polish political exiles.
- All ex-members of the Polish socialist party and of other Polish political parties.
- All "antisoviet and nationalistic elements" from districts and regions of the USSR where there existed a Polish community.
- All Soviet citizens having had some sort of contact with Polish diplomatic, consular, military, commercial, or economic representatives in the USSR.

In the case of the "German operation," the targeted categories were much the same: German ex-prisoners of war, who had remained in the USSR; German political exiles and refugees from Germany, especially workers and engineers who had come from Germany in the 1920s and in the beginning of the 1930s and had taken Soviet citizenship; "antisoviet and nationalistic elements" from districts and regions of the USSR where there existed a German community. To these "standard categories," local officials of the NKVD were encouraged to add "specific groups," which they did. In Kharkov, for example, L. Reikhman, the newly appointed head of the NKVD, ordered the following "additional" categories of people to be arrested, in the process of the "Polish operation":

- All ex–agents of the NKVD "Foreign Department" having been in charge of "Polish affairs."
- All informants of the NKVD "specialized in Polish affairs."
- All "clerical elements" having, or having had, some kind of connection with Poland.
- All Soviet citizens having "family or other suspect ties" in Poland.[76]

In Gorki, the local head of the NKVD decided to add to the "standard categories" of the "German operation," which were "too thin" in the area within his jurisdiction, another group consisting of "ex-prisoners of World

---

76 Okhotin and Roginskii, "Iz Istorii 'nemetskoï operatsii' NKVD 1937–1938," 53.

War I having been in captivity in Germany, recruited by German secret services to organize terrorist and spying activities" (441 persons were arrested in this category under Order no. 00439 in Gorky region).[77] In Sverdlovsk, the NKVD chief D. Dmitriev decided, for lack of "proper suspects" for the "German operation," to arrest thousands of Ukrainian and Russian deportees. Thus, Sverdlovsk region could boast an excellent score – 4,379 individuals arrested in operations implementing Order no. 00439, or 8 percent of the overall figure of the "German operation" (but out of these 4,379, only 122 were of German origin!).[78] As the fate of the arrested depended entirely on the zeal of local NKVD bosses, the chance of being caught and the probability of being sentenced "in the first category" varied considerably: in Armenia, 31 percent of those trapped in "national operations" were shot; in Vologda region, 46 percent; in Bielorussia, 88 percent. Krasnodar territory, Novossibirsk, and Orenbourg regions had the highest rate of "first category" victims: respectively 94 percent, 94.8 percent and 96.4 percent![79]

The case of people arrested under one of these "national operations" was swiftly examined by local *troïka* or *dvoïka* (a two-man commission comprising the NKVD chief and the procurator), who decided what punishment should be applied to the accused: the "first category" (death sentence) or the "second category" (eight to ten years in camp). The verdict was to be confirmed by Moscow, that is, by Ezhov or Vychinski (the general procurator of the USSR). Each case examined by the local *troïka* or *dvoïka* was summed up in a few lines, giving minimal information on the identity of the accused, his alleged crime, and the proposed punishment. These short abstracts were copied in a special album. When the album was full, it was sent "for approval" to Moscow, with a special NKVD messenger. Of course, neither Ezhov nor Vychinski had time to countersign every record, because each album contained several hundred cases. The records were countersigned (and the verdict of the *troïka* or the *dvoïka* thus confirmed) by high-ranking NKVD officials, who glanced through the album, ratifying the sentence in 99 percent of the cases. Ezhov or Vychinski signed only the final page of the album. In spite of this swift procedure, albums got stuck in Moscow: in July 1938, more than 100,000 cases (several hundred albums) piled up in the headquarters of the NKVD. Meanwhile, prisons all over the country were overcrowded with people waiting for their sentences to be confirmed. In order to put an end to this situation, the Politburo

77 Ibid., 55.   78 Ibid., 65.
79 Petrov and Roginskii, "Pol'skaia operatsia NKVD 1937–1938," 33.

decided, on September 15, 1938, to abolish the "album procedure" (as it was called in NKVD circles) and to set up, in every region, territory, and republic, "special *troïki*," whose decisions, as those of the extrajudicial organs implementing Order no. 00447, would not require confirmation by central authorities. These "special *troïki*" were to complete the examination of all cases related to the different "national operations" before November 15. During these two months, over 105,000 people were sentenced by the "special *troïki*," of whom over 72,000 were shot and only 137 released.[80]

We do not know precisely who was trapped in the "national operation." For the "Polish" and the "German" operations, NKVD central statistics, discovered by N. Okhotin, A. Roginskii, and N. Petrov, give information on the number of people arrested and sentenced in the different regions of the USSR. Not surprisingly, the largest group (40 percent of all people arrested in the process of the "Polish operation"; 39 percent of all people arrested in the process of the "German operation") came from the Ukraine, and in particular from its western border districts, where a large Polish community and a smaller German one lived.[81] Tens of thousands of peasants, industry and railway workers, employees and engineers, were arrested for the reason that they lived and worked "too close by the enemy." For the same reason, Bielorussian provinces gave 17 percent of the arrested under "Order no. 00485." Surprisingly, at first sight, western Siberia, southern Urals, northern Caucasus, Kazakhstan, and the Far East gave high figures of arrested people:[82] in these unruly regions, with large numbers of deportees and social outcasts and high quotas of "antisoviet" and "socially harmful elements" to "repress," local NKVD officials tended to fill in "national lines" (another term of police jargon) with their usual victims, who had little in common with those targeted by Order nos. 00439, 00485, or 00593.

A remarkable feature of the "national operations" should be underlined: until May 1938 the NKVD leadership did not seem concerned by the ethnic origin of those arrested;[83] information concerning their nationality and

80 Okhotin and Roginskii, "Iz Istorii 'nemetskoï operatsii' NKVD 1937–1938," 62.
81 According to the 1937 General Census, 656,220 Soviet citizens were Polish by nationality. Among them, 417,613 lived in the Ukrainian SSR, 119,881 in the Bielorussian SSR, 82,078 in the RSFSR.
82 For the "Polish operation," the highest figures (Ukraine and Bielorussia excluded) came from Novossibirsk region (7,444), Leningrad region (7,404), Sverdlovsk region (5988), Tcheliabinsk region (2,693), Krasnoiarsk region (2,269), Krasnodar territory (1,916), Rostov/Don region (1,478); for the "German" operation, the highest figures (Ukraine excluded) came from Sverdlovsk region (4,379), the Altaï territory (3,171), Leningrad region (2,919), Krasnodar territory (2,895), Novossibirsk region (2,645), Tcheliabinsk region (1,626).
83 On May 16, 1938, a special directive signed by Ezhov ordered local NKVD officials to mention in their reports and statistics the nationality of the people arrested and sentenced. This directive was related to an important change in ascribing nationality to Soviet citizens, introduced one month earlier, by the circular letter no. 65 of the NKVD, dated April 2, 1938. According to this text,

ethnic origin was systematically collected only after September 1938, when "special *troïki*" were set up to "finish off" the "national operations." Thus, we know that among the 36,768 individuals sentenced under Order no. 00485 ("Polish operation") by the "special *troïki*" between September and November 1938, Poles and Soviet citizens of Polish origin represented 55 percent of the total, Bielorussians 15 percent, Ukrainians 13 percent, Russians 9 percent, Jews 4 percent.[84] According to N. Okhotin and A. Roginski, Poles and Soviet citizens of Polish origin represented about 70 percent of the 140,000 persons sentenced under Order no. 00485 (i.e., 98,000 persons); during the Great Terror, approximately 120,000 Poles and Soviet citizens of Polish origin were arrested and sentenced. With one-fifth of its total group repressed, Soviet citizens of Polish origin paid the heaviest toll of all ethnic minorities forming the "Great Soviet family."[85] Soviet citizens of German origin represented 69 percent of the 55,000 persons sentenced under Order no. 00439 (i.e., 38,000 people); during the Great Terror, approximately 72,000 Soviet citizens of German origin were arrested and sentenced (i.e., 5 percent of the Soviet Germans).[86] A remarkable feature should be stressed at this point: very few Soviet Germans living in the Autonomous Republic of the Volga Germans (by far the largest community of Soviet citizens of German origin) were arrested in the course of the "German operation:"[87] obviously, ethnicity as such was not the prime criterion, as it would be two or three years later, when entire ethnic groups would be deported (among them, all Soviet Germans): in 1937–38, the Stalinist leadership and the NKVD were after all those who might have had some sort of connection or "suspect ties" with hostile foreign countries – Poland, Germany, Japan in the first place.

On November 17, 1938, the Politburo issued a top-secret decision abolishing all *troïki*, stopping all mass operations, and sharply criticizing "major deficiencies and distortions" in the work of the NKVD. According to the

nationality could no longer be ascribed on the sole basis of the declaration made by the applicant, stating he considered himself Russian, Ukrainian, Polish, Jew, German, etc. Every passport holder had to bring proof of his parent's nationality or ethnic origins; on this basis, he was ascribed a nationality by the passport-issuing authority.

84 Petrov and Roginskii, "Iz Istorii 'nemetskoï operatsii' NKVD 1937–1938," 37.

85 See note 81.

86 According to the 1937 General Census, there were 1,151,000 Soviet citizens of German nationality.

87 A total of 1,068 were arrested under "Order 00439"; a further 5,630 were arrested under "Order 00447" as "socially harmful elements." The percentage of people arrested in the Autonomous Republic of the Volga Germans was considerably lower than the average. In 1937–38, Soviet citizens of German origin living in the Autonomous Soviet Republic of the Volga Germans seem to have been considered as "better integrated" in the Soviet system than individuals of German origin scattered in "sensitive" border areas or in industrial towns. See A. German, *Istoria Respubliki Nemtsev Povoljia* (History of the Volga German Republic) (Moscow, 1996), 223–29.

Politburo resolution (sent only to a few selected party, police, and judiciary officials), "these intolerable defects[88] had occurred because enemies of the people who had wormed their way into the NKVD and into the procuracy attempted with every means at their disposal to cut off the NKVD and the procuracy from party organs, to evade the party's control and leadership, and thereby to make it easier for themselves and their confederates to continue their anti-Soviet, subversive activities."[89]

Four days later, Ezhov resigned from his post of people's commissar of the interior and head of the NKVD; in *Pravda's* terse announcement for the general public, Ezhov's resignation was due to "health reasons." Enemies were still wandering about. The NKVD, headed by Lavrentii Beria, an experienced tchekist, remained on duty. Mass repressions ended in the way they had started – by a secret resolution taken, at the highest level, by Stalin and his closest associates. Mass operations had been secret; their end was not to be publicized, and "NKVD deficiencies" were not to be discussed.

By its scope, its ruthlessness, the numbers of people trapped in the "whirlwind" of repression, arrested, sent to camp, or shot, the Great Terror of 1937–38 is indeed a unique event in the course of the short Soviet period of Russian history – even if this mass crime was largely surpassed, in death tolls, by other specific forms of murderous policies implemented by the Soviet state, which paved the way to the last major European peacetime famine – that of 1932–33 in the Ukraine, northern Caucasus, and Kazakhstan, with its 5 to 6 million victims.[90]

The Great Terror was not a single, unitary phenomenon. It was not merely another, harsher, *political* purge, related to previous party purges. It was also, and foremost, a radical, murderous form of *social* engineering, relevant to practices of mass deportation, policing, categorization, ascription, and cleansing experimented with during the 1930s. The starting point was not Kirov's murder;[91] it was forced collectivization and dekulakization. As Pasternak acutely noted, in his *Doctor Zhivago*, the "unprecedented cruelty

---

88 The Politburo resolution underlined two major defects in the work of the NKVD: "Officials of the NKVD had become unaccustomed to a meticulous, systematic work with agents and informers and had come to adopt a simplified method for conducting the investigation of cases, to such an extent that right up until the last moment they were raising questions concerning the so-called 'quotas' imposed on the carrying out of mass arrests.... Second, a major deficiency in the work of the NKVD has been the deeply entrenched simplified procedures for investigation, during which, as a rule, the investigator is satisfied with obtaining from the accused a confession of guilt and totally fails to concern himself with corroborating this confession with the necessary documents." See Getty and Naumov, *The Road to Terror*, 533–34.

89 Ibid., 535.

90 I developed this point in my "State against Its People," 146–68.

91 A point of view developed, in particular, in Conquest's *Great Terror*.

of Ezhov's time" bore the imprint of the events of the earlier part of the decade, a decade characterized by an explosive mixture of a peculiar kind of modernity, embodied by an almighty industrial and bureaucratic state, and of deep social regression, as extortion became an everyday practice, local despots proliferated, children were abandoned, millions of peasants were deported, famine spread, and cannibalism reappeared. In the wake of collectivization and dekulakization – two major and, in the eyes of the Stalinist leadership, successful operations of social engineering – the state launched a vast offensive in order to systematize and rationalize social control over a "quicksand society."[92] This long-term initiative, based on harsh policing practices inherited from the previous years, "led to an ever more acute problem of what to do with social misfits and deviants."[93] Undoubtedly, parallels should be drawn between the 1937–38 eradication campaign of all "formers" and social outcasts in the Soviet Union and Nazi eugenic cleansing taking place in Germany during the same years.[94]

---

92 This characterization of Soviet society in the 1930s was introduced by Moshe Lewin, *The Making of the Soviet System: Essays in the Social History of Interwar Russia* (London, 1985), 221.

93 Fitzpatrick, *Stalinism: New Directions*, 259.

94 Because the Soviet mass repressive operations, the planned implementation of which has just been revealed by recently declassified top-secret documents, were unknown to Nazi officials, a comparative study of Nazi eugenic and Stalinist social eradication campaigns would most certainly draw different conclusions from those presented by Ernst Nolte, in his much debated book, *Der europäische Bürgerkrieg 1917–1945*, 5th ed. (Munich, 1997), focusing on the *influence* of Soviet criminal practices on Nazi terror.

11

The Third Reich, the Holocaust, and Visions of Serial Genocide

ROBERT GELLATELY

In this chapter I want to suggest how Nazi repression and persecution as practiced between 1933 and 1939 escalated during the war into wholesale human rights abuses, mass murder, and genocide. On January 30, 1933, when Hitler was appointed chancellor, the massive killing and the disastrous war could not have been foreseen either by the German people or perhaps even by the most radical Nazis. Hitler and most others in the Nazi Party were certainly antisemitic and broadly racist, but what they wanted to do about it and other aspects of their still vaguely defined agenda was not settled. Hitler was determined to become an authoritarian ruler, even a dictator, but at the same time he also wanted to be popular, and so was bound to avoid issues likely to upset the nation as a whole. He insisted time and again that popularity was crucial in that it provided the foundation for all political authority, including his own. This point of view helps us understand why the Nazis proceeded initially with much caution on all fronts.

Unlike Stalin and many other twentieth-century dictators, Hitler wanted to establish a consensus on which he could build. Although some members of the Nazi Party, particularly the Storm Troopers, were prepared to bring about a real revolution in 1933, Hitler favored moving forward not against society but with its backing. It is not surprising, therefore, that the Nazis adopted a kind of negative selection process by which they would single out for persecution those who were on their own hate list who also happened to be regarded by many Germans as social outsiders or political enemies.

At any rate, between 1933 and the outbreak of the war, as I have shown elsewhere, Hitler succeeded in creating a hybrid regime we can label a "consensus dictatorship."[1] He legitimated his regime particularly by beating the Great Depression and tearing up the hated Treaty of Versailles. Successes

---

1 See in general Robert Gellately, *Backing Hitler: Consent and Coercion in Nazi Germany* (Oxford, 2001).

in economic and foreign policy, also in the Nazi war on traditional crime, fueled the popular will to support the new dictatorship. As in other times and places, the consensus never embraced the entire population, and pockets of opposition, grumbling, and indifference persisted. The consensus was also fluid and dynamic, and changed not only from issue to issue, but also over time. In spite of it all, however, what remains remarkable was how the majority of this highly cultured nation switched to Hitler's side after his appointment, how quickly they did so, and how so many stuck by him to the bitter end.

A crucial factor in understanding Hitler's dictatorship was how it changed over time. The most dramatic period was heralded with the coming of war in 1939. The opening of hostilities in September 1939 not only affected social life from top to bottom, but soon ushered in far harsher measures, "swift justice," and an increasing brutalization that affected the attitudes of both the dictatorship and the people. War made the regime more bloody-minded than ever, and it soon hardened people's hearts and desensitized them to all kinds of inhumanities. As the war continued, more and more people grew willing to accept with a shrug what would have been unthinkable for them when Hitler was first appointed. We can trace the desensitization process already before the war, and it was a process with fateful consequences for so many.

In what follows I discuss how the coming of the war proved to be the key factor that led from various forms of repression and persecution into genocide. The war provided the link between all previous exclusionary policies and mass murder, and from the beginning it ushered in new waves of terror and systematic killing at home and abroad. Selective massacres soon followed in the East, aimed above all at the Jews. A combination of factors culminated in the Holocaust and other mass murders at that time, but certainly the underlying racism was of central importance.

EARLY PERSECUTIONS IN A CONSENSUS DICTATORSHIP

Hitler told Germany's leading military men less than a week after his appointment that he wanted to get rid of what remained of Weimar democracy and to introduce more authoritarian leadership. He spoke of his desire for the "conquest of new living space in the east and its ruthless Germanization."[2] Although still faced by the need to deal with massive unemployment, he

2 See J. Noakes and G. Pridham (eds.), *Nazism, 1919–1945: A Documentary Reader*, vol. 3 (Exeter, 1988), 628–29.

soon began to call for the "moral purification of the body politic" and for the creation of a racially pure "community of the people."[3] Thus, even if it was going to take time to mobilize an army, and to throw off the shackles of Versailles, Hitler already contemplated the future in radical and racist terms.

From 1933 onward he began constructing the racially pure "community of the people," as well as preparing for war, by eliminating or at least confining certain groups and individuals, especially the communists and others who were already hated, feared, or merely envied by many German citizens. In the campaigns of persecution the Nazis soon introduced, we can see that the identification and treatment of political opponents and social outsiders illustrated that those in power attuned their policies to German society, history, and traditions. There was coercion and terror, but it was selective. There was no revolution in 1933 on the scale of Russia in 1917, and Hitler did not set out to break the nation to his will as did Lenin or Stalin. In Germany there was no all-out assault on society as a whole, much less civil war. Terror was used to suppress "obvious" enemies and was designed to make Hitler more popular and to win converts to Nazi teachings.[4] To this end, the new regime set out to mobilize the nation around certain relatively modest missions at first, including the elimination of recognizable social types who disturbed the peace, beggars in the streets, recidivist criminals, chronic welfare cases, and others who would not conform to well-tried German values.[5]

Once these social enemies were identified and targeted, the police, the judges, and any number of civil servants were quick to take the initiative and sought to outdo each other in their pursuit of the Nazi cause. Many authorities in state and society "below," particularly in fields such as medicine, welfare, the justice system, and so on, showed they were pleased that Hitler allowed them the flexibility and freedom to implement measures that many of them had only dared to contemplate in earlier years.

Most historians agree that in 1933 and even much later, Hitler and other Nazis had no specific plans about what should happen to the Jews in Germany. At the beginning of the new Reich the German Jews were not really social outsiders. After their full legal emancipation in 1871, they had become increasingly well integrated. Most were proud of their Fatherland,

---

3 See Max Domarus (ed.), *Hitler Reden und Proklamationen 1932–1945*, vol. 1 (Leonberg, 1973), 229–37, at 232–33.

4 For an introduction and studies of selected groups, see Robert Gellately and Nathan Stoltzfus (eds.), *Social Outsiders in Nazi Germany* (Princeton, 2001).

5 See Uli Linke, *German Bodies: Race and Representation after Hitler* (New York, 1999), esp. 37–54.

many had served with distinction in the First World War, and they were often quite nationalistic, not unlike the Jewish community in Italy.[6] However, it is also true that there were signs of dangers to come, such as the rise of more virulent strains of antisemitism. Jews, particularly in rural areas, lived apart from their neighbors, and there were some social frictions. Nevertheless, by and large many Jews in Germany, particularly among the educated elite, seem to have felt they had finally found a home in Germany. In retrospect, that hope proved to be an illusion.[7]

Although antisemitism was fundamental to the Nazi movement, it was not nearly as popular in Germany as a whole. The percentage of "believing Jews" to the total population, at under 1 percent, was small and had been declining well before Hitler came to power. Given this situation, Hitler's government initially soft-peddled its antisemitism. Instead of open pogroms on the Jews, it opted for less ostentatious and semilegal steps to begin the reversal of Jewish emancipation.[8] Exclusionary policies often pushed and pulled in contradictory directions, so much so that most historians have concluded that the Nazis had no clearly thought-out policies, much less a preordained "final solution." Beginning in 1933 the authorities of the German state and Nazi Party moved against the Jews but tended to retreat slightly if and when the people appeared to respond negatively to acts of antisemitism. That happened when the Nazis attempted a boycott of all Jewish businesses in April 1933.

Historians continue to debate how Germans responded to what happened over the years down to the war. The new regime soon made it clear that racism and specifically antisemitism was now government policy. Although most citizens certainly did not want to see violence, by the end of the prewar era, it seems many of them came to accept that there was a "Jewish question."[9] According to one study, even before the war, the population on the whole "consented to attacks on the Jews as long as these neither damaged non-Jews nor harmed the interests of the country, particularly its reputation abroad."[10] "Aryanization," that is, taking over Jewish businesses and property, impoverished the Jews and made it difficult for them to emigrate. But the

---

6 See, e.g. Alexander Stille, *Benevolence and Betrayal: Five Italian Jewish Families under Fascism* (New York, 1991), esp. 17–90.

7 See Richard Wolin, *Heidegger's Children: Hannah Arendt, Karl Löwith, Hans Jonas and Herbert Marcuse* (Princeton, 2001), 27–28.

8 According to official figures for January 1933, approximately 525,000 Jews lived in Germany. Saul Friedländer, *Nazi Germany and Jews*, vol. 1 (New York, 1997), 15.

9 See Ian Kershaw, *Popular Opinion and Political Dissent in the Third Reich: Bavaria, 1933–1945* (Oxford, 1983), 224–77.

10 David Bankier, *The Germans and the Final Solution: Public Opinion under Nazism* (Oxford, 1992), 73–74.

same process opened opportunities that many people could and did capitalize upon, to gain at the expense of the Jews.[11]

The coming of war provided an opportunity for Hitler and the Nazis to put "civilian" hesitations aside, to break out of established routine, and to embark upon the more heinous parts of their imperialist and racist agenda. In Hitler's mind, the war marked an ideological turning point, and it was no accident that he responded favorably to suggestions, put to him at the start of the war, to begin a euthanasia program. He had informed the doctors' leader back in 1935 that he intended "in the event of war to solve the problem of the asylums in a radical way."[13] Hitler kept his promise, and even backdated his secret authorization to the doctors (given in October 1939) to September 1 for the beginning of the "mercy killing operations," as if the first day of the war represented for him a declaration of war against all Germany's biological "enemies."[14]

Did Hitler and his closest associates have a carefully laid out plan by which they would proceed from persecution of various groups, sterilization of some, with a view to changing to "euthanasia" and selective mass murder, after which they would move on to genocide? Few historians would say they did.[15] On the other hand, over time as the regime incarcerated ever more broadly defined groups of social outsiders, it grew more inclined to radical solutions, especially as it began gearing up for war in 1938 and 1939. Thoughts of many people around Hitler about what to do with what was termed "lives unworthy of living" – that is, the chronically ill and hospitalized – were soon translated into practice.

Nevertheless, Germany was a nation with a tradition of the rule of law and protection of the individual. We need to recall that until 1933, sterilization was illegal in Germany, much to the frustration of race and medical experts, some of whom had been arguing for it from as early as the turn of the

---

11 Frank Bajohr, *"Arisierung" in Hamburg: Die Verdrängung der jüdischen Unternehmer 1933–1945* (Hamburg, 1997), 331–38.

12 Marcel Reinhard's phrase, "La guerre révolutionna la Révolution," refers to the great French Revolution, and is cited in Norman Hampson, *A Social History of the French Revolution* (Toronto, 1963), 132.

13 Cited in Lothar Gruchmann, *Justiz im Dritten Reich 1933–1940* (Munich, 1987), 499.

14 See Henry Friedlander, *The Origins of Nazi Genocide: From Euthanasia to the Final Solution* (Chapel Hill, 1995), 39ff.

15 For an excellent introduction to the issues and important contributions by younger German scholars, see Ulrich Herbert (ed.), *Nationalsozialistische Vernichtungspolitik 1939–1945: Neue Forschungen und Kontroversen* (Frankfurt am Main, 1998).

century. The "model" approach in the 1920s was the United States, where in 1927 even the Supreme Court (see the arguments of Oliver Wendell Holmes) upheld the constitutionality of compulsory sterilizations.[16] Many German doctors, especially in "racial hygiene" or eugenics were pleased that the Hitler dictatorship finally untied their hands to deal with people whose "defects" – whether mental, physical, or merely ones of appearance – were thought (often on dubious grounds) to be hereditary.[17] The participation of medical specialists and learned judges in the sterilization campaign of some 400,000 people helped to assure good citizens that proper procedures were being followed.[18]

Fiercer radicalization of the dictatorship came almost of itself with the opening of the shooting war. Once the German armed forces began taking casualties, and thus began losing "superior stock," it was almost inevitable, given Nazi racial-biological theory, that they would see it as necessary to eliminate "inferior stock" (the incurables) to balance off the losses. This form of euthanasia led to a minimum of just over 70,000 murders already by September 1941 and more were to follow.[19] This killing in turn opened the door to still further radical options in the name of maintaining the purity of the body politic in a time of war. Moreover, the imperialist and racist mission that opened in the East with the attack on Poland in September 1939 expanded ever more dramatically with the opening of the war against the Soviet Union in June 1941.

Without the war of conquest in the East, genocide might have been thinkable, but it was not realizable.

TOWARD THE FINAL SOLUTION

Almost as soon as war began in September 1939, given Hitler's own wishes, various resettlement schemes and occasional "ethnic cleansing" operations, genocide soon made its way from theory to practice.

First and foremost, Hitler saw far more possibilities for radical solutions to all kinds of "problem cases," chief among them from his point of view being the "Jewish question." He repeatedly uttered threats about what would happen to the Jews should "they" cause another world war. This threat

---

16 According to Stephan Kühl, *The Nazi Connection: Eugenics, American Racism, and German National Socialism* (Oxford, 1994), 24, in the United States there were 200–600 sterilizations per year before 1930; and 2,000–4,000 per year in the 1930s.
17 See Robert N. Proctor, *Racial Hygiene: Medicine under the Nazis* (Cambridge, Mass., 1988), 95–117.
18 For more on this theme, see Götz Aly, Peter Chroust, and Christian Pross, *Cleansing the Fatherland: Nazi Medicine and Racial Hygiene*, trans. B. Cooper (Baltimore, 1994).
19 For details, see Gellately, *Backing Hitler*, 100–6.

was first made in the days following the "Kristallnacht" pogrom, and was repeated in public on January 30, 1939. Over the next several years, when he reiterated this threat in public (also in private), he invariably misdated his prophesy to September 1, 1939, so that in his mind it would seem that this date marked the real beginning of the racist war against the Jews.[20] He and other Nazi leaders made this threat on more than a dozen occasions, so much so that any thinking person who heard it would have had to conclude that in fact the Jews were being done away with.[21]

Hitler took specific steps to begin the ethnic cleansing of the conquered territories soon after war began in 1939. On September 7, for example, he mentioned (and soon repeated) to his army commander in chief his wish for the "ethnic cleansing" (*völkische Flurbereinigung*) of Poland. In the first instance these measures would involve moving around the Polish population, such as by driving it out of areas that were to be made free for German settlers. Hitler's wish was transmitted by Heydrich the same day to subordinates, and it was full of momentous implications for the Polish population as a whole and for the millions of Jews among them.[22] The following day Heydrich stated simply that "the nobility, the priests and the Jews" would have to be killed off.[23]

Already on September 21 Heydrich held an important meeting in Berlin at which time he signaled the beginning of changes in anti-Jewish policies, moving from emigration to "resettlement." Heydrich told assembled police leaders in Berlin that the immediate priority or "short-term goal," was to get the Jews in western Poland moved off the land and into ghettos; to send German Jews there as well; and finally to ship there the remaining 30,000 Gypsies in Germany. The "final goal" or *Endziel* at that point was to move all Jews in the German sphere of influence to some kind of reservation in the East.[24] They would be separated from the Reich by some kind of "eastern wall."[25] It would take time to achieve even the most "modest" of these goals, and they would be reformulated on numerous occasions down the line.[26]

---

20 For a general discussion of this theme, see Ian Kershaw, *Hitler* (London, 1991), 149–51.

21 For a detailed examination, see Gellately, *Backing Hitler.*

22 On Hitler's decision, see Ulrich Herbert, *Best: Biographische Studien über Radikalismus, Weltanschauung und Vernunft 1903–1989* (Bonn, 1996), 240–49, at 241, and Helmut Krausnick and Hans-Heinrich Wilhelm, *Die Truppe des Weltanschauungskrieges: Die Einsatzgruppen der Sicherheitspolizei und des SD 1938–1942* (Stuttgart, 1981), 64–65.

23 See Michael Wildt, *Generation des Unbedingten: Das Führungskorps des Reichssicherheitshauptamtes* (Hamburg, 2002), 456.

24 See Michael Zimmermann, *Rassenutopie und Genozid: Die nationalsozialistische "Lösung der Zigeunerfrage"* (Hamburg, 1996), 166.

25 Wildt, *Generation*, 461.

26 See Christopher R. Browning, *Nazi Policy, Jewish Workers, German Killers* (Cambridge, 2000), 1–25.

Although Goebbels observed on September 28, 1939, that Hitler had "firm plans" in mind for Poland and noted that Hitler envisioned using part of the conquered area as a dumping ground for "racially inferior" Poles, who would be joined by all the Polish Jews, and even Germany's Jews as well, it was not clear when or how all this would come about.[27]

German authorities in Poland reported already for September 1939 the murder of "tens of thousands" of civilians (Jews and non-Jews).[28] By early 1940 in one area after another in Poland, there were mass shootings of Jews. The death squads also targeted the Polish elite, in what was clearly designed to be the first step in the mass enslavement and perhaps even the genocide of the Polish nation.[29]

Most historians now agree that a decision for the total physical elimination of the Jews was taken (if at all) only in the autumn of 1941. In the period from the autumn of 1939 into the first months of 1941, the Nazis considered a territorial solution to the "Jewish question," by which they meant finding a place somewhere to which the Jews could be deported. Hitler and numerous other Nazi leaders evidently continued to think in terms of some kind of reservation in the newly conquered east. Reinhard Heydrich was one of the first to use the ominous phrase "the final solution to the Jewish question" in December 1939, but it still meant finding a reservation in Eastern Europe. Hitler soon abandoned that idea, however, and in an interview for the American public said it would be inhumane to cram the Jews into some such small area. American public opinion still mattered, and by the spring of 1940 the Nazis shifted their gaze to an overseas area.[30] By May Himmler had discussed sending all the Jews to somewhere in Africa, and by June some officials in the Foreign Ministry brought up the possibility of Madagascar, an island off the eastern coast of Africa. Hitler embraced these ideas with enthusiasm. Madagascar was a French possession, and in the days after Germany defeated France, Hitler latched on to the distant island as the answer to the "Jewish question," the dumping ground he still sought.[31] The obvious problem was that Britain, not Germany, controlled the seas, so that any hope of deporting the Jews was doomed as long as Britain stayed

---

27 See Elke Fröhlich (ed.), *Die Tagebücher von Joseph Goebbels*, part 1, vol. 7 (entry for September 28 and 30, 1939), 126, 130.

28 The phrase is cited in Raul Hilberg, *The Destruction of the European Jews*, rev. ed. (New York, 1985), 1:190–91.

29 For much new information and an extensive list of the murders, see Peter Longerich, *Politik der Vernichtung. Eine Gesamtdarstellung der nationalsozialistischen Judenverfolgung* (Munich, 1998), 245–48.

30 See the excellent account, stressing the changing language used by Nazi officialdom, of Philippe Burrin, *Hitler and the Jews: The Genesis of the Holocaust* (London, 1994), 75.

31 See Magnus Brechtken, *"Madagaskar für die Juden": Antisemitische Idee und politische Praxis, 1885–1945* (Munich, 1997).

in the war. Moreover, by early 1941 Hitler was turning his thoughts to the Soviet Union, a country he identified as dominated by the Jews. It was no accident that he began to speak in public once again about his notorious prophesy (first enunciated on January 30, 1939) about what would happen to the Jews should "they" bring about another world war. He did so again on the anniversary of his appointment on January 30, 1941.

It still seems unlikely that Hitler had decided in his own mind to murder all the European Jews, not least because of the absence of the single most important precondition for the annihilation to begin, as given in his own prophesy – namely, world war, which was still many months away.

The scope of the "Jewish question" from the Nazi point of view grew in difficulty as, beginning with the attack on the Soviet Union in June 1941, the German armies captured enormous tracts of land in the East, which had large Jewish populations. They took huge numbers of Soviet prisoners, and either through willful neglect or the inability to care for them, there were hundreds of thousands of deaths within months of the opening of hostilities. Although sporadic murder of the Jews had been under way from September 1939, it quickly reached monumental proportions during the first successes in the attack on the Soviet Union. Disruption of food supplies and shortages that came with the war soon provided an additional rationale for the mass murder of both the Soviet prisoners and the Jews. The lives of those who fell under Nazi domination were viewed as incredibly cheap, and that point held particularly for the Jews but also for nearly all the Slavic nations.

The situation of the Jews who stayed in Germany during the war, often because they had nowhere to go, deteriorated over time especially after the pogrom in November 1938, but grew much worse after the war began in 1939. Their desolate status, regaled as they were with endless hate-filled speeches from the country's leaders, and subjected to shabby treatment at the hands of many of their neighbors, was formally symbolized when they were forced to wear the yellow star (from September 15, 1941). The deportations soon began, and as if to cut them off from all contact with other citizens, on October 24, 1941, it became a serious crime for any "German" even to be seen in public with a Jew.[32]

Although some historians insist that the "final solution of the Jewish question," that is, systematic murder with the aim of total annihilation of all European Jews, could not have moved from vague theory, or even a Hitler "wish," to practical reality without an order from Hitler of some kind, other

---

32 For a detailed discussion, see Robert Gellately, *The Gestapo and German Society: Enforcing Racial Policy, 1933–1945* (Oxford, 1990).

historians point to how the killing escalated in the context of the war against the Soviet Union for a wide range of reasons and did not need such an order. At any rate we have neither a direct order from Hitler, nor anything but circumstantial evidence that he ever issued one. As best we can reconstruct what happened, it would seem that he likely issued some sort of verbal wish or merely agreed to proposals put to him for the genocide to begin sometime in the autumn of 1941. Although until then Hitler had said that the solution to the "Jewish question" would come after the victorious war against the Soviet Union, by yielding to demands from various regional leaders who wanted to send the Jews from their areas to the East already in September, Hitler removed that obstacle, so that all options were now opened, including systematic mass murder. The first deportation trains of Jews from Germany left on October 15, 16, and 18, 1941, from Vienna, Prague, and Berlin.[33] Whereas until this point in time Germany sought any means possible to get rid of the Jews within its territory, on October 23, head of the Gestapo Heinrich Müller issued the not insignificant order that henceforth all Jewish emigration was forbidden, which meant at the very least that all the Jews were now to be deported to the East.[34]

In order to systematize what was happening to the Jews – some of them were simply shot out of hand on arrival in the East, while mass shootings of local Jews were already commonplace – a meeting was called by Heydrich for December 9 to discuss the full scope of the "final solution," which by this point meant the mass murder of all the Jews in Europe. This was the call for what became the Wannsee conference, but it was postponed (until January 20, 1942) likely because of the Japanese attack on Pearl Harbor and entrance of the United States into the war. Hitler took the fateful step of declaring war on the United States on December 11, and for the first time since 1918, the world was at war. Thoughts Hitler seems to have had about holding the Jews as hostages to keep America in line now vanished. In meetings he held with top officials on December 12 it seems clear that Hitler took the occasion to turn up the inflammatory rhetoric, for example, by repeating again his own public "prophesies." These stated that if the Jews brought about world war, they would pay. Having declared war on the United States the day before, he thus also perversely fulfilled the precondition for his declaration of war on the Jews. Merely repeating on December 12 his prophesy just hours after world war finally had come about may have been all that was needed to accelerate the process into a determination to kill all the European

---

33 See also, for the background, Wildt, *Generation*, 616.
34 Ibid., 626.

Jews. In fact, of course, mass murder was already well under way. Even mobile gas vans had begun working in late 1941 at Chelmo and Belzec. These relatively "modest" facilities alone killed hundreds of thousands of people. In addition, Nazi death squads roamed behind the advancing Wehrmacht and soon escalated the killing to include women and children, in addition to men and boys. When we read the reports of these death squads, most of them led by men who were highly educated, we can only shudder.[35]

The Holocaust developed in several short stages, particularly after the invasion of the Soviet Union began. Mass shooting of Jews took place almost immediately and by the end of 1941 already as many as 1 million may have been killed. In a number of areas in the East local Nazi bosses competed with each other to clear "their" areas of Jews, and there was the additional pressure of food shortages. It was in this context, toward the end of 1941, that Hitler's declaration of war on the United States could be taken as a signal to kill all the Jews, precisely as threatened in his oft-repeated prophesies.

The world war finally began on December 11, 1941, and it was certainly no accident that thereafter the mass murder of the Jews accelerated dramatically. The single greatest period of killing took place between March 1942 and February 1943. In March 1942, 75 to 80 percent of all the victims who would eventually die in the Holocaust were still alive, while 20 to 25 percent were dead. During the next year, these percentages were reversed. But while the killing was concentrated into that twelve-month period, murder of the Jews continued to the end of the Third Reich, and this killing, in the context of the increasingly horrendous war against the Soviet Union, provided the backdrop to the plans and practices for the genocide of other people.[36]

We also need to recall that the Holocaust was a multinational operation. Certainly there is no doubt that the headquarters was in Berlin. However, much of the rounding up and even the killing needed the collaboration of the local people. Many peoples in Europe, including Poles, Ukrainians, Romanians, Croats, Lithuanians, and others, also did the killing, often with enthusiasm.[37]

---

35 For the complete reports, see Peter Klein (ed.), *Die Einsatzgruppen in der besetzten Sowjetunion 1941–42: Die Tätigkeits- und Lageberichte des Chefs der Sicherheitspolizei und des SD* (Berlin, 1997).

36 This point is made by the remarkable study of Christopher R. Browning, *Ordinary Men: Reserve Police Battalion 101 and the Final Solution in Poland* (New York, 1992), xv.

37 For an account of massacres in one town (Soviet and Nazi inspired) in Ukraine, often with the participation of local citizens, and discussion of a controversy surrounding photographic evidence, see Bernd Boll, "Złoczów, July 1941: The Wehrmacht and the Beginning of the Holocaust in Galicia," in Omer Bartov, Atina Grossmann, and Mary Nolan (eds.), *Crimes of War: Guilt and Denial in the Twentieth Century* (New York, 2002), 61–99.

We know that in spite of everything some Jews survived in the underground in Germany and elsewhere. They could hardly have done so without support from non-Jewish citizens. On the other hand, it has to be said that inside Germany there was little resistance. Bulgaria shows, or at least suggests, what might have happened, had the people stood up for justice. There the Eastern Orthodox Church as well as many prominent individuals and social institutions came out in order to protect the Jews, with the upshot that nearly the entire Jewish community of 50,000 survived the war.[38] On the other hand, we know that elsewhere some people took advantage of the situation to settle accounts with the Jewish community, and when that occurred the annihilation was nearly complete.

ACTIONS AGAINST "GYPSIES" AND POLES

We have already seen hints that at the same time as the Nazis radicalized their policies toward the Jews they did the same for the Sinti and Roma, the group called the "Gypsies." The Nazis moved from the persecution of the Sinti and Roma to their deportation and eventually escalated to annihilation, just as they did for the Jews. Sinti and Roma were by tradition wanderers across Europe who came to be regarded especially in the modern era of state making and nation building as rootless and apart. Although in Germany they constituted only a tiny minority, under Hitler's dictatorship they caught the official eye. The Nazis pursued them not only because they did not fit in and were thought to be prone to crime, but also on racial grounds. Local officials in some places took advantage of the opportunities opened under Hitler's dictatorship to get rid of such "problem cases."

The criminal biologists and scientists like Dr. Robert Ritter who studied the Sinti and Roma concluded that the most dangerous variety and the majority group were those of mixed race. The initial recommendation was that they be confined in camps of some kind, but once the war began, these officials pressed for more. The radical options that opened with the war soon edged leaders like Heinrich Himmler of the SS to think about eliminating the "Gypsy plague." Himmler thought that some "pure-bred Gypsies" might be allowed to live, but there really was no place for these people as a whole in a Nazi-dominated Europe. We can see certain parallels in the definition, registration, confinement, and deportation of the Gypsies and the Jews. We do not know how many Sinti and Roma were

---

38 See Tzvetan Todorov, *The Fragility of Goodness: Why Bulgaria's Jews Survived the Holocaust* (Princeton, 2001), and Michael Bar-Zohar, *Beyond Hitler's Grasp: The Heroic Rescue of Bulgaria's Jews* (Holbrook, Mass., 1998).

murdered. Some scholars suggest that around 100,000 were killed, but others go as high as one-half million. The death-book of the "Gypsies" in Auschwitz conveys a sense of systematic murder that looks and feels like genocide.[39]

The fate of other nations and ethnic groups was also debated among the Nazis during the war and several of them might well have culminated in genocide. One immediate issue already in October and November 1939 was what to do with the millions of non-Jewish Poles. By tradition, the Poles were not highly regarded in Germany, and there was a good deal of resentment toward Poland because it had gained land at Germany's expense in the peace settlement of 1919. This hostility and hatred was magnified many times in the Third Reich.

If we read through the documentation that survives of the plans that were bantered about among leading Nazi officials, including Hitler, there can be no question but that they wanted to eliminate Poland as a recognizable nation and culture. We can term this cultural genocide, but given how other discriminatory programs quickly degenerated into mass murder, it is also conceivable that in due course there would have been something approaching a genocide of the Polish people.

Genocidal intent seems to have been more or less assumed in discussions of the Poles by a wide range of Nazi officials and planners. By "intent" I mean that there was a desire to erase the Polish state, nation, and culture from the face of the earth. The Poles were to be deprived of leaders, education, and their culture and treated as slaves. As early as October 12, 1939, Hitler ordered that the western section of Poland be "Germanized," cleansed of Poles, and "returned" to Germany. For the time being its eastern part was to go to the Soviet Union. Many Poles were murdered on the spot in 1939 and into 1940 – also by the Soviets who invaded Poland from the east at that time. The Soviets carried out their own mass murders in their area and shipped no less than 2 million Poles to Siberia. The Nazis and the Soviets seemed to share the view that the Polish nation should disappear.[40]

The Nazis converted the central section of Poland into the General Government under Hans Frank.[41] At a meeting with the head of armed forces on October 17, 1939, Hitler said he did not want to turn this area into a "model state along the lines of German order" but (at that stage) to

---

39 The standard work on the topic now is Zimmermann, *Rassenutopie und Genozid.*
40 For this and other excesses, see Krausnick and Wilhelm, *Die Truppe,* 63–106, at 93.
41 Horst Rohde, "Hitlers erster 'Blitzkrieg' und seine Auswirkungen auf Nordosteuropa," in Klaus A. Maier, Horst Rohde, Bernd Stegemann, and Hans Umbreit (eds.), *Das Deutsche Reich und der Zweite Weltkrieg* (Stuttgart, 1979), 2:139ff.

make it a kind of dumping ground that would allow the Nazis "to cleanse the Reich of Jews and Poles."[42]

Polish men, women, and children were immediately forced to work in Germany, to help make up for growing labor shortages. Soon the Nazis demanded so many, that it would have been economically and socially impossible for any "Poland" to exist and for its culture to replicate itself. A sense of the status of the Poles is conveyed by Gestapo guidelines on their treatment. They were given a set of nine rules as to the "duties of male and female civilian workers of Polish nationality during their stay in Germany." They were confined to their workplace and to their billets after curfew and excluded from using public transport except with special permission. The Poles were the first in Germany to be forced to wear a badge – a purple "P" – sewn to all their clothing. In addition, "all social contact with the German people" was expressly prohibited, including visits to theaters, cinemas, dances, bars, and churches in their company. Regulations stipulated that any Pole "who has sexual relations with a German man or woman, or approaches them in any other improper manner, will be punished by death."[43]

By 1944, there were 1.7 million Poles working in Germany, all of them subject to mistreatment and "police justice." What would have been left of a recognizable Polish nation in an expanding Third Reich? Not much. One recent estimate of Polish losses in the war puts the death toll at just over 6 million, half of them Polish Christians and half of them Polish Jews.[44] Put another way, an average of 3,000 Polish citizens died each day of the occupation.[45] Most of the Polish Jews died in gas chambers or were shot on Polish territory as part of the "final solution." Most "ordinary Poles" were worked to death or executed on an "individual" basis.

PLANS FOR SERIAL GENOCIDE AND THE GENOCIDAL MENTALITY

Instead of exploring the new accounts of the microlevel that are beginning to appear, which are crucially important because that is where genocide happens, I want to draw attention to the macrolevel, to the planners and the experts who studied the East and who drew up ethnic, political, and

---

42 *Der Prozess gegen die Hauptkriegsverbrecher vor dem Internationalen Militärgerichtshof* (Nuremberg, 1949), vol. 26, doc. 864-PS, 377ff.
43 Bundesarchiv Berlin: R58/1030, 42ff.
44 Richard C. Lukas, *Forgotten Holocaust: The Poles under German Occupation, 1939–1944* (Lexington, Ky., 1986), 39. For a broader examination, see Yisrael Gutman and Shmuel Krakowski, *Unequal Victims: Poles and Jews during World War II* (New York, 1986).
45 Michael Burleigh, *The Third Reich: A New History* (London, 2000), 416.

economic blueprints for the future in which they outlined what I would term serial genocides.[46] In this brief section I want to underline not so much what happened, but to study these plans as a way of helping us understand the genocidal mentality that apparently gripped large numbers in the German elite during the war. That mentality also partly filtered down to the millions in the armed forces.[47]

One of the most infamous blueprints is the "General Plan East" (GPO). It was initially formulated on Himmler's inspiration in 1940 but went through at least five successive stages and as many as three major revisions. The GPO was one among many others, similar in their radical views and recommendations for future ethnic cleansing operations.[48]

The first version of the GPO was ready by July 15, 1941, just weeks after the beginning of the attack on the Soviet Union. The plan, which was worked out by a Berlin professor, Konrad Meyer, at his university institute, was developed for Himmler's Reich Commission for the Strengthening of German Nationhood (RKF). No copies of this first plan survive.

A second GPO was drafted by November 1941 by Reinhard Heydrich's Reich Security Main Office (RSHA). Heydrich spoke in general terms about it without mentioning the plan as such, in early October 1941 in Prague. Enough is known of that document to establish that it called for the resettlement of 31 million people from the occupied eastern areas. Likely at the end of 1941 or early in 1942, the blueprint was completed, evidently by the SD (Security Service, Office III B of the RSHA).

Although no copies of this second GPO survive either, we do have a detailed analysis of it, dated April 27, 1942, by Dr. Erhard Wetzel, the expert on race issues in the Reich Ministry for the Occupied Eastern Areas. We can deduce a great deal from Wetzel's remarks. Evidently, 10 million Germans or "Germanic people" were to be resettled over a thirty-year period after the war. They were to replace most of the native population from the area between Russia and Germany, estimated at about 45 million people, of whom 31 million were declared to be "racially undesirable" and who were to be sent to western Siberia. About 14 million of the conquered people were to remain, but only to be used as slaves. Those deported would have included 100 percent of all the Jews, about 80 to 85 percent of the Poles,

---

46 For a study of how "ordinary Poles" murdered the Jews in their village, see Jan T. Gross, *Neighbors: The Destruction of the Jewish Community in Jedwabne* (Princeton, 2000).

47 For a brief introduction, see Saul Friedländer, "The Wehrmacht, German Society, and Knowledge of the Mass Extermination of the Jews," in Bartov et al., *Crimes of War*, 17–30.

48 See Czeslaw Madajczyk (ed.), *Vom Generalplan Ost zum Generalsiedlungsplan* (Munich, 1994); and Mechtild Rössler and Sabine Schleiermacher (eds.), *Der "Generalplan Ost." Hauptlinien der national-sozialistischen Planungs- und Vernichtungspolitik* (Berlin, 1993).

75 percent of the White Russians, and 64 percent of the west Ukrainian population. Given these percentages, it would have been impossible for any of these nations to survive as cultures or nations in any meaningful sense, so that these plans explicitly accept that all four of these nations would for all intents and purposes cease to exist. These plans in effect, therefore, called for nothing less than serial genocide.

Far from thinking the plans were utterly outlandish, Wetzel's main concern was that the GPO underestimated the scope of the problem and the number of people in the East. By his calculations there were not 45, but 60 to 65 million. If the 14 million people mentioned in the plan remained in their homelands, to be worked as slave labor, that meant that there would be 45 to 51 million people who would have to be deported over the next generation or so after the war. According to Wetzel, the plan also overestimated the number of Germans and "Germanic people" who could be settled in eastern Europe: there would be only 8 million, not 10 million of them. He did not object to the idea that around 20 million Poles would be forcefully deported to Siberia. He still thought it was technically feasible, over a thirty-year period, to deport somewhere between 700,000 and 800,000 Poles *each year*, and he even calculated how many trains would be needed. Given what we know about the death rates during Nazi deportations, we can imagine that this process would certainly have entailed murder on a massive scale.

Wetzel considered it practical and realistic, to mention another example, to ship "several millions of the most dangerous Poles" to Brazil. In exchange Germany would somehow reacquire Germans already settled there. Even the stuffy old Foreign Office (according to Wetzel) thought this idea was "not uninteresting." In other words, by the end of 1941 not only was the "final solution" in full swing on the ground, but even the pencil pushers and the expertocracy had begun to think the unthinkable.

The magic number of about 30 million and more "excess" people seemed to be in the air among German planners in the early days of the invasion of the Soviet Union. Not only did Himmler talk about the decimation of the Soviet peoples by 30 million at the beginning of 1941, but almost at the same time plans were formulated by Herbert Backe of the Ministry of Agriculture, for the mass starvation of that number of people in the urban areas of the Soviet Union and elsewhere. Faced with drastic food shortages, the inability to feed the German invading forces, and the unwillingness to cut the rations of the German population on the home front, Backe conceived of the idea of letting millions of Soviet people starve to death.[49]

49 See Götz Aly and Susanne Heim, *Vordenker der Vernichtung* (Hamburg, 1991), 365–94.

The first mention we have of this plan, surely the greatest starvation plan in world history, was briefly recorded at a State Secretaries' meeting held on May 2, 1941. The notes of the meeting mentioned that in the course of the coming war "undoubtedly x million people will starve."[50] Although the key authorities sought, without success, to get Hitler's signature, he approved of the idea, and a wide circle of people concerned with the coming invasion began to discuss the implications of this plan in detail.[51] The agricultural branch of the Economic Staff (East), for example, on May 23, 1941, came up with a detailed outline of the situation they thought would develop when war came against the USSR. The long report of the meeting noted that "many tens of millions of people" in certain areas "were superfluous" and would either die or be shipped to Siberia. Any effort to save them from starvation was deemed unacceptable, because that could only happen at the cost of provisioning Western Europe and especially Germany.

There is another important point to keep in mind: this report, like others at the time, often mentioned that the railway system of the USSR was inefficient and hardly capable of moving so many people to Siberia. Thus, calling for "resettlement in Siberia" was in effect another of the many code words for mass murder.[52]

As it turned out, it proved difficult to starve all these people, because they could not be confined behind fences or in a ghetto where supplies could be kept from them. But if the plan could not be implemented, the principles behind it informed the thinking of many of the leaders involved in the war in the USSR, certainly in the battles against Leningrad and Stalingrad. The ominous number of 30 million circulated in various conversations among the leaders of the invading forces, like Quartermaster General Wagner. Leaders of the military, the SS, and all the civil authorities knew and apparently accepted some kind of starvation plan, encapsulated by one man in the phrase that there were "40 million too many Russians! They must 'pass away,'" which is to say, must be starved to death. There was no way to stop so many people from finding ways of getting food on their own. Nevertheless, the plan was implemented where possible, above all against captive Soviet prisoners of war and ghettoized Jews, neither of whom could escape their confinement nor establish satisfactory ways to feed themselves.[53]

50 See Dokument 2718-PS: Aktennotiz der Staatssekretäre vom 2. Mai 1941, in *Der Prozess*, 31:84.
51 Christian Gerlach, *Kalkulierte Morde: Die deutsche Wirtschafts- und Vernichtungspolitik in Weißrußland 1941 bis 1944* (Hamburg, 1999), 46.
52 See Dokument 126-EC, Bericht des Wirtschaftsstabes Ost, in *Der Prozess*, 35:135–57; also Gerlach, *Kalkulierte Morde*, 49.
53 Gerlach, *Kalkulierte Morde*, 54.

Hitler himself set the murderous tone and privately remarked that the invading forces should treat the people in the Ukraine or White Russia as he believed the Indians had been treated in America. When it came to taking food the Germans needed, no thought should be given to whether the people in the East starved. Hitler's calculations were based on an utter disregard for the fate of the Slavic people. Indeed, he was of the view that the invaders should avoid entering these despised Russian cities altogether, which he said "must completely die away" (*müssen vollständig ersterben*).[54]

Even when easy victories against the USSR began to become difficult, Himmler continued to fantasize about a racist-inspired future empire and, at the end of January 1942, again asked Konrad Meyer to work out plans. A new draft was ready by May but again rejected by Himmler as too modest. He only got what he wanted at the beginning of 1943, in the form of a General Settlement Plan (*Generalsiedlungsplan*). Some of this document has survived, mostly population statistics and tables, as well as maps. It dealt with population transformations of the area from the Baltic to the Crimea and from Leningrad to the west. It also took into account the population of Germany proper, the so-called Germanic lands, such as the Netherlands and Norway, and the overseas Germans (*Volksdeutsche*), who would be available for resettlement in the East. This monstrous plan came to fruition at a time when the war had already taken a turn for the worse. One can scarcely imagine what the plan might have looked like had Germany actually been winning.

The visions of the future were also propagated by numerous other experts well down the line of command. For example, RSHA planner Hans Ehlich spoke in Salzburg in December 1942 to a meeting of student leaders. Ehlich wondered aloud how Germany would deal with the 70 million "racially foreign people" in the postwar era. Included in this group were people from the Baltic countries, Czechoslovakia, and Poland. He noted that if the best approach to protect the German body politic would be "expulsion" and "destruction" of these people, given the large numbers involved he supposed it would be impossible completely to replace their labor power. Therefore one would also use, alongside expulsion and destruction, also "assimilation" (*Umvolkung*), by which consideration would be given to individuals who passed race tests and already had some German blood in their veins. What would actually become of Poles was left up in the air, and the Jews were not even mentioned as such, for their fate was to a large extent already sealed.

54 See Werner Jochmann (ed.), *Adolf Hitler: Monologe im Führerhauptquartier 1941–1944: Die Aufzeich-nungen Heinrich Heims* (Munich, 1980), 90–91 (for the evening of October 17, 1941).

It would seem implausible to suppose that these nations and ethnic groups, above all Jews, to some extent also the Poles and most Slavic people, could really have been granted peaceful coexistence inside Hitler's New Order.[55]

There were many other planners in the East, more humble folk like sanitation engineers, city and landscape architects, and town planners. One drew up a new plan in 1940 for Warsaw by which 1.5 million Poles and Jews would be driven out and replaced by 100,000 Germans. We now know from quite recent revelations that some of these planners, far from being mentally deranged, included a number of men who became noteworthy historians in Germany after 1945. There never seemed to be a shortage of visionaries, many drawn from academia. Even if their plans came to nothing, this shows not that these professors were somehow superfluous to what happened but that they shared in the broader social, political, and racist consensus.[56]

The mentality of the conquerors and the intellectuals who supported them reminds one of late nineteenth-century imperialists in Africa. Hans Frank, governor general of Poland, stated his vision in no uncertain terms in early 1944: "[W]e can make mincemeat out of the Poles and the Ukrainians and all the other people hanging around here" later on, but for the moment he thought that tactical "statesmanship" was called for.[57]

WAR OF ANNIHILATION

As the planners continued to work away, the war in the USSR itself raged on. I have already suggested how this war unleashed genocidal processes, but it is important to underline more specific genocidal aspects of the Nazi-Soviet conflict itself. Hitler said on many occasions that his dreams of race and space inevitably would involve war with the USSR. Operation Barbarossa, the attack on the Soviet Union, was set for mid-1941. Even before it began Hitler insisted it was to be a *Vernichtungskrieg*, or war of annihilation unlike any other in history. Planning began in earnest in July 1940 when Hitler stated again that it would not be enough just to win the war but that the Soviet state had to be "utterly destroyed." After the "inferior race" was conquered, the Soviet peoples, like the Poles, were to become "a people of leaderless slave laborers."[58]

---

55 See Karl Heinz Roth, " 'Generalplan Ost' – 'Gesamtplan Ost': Forschungsstand, Quellenprobleme, neue Ergebnisse," in Rössler and Schleiermacher, *Generalplan Ost*, 25–117, at 43.
56 See my review of the issue and a symposium on the theme in <http://hsozkult.geschichte. hu-berlin.de/rezensio/symposiu/versfrag/sympos.htm>.
57 Cited in Burleigh, *The Third Reich*, 456.
58 Hans-Adolf Jacobsen, "The Kommissarbefehl and Mass Executions of Soviet Prisoners of War," in Helmut Krausnick et al., *Anatomy of the SS-State* (London, 1968), 508–9.

He was not alone in repeatedly insisting on "the utmost brute force" and said this war was going to be unlike anything seen before. When the invasion began it was by far the largest in world history. Himmler's attitude on the eve of the attack was that he had "no interest in the fate" of such people. "Whether they thrive or starve to death concerns me only from the point of view of them as slave labor . . . in all other respects I am totally indifferent."[59]

In the beginning Operation Barbarossa was unstoppable, and the Germans took vast numbers of prisoners, so many in fact that it was possible to murder the Jews without giving much thought to concerns about their lost labor power. Numerous Soviet prisoners were shot out of hand, but many thousands were confined in camps, including some inside Germany, where it was well known locally that the men were starving to death and were otherwise in desperate shape. The mayor of at least one town wanted to have the road to the camp opened so that ordinary Germans could go to see for themselves "these animals in human form" and imagine what would have happened if "these beasts" had conquered Germany.[60]

To illustrate the net effect of how Soviet prisoners were treated, we need only look at one German report from May 1, 1944. It states that by then the Germans had taken a total of 5,165,381 prisoners. The report speaks about a "wastage" of 2 million (i.e., they died). Another 1,030,157 were supposedly "shot while trying to escape," while 280,000 perished in transit camps, bringing the total to 3.3 million. By 1945, out of a grand total of 5.7 million prisoners of war, no less than 3.3 million of them died in captivity. We have to recall, however, that the Germans often made sure there were no prisoners to take and had largely stopped taking any by the time of this survey.[61]

The civil population in one place after another across the occupied areas of the Soviet Union was simply allowed to starve to death, deported to work as slaves in Germany, or exploited on the spot. Mass starvation, however, almost inevitably accompanied the German invasion, because the troops were expected to live off the land, which in many cases had already been combed through for provisions by the retreating Soviet forces. Deliberate starvation was part of the great sieges such as the one at Stalingrad and the other at Leningrad, but we can see the effect of the occupation in many less

---

59 Jacobsen, "Kommissarbefehl," 510.
60 See note of the Bürgermeister Wietzendorf (August 28, 1941) to the Landrat in Soltau, reprinted in full in the corrected and extremely important exhibition catalog: Hamburger Institut für Sozialforschung (ed.), *Verbrechen der Wehrmacht: Dimensionen des Vernichtungskrieges 1941–1944* (Hamburg, 2002), 261.
61 Jacobsen, "Kommissarbefehl," 531.

well known areas like Charkov, a city with a population of nearly 1 million before nearly half of them left with the Soviet evacuation. Located on the road to Stalingrad in the southeast of the country, Charkov was already in terrible shape when the Wehrmacht arrived. Nevertheless, the German Armed Forces were told to live off the land, which meant seizing provisions where they could be found and that left very little for the native population. During each month of the German occupation, hundreds starved to death.[62]

Starvation was magnified many times in cities like Leningrad where major battles took place. The siege of the city lasted from September 8, 1941, to January 18, 1943. Hitler and other leaders repeatedly said they did not even want it to surrender, nor did they wish any of the civilian population to escape. In this battle alone, according to official Soviet figures, civilian losses were put at 632,253, the vast majority of them dying from starvation, but the losses in fact were higher.[63] Hitler told Goebbels that Leningrad should disappear, for it would be impossible to feed its 5 million inhabitants after the battle was won.[64] Even on the ground by the winter of 1942 the death rate just for this city was estimated at between 4,000 and 5,000 per day before the registration system broke down.[65]

The Slavic peoples suffered enormous losses. A reliable and conservative estimate puts the losses of the Soviet Union alone at around 25 million, of whom two-thirds or so were civilians. Some Soviet historians have only recently suggested the number of dead may have been twice as large in total, ranging close to 50 million.[66] Although we have to be very careful with these kinds of statistics, there is no disputing the fact that the Soviets suffered by far the greatest casualties in the war. There should be no question in anyone's mind that if the Nazis had won that war against Stalin, the results for the peoples of the Soviet Union would have been even more catastrophic.

CONCLUSION

Just as the regime grew more radical over time, so too did the population in Germany become willing to accept more far-reaching measures. Once the war came, the Nazis quickly brushed aside traditional moral and legal reservations, and at the same time adopted steadily more expansive imperialist missions. Successes on the battlefield in 1939 and 1940 and at first also in the war against the Soviet Union fueled Hitler's ambitions as never

---

62 For a selection of the documents, see Institut für Sozialforschung, *Verbrechen der Wehrmacht*, 299–346.
63 See Richard Overy, *Russia's War: A History of the Soviet War Effort, 1941–1945* (Harmondsworth, 1998), 112.
64 See Ian Kershaw, *Hitler: Nemesis* (New York, 2000), 480–81.
65 Overy, *Russia's War*, 107.   66 Ibid., 287–89.

before. These victories also won converts to his cause and certainly to the Hitler cult. They also brought on board even more of the country's leading experts, members of the business, military, and academic elite. The new racist discourse that had taken shape well before the war now grew bolder and increasingly impatient with any reservations.

Many of the inhabitants of the conquered eastern areas were slated for slavery at best, mass murder at worst. Hitler does not seem to have given any real thought to what a postwar Reich would look like, with no vision of a European community. For him, one successful war would lead almost inevitably to the next. In the meantime, German needs would everywhere take precedence. Even most of the people who were not going to be killed outright in the East were to survive merely as slaves. Vast resettlement schemes were drawn up, growing more expansive with each draft. Anyone who stood in the way of the realization of what Hitler called the "Garden of Eden," anyone who looked askance at their conquerors was to be killed.

We can identify under Nazism a very particular linguistic turn. In that discursive context, the unthinkable – that is, organized and even serial genocides, the wholesale transfer of populations, and the use of mass starvation as "rational" policy – came to be seen as thinkable and practicable. Given an acceptance of the first principle, that the Germanic "race" was superior and must dominate the "inferior," then the complete obliteration of those who were undesired, superfluous, or threatening became a "rational" option. So there was science, modernity, and genocide but, alongside them, also atavism and barbarism.

Although we can point to some similarities in Nazi plans and actions for Jews and Slavs, there was and remained one crucial difference: in principle Jews could never be saved, never convert, nor be assimilated. Some Slavs, at least if they passed "scientific" race tests – tests that were in fact sheer quackery – could become assimilated or naturalized Germans. When Hitler himself dreamed out loud about the East as late as in May 1942, he talked about settling "soldier-peasants" (*Wehrbauern*) there. Germans would be brought back from America, and over decades population policies would be pursued to bring the German population of the area up to 250 million. It would be hard to imagine the Germans fostering the national and ethnic independence of non-Germans in this new eastern Reich, which Hitler regarded as Germany's colonial empire. Walls would again be built as in Roman times to separate Europe from Asia.[67]

---

67 *Tagebücher von Goebbels*, T. 2, 4:362–63 (entry May 24, 1942).

Scholars interested in explaining genocides rightly focus on the murderous events in the field. In this chapter my plea is to expand the study also to include the plans of the politicians, the enforcers, as well of the experts in order to contextualize genocidal theory and practice. Looking at the wide range of Nazi plans tells us a great deal about the genocidal mentality that was directly related to the killing.

Regarding the events of the Holocaust and Second World War from a somewhat different vantage point, I would like to suggest that it may be time to rethink our general interpretation of the Second World War. It was not essentially about "Saving Private Ryan" but was overwhelmingly a race war. The main aggressor in Europe was Germany. In its race war against the Jews, it murdered an estimated 5 to 6 million people. The Nazis also went after the "Gypsies" and would have killed them all except for a handful of "pure-breeds" who would be kept alive as curiosities or museum pieces.[68]

These genocidal campaigns were carried out simultaneously, and reinforced each other. Moreover, independent or semiindependent genocidal processes can be seen during the war in countries like Romania.

This is not the place to discuss the ethnic cleansing carried out by the Soviets during the war and how the Polish and Czech governments and people after the defeat of the Third Reich drove out millions of Germans using the most brutal methods imaginable.[69] These stories are only now reaching a broader audience, and they remind us of how the Second World War provided the context for genocide and ethnic cleansing on a scale unlike anything seen in history.

A half century has passed since the end of the war, and we continue to learn about the scale of the abuses, the persecution, the murder, and the mayhem. We have made great strides in historical research, but it is no less clear that much work remains to be done to clarify and to explain what happened.

---

68 The death toll ranges between 200,000 and 300,000.
69 See esp. Norman M. Naimark, *Fires of Hatred: Ethnic Cleansing in Twentieth-Century Europe* (Cambridge, Mass., 2001), 85–138.

12

Reflections on Modern Japanese History in the Context of the Concept of Genocide

GAVAN McCORMACK

The twentieth century was marked by nothing so much as the intensity of state-sponsored violence and terror. Historians struggle to come to terms with this by making generalizations, weighing and measuring, setting events to a scale. Genocide, understood in broad terms as the attempt to wipe out whole peoples, has been allocated the polar position among such crimes, and among genocides, the Holocaust, understood as the attempt to exterminate the whole of the Jewish and Romany peoples (among an even broader range of categories), the place of absolute and unqualified evil.[1] A prominent thread in the literature is that which insists that the only true case of genocide is the Nazi, because only the Nazis tried to achieve the annihilation of an entire people.[2] However, it is reasonably clear now that in the evolving construction of the crime of genocide, the "classic" case of the Holocaust has been slowly extended to include at least three major examples: the "Aghet" massacre of Armenians by the Turkish empire between 1914 and 1923; the Khmer Rouge mass murder of Vietnamese, Cham Muslims, and other minorities and finally of urban Khmer between 1975 and 1979 in Cambodia; and the massacre of the Tutsi people in Rwanda in the 1990s.[3] In that

---

1 Although crimes were committed against many groups, from the "six million Jews who were murdered in German concentration camps" to the "countless citizens of the Soviet Union and Poland," the Sinti and Romany Gypsies, the homosexuals, and mentally ill, and all those killed for religious or political beliefs, as well as the German people themselves, first and foremost the members of the resistance, the term "Holocaust" is commonly applied to the first of these. (The list here taken from President Richard von Weizsäcker's speech to the German Bundestag, May 8, 1985, reprinted in Geoffrey Hartman [ed.], *Bitburg in Moral and Historical Perspective* [Bloomington, 1986].)

2 Steven R. Welch, "A Survey of Interpretive Paradigms in Holocaust Studies and a Comment on the Dimensions of the Holocaust," paper presented at the Workshop on Comparative Famines and Political Killings, Genocide Studies Program, Yale University and History Department, University of Melbourne, August 1999 <http://www.yale.edu/gsp>.

3 Christian P. Scherrer, "Preventing Genocide: The Role of the International Community," Summary of a report to the Stockholm International Forum on the Holocaust, January 26–28, 2000 <http://preventgenocide.org/prevent/scherrer.htm>.

same vein, the Report of the Preparatory Commission for the International Criminal Court, in drawing up in July 2000 a systematic set of criteria by which acts of genocide might be identified, was also furthering the process of converting genocide from a unique evil to a particular, but possibly widespread, kind of state crime.[4]

The question addressed in this chapter is whether the notion of genocide can be applied to the policies and actions undertaken by imperial Japan against its neighbor countries from the late nineteenth through the first half of the twentieth century. Although the focus is modern, it is also necessary to consider some older moments that still cast a long shadow over relations between Japan and its neighbors.

There are obvious difficulties. Nobody accuses the imperial Japanese government or army of a design to wipe out the people of the United States or Britain or the (Dutch) East Indies or elsewhere, much less of any such design against the Chinese (or other Asian) people. As for Korea, under the Japanese imperial regime there was no state of war, and economic development and population growth were both rapid. Prima facie at least, whatever Japan was doing in China and Korea, it seems difficult to describe it as genocidal, and as a matter of fact, until Iris Chang's book – *The Rape of Nanking: The Forgotten Holocaust of World War II* – the question of "genocide" had rarely if ever been considered.[5] Chang for the first time explicitly equates Nanjing and "The Holocaust," Japanese military atrocities and the Nazi "final solution." Her book, however, though widely sold and reviewed in the United States, had little impact elsewhere and was widely criticized by scholars for its blockbuster, sensationalizing approach. Although directing fresh international attention to Nanjing, it seems to have exercised little lasting influence over the question of legal or philosophical construction of the events.[6]

However, the definition of genocide adopted in 1948 by the United Nations (and continued in the work of the Preparatory Commission for the International Criminal Court in 2000) is actually very broad, encompassing "acts committed with intent to destroy, in whole or in part, a national,

---

4 <http://www.un.org/law/icc/statute/elements/elemfra.htm>.

5 New York, 1997. For a comment by this author, see *China Journal*, no. 43 (January 2000): 228–31. For a recent volume of critical essays on Nanjing, see Joshua Fogel (ed.), *The Nanjing Massacre in History and Historiography* (Berkeley, 2000). See also Timothy Brook (ed.), *Documents on the Rape of Nanking* (Ann Arbor, 1999).

6 As several Japanese scholars have noted, there is a certain similarity in tone and content between Chang's book and the 1997 volume by the Japanese neonationalist cartoonist Kobayashi Yoshinori: both simplified, self-righteous, emotional, stressing national stereotypes, and hugely popular in their respective countries.

ethnical, racial, or religious group."[7] In its original form, as adopted in 1946 by the UN General Assembly, it was even broader, including crimes committed for "political" motives, but pressure from the Soviet Union, where Stalin was presumably anxious to avoid his purges being subjected to genocidal scrutiny, led to its deletion.[8] Because of the restricted definition adopted in 1948, killings that occur in revolutionary or counterrevolutionary contexts, for political reasons, have commonly been excluded from "genocide." Nevertheless the qualifying phrase added in 1948, "in whole or in part," opens the definition to quite wide potential application, and there would seem to be at least a strong a priori case for considering events in Nanjing, and elsewhere, under such a rubric. On the same logic, mass political killings, whether by Stalin or Mao (between 1949 and 1980) or by Suharto in Indonesia, especially in 1965–66, would also be seen as genocidal, the exemption opened for Stalin in 1948 being effectively closed through the adoption of a literal interpretation of the terms of the convention.[9] There would likewise seem to be a strong case for considering acts of the United States government at various times during this century genocidal. To take just one example: was not the bombing of Hiroshima and Nagasaki, for example, designed to kill the citizens of those cities because they were part of the Japanese national group? To this problem we will return.

Everyone, including all post-1945 Japanese governments, agrees that crimes were committed by imperial Japan. Where the differences arise is when it comes to locating those crimes on some comparative frame of criminality. Neither government nor nongovernment organizations in Japan see Japanese criminality as genocidal. The result is that the killing of 6 million people in the European context is regarded as more seriously criminal than that of approximately 10 million in Asia, the one genocidal, the other not. Although explicit moral or legal justification is rarely given, because the suffering of the victims on all sides is equal and absolute, a greater measure of evil *intent* is implicitly attributed to the European side.[10] Such a claim is subjective and unverifiable.

---

7 Acts including killing or causing serious bodily harm to members of such group, or inflicting conditions calculated to bring about its physical destruction, to prevent births within the group, or to transfer children forcibly out of the group. See "Convention for the Prevention and Punishment of the Crime of Genocide," adopted by Resolution 260 (111) A of the UN General Assembly, December 9, 1948 <http://www.preventgenocide.org.law/convention/text.htm>.

8 Robert Cribb, "Genocide in the Non-Western World," *IIAS* (International Institute for Asian Studies, Leiden), Newsletter, no. 25 (July 2001): 6.

9 This is the position taken by Cribb.

10 Foreign visitors to the United States have to fill in series of forms, including one (1-94W Nonimmigrant Visa Waiver) that asks as to their possible involvement in espionage, sabotage, terrorism "or genocide; or between 1933 and 1945 were you involved, in any way, in persecutions associated with

If the fabric of genocide is woven in the narrow sense out of the Holocaust of the 1930s and 1940s, and secondly out of the Armenian, Cambodian, and Rwandan atrocities of the 1910s, 1970s, and 1990s, then the case for extending it to incorporate Japan must argue plausibly that the Japanese record, especially in the 1930s and 1940s, is legally and morally on a par with the Nazi, Khmer Rouge, Turkish, and Rwandan genocides, and it must also argue that it was more repugnant than the other famous examples, including the American, of twentieth-century state violence. That presents difficulties. Excluded from consideration are some extremely violent and atrocious acts, including Stalin's slaughters of the 1920s and 1930s and Mao Zedong's of the 1950s to 1970s, both of them because they were mass killings for *political* rather than for "national, ethnical, racial, or religious" reasons, and therefore not genocidal. Even more difficult is the fact that the kinds of killings for which major Western countries have been responsible, in colonial wars or in counterrevolutionary and counternational liberation struggles, are excluded from the genocidal frame. If Japan is to be seen as genocidal because of *its* colonial and imperial crimes, then the question of the liability of the major Western powers to such charges stemming from their colonial (or postcolonial) record would also have to be reopened, not to mention the violent assault of the powers of the New World upon the aboriginal inhabitants of the New World, continuing till recent times with policies aimed at the destruction of aboriginal cultures by many advanced industrial states (including Australia).[11]

If, on the other hand, the notion of genocide is constructed more broadly, to include large-scale state-sponsored killings, from Stalin to Mao and Suharto, by the simple device of treating the words "in whole or in part" literally, then the case for including Japan is much more straightforward. In fact, it is scarcely open to contest.

In East Asia, in place of the term "genocide" the commonly used terms for great, state-sponsored killings have been terms meaning "great massacre" or "great slaughter" (*gyakusatsu* or *daigyakusatsu*). The literal Japanese term for genocide – *minzoku zetsumetsu* (composed of characters meaning, literally, "racial extermination" or "national extermination") – is reserved,

---

Nazi Germany or its allies." The U.S. government shows no interest in possible Japanese or other perpetrators of crimes against humanity, including genocide.

11 The forced removal of aboriginal children from their families by Australian governments until relatively recent times has been described as genocidal under Article 11 (e) of the 1948 Convention. See Ronald Wilson, *Bringing Them Home: Report of the National Inquiry into the Separation of Aboriginal and Torres Strait Islander Children from Their Families*, Human Rights and Equal Opportunity Commission, (Sydney, 1997). The Australian government has angrily rejected the charge. See also Colin Tatz, "Genocide in Australia," *Journal of Genocide Research* 1, 3 (November 1999): 315–52.

whether in this unfamiliar compound or in its Romanized Japanese form, *jenosaido*, for discussions of Nazi war criminality or "ethnic cleansing."[12]

Of course, even Japanese nationalists and neonationalists concede that Japan may have committed "excesses." What they describe as "Japan's theocratic state under the emperor as high priest" may once have fought "a slightly high-handed patriotic war," but they believe it did not commit "crimes against humanity" such as would warrant its inclusion with Nazi Germany in the category of "historically unprecedented terror state" or "grotesque sex crime state"; Japan, they insist, is neither outlaw nor monster.[13] Its crimes were "ordinary" ones, not the extraordinary crimes of genocide. Not only in relation to the Holocaust, but also in comparison with the U.S. bombing of Hiroshima and Nagasaki (and other Japanese cities) in 1945, or many other twentieth-century crimes, they argue that what Japan did was relatively trivial. In terms of subsequent world history, it seems true enough. Gregory Clark recently observed, "The Dutch in postwar Indonesia, the French in Indochina and Algeria, and the U.S. and Australia in Indochina all behaved as badly as Japan did in Southeast Asia," and yet "[n]one of these governments," he points out acidly, has shown "any great willingness to apologize and make amends."[14]

Clark's point is one that is heard often in Japan. Any case for declaring Japan one of the handful of twentieth-century genocidal states must meet the objection that it does so by employing double standards to justify the exemption of major Western countries from the same list. Unofficial Western (especially U.S.) demands for Japanese admission and apology for war and atrocity responsibility that are not matched by any similar sensitivity to the war crimes committed by the United States and its allies are bound to be seen as hypocritical. As Sakai Naoki observes, there is a notable lack of symmetry in the way that U.S. atrocities at Son My and My Lai recede in the American collective memory, while those committed by the Japanese at Nanjing and elsewhere do not.[15] All late twentieth-century discussion of war crimes, responsibility, and punishment has to address the sort of doublethink that assumes such criminality is absent on the part of the West, especially the United States. The credibility of the newly established International Criminal Court, to which President Clinton committed the

12 The Chinese term uses slightly different characters, *zhongzu miejue*, but with essentially the same meaning.
13 Gavan McCormack, "Nationalism and Identity in Post-Cold War Japan," *Pacifica Review* 12, 3 (October 2000): 249–65, at 250.
14 Gregory Clark, "Japan Has No Monopoly on Obscuring Past," *Japan Times*, November 6, 2000.
15 Sakai Naoki, Takahashi Tetsuya, Sun Ge, and Dai Jinghua, "Sensō no kanjō," *Sekai* (November 2000): 190–205, at 194.

United States in one of his last acts as president in December 2000 (although there is no chance of ratification or implementation by the Bush
administration or Congress), must depend on its demonstrating that it takes
as seriously evidence of crimes against humanity by powerful figures in the
Western world as it does by those who represent discredited and often collapsed or collapsing regimes of the Third World. However unlikely it may
seem, the recent attempt to argue the case for prosecution of Henry Kissinger
before this tribunal on charges of genocide and crimes against humanity assumes importance in this context.[16]

To resume this introductory comment, the following are the major problems involved in any move to add imperial Japan to the select "black list"
of genocidal powers of the twentieth century:

1. In East Asia, neither defenders nor critics of Japanese imperialism, colonialism,
   and militarism, nor scholars who specialize in interpreting and understanding
   it (with some very recent exceptions discussed below), use the term.
2. In the China War context (1931–45) where casualties were huge, for genocide
   to be proved it would have to be shown that those casualties were not the
   consequence of "conventional" military operations as commonly conducted
   by other countries at the time, but part of a design to "destroy, in whole or in
   part, a national, ethnical, racial or religious group." (However, if "anti-Japanese"
   resistance elements constitute "part" of the Chinese national group, as surely
   they do, then plainly Japan, which tried very hard to wipe them out, is guilty
   of genocide under the broad interpretation of the term.)
3. In the Korean context, Japanese colonialist policy was undoubtedly designed
   to destroy "Korea" as a "national group" by assimilating it within Japan. However, such measures by other twentieth-century colonialist regimes have not
   elsewhere been held genocidal. There has been, so to speak, a colonialist exemption, and if that exemption is to be now closed, both logic and morality
   demand that it be closed against all colonialist powers, not just Japan. In the
   overall context of the century, the use of the term "genocide" carrying as it
   does extreme legal and moral oppobrium, to describe acts committed by imperial Japan but not to describe any acts committed by the Western powers
   must be problematic. If Japan was genocidal in China or elsewhere in Asia,
   what then shall we say of the French in Algeria or Indochina, the Americans
   in Korea and Indochina and the Gulf, the Russians in Chechyna?

In what follows, let me consider the record of Japanese colonialism and
war in relation to Korea and China (including the crime of mass mobilization of women throughout Asia for purposes of sexual slavery), with brief
reference also to two special cases of the Japanese treatment of prisoners of
war and engagement in bacteriological or chemical warfare, to consider the

---

16 Christopher Hitchens, *The Trial of Henry Kissinger* (London and New York, 2001).

possible relevance of the concept of genocide as a category of interpretation and understanding.

CHINA

The total Chinese casualty figure in the war with Japan that began with Japanese aggression in the northeastern region of the country in 1931 and spread through the rest of it from 1937 is impossible to know. Dower summarizes the evidence to conclude that "in the end it is necessary to speak of uncertain 'millions of deaths.'" He goes on: "Certainly it is reasonable to think in general terms of approximately 10 million Chinese war dead, a total surpassed only by the Soviet Union."[17]

The best-known, and most infamous, episode in this long war was unquestionably the events of December 1937 in Nanjing, referred to by apologists as an "incident" and by others as a "massacre," "great massacre," or "rape" (the latter only rarely, and then in the romanized form rather than the Sino-Japanese term *gōkan*). In theory, at least, there would seem little difficulty in formally representing Japanese actions in Nanjing as genocidal under the terms of the UN definition because it was a case of killing members of a national group, with intent to destroy them "in whole or in part" because they were members of that group. The subjective experience of the residents of Nanjing (and of countless other cities, towns, and villages in China subject to the operations of the Imperial Japanese Army) involved no less terror than was experienced by the Jewish victims of Nazism or the other victims of recognized genocidal violence. But it could not be considered genocidal if what happened was a series of regrettable, tragic consequences of war attendant upon the temporary breakdown of discipline (as nationalists and neonationalists argue), or if genocide is by definition a term specific and exclusive to Europe (as critics have assumed).

What can be said of Nanjing now is the following: the Japanese army landed at Hangzhou Bay in late November, entered the Chinese walled city of Nanjing on December 12, conducted victory celebrations there on December 17, and continued "mopping up" and "pacification" campaigns in neighboring districts through January of 1938. Chinese victims, both military and civilian, were many. Precise numbers cannot be known, but the Nanjing Museum's figure of 300,000 seems improbably high, inflated perhaps by righteous patriotic outrage, while conservative Japanese estimates of 30,000 to 40,000 are almost certainly too low, deflated by (misplaced)

---

17 John Dower, *War without Mercy: Race and Power in the Pacific War* (New York, 1986), 296.

patriotic righteousness. The question of numbers is, of course, a serious one and historians rightly strive to clarify the record, but with a very few absolute deniers excepted, the emerging Japanese consensus would seem to be that around 200,000 Chinese people were killed, of whom perhaps half were "prisoners of war," and that the killings were either deliberate or else a spontaneous and prolonged outburst of unplanned brutality by Japanese forces, in either case with responsibility borne by the Imperial Japanese Army command and therefore the Japanese government.[18] The evidence is unequivocal that many innocent people were killed.[19] Strictly speaking, therefore, the 1948 definition would seem to cover such events but in fact, except for Chang, it has not been invoked. The event is variously seen (by nationalists and neonationalists) as part of the tragedy of war, or (by critics) as a "massacre" or a "great massacre."

More than sixty years after the event, the question of whether a massacre occurred in Nanjing in December 1937 – and if so, of what scale and character it was – is still debated in Japan. But some progress has undoubtedly been made, especially in this past decade. The idea that "Japan" in general somehow is still in "denial" mode over Nanjing, or that its school history texts still ignore it, is no longer true. Thanks to the long struggle of journalists like Honda Katsuichi, scholars like Ienaga Saburō (who fought the question of censorship of history texts in the court system for three decades), and many professional historians, a consensus has emerged on the broad outlines of the horror of 1937–38, and the "deniers" have plainly lost ground.

In the 1990s prime ministers and the emperor apologized for Japan's colonialism and aggression and referred to the massive suffering inflicted on millions of people. Textbooks were revised to incorporate, however briefly, reference to Nanjing, "comfort women," and other aspects of the war.[20] Various spokespersons for the government issued statements confirming official recognition that many noncombatants were killed during the capture of Nanjing.[21] In September 1999 the Tokyo District Court likewise held that the atrocity known as the Nanjing Massacre definitely happened. According to the judgment, the scale of the devastation could not be known, but it was an act of indefensible, imperialist, planned colonial aggression against

---

18 This assessment is owed to Professor Yoshimi Yoshiaki, personal communication, Canberra, November 4, 2000.

19 For a recent Japanese summary of the evidence, see Nankin jiken chōsa kenkyūkai (ed.), *Nankin daigyakusatsu 13 no uso* (Tokyo, 1999).

20 Gavan McCormack, "The Japanese Movement to 'Correct' History," in Laura Elizabeth Hein and Mark Selden (eds.), *Censoring History: Citizenship and Memory in Japan, Germany and the United States* (New York, 2000), 55–73.

21 Nankin jiken chōsa kenkyūkai, *Nankin daigyakusatsu hiteiron 13 no uso* (Kashiwa shobō, 1999): 1–2.

the Chinese people, in clear breach of international law, and the damage and suffering it caused is beyond question, for which Japan should apologize sincerely to the Chinese people.[22] It was a landmark decision, even though the court went on to declare that, while the victims deserved an apology from the government of Japan, they had no legal entitlement to redress. Some fifty cases seeking redress for wartime suffering are currently before the Japanese courts. The process may be belated, slow, and sometimes equivocal, but Diet, judiciary, media, and education circles are grappling in one way or another to come to terms with the horrors of the war. However, genocide has, to date, formed no part of the debate, in or out of the courts, and while in Germany over 10,000 cases of Nazi war criminality have been tried in German courts (with 6,000 guilty verdicts being handed down), in Japan the notion of criminal responsibility, if considered at all, has been treated in the most abstract way.

While attention focuses on Nanjing, much of the rest of the war is forgotten. Yet the war as a whole was characterized by mayhem, slaughter, rape, and arson, and the wave of violence that swept across cities and countryside around Nanjing from November 1937 to January 1938 was not qualitatively different from the rest of Japan's war on China between 1931 and 1945. Indeed, the sad fact is that China as a whole was Nanjing writ large; and that what was different about Nanjing was that there were many observers, including foreigners, who were able to report it. In particular the countryside of North China was punctuated with mass graves, "ten thousand people pits" (*wanrenkeng/banjinkō*), or "people reducing kilns" (*lianrenlu/renjinro*); countless villages were burned to the ground and their population either killed or driven off into walled compounds, and countless women were raped. For Chinese historians, therefore, and also for many Japanese historians, Nanjing was part of a broad movement that, in terms of deliberation and quantity, and in the context of these huge campaigns to drain the water from the pond in which the guerrillas swam, was "total war" (though never actually declared a war, and thus prosecuted free of the inhibitions demanded by the international laws of war), ruthlessly prosecuted by modern, mechanized, forces against a largely civilian, often peasant population, with immense casualties. Particularly from 1940 in North (and Central) China the official Japanese policy of rooting out resistance by a series of "absolutely extinguish, pacify, and punish" operations, designed to concentrate the population in militarized encampments and to turn the open countryside into "unpopulated

22 Gavan McCormack, "Nationalism and Identity in Post–Cold War Japan," *Pacifica Review* 12, 3 (October 2000): 249–65, at 252.

zones" (*mujin chiku*), meaning free fire zones, was understood as a policy of "three alls" (*sankō sakusen*) that meant "kill all, burn all, loot all."[23] These North China campaigns certainly merit consideration under the rubric of genocide, alongside the better-known horrors of Nanjing, but once again, the case is rarely put in those terms.

Furthermore, although the Japanese poured huge forces into China, because it was no war, merely an "incident," no provision or plan was made for taking or holding prisoners, many of whom were ill-treated, often tortured or killed. In terms of the 1948 UN Convention, such acts had no legal or military justification, and therefore might be construed as committed with "intent to destroy" part of a "national group" – that is, those members of the national group who dissented from the Japanese agenda.

This phase of the Japanese war in China constitutes a major link in the history of twentieth-century counterguerrilla warfare that began with the U.S. efforts to crush nationalist resistance in the Philippines after the war with Spain at the beginning of the century and ended with the Russian attempts to crush Chechnyan resistance.[24] The case for viewing such counterguerrilla operations as genocide, rather than as covered by "military exigency," seems plain enough. As Jean-Paul Sartre observed to the Russell Vietnam War Crimes Tribunal, "the only anti-guerrilla strategy which will be effective is the destruction of the people, in other words, the civilians, women and children," namely, torture and "genocide," exactly what he and others believed was the tactic adopted by the United States in Vietnam.[25] For Japanese crimes falling under this category to be seen as genocidal, much twentieth-century history of like actions would have to be reassessed too.

KOREA

Strictly speaking, the search for the criteria of genocide in Japan's prewar regime would almost certainly concentrate on a country with which Japan was never at war: Korea. Here the evidence for a systematic attempt to destroy a national group, the Korean nation (by assimilating it), is plain. Furthermore, in Korea, there is no Auschwitz or Dachau, no Nanjing or Harbin, yet countless Korean proponents of national autonomy were tortured and

23 Himeta Mitsuyoshi and Chen Ping, *Mo hitotsu no sankō sakusen* (Aoki shoten, 1989), esp. 133–34. And see Gavan McCormack, *The Emptiness of Japanese Affluence* (1996; New York, 2001), ch. 6, "Remembering and Forgetting: The War, 1945–1995," 225–84.

24 On the former, John R. M. Taylor, *The Philippine Insurrection against the United States*, 5 vols. (Pasay City, 1971).

25 Jean-Paul Sartre, "On Genocide," Russell Vietnam War Crimes Tribunal <http://www.homeusers. prestel.co.uk/littleton/v1217sar.htm>.

killed between 1894 and the incorporation of Korea as the Japanese colony of Chosen in 1910, culminating in the suppression of the great nonviolent resistance movement of 1919 (in which Korean sources report over 7,500 people killed and 45,000 injured),[26] and the extinction of Korea as a national unit "in whole" rather than "in part" was a consistent, fundamental, Japanese national policy. An Chung-Gun, the Korean patriot who in 1909 assassinated the Japanese regent and thus precipitated the transition, is hailed and commemorated by Koreans in both North and South as a national hero; in Japan he is reviled as a terrorist. The Japan-Korea relationship is pivotal in modern East Asian history but cannot be understood without reference to the deep roots of the modern relationship: the sixteenth century.

The Sixteenth Century

The debate on genocide proceeds from the assumption that only modern events should be considered, and that it would serve no purpose for the destruction of Carthage, for example, to be declared genocidal. Yet in East Asia the burden of premodern history weighs heavily on the present. As the sixteenth-century Japanese historian, Mary Elizabeth Berry, has remarked, "I have wondered whether the scale of twentieth century atrocity has reduced the gravity of our response to the past. Perhaps our attention to the institutional brutalities of modern states has also led us to slight pre-modern brutality."[27] Japan experienced a long period of violence and civil war from around 1467 to the beginning of the seventeenth century. In the late sixteenth century, the coalition of forces led by the warlord (to give him a modern designation), Toyotomi Hideyoshi, victorious in the civil war, proceeded to demilitarize the country, seizing swords and other weapons and melting them down. But the violence and turmoil had their own momentum, for which mere stability was no satisfaction. While pacifying Japan, Hideyoshi therefore resolved to conquer China and establish a new world order. Whether or not Berry is right that he craved above all "homage," not control, his ambition disrupted first Korea, then China and indirectly the world.[28]

When Korea refused to recognize and defer to the new order, Hideyoshi in 1592 launched a war against it. Eventually he lost, but his forces, around 160,000 men in all, armed with modern (matchlock) firearms and seasoned from generations of warfare, inflicted deep wounds and only withdrew from

---

26 Chong-Sik Lee, *Japan and Korea – the Political Dimension* (Stanford, 1985), 7.
27 Mary Elizabeth Berry, *The Culture of the Civil War in Kyoto* (Berkeley, 1994), xv.
28 Ibid., 216.

a second phase of warfare, in 1598, after his death. In terms of period, this was certainly premodern, but it pitted large armies, equipped with modern firearms and discipline, in a systematic attempt to conquer a neighbor state; it was modern in the degree of its mobilization of people and resources. Was it also genocidal?

Hideyoshi rewarded his commanders in proportion to the number of enemies they could show they had slaughtered. They could prove the numbers by delivering back to headquarters in Japan the noses of those killed. Heads might have been more satisfactory, and in the case of commanders were required, but they were heavy and difficult to transport, ears were complicated since people had two, but noses were an irrefutable, distinctive, and conveniently small human attribute. Hideyoshi's forces were assigned quotas – three Korean noses for each Japanese soldier.[29] Pickled in great barrels, they were despatched back to Japan, where they were duly counted and rewards meted out accordingly. One meritorious Japanese clan, the Nabeshima, sent back 29,251 noses, but thousands of others were sent back by other commanders with no overall count surviving. Various counts point to a figure between "not less than 100,000" and about 200,000 noses being brought back from Korea to Japan.[30] Several tens of thousands were buried in front of the Great Buddha hall at Hōkōji Temple in Kyoto, where to this day the *Mimizuka* (literally "Ear Mound") remains, a nondescript place now partially swallowed by suburbs, before which it is hard to stand without feeling the blood chill.

Like Nanjing much later, there would be a wide discrepancy in detail, especially numbers, but not in the essential facts of the slaughter.[31] The burial mound was throughout premodern and modern Japanese history till very recent decades a celebrated place of pilgrimage, a monument to Hideyoshi's triumphs and his clemency (for having the defeated enemy given a Buddhist repose).[32] And at Fujisaki Shrine in Kumamoto, Katō Nagamasa is commemorated and the autumn festival is known as *Boshita-sai*, probably short for *Chōsen o horoboshita* ("the devastation of Korea").[33]

Korean culture as of the late sixteenth century was in many, perhaps most (save warfare) respects, more developed than Japan's. Consequently it was not just noses that Hideyoshi and his commanders plundered. The

---

29 Kim Hong-kyu (ed.), *Hideyoshi, Mimizuka, yonhyakunen* (Tokyo, 1998), 66.
30 Ibid., 74, for the lower figure, and Kim Pong-Hyun, *Hideyoshi no Chōsen shinryaku to gihei tōsō* (Tokyo, 1995), 378, for the higher figure. Both, however, are in broad agreement and careful to stress the impossibility of knowing accurately.
31 Kim Pong-Hyon, *Hideyoshi no Chōsen*, 375–78.
32 Kim Hong-kyu, *Hideyoshi*, 78ff.
33 Nukii Masayuki, *Hideyoshi to arasotta Chōsen bushō* (Tokyo, 1992), 184.

living, the most famous being the potters, were also seized in large numbers. After fourteen or so generations, their descendants still retain a distinctive identity and remember their Korean origins. Not only potters, but doctors, printers, artisans in wood and metal, paper makers, scroll makers, painters, dyers, weavers and spinners, garden designers and experts, and scholars were seized and brought back to Japan, along with printing presses, the "high tech" items of their time, many cultural treasures, and, perhaps the greatest prize, Korea's young women. How many of them were seized is impossible to know, but an estimate of 50,000 to 60,000,[34] in a total figure of "no less than 100,000" Koreans transported to Japan, has been suggested in various scholarly accounts.[35] Other Koreans were sold as slaves, or exchanged for guns, silk, or other prized foreign goods, either directly or via third-country slave traders, to many countries, some finishing up as far away as Portugal.

In short, it seems that a case might be made for considering this war genocidal, but the fact is that it almost never is discussed in these terms. The reasons might be either spatial or temporal: perhaps genocide is a European cultural construct, or perhaps considerations of genocide are guided by a statute of limitations, so that events of 70 years ago, Nazism, and (perhaps) of ninety-odd years ago (Armenia), may be accepted as part of the debate, but those of 400 years ago must be disqualified from consideration. But it is not easy to formulate any moral principle to justify such distinctions. If genocide is to be reconstituted as a universal, cross-cultural and cross-temporal criminal phenomenon, then these events surely deserve consideration.

After the Japanese withdrawal from Korea, the adoption of a policy of national isolation ushered in two centuries of peace. However, because the legacy of violence and brutality was not critically addressed, Hideyoshi was eulogized as the commoner who rose from the ranks, and modern Japan was destined from the nineteenth century to revive both his dreams of continental empire and his ruthless methods of accomplishing them. There was no debate in Edo Japan on all this, no regrets save over the mission having ended in defeat and withdrawal.

The Twentieth Century

As the "feudal" East Asian order crumbled before the advances of Western imperialism in the nineteenth century, China, Japan, and Korea were all shaken by political, economic, and social upheaval. In Japan, two decades of

---

34 Kim Pong-Hyon, *Hideyoshi no Chōsen*, esp. 382–89.
35 Kim Hong-kyu, *Hideyoshi*, 127.

disorder culminated in the emergence of the modernizing Meiji state (1868), but in Korea the peasant and antiimperialist war known as the Tonghak erupted two and a half decades later. It triggered interventions from both Ch'ing dynasty China and Meiji Japan, opening the way, first to semicolonial encroachment, then, in 1910, to full absorption. Recent scholarship on the Tonghak Peasant War of 1894 draws a picture of between 300,000 and 400,000 injured and some 50,000 killed in the brutal Japanese suppression campaigns, and shows that mass killings were in accordance with specific orders from Imperial Army Headquarters in Hiroshima.[36]

From around 1920 to 1945 overt military violence was uncommon, but the structural incorporation and subordination of Korea as Japan's colony was extremely thorough and the shift from "military" to "civil" rule was consistent in the ruthless suppression of any sentiment for Korean independence. Korea was known to the world as Chosen. The land was appropriated by mostly absentee Japanese landlords, the harvest was appropriated to relieve the food problems in Japan, driving many locals to the brink of starvation. Policies adopted to incorporate, assimilate, and thereby extinguish Korea as a separate political, national identity were adopted, including the imposition on Korea of subordinate political status (Japanese rule), of Japanese state Shinto religion, and of Japan's emperor and his imperial ancestors as gods, of Japanese names to replace Korean names, and of Japanese language for Korean language. Speaking Korean was punished, the work on a Korean dictionary stopped, and (in 1942) the members of the Korean Institute of Linguistics all arrested (twenty of them dying in prison). "Love the country" (i.e., Japan) days were instituted in schools, shrines to the Japanese imperial family gods were turned into focal points in all towns, flag wavings and recitals of Japanese imperial rescripts were instituted. Ultimately, as the system of total mobilization was adopted from 1942, around a million young Korean men were mobilized to work the mines and construction sites in Japan itself, and quite a few thousands directly into low-ranking positions in the Japanese military itself, while tens of thousands of young Korean women, most of them between the ages of sixteen and nineteen, were mobilized as "comfort women" to service sexually the Imperial Japanese Army.

Korea's separateness, its history and memory, traditions and religion, were crushed, its language, its people's names, and many of its bodies, especially

---

36 Cho Kyon-Dal, "Gitan no minshū hanran – Togaku to Kango nōmin sensō" (Iwanami shoten, 1998). See also Inoue Katsuo, "Nihongun ni yoru saishō no higashi Ajia minshū gyakusatsu," *Sekai* (October 2001): 238–47, at 245. In his paper to the International Conference on the 21st Century Significance of the Tonghak Peasant Revolution, Chonju, Korea, May 2001, Inoue used the term "genocide" in brackets as the equivalent of "gyakusatsu" or mass killing. (See also Hahn Seung-hun, "Tōgaku nōmin kakumei to Ajia no atarashii rekishi," *Sekai* [October 2001]: 248–56.)

those of its youth, appropriated. However, the attempt to extinguish Korea as a separate identity, culture, and state, and to absorb it within Japan, was not even considered criminal by the International Military Tribunal for the Far East that sat in Tokyo from 1946.[37] That tribunal included the major colonial powers of the time, and however harsh and brutal to the contemporary conscience, in the records of colonialism it is hard to find anything unique about Japanese practice. Although bitterly resented by Koreans to this day, the policies and acts associated with the forced assimilation of Korea have rarely been considered in "genocide" terms.

Furthermore, as Takahashi Tetsuya notes, the category of crime against humanity, first addressed in the judgment at Nuremberg, later held so serious that immunity from prosecution due to passage of time was removed, and then developed into a fundamental concept in the various trials leading up to the International Criminal Court's Tribunal hearings on Yugoslavia from 2000, was not addressed in Tokyo.[38] There, such crimes were not distinguished from "ordinary" crimes of war or against peace. The sexual slavery of women, for example, was not treated as criminal. Indeed the Allied occupation forces relied on a very similar process of mobilization of young women to provide sexual outlets for their soldiers in peace as had the Japanese army during war.[39] It took nearly five decades after the war ended before the first victim of the "comfort women" system, a Korean, in 1991 came out to speak of her experiences and demand justice. In Tokyo in December 2000 a Women's International War Crimes Tribunal on Japan's Military Sexual Slavery was conducted by women's groups from throughout the region.[40] One Japanese scholar has observed that, in a sense, the suffering of the women victims of these crimes has been even deeper than that of survivors of the Holocaust, because it has been compounded by a sense of shame that has lasted through their entire lives.[41] The societies and governments of East Asia share a complicity in the crime by participating in its cover-up and enforcing silence and guilt on the women victims for fifty years.

Had the Tokyo tribunal addressed the category of crimes against humanity, the criminality of the "comfort women" system and the "enslavement" of the Korean people (in the words of the 1943 Cairo Declaration) would have been plain. The deep reluctance on the part of spokespersons of the

37 The enslavement of Dutch women was the subject of prosecution in separate trials conducted by Dutch authorities in Batavia in the East Indies (Indonesia).
38 Takahashi Tetsuya, "Rekishi to sabaki," *Sekai* (December 2000): 98–107.
39 On this latter point, Yuki Tanaka, *Japan's Comfort Women: Sexual Slavery and Prostitution during World War II and the US Occupation* (New York and London, 2001), esp. ch. 5 and 6, 110–66.
40 <http://www.jca.apc.org/vaww-net-japan/>.
41 Takahashi Tetsuya, "Rekishi to sabaki," 100.

Japanese state to concede wrong, let alone criminal responsibility, for its Korean record has long bedeviled Japan-Korea relations. Between Japan and South Korea a Cold War accommodation was reached under U.S. pressure in 1965, in which war responsibility issues were elided and emphasis placed on restoring of economic links. More than half a century since the collapse of Japanese imperial control, a settlement between Japan and North Korea has still to be negotiated.

The systematic attempt to crush Korea's political, cultural, and religious identity might seem directed at "the destruction of a national, ethnical, racial or religious group," but the record of Japanese colonialism in Korea is complex. To stop at the repressive aspects of the colonial system would be to neglect the fact that considerable economic growth was also accomplished. The context in Korea was one of imperialism but not war, and the Japanese system relied, especially after 1920, on securing the consent of a substantial element of the Korean elite. Population grew. Korea was "modernized," and industrialization pursued – a rare phenomenon in a colony. Furthermore, of no small significance, while resistance was crushed, sometimes brutally, the people were not on the whole, especially after 1920, subject to mass killings. Order prevailed. It may be that the process was all oriented toward the strengthening of the Japanese imperial system, but a huge social and economic transformation took place all the same.[42] Whether historical understanding would be advanced by insisting that Japanese colonialism be categorized along with the crimes of Nazism and the Khmer Rouge may be doubted.

TWO SPECIAL CASES: PRISONERS OF WAR AND GERM WARFARE

However the operations of Japanese armies in neighboring Asian countries be characterized, a genocide discussion should probably also take into account two special cases: the treatment of prisoners of war (POWs), and the cultivation of weapons of mass and indiscriminate killing, chemical and bacteriological, with a view to their employment for genocidal purposes, even if the intent was not executed.[43] A case could be made that Japan's crimes against POWs during the Second World War were extreme, and such a case has often and eloquently been argued.[44] The death rate among prisoners

---

42 Gavan McCormack and Stewart Lone, *Korea since 1850* (Melbourne and New York, 1993).
43 By this I mean that the genocidal dimension was not implemented. Chemical and biological warfare were both conducted by Japan in China in a limited, essentially experimental way.
44 Gavan Daws, *Prisoners of the Japanese: POWs of World War II in the Pacific* (New York, 1994); Yuki Tanaka, *Hidden Horrors: Japanese War Crimes in World War II* (Boulder, 1996).

of the Japanese was many times higher than that among prisoners of the Nazis, although much lower than in the case of other theaters – such as the Russian and German prisoners on the eastern front in World War II.[45] It is also at least plausible that there was a plan to murder all POW survivors if Japan was defeated, and that the plan was not implemented only because of the suddenness of the final events and the breakdown of Japanese army command.[46] Certainly many POWs believed they were destined for a "final solution" when the time came. Daws concludes from his study that

The Japanese were not directly genocidal in their POW camps. They did not herd their white prisoners into gas chambers and burn their corpses in ovens. But they drove them toward mass deaths all the same. They beat them until they fell, then beat them for falling, beat them until they bled, then beat them for bleeding. They denied them medical treatment. They starved them.... They sacrificed prisoners in medical experiments. They watched them die by the tens of thousands from diseases of malnutrition like beriberi, pellagra, and scurvy, and from epidemic tropical diseases: malaria, dysentery, tropical ulcers, cholera. Those who survived could only look ahead to being worked to death. If the war lasted another year, there would not have been a POW alive.[47]

But the POWs were by definition a multinational, multiethnic group.[48] Even had they all been killed, it would therefore have amounted to a massacre, a slaughter, but not genocide. Furthermore, most agree now that the treatment of Asian POWs in Southeast Asia was substantially worse than that of Europeans, while for the Chinese, the war brought a wide range of possible outcomes: slaughter, capture, and imprisonment (but as prisoners in ordinary prisons, not POW camps protected by international law), or even incorporation as part of "puppet" forces fighting on the Japanese side. When the war in China ended, there were no prison camps to be thrown open, few prisoners to be liberated. Whether the cause of subjecting state violence to legal sanction would be advanced by having the label of genocide attached to the treatment of the relatively small numbers of Western prisoners but not to the treatment of the masses of the people of Asia seems doubtful.

45 The death rate in the case of Australian prisoners was 3 percent for those held by Germany and 36 percent for those held by Japan. However, for German and Russian prisoners on the eastern front in World War II, it was 45 and 60 percent respectively. Hank Nelson, "Prisoner-of-War Death Rates: Some Comparisons," in Gavan McCormack and Hank Nelson (eds.), *The Burma-Thailand Railway: Memory and History* (London, 1993), 162–65.
46 See "Saigo no shodan" (Final disposal), in Yui Daizaburō and Kosuge Nobuko, *Rengokoku horyō gyakutai to sengo sekinin*, Iwanami bukkuretto, no. 321 (1993): 37–38.
47 Daws, *Prisoners*, 18.
48 Ibid., passim; see also McCormack and Nelson, *Burma-Thailand Railway.*

As for the problem of chemical and bacteriological warfare preparations, and partial or experimental deployment, the considerable literature on this could be summarized by saying that many atrocities were committed by Unit 731 in Harbin and its subbranches elsewhere in China.[49] Research and development work designed to manufacture racially or ethnically discriminatory pathogens to wipe out particular peoples was conducted, and in the process many lives were lost. The grand campaign to which it was oriented was never launched, however, so that it amounted perhaps to conspiracy for genocide, or planning toward genocide, rather than the thing itself (although some thousands of people nevertheless fell victim to it). To my knowledge, however, none of the experts who have worked on these matters chooses to characterize these crimes as genocidal. In any case it is necessary to recall that superpower strategy, to the end of the twentieth century and even at the beginning of the twenty-first, has been based on the development and stockpiling of weapons capable of destroying not only particular peoples but all people. Such plans may not be considered as genocidal, however, because the crime as defined in 1948 did not include the planning or working toward indiscriminate or general human slaughter, only cases in which members of a particular "national, ethnical, racial or religious group" are targeted.

THE GENOCIDAL COMPLEX

To the extent that the historical record makes possible the identification of some elements of a "genocidal" or "protogenocidal" mind-set, understanding the history becomes one condition for blocking, or at least contesting, its repetition. Robert Lifton has argued that the possibility of genocidal violence becomes high in situations of what he calls "extreme historical trauma, confusion and chaos," in which there emerges "a group with a revitalizing ideology that becomes genocidal by feeding on an impulse to destroy what I call the designated victim."[50] It is an analysis that seems to fit well the circumstances of the European Holocaust and also the circumstances in Turkey, Cambodia, and Rwanda, but much less obviously those of 1930s and 1940s Japan, where social and political order never broke down. However, what is characteristic of the "revitalizing ideology" is the way that a line is drawn

---

49 See the various works of Tsuneishi Kei'ichi, the authority on this subject, or, in English, Sheldon H. Harris, *Factories of Death* (London and New York, 1994).
50 Robert Lifton, quoted in Paul Grondahl, "Writer Studies Why We Hate," *Times Union*, November 2, 2000 <http://www.timesunion.com>.

between inside and outside, "us" and "them," so that the "designated victim" can be identified and victimized, "our" society cleansed.

The process of establishing the inside and outside of national identity involved in the premodern and modern Japanese case to an unusual degree the construction of "Japan" as a superior, unique, divine, blood and history united people, different from their neighbors and destined to rule over them. The way that the line was drawn reflected a sense of vulnerability and crisis, and undoubtedly facilitated from time to time the direction of large-scale, state-directed Japanese violence against neighbors. This mentality remains strong. Japan has had consistent difficulty in conceiving of a common "Asian" identity and destiny, resorting instead to atavistic notions of a unique Japanese identity, commonly constructed around the institution of the emperor. Although Lifton's "extreme historical trauma," of the depth that was experienced in Turkey, Germany, Cambodia, and Rwanda, has not been known in modern Japan, the ideology of Japanese superiority and uniqueness, codified in the prewar and wartime years as *kokutai* (national polity) persists.

Even as internationalization of the economy and political and social engagement with the region and the world reaches unprecedented levels, so, in contrapuntal tension, does the insistence on Japan's uniqueness, as a "monoracial society" and a "natural community" (*shizen kyōdōtai*), unlike polyglot countries such as the United States, mere nations "formed by contract."[51] The representation of Japan as a blood-defined nation, a "land of the gods centered on the emperor,"[52] superior and distinct, on which conservative bureaucrats and politicians continue to insist, has marked similarity to the rhetoric of "ethnic cleansing" elsewhere in the world. The movement to construct a "bright" Japan, and a "proud" Japanese identity is backed by prominent corporate as well as political and intellectual figures. Its capacity for mass mobilization is evident in the recent campaigns for textbook revision, and for the reinstatement of imperial symbols.[53] Inside the National Diet, members who insist on the justice of the war's cause and firmly oppose any apologies organize groups with names such as the Dietmembers League for a Bright Japan and the Dietmembers League for the Passing on

51 Words used by Nakasone Yasuhiro, prime minister in the mid-1980s and Japan's elder statesman through the end of century. See Gavan McCormack, "Kokusaika: Impediments in Japan's Deep Structure," in Donald Denoon, Mark Hudson, Gavan McCormack, and Tessa Morris-Suzuki (eds.), *Multicultural Japan – Palaeolithic to Postmodern* (Cambridge, 1996), 265–86, at 275–76.
52 Prime Minister Mori Yoshiro's formulation, May 15, 2000. See Gavan McCormack, introduction to *The Emptiness of Japanese Affluence*, 2nd rev. ed. (New York, 2001).
53 McCormack, "Nationalism and Identity in Post–Cold War Japan."

of a Correct History, whose formulations match those by nationalist and rightist leaders such as Joerg Haider in Austria and Jean-Marie Le Pen in France.

If there is a protogenocidal or ethnic cleansing sort of mind in Japan, it is not manifest in active discrimination against racial minorities (at least on a scale comparable with Europe), and it certainly does not include any idealization of the peasant soul.[54] To the extent that contemporary Japanese identity politics is characterized by a powerful trend toward returning to the formula of premodern and imperial Japan, the debate over identity thus has profound implications.

CONCLUSION

Fifty-seven years after the end of its various wars and the liquidation of its colonial empire, Japanese courts have yet to arraign, much less convict a single person for any war crime. The many war crimes trials that followed World War II meted out a lot of punishment – though in the Japanese case nearly all at the lower, field levels rather than at the level of command and real responsibility – but signally failed to settle the issues of guilt and responsibility to the satisfaction of the Japanese community, even less of those who were actually punished. Paradoxically, the war crimes trials that, virtually uniquely, seem to have accomplished moral regeneration in the guilty were those conducted in China at the direction of Zhou Enlai. There, a thousand Japanese soldiers were imprisoned and, instead of punishment, simply encouraged to recall and record the details of their lives and deeds as soldiers, including their participation in mass killing, rape, and pillage in the course of the extermination campaigns.[55] What is unique about this group is the fact that their spell in Chinese prisons between 1945 and 1956 seems to have stirred their conscience in a profound way that lasted, for many at least, a lifetime, and served as a powerful voice in Japanese society for truth and reconciliation. Yet in official Japan, those responsible for both Japan's

---

54 Compare Ben Kiernan's hypothesis that two qualities intrinsic to genocide are persecution of minority races and idealization of the peasant population. Quoted in Lisa Asato, "Genocides Share Common Aspects," *Ka Leo On line* <http://www.kaleo.org/1999/11/30/1news.html>. See also Ben Kiernan, "Sur la notion de génocide," *Le Débat* (March–April 1999) <http://www.yale.edu/gsp/Debat-Kiernan.htm>.

55 The Chūgoku Kikansha Renrakukai (Association of Returnees from China). See <http://www.tyuukiren.org>. For a recent example, Hoshi Toru, "Chūgoku e 'kikyō' shita Nihonjin senpantachi," *Shūkan kinyōbi*, October 13 and 20, 2000, 52–55 and 30–31. See also the 1990 documentary film produced by NHK and entitled *1,064 Nin Senpan no Jihaku* (Confessions of 1,064 war criminals). The psychoanalyst Noda Masaaki has written a penetrating analysis of the mind-set of these soldiers: *Sensō to zaiseki* (War and criminal responsibility) (Iwanami shoten, 1998).

aggressive ventures into Asia, in the sixteenth and twentieth centuries are to this day seen as heroes.

The search for judicial machinery to restrain and punish acts of genocide continued after World War II, but the record has been mixed. When genocide, as widely agreed, occurred in Cambodia and Rwanda in the 1970s and 1990s respectively, the major powers in the United Nations (including the United States) insisted on the Khmer Rouge retaining its seat in the United Nations in the one case and stood aside, declining any intervention while nearly a million people were slaughtered, in the other. The great slaughters that occurred in China between 1949 and 1980 and in Indonesia in 1965 and 1966 have not commonly been described as genocidal for the reason that, like those occurring under Stalin, they were politically motivated. Increasingly, however, a consensus seems to be evolving toward the position that the "political exemption" of the 1940s should be closed by the literal interpretation of the term "in part" in the expression of the convention "intent to destroy, in whole or in part, a national, ethnical, racial or religious group."

End-of-century initiatives included, at the public level of states and international institutions, the establishment of the International Criminal Court and the opening of various trials under its auspices; and, at the level of civil society, the convening in Tokyo in December 2000 of the Women's International War Crimes Tribunal on Japan's Military Sexual Slavery. This latter was a "tribunal" in the tradition of the Russell Tribunal of 1966–67 on U.S. war crimes in Vietnam. Organized by women from various groups of civil society throughout the region, it was designed to redress the long failure of official Japan to concern itself with war crimes and the failure of the international community adequately to address crimes against women in particular. It formally heard evidence on the "comfort women" system practiced by imperial Japan and took some steps toward assigning responsibility for it, most notably by finding Japanese emperor (and commander in chief) Hirohito guilty. It was an important step toward the restoration of justice, human rights, and dignity to the victimized women, and a pressure on the international community to end the cycle of impunity for violence against women in wartime and conflict situations. But even in this "citizen's tribunal," representing the voice of civil society from throughout the region and making a great, late-century contribution toward elucidating the problems of war, violence, and gender, neither the victims, nor their legal representatives, sought recourse to the law of genocide.

The problem of drawing up a taxonomy of state-led mass killing in the twentieth century is no mere academic pursuit. More than in any other

sector of criminal law the goals of punishment and deterrence are major social policy objectives. State-sponsored violence was a scourge of the
twentieth century. But it is far from clear that advances in the identification,
prosecution, and punishment of the specific crime of genocide will serve to
neutralize or block it in the twenty-first. The bedrock of the problem may
be twofold. On the one hand, the crime of genocide, often conceived and
in the courts and history texts reserved for the crimes of Nazism against the
Jewish people, has only slowly been expanded from the special, unique evil
of the Nazi slaughter of the Jews to a general and universal category of war
crime. The process does not move smoothly. The legal and moral reasons
for singling out one particular form of state violence, genocide, as the systematic attempt to exterminate whole races, from the systematic attempt to
exterminate the part rather than the whole of racial or ethnic groups, was
tied in its origin to political expediency and had little to do with a defensible
moral or legal principle. On the other hand, the twentieth century is too
rich in precedents of "victor's justice," where the acts of the defeated were
declared utterly depraved (and genocidal) while similar acts on the part of
the victor were justified. Both of these problems cast a shadow over the
effort to achieve generalized justice and to punish and deter all forms of
state violence.

PART IV

Genocide and Mass Murder since 1945

13

"When the World Turned to Chaos"

1965 and Its Aftermath in Bali, Indonesia

LESLIE DWYER AND DEGUNG SANTIKARMA

In May 1998, when Suharto stepped down from the presidency of Indonesia, a torrent of talk was unleashed about the past, present, and future of the country he had ruled for more than thirty-two years. As censorship of the media was lifted and as laws prohibiting the formation of political parties were repealed, a newly vibrant civil society began to overflow with optimism and openness. From the halls of the People's Consultative Assembly in Jakarta to the small *warung* food stalls that serve as gathering places for the archipelago's poor, one word was being uttered that seemed to condense a national consciousness: *reformasi*, the new era that would leave the legacy of Suharto's "New Order" regime behind.

But even as Indonesia was looking to its future with a heady sense of hope, the fall of Suharto saw stories emerge into public culture that had long been silenced. Reports began to be heard of military murders, torture, and sexual violence in Aceh and East Timor. Tales began to be told of the everyday terror of living under a regime committed to surveillance of its population and to spectacles flouting its military might. And people began – some haltingly, some looking warily over their shoulders, and a few more boldly – to speak about the inaugural events of Suharto's rule: the violence of 1965, in which up to 1 million people were brutally killed over the span of a few bloody months.

Today, in the aftermath of the initial euphoria of reform, with communal violence continuing across Indonesia, we believe that it has become even more urgent to address the events that brought Suharto to power and to understand how they continue to haunt national and local imaginations,

This essay was first prepared for a conference on comparative genocide in Barcelona, December 6–10, 2000, organized by Robert Gellately and Ben Kiernan and funded by the Harry Frank Guggenheim Foundation. Our work is based on field research in Bali, Indonesia, funded by a MacArthur Foundation Global Security and Sustainability Research and Writing Grant for collaborative research.

provoking conflict, mistrust, and fear of political articulation or action. For the events of 1965 are not simply historical happenings made distant by the passage of time, or fading memories subject to remembering or forgetting or revision. The bloodshed of 1965 has soaked into Indonesia's social landscape, shifting cultural, religious and political topographies, and shaping possibilities for speech and social action.

EXPLAINING VIOLENCE

In the early 1960s, Indonesia was home to the largest communist party in Southeast Asia, the Partai Komunis Indonesia or PKI. Enjoying the tacit support of then-president Sukarno, whose self-professed philosophy of NASAKOM – nationalism, religion, and communism – attempted to appeal to and encompass a broad ideological spectrum, the PKI was an established force on the political scene. But as Sukarno's government wobbled under economic and political pressures, tensions between the left (represented by the PKI, the Partai Sosialis Indonesia [PSI], and a host of local groups concerned with issues ranging from land reform to labor rights to literature) and the right (represented by the Partai Nasionalis Indonesia [PNI], its affiliates, and a coalition of Islamic parties) began to intensify. On September 30, 1965, six army generals were murdered in what the government claimed was a coup attempt sponsored by the PKI. According to official state history, a then-unknown General Suharto stepped in, frustrating the coup, and, in the name of order and stability, relieving Sukarno of his duties.[1] Over the next few months, Suharto's new regime carried out a military and symbolic offensive against Indonesia's left, executing and jailing those suspected of having ties to the communist party, encouraging communities to "cleanse" themselves of subversive elements and, in the process, redefining "politics" as something dangerous, divisive, and antinational. By February 1966, when the mass violence finally died down, up to 1 million Indonesians were dead and another 80,000 others were jailed without trial as political criminals.[2] As

---

1 This is obviously a very abbreviated history of events that, even now, remain shrouded in secrecy and silence. For discussions of the alleged coup attempt and the massacres that followed, see Benedict Anderson and Ruth McVey, *A Preliminary Analysis of the 1 October 1965 Coup in Indonesia* (Ithaca, 1971); Robert Cribb (ed.), *The Indonesian Killings of 1965–66: Studies from Java and Bali*, Monash University Centre of Southeast Asian Studies Papers on Southeast Asia no. 21 (Clayton, 1990); Harold Crouch, *The Army and Politics in Indonesia* (Ithaca, 1978). For an overview of the events of 1965 in Bali, see Geoffrey Robinson, *The Dark Side of Paradise: Political Violence in Bali* (Ithaca, 1995).

2 It has been notoriously difficult for scholars to collect accurate data on the numbers of people killed and imprisoned during 1965–66, both because the military has closely guarded its data and because so many of the killings were carried out not by military personnel but by civilians in rural villages. Cribb, *Indonesian Killings*, provides a summary of estimates ranging from 100,000 to 2 million, and

the New Order sought to consolidate its control of the country, it elaborated the events of 1965 into something of a mythic charter for the state, justifying its rigid rule as a protection against an ever present threat of subversion and its repressive policies as insurance of national security and unity.[3]

Numerous explanations have been offered for the events of 1965. According to the New Order state, the violence that swept Indonesia in the months following the alleged coup attempt was a reasonable – if somewhat regrettable in its intensity – popular outpouring of emotion in response to a threat to the beloved nation's security. The military's role in 1965 was, Suharto and his subordinates claimed, limited to safeguarding national order by rooting out the PKI instigators of the violence.[4] Most Western news accounts of the time tended to strangely echo these claims by the state that the violence was a product of the uncontrollable masses, describing Indonesians slaughtering each other in a mad frenzy, betraying their cultural propensity for falling into mass trance or running *amuk* or simply demonstrating their Third World savagery.[5] Even the U.S. ambassador to Indonesia at the time, Marshall Green – who, it was later reported, oversaw the supply of CIA-compiled lists of alleged communists to the Indonesian military – retrospectively explained the violence as an understandable local reaction to culturally alien forces, claiming "the bloodbath visited on Indonesia can be largely attributed to the fact that communism, with its atheism and talk of class warfare, was abhorrent to the way of life of rural Indonesia, especially in Java and Bali, whose cultures placed great stress on tolerance, social harmony, mutual assistance ... and resolving controversy through talking issues out in order to achieve an acceptable consensus situation."[6] And, of

Robert Cribb, "The Indonesian Massacres," in S. Totten, William S. Parsons, and Israel W. Charny (eds.), *Century of Genocide: Eyewitness Accounts and Critical Views* (New York, 1997), concludes that a reasonable figure is around 500,000. We would estimate that the totals may be even higher than Cribb's estimates, given our research into the important role that extramilitary killings played in Bali.

3 For discussions of the place that 1965 has held in state discourse and public culture, see Benedict Anderson, *Language and Power: Exploring Political Cultures in Indonesia* (Ithaca, 1994); John Pemberton, *On the Subject of "Java"* (Ithaca, 1994); James T. Siegel, *A New Criminal Type in Jakarta: Counter-Revolution Today* (Durham, N.C., 1998); Mary Margaret Steedly, *Hanging without a Rope: Narrative Experience in Colonial and Postcolonial Karoland* (Princeton, 1993).

4 An official state version of the events is offered in Nugroho Notosusanto and Ismail Saleh, *The Coup Attempt of the "September 30 Movement" in Indonesia* (Jakarta, 1968).

5 Probably the best known of these journalistic accounts is John Hughes's Pulitzer Prize–winning *Indonesian Upheaval* (New York, 1967), which includes chapter titles such as "Punishment in the Paddies" and "Frenzy on Bali." Robinson (1995) also discusses journalistic representations of violence in Bali. For an analysis of how the concept of *amuk* as a culture-bound disorder unique to ethnic Malays was used by the New Order state to pathologize political resistance, see Byron Good and Mary-Jo DelVecchio, " 'Why Do the Masses So Easily Run Amuk?': Madness and Violence in Indonesian Politics," *Denpasar Latitudes Magazine* 5 (June 2001).

6 Marshall Green, *Indonesia: Crisis and Transformation, 1965–1968* (Washington, D.C., 1990), 59–60. Cited in Robinson, *Dark Side of Paradise*, 277.

course, in the years that followed the violence, when mass tourism invaded the archipelago, the history of 1965 was written over by commercial images of Indonesia as a land of peaceful, harmonious, artistic peasants, far removed from the turbulent mainstream of modernity.[7] The violence, when it was footnoted in tourist guidebooks, was reassuringly described as an anomalous occurrence, the product of a troubled time unlikely to ever repeat itself.

Understandably, many scholars and activists trying to understand the events of 1965 have been dissatisfied with these kinds of explanatory frameworks. The majority of their reports have focused on documenting the role of the Indonesian military in carrying out killings, supplying right-wing paramilitary gangs with logistical and intelligence support, and provoking local communities to participate in the violence by way of propaganda campaigns against the PKI and threats against those who refused to participate in "cleansing" communism from the body politic. Geoffrey Robinson, in his sustained analysis of the political conflicts in Bali that led up to the 1965 violence, goes so far as to explicitly eschew analyses that privilege "Balinese culture," arguing that we can only understand what happened by reference to the long-standing class, caste, and party conflicts, many of them a direct result of colonial relations of power, which divided Bali in the decades leading up to 1965. Based on interviews with well-known local leaders and a careful reading of newspaper accounts from the period, Robinson argues that the violence was attributable not to cultural particulars unique to Bali but to military manipulations and broader currents of sociopolitical conflict. He writes:

For if the religious and cultural passion of Balinese can help us to understand the intensity of the violence once it had begun, it cannot plausibly explain how the idea of annihilating the PKI developed, how the mass violence started, and why it started when it did. Arguments about religious passion and "frenzy" give the impression that the causes of the violence are as exotic and mysterious as the people of Bali are reputed to be, and that these causes are simply not decipherable or amenable to rational explanation. Yet the weight of historical evidence suggests that such factors were important in accelerating the violence principally to the extent that they converged with and were reinforced by political and military developments in Bali, in Indonesia, and beyond.[8]

Elite politics and military intervention have also been the primary focus of a new generation of Indonesian scholar-activists, who have begun in the post–New Order era to gather facts about the killings that can, they hope,

7 See Robinson, *Dark Side of Paradise*, and Adrian Vickers, *Bali: A Paradise Created* (Harmondsworth, 1989).
8 Robinson, *Dark Side of Paradise*, 278–79.

be used to prosecute Suharto and his supporters for crimes against humanity or to create victims' advocacy programs.

We support these efforts to challenge the falsehoods of New Order narratives and the often-racist reductionism of journalistic or touristic accounts. We also respect attempts to help the victims of the violence by acknowledging their continuing suffering and addressing it through activist means. Yet in our ethnographic research on the violence of 1965 and its continuing aftermath in Bali we have encountered complex weaves of power, culture, emotion, and ritual that cannot be satisfactorily explained by analyses that rely on theories of politically motivated agency. We are faced with the fact that the agency of the political actor is always relational, situated, and mediated both by embodied experience of living within networks of power and the interpretive understandings he or she attributes to such power. Likewise, the victim of political violence is caught up in tangled webs of terror that even the most careful historical analysis is hard pressed to pull apart. Indeed, while our ethical and political commitments may push us toward clear definitions of "victims" and "perpetrators," the historical and cultural complexities in which these categories are embedded frequently makes such a task quite difficult.

The present and past situation in Bali throws such concerns into sharp relief. In contrast to many events of mass violence elsewhere in the world, the killings of 1965–66 in Bali – which have been estimated to have taken the lives of some 100,000 Balinese, or 7–8 percent of the island's population, over a period of less than six months[9] – cannot, we argue, be easily understood as a result of hostilities between clearly defined groups of people. Although there were serious conflicts in Bali between the organized political left and the organized political right, much of the bloodshed was in fact, we have found, motivated by social conflicts that were local, diverse, and shifting, conflicts that crosscut and shaped formal political allegiances and that were then manipulated by the state to give particular forms to the violence. These conflicts erupted over issues of caste, over access to and ownership of land, over economic inequalities, and over status and inheritance within extended families. The violence also worked to exploit and intensify existing inequalities between classes and between genders, underscoring the marginality of women and the poor.

These conflicts did not, however, always map clearly onto party divisions or result in the same outcomes. For instance, caste conflicts had been

---

9 In Bali, as elsewhere in Indonesia, these numbers are difficult to estimate with accuracy. Robinson, ibid., cites a figure of 80,000 people killed. Vickers, *Bali*, cites a figure of 100,000. Balinese activists currently working to gather facts on the killings also tend to use a figure of 100,000.

intensifying in Bali since at least the 1920s, when an anticaste movement first took organized form. By the early 1960s, these tensions were openly acknowledged in many areas of Bali, and numerous local *banjar* – the traditional social unit responsible for organizing customary law (*adat*) and community-wide ritual – had formally split into separate high-caste (*triwangsa*) and commoner (*sudra*) *banjar*. However, membership in political parties did not always follow one's caste status. In some villages, especially where the traditional aristocracy was powerful enough to have had privileged access to modern education, it was they who formed the core of the local leftist organizations' memberships. In other villages, especially those where the left-sponsored land reforms of the 1950s and early 1960s had put substantial dents in royal land holdings, it was the commoners who supported the leftist groups and the aristocracy who opposed them. And in still other villages, traditional patron-client (*panjak-parekan*) ties between aristocrats and commoners included shared party affiliations. Likewise, when the violence erupted in Bali in late 1965, it exploited caste conflicts differently according to these local political configurations. In some villages it was mainly those of the priestly (*brahmana*) caste – communists and noncommunists alike – who were killed, in others the aristocracy (*satria*), and in still others the commoners (*sudra*). In other locations, caste seems to have had little to do with the patterns the violence took.

In some cases, it would indeed even be inaccurate to say that killings were motivated by sociopolitical conflicts, at least in the manner that we normally understand such phenomena. Most of the personal narratives that we have heard claim that while there were indeed many Balinese who were known to be and who identified themselves as communists, a majority of those killed went to their deaths denying such affiliation. In many cases, the label "communist" was attached to victims and, by extension, to their family and friends and even casual acquaintances once they were dead, as an after-the-fact explanation of their fate. Contemporary Balinese tell stories of people being killed over land, over inheritance, and over more personal problems such as long-remembered insults or sexual jealousy. But events or emotions other than political allegiance that might have provoked people to kill were post facto subsumed by a grand state-sponsored narrative of party participation, these alternative narratives dismissed as the products of ignorance, sentimentality, or subversive inclinations.

We have also heard stories of how, when it became clear that no one with even the loosest of ties to the PKI – such as once having lent one's truck to a known PKI member or once having attended a PKI-sponsored arts performance – would be spared, many Balinese who feared being condemned asked family members to kill them, preferring to die at the hands of someone they trusted would carry out the necessary rituals to ensure the soul could be reincarnated, rather than at the hands of the military or paramilitary gangs, who "disappeared" alleged communists and dumped their bodies in the ocean or in secret mass graves. Others "turned themselves in" at their local *banjar* or village temple, where the ritual offerings that are normally made upon one's death were prepared and where community members would join together to kill them. Others committed suicide rather than be tortured or "disappeared," or drank poison publicly as a way of "proving" they were not communists. In our discussions with victims and killers alike, it has become clear that few people felt at the time that there were clear "sides" to take or free options for action or restraint. As Robinson describes in his account of 1965 in Bali, the military made it clear through a concerted propaganda campaign that a refusal to participate actively in the project of "cleansing" communism from the national body politic would be taken as an admission of one's own guilt. Yet even if there were few "real communists" in a particular village, there were severe pressures to create some by whatever social and symbolic elaboration necessary. And what has also been left out of most accounts of 1965 is a "second wave" of death and destruction, where substantial numbers of those who felt "forced" to kill friends or family members later took their own lives, and where symbolic and political networks that support everyday life were shredded by traumatic memory.

THE SOCIAL LANDSCAPE OF VIOLENCE

In order to better understand the complex nature of these conflicts and their continuing aftermath, we have been conducting ethnographic research in Kesiman, Bali, an "urban village" located on the eastern outskirts of the capital city of Denpasar. Between November 1965 and February 1966, approximately 500 people were killed in Kesiman, out of a total population of around 4,000 people. Another 300 were jailed or placed in work camps, while several dozen more fled the region, most never to return. Kesiman is known to have experienced some of the worst violence in Bali, with residents remembering the height of the terror as a time when the streets were littered with body parts, innards, and blood and the rivers were overrun with the stench of death.

One of the most important insights that people in Kesiman have shared with us is the fact that the violence of 1965 is not simply an event of the past against which Balinese can take a distanced stance. In contemporary Bali, it is not something that one can intentionally choose either to "remember" by way of, say, a Truth Commission or a revamped national curriculum, or to "forget" by way of erasure from the mass media or official histories or through more personal attempts at repression. Rather, the events of 1965 have channeled and dammed possibilities for speech, social and political action, and religious and cultural meaning. Violence continues to reverberate through social networks, marking everyday life and molding aspirations for the future.

In part, this endurance of the events of 1965 has been an effect of the New Order state's persistent attempts at commemoration and symbolic control of the violence. Suharto's regime created an official history of 1965 and deployed it to advertise its claims to rule and to justify its repressive social and political policies. Under Suharto, public debate of the events was banned, and alternative analyses of both the alleged coup and the violence that followed were censored. Alleged communists, who had previously been known as neighbors and relatives and friends, became socially alienated through official discourse, painted as shadowy, sadistic figures laying in wait for a chance to undermine the nation, which needed to be protected by a vigilant military and a powerful system of state surveillance. For a new generation of Indonesians, the halting tales their parents told of the events were drowned out by the insistent rhetoric of the New Order, which staged regular "remembrances" of the alleged coup and the state's victory over communism, and which spread images of communist evil and bloodthirstiness through the school curriculum and through such propaganda pieces as the film *Penghianat G/30/S* (The September 30th Movement Traitors), which was screened on public television and in classrooms each September 30. Up until Suharto's fall – and even after – state officials have tended to dismiss social and political protests as the work of "formless organizations" (*organisasi tanpa bentuk*) of communist sympathizers or as the result of provocation by remnants of the PKI.

The continuing power of 1965 to shape Balinese social life and subjectivity has also been an artifact of the patterns that the violence itself took in Bali. Violence embedded itself in local communities and kin groups, as neighbors killed neighbors and relatives killed relatives. There were few social units, whether familial, religious, or community-based, that were not fractured by deaths, disappearances, and arrests. Post-1965, those who were alleged to have communist ties saw their mobility limited by the state, which placed them under constant military and local governmental surveillance. A few Balinese succeeded in moving elsewhere on the island, attempting to leave their pasts behind, but the vast majority remained in their original communities, where they came face to face with those who had terrorized them or those they had terrorized while attending village temple ceremonies, shopping in the market, or walking their children to school. Patterns of everyday life, speech, and social interaction shifted to accommodate memories of violence and fears of further reprisals, with silence and submission to power the preferred strategies.

One social arena that changed dramatically in the years following the violence was kinship relations. Families were broken apart by deaths and arrests, with the pain of these losses compounded by social sanctions against public mourning for the dead, who were demonized by the New Order state as dangerous criminals who deserved their fate. Especially in those cases where the bodies of the dead were never recovered and the religious rites that would ensure them a place in the pantheon of divine ancestors were never able to be performed, there remain ragged gaps in social networks. Normally, Balinese Hindus – unlike Hindus elsewhere – are reincarnated back into their extended families, usually within a generation or two of their death. But since 1965 there have been less than a handful of those killed in the violence who have returned to their families in Kesiman. History has, however, returned in the form of stories circulating through public culture that locate the family as the site of traumatic memory or karmic retribution. In Kesiman, there is the story of the well-known killer who boasted of hacking his victims apart whose child was later born without legs or arms. There is the story of the PNI member who killed one of his brothers, a member of the PKI, and later killed himself. Ten years after the events, the surviving brother's wife gave birth to a child who, a traditional psychic (*balian peluasan*) informed her, was the reincarnation of the murdered PKI brother. The child, once it became public who he was, was shunned as a "PKI child" within his staunchly nationalist family and, affected by that experience, has now grown up to be an activist working to collect data on the killings.

After 1965 these fragmented Balinese families were perversely knit back together by the infamous "clean environment" (*bersih lingkungan*) policy of the New Order government, which claimed that spouses, parents, siblings, children, and grandchildren of those marked as communists were "infected" by "political uncleanliness" and thus to be barred from political participation. Extended kinship networks became fraught with suspicions and tensions, as "clean" segments of families grew resentful of being linked to their "dirty" relatives, and as those who had been terrorized or had experienced the deaths of close family members suspected their more distant relatives of having offered the information that led to their victimization. The family also became an important site for political surveillance, with older relatives whose memories of the violence were still strong monitoring the younger generation for actions that could be interpreted by the state as political, thus risking new repressions on the entire family. These tensions were sometimes compounded by family members who manipulated their relatives' political marginalization to claim communally held land as their individual possessions, taking advantage of the victims' fear of the government apparatus for personal gain.

The events of 1965 also seem to have left long-lasting effects on gender relations. In the early 1960s, many Balinese women were highly politicized. Members of Gerwani (the Indonesian Women's Movement), a leftist group with ties to the PKI, were active in labor issues, populist art, and education. With the ascendancy of the right-wing PNI – which had very few women members – to power, women's political participation was virtually halted. State rhetoric of the time painted Gerwani members as sexually degenerate, claiming that they had danced naked in front of the generals in Jakarta before castrating them, gouging their eyes out, and leaving them to be killed by their PKI comrades in the attempted coup. In Bali, reports were printed in the newspapers that local Gerwani women had prostituted themselves to members of the military in exchange for arms.[10] In these discourses, women's political agency was equated with an uncontrolled and predatory sexuality, playing upon Balinese patrilineal gender ideologies that see a woman's sexuality and reproduction as properly under the control of her male relatives. To this day it is still the case that very few Balinese women are active participants in local or regional politics or in nongovernmental activist organizations. Although many Balinese women are quite aware of political events, few have publicly organized in political or social welfare groups.

Many women victims of 1965 also continue to be traumatized by the deep and decisive silence that surrounds their experiences. While stories circulate quietly through Kesiman about those who were killed or imprisoned there is an almost absolute silence about those who were raped or sexually tortured by the paramilitary gangs or in the jails. Few speak, even within their families, of the frequent sexual violence against women that occurred during 1965. Few talk about how in January of 1966 thousands of women, most of them young teenagers not yet married whose male relatives had been marked as communists, were rounded up and brought by paramilitary patrols to government offices. There they were taken, one by one, into rooms where they were stripped naked in front of the paramilitaries

10 See Robinson, *Dark Side of Paradise.*

and vaginally "examined" for signs of sexual activity, which, it was claimed, could identify them as Gerwani women. The humiliation, assaults, and frequent rapes that accompanied these "examinations" have not become part of the public discourse or academic analyses of the events of 1965. Nor have the stories of what happened to tens of thousands of women after 1965 come to light. Women who lost husbands in the violence were forced not only to shoulder the economic burdens of caring for their children alone but were frequently isolated within their husband's families as unpleasant reminders of what had happened. The thousands of Balinese women who were jailed for alleged communist affiliations also faced, upon their release, frequent refusals on the part of their husbands' families to reclaim their children, who in Bali are considered to belong to the paternal line. Not only were these women thought to be politically dangerous but they were considered, because of their suffering, to be more likely to engage in black magic and thus be doubly menacing, even to their own children.

After 1965 an economic split also developed in Balinese society between those who were given places in an increasingly large civil service bureaucracy and those who were banned from participation. Under the New Order, a "clean environment letter" (*surat bersih lingkungan*) was a prerequisite for obtaining a job – no matter how menial – in a government office, in a school or university, or in a corporation with ties to the government, such as a utility company or a hotel or travel service company in which the state held a stake. This letter – which was also required to obtain a passport or a permit to move to a different district, to become a formal member of a non-governmental organization (NGO) or a social welfare foundation (*lembaga swadaya masyarakat* or LSM), to become a journalist, or to claim a high school or university scholarship – was given only to those who were considered free of ties to the Communist Party or to those who commanded sufficient financial and social resources to make high-placed bribes. The "clean environment" requirement ensured that the victims of 1965 included not only those killed or imprisoned but their descendants – known popularly as "*anak PKI*" or "children of the communist party" – a policy that politically and economically disadvantaged hundreds and thousands of Balinese.[11] This policy helped not only to centralize the power of the state but worked to concentrate power in the hands of village-level leaders, who gained economic rewards and political influence by overseeing the distribution of these coveted documents.

---

11 In our field site of Kesiman, we estimate that some 40 percent of the current population was, during the New Order, considered to have an "unclean environment."

Beginning in the late 1970s, when mass tourism caused land values to multiply dramatically, those marked as "unclean" were often pressured by local politicians to sell their land for cut-rate prices to tourism developers in government-brokered deals. Those who refused to sell were labeled "subversives" blocking the pace of development. Those victims who did manage to succeed without government patronage or protection, especially those in the increasingly lucrative tourism industry, which offered many victims their only option for economic advancement, found themselves pressured into an even deeper silence about the events of 1965, both to protect themselves from state reprisals, which grew more likely as they grew more wealthy and socially visible, and to maintain the touristic image of Bali as a traditional oasis of peace and harmony.

Even the most basic aspects of human life were thrown into question in the wake of 1965, as violence and the languages people use to comprehend it worked through the body, which became not just a material object but a symbolically and politically charged site for expressing and reading power. During 1965, bodies were often used to effect violent shifts in social meaning. Deaths, disappearances, torture, and fears of physical harm were, of course, central to many people's experiences of the time. Torture was used as a tool of power both by the military and paramilitary gangs. Sexual violence was an ever present threat, targeting both women and the husbands and brothers who had an interest in their purity. Family members of victims were often physically marked, as was the case with one eight-year-old Kesiman boy who to this day bears the scars of having hot oil thrown on him by his father's killer. And bodies were also manipulated in more charged and complex ways as well. In Kesiman, the paramilitary gangs would often kill their victims by hacking them apart. They would then take most of the body parts away from the killing ground, dumping them somewhere secret, leaving only the innards behind in a pile in front of the victim's house. Here the body became not simply the means of death but a vehicle for effecting more traumatic symbolic and ritual violence. By dismembering bodies and dispersing the parts, killers made bodies nonsensical, materially incoherent, effecting transformations with highly disturbing emotional and ritual effects. Most people interpreted these practices as tactics designed to ensure continuing distress to victims' families by upsetting established ritual practice regarding the dead, leaving emotional effects that linger in the present. To this day in Kesiman there are still serious debates about the implications of the fact that many victims remain uncremated, as well as concerns about whether in the present one's body must be whole – for example, whether one must save a body part that has been amputated – to be "properly" cremated.

VIOLENCE AND RITUAL REFIGURINGS

Similar to other posttraumatic situations elsewhere, in Bali one of the most enduring legacies of 1965 has been a continuing sense of epistemic uncertainty. Many people refer to the period of violence as *gumi uwug* – when "the world turned to chaos." They describe it as a time when familiar certainties were shattered, when the routines of everyday life were fractured by unpredictability and terror, and when regular cycles of ritual were replaced by strange and fearful supernatural occurrences. Especially in cases where bodies were disappeared, or mutilated and scattered, there remains an overriding social sense of something unfinished still haunting communities, both in the form of the unknown fate of loved ones and the fear that their souls, not having received the necessary death rituals, are still lingering unsettled around their families. Indeed, one of the most problematic aspects of explanations of 1965 that privilege the role of formal political allegiances in provoking violence is that they fail to capture the widespread sense on the part of Balinese themselves that 1965 is something that they cannot – or that they refuse – to explain in rational terms. "Why are you asking me about what happened to my husband?" one woman asked us. "I know and you know that nobody knows."

There is indeed something of this absence of sense that we believe it is important to preserve when writing about 1965. The logic of social scientific analysis or the weight of historical data is hard pressed to "explain," to take only one more disturbing example, the case of a teenage woman member of Gerwani who was publicly hacked apart in the village temple by a group of men who claimed to be afraid that her presence in the village would bring down the wrath of the paramilitary gangs upon the whole community. We remain incapable of "understanding" why she was taken, before being killed, to a village priest to have a public tooth-filing ceremony performed, even though we "understand" that according to Balinese culture, one's pointed canine teeth – the mark of lust and animality – must be filed down, preferably in young adulthood and always before one's cremation ceremony, which frees the soul to become a deified ancestor and eventually to be reborn into the family. Even if we acknowledge the public threats by the military against communities that failed to act against communism, the severe social tensions that alienated neighbors from each other, or even the gender ideologies that made it possible to see a politically active woman as a dire threat to the entire community, it is difficult to "explain" how such a sequence of human actions could have occurred. We are still left with the inadequacy of our theoretical frameworks to explain the chillingly careful brutality that characterized the violence – an inadequacy that is certainly not unique to the Balinese case. As Valentine Daniel has written in his anthropological account of violence in Sri Lanka, "violence is such a reality that a theory which purports to inform it with significance must ... conspicuously 'stand apart' from it as a gesture of open admission to its inadequacy to measure up to the task."[12]

However, if we explore more deeply the tales of confusion and unpredictability told by residents of Kesiman, they begin to take on a certain focused pattern. For most people's stories, besides speaking of party allegiances or conflicts over caste or land or family relations, use images and idioms of the supernatural or *niskala* world as primary plots and motifs. In Kesiman, the paramilitary gangs were widely considered to have used black magic (*pengiwa*) to make themselves invulnerable (*kebel*) to counterattacks, to blind their victims with a supernatural darkness (*pepeteng*), or to make their weapons more potent. Their victims, it is said, were not only those suspected of communism but those who are called *anak sakti*, humans who possess supernatural abilities. Traditional healers and psychics (*balian*), or people who were known as powerful practitioners of magic, were among the most common victims. It was usually these *anak sakti* whose blood was drunk by their killers, who believed this would keep them safe from their avenging ghosts. Killers would also take care to dispose of the bodies of supernaturally powerful victims in the same way that Balinese treat the bodies of ritually sacrificed animals (*caru*), hoping that by this ritual manipulation their victims would be transformed into benevolent spirits guarding the area rather than violent spirits who would bring down chaos as retribution. Not only was the supernatural used to organize the outcomes of the violence, but patterns of violence also followed supernatural ties, with students of well-known psychics (*balian*) doing battle between themselves as the violence raged.

Some analysts of the events of 1965 have mentioned these ritual or supernatural aspects of the violence in Bali. Journalistic accounts tell tales of killers drinking victims' blood or appearing to have fallen into the kind of trance state that accompanies certain rituals or preparing religious offerings before murdering alleged communists, although without explaining the meanings of these phenomena in Bali. While we agree with Robinson that the ritual aspects of the violence cannot be taken as a comprehensive "explanation" of the events, one that locates violence in exoticized cultural difference, we argue that it is only by understanding the political and semiotic role they played in the violence that we can obtain a clear picture of the events. In fact, we argue that one key to understanding the power and meaning of the violence of 1965 is to be found within this domain of the supernatural.

12 E. Valentine Daniel, *Charred Lullabies: Chapters in an Anthropography of Violence* (Princeton, 1996).

We argue that along with exploiting modern sociopolitical conflicts, the violence of 1965 in Bali revitalized a traditional, culturally elaborated discourse of fundamental social uncertainty centered around the supernatural figure of the *leak*, a human who is capable of changing his shape into a fearsome demon, causing madness, illness, or death to his chosen victims. According to Balinese belief, anyone can become a *leak* after pursuing the necessary knowledge, and there is little way to tell who is capable of this transformation and who is not, unless one has pursued these esoteric arts oneself. Most *leak* are believed to choose their victims from within their close social and familial networks. Motivated by jealousy or offense at a perceived slight, they prey on spouses, siblings, cousins, and especially in-laws. Acknowledging this culturally vital belief that even the most intimate of relations can turn against one and that one can never truly know the character of another, it becomes somewhat easier to grasp the manner in which Balinese became capable of, first, imagining those who were known to have had little to do with communism to be in fact communists and then brutally killing them within their own families and communities. Just as one's brother or one's wife could secretly be a *leak*, one's close friend or relative could, without others realizing it, be a communist. It is striking to note here that while the military abducted and murdered people during the daylight hours, intracommunity violence in Kesiman during 1965 always took place at night, the time when *leak* transform themselves and attack their victims. In addition, the military, intentionally or not, aided in intensifying this supernatural discourse by calling communists the *musuh dalam selimut*, "the enemy in the blanket," who could be found hidden in one's intimate space. In Bali, this was easily read as an equivalence between communists and *leak*, or between political and supernatural power. This discourse of *leak* reflects a cultural belief in the instability of selfhood and the fragility, or even menace, that potentially exists within everyday social interactions. It also points to the fact that in Bali, motivation or agency cannot be reduced to worldly politics or even to what we consider to be rational frameworks.

POSSIBILITIES AND PROBLEMS OF RECONCILIATION

De otak-atik buin pianak tiange nak sampun dadi dewa (Don't mess around with my child anymore, he's already become a god).
Elderly Balinese woman speaking about her son's death in 1965

In October 1999 Abdurrahman Wahid became Indonesia's first democratically elected president. In March 2000 he publicly addressed the issue of 1965, apologizing for the role that ANSOR – the youth wing of NU, the

Muslim organization that he had chaired before assuming the presidency –
had played in the violence.[13] He abolished the state's "clean environment"
policy, restoring – at least in law – the civil rights of former political prisoners and the families of those claimed to have been allied to the Indonesian
Communist Party. No longer were former political prisoners to be forced
to report monthly to military authorities or to carry special identification
cards marked with their status. No longer were the families of those killed
to be barred from positions in government or education. For the first time
in thirty-four years, alternative narratives of the events of 1965 began to be
printed in the mass media, narratives that questioned the role of the state in
sparking the violence and that called for inquiries into the events and into
the status of the victims. And a number of scholars and activists who had
long been prohibited from carrying out research on 1965 became – at least
formally – free to pursue projects.

Since Wahid came to power, a number of nongovernmental organizations
have formed in Indonesia, devoting themselves to collecting data on the violence and developing programs to address the continuing impacts of the
events. A number of prominent scholars and activists, including Indonesia's
most famous novelist and political dissident, Pramoedya Ananta Toer, have
formed a working group of historians publicly committed to reevaluating the
official history of 1965 and publicly disseminating new truths. Pramoedya
is also one of the founders of an association called Victims of the New
Order (Korban Orde Baru), composed mainly of prominent political dissidents and those jailed for their association with the PKI. The National
Commission for Human Rights (KOMNASHAM) has begun discussions
over creating a National Truth and Reconciliation Commission (Komisi
Nasional Kebenaran dan Rekonsiliasi) that would call citizens to witness to
the abuses they suffered at the hands of the New Order state, including the
abuses perpetrated during 1965.

In Kesiman, however, few people have expressed much enthusiasm for
any of the projects proposed by these advocacy groups. The proposal to
create a national "Commission for Historical Truth" (Komisi Kebenaran
Sejarah), which would rewrite the national school curriculum and publicly
disseminate eyewitness histories, was dismissed by most Kesiman residents

---

13 Wahid's apology did, however, create serious controversy within Indonesia's Islamic community,
which forced him to announce that he was apologizing as an individual rather than as the president
or as a spokesman of NU. Several months after this announcement, Wahid also suggested that the
government repeal its 1966 ban on the Communist Party, a proposal which met with such violent
reaction by the Indonesian right that there were, for several months afterward, rumors that he would
be forced to resign over the issue. Activists working to gather data on the killings as well as high-profile
former political prisoners have also been victims of death threats and violent attacks.

we spoke to as either irrelevant or suspect. "We already know what really happened," one elderly woman claimed. "All we want is to stop being persecuted." Others doubted the sensibility of such a project, echoing a broader belief that obtains in Bali that "history" is never "true" but is always a positioned creation of those who currently hold a preponderance of power. We were told that just as Balinese family genealogies are regularly rewritten to claim higher status for descendants, so history is always changing to suit the political needs of the present. This stance is, in fact, as much a practical as a philosophical one: such history runs the risk of being used against one if and when the power structure changes again. No one, Kesiman residents realize – as much or more so as professional observers of Indonesian politics admit – can guarantee that the current government will sustain itself or its stance on 1965. And given that the violence occurred not just between social or political groups but within families, temple congregations, and villages, many people are quite frightened that to tell their stories openly would be to risk reprisals – either physical, economic, political, or supernatural – from those with whom they remain, by necessity, in everyday contact.

This is not, of course, to say that victims of 1965 and their families do not have aspirations for social and political change, or hopes for emotional and community healing. Most of the victims and their families in Kesiman are strong supporters of President Abdurrahman Wahid, wary of what might happen once Wahid's government fell, especially given his vice president and successor Megawati Soekarnoputri's strong ties to former leaders of the PNI. Many people have expressed hopes that a reconciliation process might include the recovering of bodies and complete ceremonies for those who were never cremated, bringing emotional as well as ritual closure. But just as many Balinese believe that the strongest sparks of the violence were lit within their communities rather than by the translocal forces of the state or the political parties, so they believe that healing, if and when it comes, must be locally based.

14

Genocide in Cambodia and Ethiopia

EDWARD KISSI

In his book, *Revolution and Genocide* (1992), political scientist Robert Melson pointed out that revolutionary states were the chief perpetrators of genocide in the twentieth century. He included Cambodia, Ethiopia, and Rwanda in his examples of genocides that occurred in the context of revolutions accompanied by war. But Melson is careful to note that not every revolution in the twentieth century led to genocide and not every genocide in the twentieth century was the consequence of revolution.[1] In the 1970s Ethiopians and Cambodians thought that the revolutions that took place in their society would improve their economic conditions. Instead, the Ethiopian revolution claimed the lives of 1.2 million to 2 million people out of a pre-revolutionary population of 45 million.[2] That death toll was comparable to the 1.7 million to 2 million Cambodian lives lost during the Cambodian revolution.[3] The estimated population of Cambodia before the revolution was 8 million. Some scholars, and other writers, have characterized these death tolls in the course of the two revolutions as genocide.

This chapter uses the comparative method to contribute to the debate on the relationship between revolution and genocide and the nature of the killing that took place during the Ethiopian and the Cambodian revolutions. The chapter argues that a case for genocide, as strictly defined in the UN Genocide Convention, can be established against the Cambodian Communist Party (a.k.a. the Khmer Rouge or the Angkar) from the overwhelming evidence of its selective and systematic annihilation of ethnic, racial, and religious groups. The Khmer Rouge leadership was able to commit

---

1 Robert Melson, *Revolution and Genocide: On the Origins of the Armenian Genocide and the Holocaust* (Chicago, 1992), xvi, 1.
2 Paulos Milkias, "Mengistu Haile Mariam: Profile of a Dictator," *Ethiopian Review* (February 1994): 51.
3 Patrick Heuveline, "Between One and Three Million: Toward the Demographic Reconstruction of a Decade of Cambodian History (1970–1979)," *Population Studies* 52 (1998): 59.

crimes of that magnitude because of the uncontested power and control
it exercised during the three years, eight months, and twenty days of its
revolution in Cambodia (April 1975–January 1979). A different situation
existed in revolutionary Ethiopia. Throughout its seventeen years of rule
(September 1974–May 1991), Ethiopia's revolutionary military government
(a.k.a. Dergue) faced determined armed opposition from numerous "liberation fronts." Unlike the Khmer Rouge, the Dergue fought and targeted
armed political opposition groups. Under the UN Genocide Convention,
the crimes of the Dergue would not constitute genocide. But the Ethiopian
experience raises a problem in the definition and prosecution of genocide.
In Ethiopian law, the killing of people on grounds of their political beliefs
or opposition to the state is a form of genocide. Herein lies the problem
about the prosecution of genocide in cases where national and international
laws of genocide diverge on the key issue of definition of the crime.

ETHIOPIA, CAMBODIA, AND THE GENOCIDE DEBATE

The Empire of Ethiopia and the Kingdom of Cambodia ratified the United
Nations Genocide Convention (UNGC), in 1951. Thus, the two monar-
chies assumed legal and moral obligations to prevent and punish genocide.
Six years after ratifying the Genocide Convention, Ethiopia incorporated
the terms into its Penal Code of 1957. Ethiopia was also the first member
of the United Nations to define genocide broadly to include the protection
of political groups in its national law on genocide. Thus in Ethiopian law,
"genocide" is defined as acts committed "with intent to destroy, in whole
or in part, a national, ethnic, racial, religious or political group."[4]

After the overthrow of the Khmer Rouge in January 1979, the new
leaders of Cambodia began a trial of the leaders of the Khmer Rouge
for genocide. Similarly, in 1991, when the Dergue was ousted, the successor regime, the Ethiopian Peoples Revolutionary Democratic Front
(EPRDF), organized by the victorious opposition political group, the Tigray
Peoples Liberation Front (TPLF), began a domestic trial of members of
the Dergue, and their leader Mengistu Haile Mariam, for "genocide." In
its indictments against the Dergue, the Ethiopian Central High Court argued that the Ethiopian revolutionary government committed "genocide"
under Ethiopian law by "undertaking, organizing and employing different investigation techniques, torture, killing, firing squads, cleansing campaign[s], summary execution[s] and red terror" against "politically organized

---

4 Empire of Ethiopia, *Penal Code of the Empire of Ethiopia of 1957* (Addis Ababa, 1957), 87.

multinational social group[s]," and by placing members of the targeted political group "under living conditions calculated to result in their death."[5]
Genocide trials in Cambodia and Ethiopia have ignited a debate about the
nature of the two revolutions and the killings that the Dergue and the Angkar
sanctioned.

Scholars who study the Cambodian revolution continue to debate the
extent to which the killings in revolutionary Cambodia could be characterized as genocide. Michael Vickery, David Chandler, and Serge Thion argue
that the Khmer Rouge leadership never intended to use its revolution as
a mechanism for destroying particular groups of people. David Chandler,
for instance, insists that comparing Pol Pot to Hitler has "little explanatory
power" beyond making him "a household word, synonymous with genocide ... and everyone's worst fears of communism." Chandler considers
the deaths in revolutionary Cambodia as the unintended consequence of
a social revolution in which "lower ranking cadres and officials fearful of
reprisals ... made unworkable demands on the people under them." Serge
Thion has argued that the Khmer Rouge leadership never had the power
and control required for the commission of the atrocities of which they are
accused.[6] Anthony Barnett and Ben Kiernan disagree. They contend that
revolutionary Cambodia was tightly controlled by the Khmer Rouge leadership. In Kiernan's view, the Khmer Rouge leadership achieved "successful
top-down domination" and accumulated "unprecedented" power.[7]

The intent of the Dergue to kill political groups opposed to it has never
been disputed in the scant literature on the Ethiopian revolution. That is a
fact. The bone of contention is over which concept of genocide – the international (UN) or the Ethiopian – should be applied in the Ethiopian genocide trial and who can be defined as the perpetrators of genocide. Those who
dispute the characterization of the Dergue's crimes as "genocide" point to
its implication as a deliberate attempt to destroy groups of people because of
their ethnic background and religious beliefs. They also criticize the focus on
the Dergue as the sole perpetrator. The journalist, John Ryle, has argued that

---

5 Transitional Government of Ethiopia, Central High Court, *Genocide and Crimes against Humanity*,
part 1, Unofficial Draft Translation (Addis Ababa, October 1994), 8.
6 Michael Vickery, "Democratic Kampuchea: Themes and Variations," in David P. Chandler and Ben
Kiernan (eds.), *Revolution and Its Aftermath: Eight Essays* (New Haven, 1983), 101, 112; David P.
Chandler, *The Tragedy of Cambodian History: Politics, War, and Revolution since 1945* (New Haven,
1991), 1; David P. Chandler, *Brother Number One: A Political Biography of Pol Pot*, rev. ed. (Boulder,
1999), 115, 161; Serge Thion, "The Cambodian Idea of Revolution," in Chandler and Kiernan,
Revolution and Its Aftermath, 28.
7 Anthony Barnett, "Democratic Kampuchea: A Highly Centralized Dictatorship," in Chandler and
Kiernan, *Revolution and Its Aftermath*, 212, 216; Ben Kiernan, *The Pol Pot Regime: Race, Power, and
Genocide in Cambodia under the Khmer Rouge, 1975–1979* (New Haven, 1996), 26–27.

"on the face of it, the genocide charge seems odd. The Dergue was undoubtedly responsible for terrible crimes, but it was not, in any ordinary sense,
guilty of genocide: it did not . . . kill people on the grounds of race or creed."[8]
Merera Gudina, an Ethiopian of Oromo ethnicity, and a former member
of the opposition political group, All Ethiopian Socialist Movement, who
was tortured by the Dergue, agrees with Ryle. In his view, the Dergue's
killing campaigns transcended the boundaries of ethnicity, class, and gender
because the revolutionary regime randomly targeted people including
children as tender as ten and thirteen years of age, whom the regime
considered as "operatives" of the Ethiopian Peoples Revolutionary Party
(EPRP), the armed political group that posed the greatest threat to the
power of the Dergue.

Some commentators see revolutionary Ethiopia as similar to revolutionary Cambodia. The journalist Robert Kaplan has described revolutionary
Ethiopia as the "The African Killing Field." He argues that "the manner in which Ethiopians died evoked the well-known slaughter of millions
of Cambodians by the Khmer Rouge."[9] Critics of this comparison such as
Merera call for clear distinctions to be drawn between the Ethiopian and the
Cambodian revolutionary regimes. Those distinctions, they argue, should
acknowledge the fact that the Dergue was motivated by a desire to stay
in power and not an ideology to change and purify the ethnic demography of Ethiopia by destroying particular ethnic groups as the Angkar did in
Cambodia.[10]

Other analysts place the blame of murder equally on the Dergue and
its armed political opponents (EPRP; All Ethiopian Socialist Movement;
Oromo Liberation Front [OLF]; Afar Liberation Front [ALF]; Western
Somalia Liberation Front [WSLF]; and others). Ethiopian scholar Hagos
Gebre Yesus describes what happened in revolutionary Ethiopia as "national
nihilism" in which the Dergue stands as guilty of murder against its political
opponents as those opponents do against the Dergue.[11] The controversies
over state-sanctioned killing of groups in Ethiopia and Cambodia highlight the efforts of scholars and other commentators to distinguish between
genocide and other crimes against humanity.

Historian Frank Chalk's and sociologist Kurt Jonassohn's research definition of genocide as "a form of one-sided mass killing in which a state or

8 John Ryle, "An African Nuremberg," *New Yorker*, October 2, 1995, 52.
9 Robert Kaplan, "The African Killing Fields," *Washington Monthly* 28, 8 (September 1988): 32.
10 Author's interview with Merera Gudina, Addis Ababa, April 17, 1999.
11 Hagos Gebre Yesus, "The Bankruptcy of the Ethiopian Left – Meison-EPRP, a Two-Headed Hydra:
   A Commentary on the Ideology and Politics of National Nihilism," in Joseph Tubiana (ed.), *Modern
   Ethiopia: From the Accession of Menelik II to the Present* (Rotterdam, 1980), 455.

other authority intends to destroy a group, as that group and membership in it are defined by the perpetrator," lends theoretical clarity to what happened in Cambodia and Ethiopia in the early 1970s.[12] In Cambodia and Ethiopia, it was the perpetrators of genocide who defined the boundaries of the group to be destroyed. The research definition of genocide as "a one-sided mass killing" may not be an adequate hypothesis for studying the Ethiopian case of mutual killing by well-armed antagonists. It becomes applicable, however, when the victims are unarmed civilians and when the killings form part of a deliberate attempt to destroy the target group.

The task of comparing the Ethiopian and Cambodian cases of state-organized murder of groups should involve the resolution of three key questions. First, why did the Khmer Rouge and the Dergue target different people in their revolution? Second, why did they succeed or fail to kill a substantial number of the target group? Third, is the UN Genocide Convention the sole authority for determining genocide?

DEFINING THE EXPENDABLE

The key difference between what occurred in Cambodia and Ethiopia was that the murders in Ethiopia were more random and arbitrary than selective and systematic. That was due to the varying degree of power and control which the Dergue and the Angkar exercised and the different cultural systems in which the two revolutions occurred. In late 1975 and early 1976, the Khmer Rouge, which had won a decisive victory in the Cambodian civil war (1970–75), sought and killed former soldiers, policemen, and officials of the defeated Lon Nol regime.[13] Other targets included the city people, categorized as "new people." This group comprised "men, women, girls, boys, and babies who did not live in [Khmer Rouge] 'liberated zones' during the civil war." Because they lived in the "enemy's zone" during the civil war, the Khmer Rouge not only suspected their loyalty but also regarded them as contaminated and, therefore, expendable in the "new" and "pure" society it wanted to create. The "new people" provided the labor force for building the massive irrigation dikes, maintaining rice fields, and constructing dams and villages in malaria-infested areas. Many perished under these hazardous conditions. Others died of misdiagnosed and mistreated illnesses.[14] Here

---

12 Frank Chalk and Kurt Jonassohn, *The History and Sociology of Genocide: Analyses and Case Studies* (New Haven, 1990), 23–26, 27–32.
13 Chandler, *Brother Number One*, 124.
14 Ibid., 117. See also Ben Kiernan, "The Cambodian Genocide – 1975–1979," in Samuel Totten, William S. Parsons, and Israel W. Charny (eds.), *Century of Genocide: Eyewitness Accounts and Critical Views* (New York, 1997), 342.

is clear evidence of the imposition of conditions on a group calculated to bring about its eventual destruction. The now confident Khmer Rouge did not spare intellectuals, doctors, lawyers, teachers, and civil servants whose Western education marked them, in Khmer Rouge anti-Western ideology, as impure Khmers. From Chalk and Jonassohn's research definition of genocide, one can argue that it was the Khmer Rouge's ideology of purity that converted doctors, merchants, and other members of the Cambodian national group into political enemies to be destroyed. Only Pol Pot and his Paris-educated group escaped the slaughter of Western-educated intellectuals, the supposedly contaminated.

The Khmer Rouge also targeted religious and ethnic groups such as monks, Muslims, Christians, Chams, Chinese, Vietnamese, and foreigners, "mainly Thai and Lao," for annihilation.[15] A September 1975 party document celebrated the regime's "ninety to ninety-five percent" success in eradicating "the foundation pillars of Buddhism."[16] An intent to "wipe out religion" from Cambodia is evident in the persecution of Buddhist monks and Muslim clerics, the dominant religious groups in Cambodia. Through direct massacres and indirect forms of persecution, such as the disrobing of monks and closure of Buddhist temples, the Khmer Rouge eliminated a substantial number of monks and undermined the bases of their faith. According to Kiernan, by the end of the Cambodian revolution in January 1979, possibly "fewer than 2,000 of Cambodia's 70,000 monks" had survived.[17]

The Dergue intimidated a handful of religious groups, but did not zealously exterminate them as the Khmer Rouge did. That was because the objectives of Ethiopia's soldier-revolutionaries were limited to preventing ethnic nationalism from leading to the breakup of Ethiopia as one country. The Dergue seized the land and other property of the Ethiopian Orthodox Church in the secessionist province of Eritrea in northern Ethiopia. The intent was not to impose conditions aimed at destroying members of the church but rather to weaken popular support for the secessionist Eritrean Peoples Liberation Front (EPLF) by redistributing church property in Eritrea to supporters of the Dergue's national unity ideology. In Wollo, in northeastern Ethiopia, local Dergue cadres intimidated, but did not kill, the clergy of

---

15 Anthony Barnett, Chanthou Boua, and Ben Kiernan, "Bureaucracy of Death," *New Statesman* 99 (May 2, 1980): 671. Also see Kiernan, "The Cambodian Genocide – 1975–1979," 340–43.

16 Chanthou Boua, "Genocide of a Religious Group: Pol Pot and Cambodia's Buddhist Monks," in Timothy Bushnell, Vladimir Shlapentokh, and C. K. Vanderpool (eds.), *State-Organized Terror: The Case of Violent Internal Repression* (Boulder, 1991), 235; Kiernan, "The Cambodian Genocide – 1975–1979," 340.

17 Kiernan, "The Cambodian Genocide – 1975–1979," 340.

the Mekane Yessus Church, a Protestant denomination. The cadres "feared [the church] as an undesirable competitor ... for peasant loyalty" in a revolution led by soldiers needing peasant support, in an agrarian society, to succeed.[18] Here, it was political power rather than antireligious ideology that motivated the Dergue and its followers. Ironically, Ethiopia's Christian and Muslim religions "experienced unusual growth in membership" despite these isolated instances of harassment. More than 300,000 Christians took part in the famous Kulubi pilgrimage in honor of Saint Gabriel and "ten times as many people participated in the Ethiopian Orthodox Church's Maskal festival" during the revolutionary period as compared with the preceding decades. Ulrich Meister is therefore correct in arguing that "it would be a gross exaggeration to speak of a general persecution of religion" in revolutionary Ethiopia.[19] In the same way, despite the fierce repression of ethnic insurgencies, it would be an exaggeration to speak of a systematic persecution of ethnic minorities in Ethiopia under Mengistu. That certainly cannot be said of Cambodia under Pol Pot.

The physical fate of ethnic minorities under the Khmer Rouge was much worse than under the Dergue. At the beginning of the Cambodian revolution, the Khmer Rouge banned, in a decree, the existence of the ethnic Vietnamese, the Chinese, and Muslim Cham as well as twenty other ethnic minorities. According to Kiernan, these ethnic minorities "made up over 15 percent of the [prerevolutionary] Cambodian population."[20] The Khmer Rouge expelled and directly massacred the entire Vietnamese population of Cambodia. Besides the Vietnamese who suffered a "campaign of systematic racial extermination," the Chinese suffered "the worst disaster ever to befall any ethnic Chinese community in Southeast Asia."[21] By 1979 "only 200,000 Chinese" out of their population of 425,000, in 1975, had survived. But Kiernan is very cautious in characterizing the Pol Pot regime's annihilation of the Chinese as racially motivated. He suggests that the Khmer Rouge targeted the Chinese in Cambodia because the party leadership viewed the predominantly urban Chinese as the "archetypal city dwellers" the revolution aimed at eliminating.[22] Here, as Kiernan suggests, it was "geographic" origin more than racial identity that marked

---

18 Ulrich Meister, "Ethiopia's Unfinished Revolution," *Swiss Review of World Affairs* 33, 2 (May 1983): 17. This observation is corroborated in author's interview with Andreas Eshete, an Ethiopian intellectual, Addis Ababa, May 5, 1999.
19 Meister, "Ethiopia's Unfinished Revolution," 17.
20 Kiernan, "The Cambodian Genocide – 1975–1979," 340; Elizabeth Becker, *When the War Was Over: The Voices of Cambodia's Revolution and Its People* (New York, 1998), 253.
21 Kiernan, "The Cambodian Genocide – 1975–1979," 340–41, 343.
22 Ibid., 341.

the Chinese as expendable enemies of a revolution with an antiurban ideology.

Given the Pol Pot regime's ideological distaste for urban groups, viewed as an exploitative economic class, Kiernan is correct that the Chinese stood as the most visible relic of the old order. But it can also be argued that the killing of the Chinese in Cambodia was racially motivated. The Chinese were one of the racial groups whose existence the Khmer Rouge outlawed. Their language was banned. Khmer Rouge exposure of the Chinese to conditions of hunger and disease had the intent of stifling the survival and biological reproduction of the Chinese as a racial group. The ethnic Chams also suffered systematic state terror on grounds of their ethnicity and religion. About 100,000 of an estimated Cham population of 250,000, at the time of the revolution in 1975, had perished by the time the Khmer Rouge regime was overthrown by Vietnam in January 1979. A decision of the Khmer Rouge leadership to "break up" the Cham people and impose upon them conditions harmful to their survival as an ethnic group was made in early 1974. As Kiernan notes, "[t]heir distinct [Muslim] religion, language and culture, large villages, and autonomous networks threatened the atomized, [and] closely supervised society that the Pol Pot leadership planned."[23] Here was a religious group that was seen by the Khmer Rouge as a threat to its idea of a new secular society.

The intent of the Khmer Rouge to destroy the Cham people by un- dermining their physical and spiritual well-being is also apparent in other acts. The Khmer Rouge compelled the Cham people to eat pork and raise pigs – acts that violated their religious beliefs. The Angkar also seized and destroyed all copies of Cham religious texts including the Koran, banned the Cham language and the traditional Cham sarong, closed Cham schools, and prevented Cham women from wearing their hair in the customary long style.[24] The Khmer Rouge used its overwhelming military might to crush the Cham people who resisted these policy impositions. By the end of the revolution, the Khmer Rouge had also reduced the Thai minority population, numbering 20,000 in 1975, "to about 8000." And only 800 of the 1,800 families of the Lao ethnic minority group survived. The Khmer Rouge wiped out the entire 2,000 members of the Kola minority group.[25]

The overt racial killings in Cambodia went beyond targeted individuals to include members of their families. This is where different cultural systems

---

23 Ibid., 341, 342.
24 Ibid.; "Phnom Penh Radio Specifies New Tasks," FBIS Daily Report, April 28, 1975, H9.
25 Kiernan, "The Cambodian Genocide – 1975–1979," 341–42. For a statistical table of the "approx- imate death toll" of the Cambodian revolution, see 343.

distinguished Khmer Rouge atrocities from the Dergue's. In Khmer Rouge notions of justice and purity, those who associate with a "guilty person" are regarded as equally tainted. Consequently, the targets for murder included the wives and orphaned children of the regime's "enemies."[26] Anthropologist Alex Hinton has argued that Khmer Rouge determination to destroy whole families had its origins in "the Cambodian cultural model of disproportionate revenge." The purpose of revenge in Cambodian culture, according to Hinton, is "to completely defeat the enemy" by obliterating the family line of the deceased because of the belief that "someone in the deceased foe's family [might] disproportionately avenge the death." As Hinton argues, the Khmer Rouge leadership manipulated this element of Cambodian culture in its exhortation of cadres to settle their "class grudge."[27]

David Chandler has noted that Pol Pot's speeches acquired "a more menacing tone" from 1977 onward when he exhorted party cadres to eliminate "enemies," "traitors," and "ugly microbes."[28] Given the cultural system of Cambodia, described by Alex Hinton, these exhortations constituted incitement to murder or official endorsement of murder. One can also draw a relationship between the determination of the Khmer Rouge to kill "traitors" and "ugly microbes" and the rigorous documentation of "life histories" and "confessions" of "enemies" the party's bureaucrats compiled.[29] Thus revolutionary Cambodia, more than Ethiopia, earned its image in contemporary memory as a "killing field."

The Dergue initially targeted a restricted class of "enemies": former officials of the Haile Selassie regime. It executed fifty-nine of them on November 23, 1974, after a general meeting where Dergue members "deliberated [and] agreed upon the execution."[30] The Dergue must have been motivated to kill the officials for two reasons. First, it likely felt a need to spill blood as a way of binding its diverse members together in a common guilt of shedding blood. Second, and perhaps more important, the

---

26 Joan Criddle and Teeda Butt Mam, *To Destroy You Is No Loss: The Odyssey of a Cambodian Family* (New York, 1987), 147, 153; Kiernan, *The Pol Pot Regime*, 198, 243.

27 Alex Hinton, "A Head for an Eye: Revenge, Culture, and the Cambodian Genocide," paper presented at the 1997 meeting of the Association of Genocide Scholars, Montreal, 1–4. See also Becker, *When the War Was Over*, 189.

28 Speech quoted in Chandler, *Brother Number One*, 129.

29 For details of the bureaucracy of murder in Cambodia, see David Chandler, *Voices from S-21: Terror and History in Pol Pot's Secret Prison* (Berkeley, 1999).

30 The Special Prosecutor's Office (SPO) has the minutes of this meeting containing information about which Dergue members were present, the comments they made, and the "order" they gave that sealed the fate on the sixty ex-officials. See Ethiopian News Agency, *State Terrorism on Trial: Genocide and Crime against Humanity, 1974–1991* (Addis Ababa, 1998)), iv; Transitional Government of Ethiopia, *Genocide and Crimes against Humanity*, part 1, 8–9; and also Mary Anne Weaver, "Annals of Political Terror," *New Yorker*, December 28, 1992–January 4, 1994, 106.

Dergue executed the officials probably to prove its revolutionary credentials to the more radical civilian opponents of the military regime. After all, these officials had been demonized, since the 1960s, by the same civilian opponents of the Dergue. Like those of the Khmer Rouge, the Dergue's targets constantly changed and the scope of state-sanctioned murder of groups in Ethiopia widened as the revolution progressed. Apart from the "routine practice of killing [active] political opponents," the Dergue also marked for elimination tens of thousands of "innocent people" whom it defined as "bandits," "puppets of imperialism," "counter-revolutionaries," "anti-unity" and "anti-Ethiopia elements."[31] These categories of "enemies" included civil servants, priests, teachers, students, and teenage children who had joined the EPRP or participated in its activities. Here, it was not a culture of disproportionate revenge that spurred the killings. It was a political culture of unquestioned obedience to the state and its leader.

The Mengistu regime officially sanctioned the Red Terror campaign of total "extermination" of the EPRP as a political group in State Proclamation 121 of 1977. This was certainly the most systematic state-organized campaign of annihilation of political opponents in the history of Ethiopia. Between February 1977 and March 1979, the Dergue issued "hundreds of orders" and "directives" to state agents and revolutionary cadres to kill. It also received "reports of summary executions," "torture and extra-judicial killings" of EPRP members.[32] With orders to kill, zealous state cadres took the killing of the Dergue's political opponents as a heroic adherence to the regime's idea of "socialist patriotism."

Anti-Dergue groups such as the EPRP were equally as guilty of murder as the Dergue. The "White Terror" campaign of assassination of Dergue officials and their supporters that the EPRP started in early 1976 partially triggered the Dergue's brutal "Red Terror" killing spree. The Dergue called its political killings "Stalin's whip" or "a lesson in extermination" of the leaders, members, and sympathizers of the EPRP.[33] Here is clear evidence of the intent of the Dergue to destroy its political opponents. Members and supporters of the EPRP and the TPLF also took "informal [steps] to eliminate [one another]." The leaders and supporters of the EPRP labeled members of the TPLF as *tebaboch* (narrow nationalists) and "pass[ed] death sentences" on them. The TPLF in turn labeled the leaders and supporters

---

31 Ethiopian News Agency, *State Terrorism on Trial*, pp. i, ii, 10, 20; author's interview with Yeraswork Admassu, Addis Ababa, May 4, 1999.
32 Ethiopian News Agency, *State Terrorism on Trial*, v; Dawit Wolde Giorgis, *Red Tears: War, Famine and Revolution in Ethiopia* (Trenton, N.J., 1989), 22.
33 Kiflu Tadesse, *The Generation, Part II: Ethiopia: Transformation and Conflict* (New York, 1998), 114.

of the EPRP as *adisochu neftengoch* (the new chauvinists) and marked them for annihilation. As Medhane Tadesse argues, the relationship between the EPRP and the TPLF in 1976 and 1977 (the period of the White and Red Terror killing campaigns) was characterized by "killing and counter-killing."[34] The EPRP also carried out death sentences on members of the All Ethiopian Socialist Movement who cooperated with the Dergue. The TPLF labeled them as "bootlickers" and "*banda* intellectuals" (meaning collaborators and quislings).[35] The Ethiopian case highlights two key facts often overlooked. First, the death toll cannot be attributed to the Dergue alone. Second, many Ethiopians were killed in the name of not lofty political ideologies but rather empty revolutionary slogans.

After eliminating the already weakened EPRP, the Dergue next turned its attention to the ethnopolitical groups. It imprisoned and tortured "hundreds of people belonging to the Oromo ethnic group" in Addis Ababa, the capital city, on grounds of being Oromo, and therefore, likely to have sympathies for the Oromo Liberation Front (OLF). Similarly, by linking Tigrinya-speaking Ethiopians from Tigray, in northwestern Ethiopia – the closest linguistic kinsmen of the Eritreans – to the Tigrayan Peoples Liberation Front, the Dergue attempted, but failed, to transform its persecution of political groups into mass murder of people on the basis of their biological affinity with members of ethnopolitical opposition groups.[36] The Dergue failed to turn political mass killing into ethnic massacre because of the political conditions under which it conducted its revolution. Unlike the Khmer Rouge, the Dergue faced a formidable domestic political opposition. It had no total control over Ethiopian society or monopoly over the instruments of terror. There are some lessons here. States may take the initiative to destroy a group in a top-down structure of murder. But the decisions of local people and their participation in state-directed murder are significant. The Ethiopian case suggests that genocide is an interactive process of murder in which states and mobilized individuals and groups actively participate or refuse to kill target groups for different reasons. Since a majority of Ethiopians resented the Dergue's dictatorship, disobedience of the state's orders to kill ethnic groups appeared as the greatest form of resistance against a brutal regime.

---

34 Medhane Tadesse, "EPRP vs. TPLF: The Struggle for Supremacy over Tigray, 1975–1978," paper presented at the department seminar, Department of History, Addis Ababa University, June 29–July 2, 1995, 8–9.
35 Ibid. Also author's interview with Merera Gudina, Addis Ababa, April 19, 1999; *Abyot, Information Bulletin of the EPRP* 1, 3 (February–March, 1976): 25–26.
36 Ethiopian News Agency, *State-Terrorism on Trial*, 19.

RESETTLEMENT: A CONTESTED CASE OF MASS DEPORTATION

The Dergue and the Khmer Rouge both used "evacuation" to achieve some measure of control. In Ethiopia it was called "resettlement." The Khmer Rouge succeeded in establishing control through deportations. The Dergue failed to use resettlement to achieve the same purpose. The Dergue did not evacuate urban areas and relocate their populations in the countryside with disastrous results as the Khmer Rouge did in April 1975. However, it did resettle masses of perceived political dissidents, as the Khmer Rouge resettled the people of Cambodia's Eastern Żone, a region that shared a boundary with Vietnam. Ben Kiernan has estimated that in six months the Khmer Rouge wiped out more than 100,000 people, about one-seventeenth of the population of the Eastern Zone.[37] Peter Niggli has estimated that about 100,000 people died in the resettlement process in Ethiopia or after their arrival in resettlement camps.[38]

The similar death toll of "resettlement" in Ethiopia and "evacuation" in Cambodia has attracted some comparisons. In an article captioned "Today's Holocaust," the *Wall Street Journal* characterized mass death of Ethiopians from the Dergue's resettlement program as "government-organized group murder" which "shape[d] up as a mass extermination on the order of the Khmer Rouge killing fields."[39] But was the scope and intent of mass deportation of groups in Ethiopia and Cambodia similar?

Pol Pot's treatment of Eastern Zone cadres bore the closest resemblance, in recent memory, to the Holocaust. There is a consensus among scholars who study Cambodia that the Eastern Zone was the initial exception to the widespread horrors in Cambodia. It was the only place in revolutionary Cambodia where the 1.7 million inhabitants practised Buddhism and ate and dressed well.[40] Economically, the Eastern Zone was important because of its rubber plantations and important rice-growing areas. Its strategic location as a border post gave it immense political significance in Vietnamese-Cambodian relations.[41] In a revolutionary society where the Khmer Rouge wanted to achieve uniformity of policy, the relative autonomy

---

37 Kiernan, "The Cambodian Genocide – 1975–1979," 343.
38 Peter Niggli, *Ethiopia: Deportations and Forced Labour Camps: A Study by Peter Niggli on Behalf of Berliner Missionswerk* (Berlin, 1986); "Today's Holocaust," *Wall Street Journal*, January 27, 1986, 24.
39 "Today's Holocaust," *Wall Street Journal*, January 27, 1986, 24. See also Robert Kaplan, *Surrender or Starve: The Wars behind the Famine* (Boulder, 1988), 106, 110; Jason Clay and Bonnie Holcomb, *Politics and the Ethiopian Famine, 1984–1986*, 2nd ed. (Cambridge, Mass., 1986), 193; Médecins Sans Frontières (France), "Mass Deportations in Ethiopia," *Confidential Report* (December 1985): 51, 65.
40 Kiernan, *The Pol Pot Regime*, 205, 209; Chandler, *Brother Number One*, 127; Becker, *When the War Was Over*, 179–80; Michael Vickery, *Cambodia, 1975–1982* (Boston, 1985), 132, 137–38.
41 Becker, *When the War Was Over*, 178.

of the Eastern Zone caused the party leadership enough displeasure. And Pol Pot demonstrated that displeasure by sending loyal Southwestern troops to the Eastern Zone in May 1978 to bring it in line with state policies. The purification of the Eastern Zone, in 1978, took the form of direct massacres of cadres, heavier work schedules, and deportations of "tens of thousands" of the inhabitants of the zone to the northwestern provinces. According to Kiernan, the Khmer Rouge leadership gave each Eastern Zone cadre evacuated to the northwestern province of Pursat a blue scarf not as a token of loyalty to the state but as a "sign" to distinguish them from other Khmers. The object of this unusual identification was to make cadres of the Eastern Zone more visible as the dissident and impure Khmers to be exterminated.[42]

A different kind of evacuation took place in Ethiopia. The Dergue intended to move 1.5 million people from northeastern Ethiopia to southwestern Ethiopia.[43] Mengistu gave the reasons at an emergency meeting of Dergue officials in February 1985:

Almost all of you here realize that we have security problems. The guerrillas ... operating in many of these areas do so with great help from the population. The people are like the sea and the guerrillas are like fish swimming in that sea. Without the sea there will be no fish. We have to drain the sea, or if we cannot completely drain it we must bring it to a level where they will lack room to move at will, and their movements will be easily restricted.[44]

Mengistu's rationale sounds like Pol Pot's reasons for moving people from the Eastern to the Northwestern Zone. But the meaning intended in Mengistu's statements was not to brutally exterminate the ethnic populations of those guerrilla areas but to relocate those perceived to be assisting anti-Dergue groups. By putting "people who ... [had] accepted the revolution along sensitive parts" of the country and removing those who had not, and were accessible to opposition groups to distant lands, in the southwest, the Dergue hoped to deprive its armed opponents of potential recruits and gain intelligence information from its loyalists on the activities of the OLF in southwestern Ethiopia.[45] It failed.

What increased the death toll of resettlement in revolutionary Ethiopia was the zeal of soldiers and party enthusiasts to enforce the program despite

---

42 Ben Kiernan, "Genocidal Targeting: Two Groups of Victims in Pol Pot's Cambodia," in Bushnell, *State-Organized Terror*, 213–15.
43 Giorgis, *Red Tears*, 288–89.
44 Statement attributed to Mengistu Haile Mariam in ibid., 298.
45 Ibid., 288–89. Giorgis's point is confirmed in author's tape interview with Tesfaye Mekasha, former vice-minister of foreign affairs in the imperial government, Addis Ababa, July 30, 1995.

the refusal of the peasants to resettle. Here, Mengistu's personal interest in resettlement, in a political culture in which the leader commanded popular reverence, turned the program into the pet project of revolutionary cadres. Party cadres and peasant association chairmen competed to earn state medals and Mengistu's praise for resettling the largest number of people.[46] Mengistu personally endorsed the execution of peasants who resisted resettlement.[47]

Clashes between indigenous ethnic groups and resettlers and attacks on settlements by anti-Dergue groups also increased the death rate in the settlements. The EPRP, for instance, attacked and killed many people in the settlement camp in Pawe, in Gojjam, in northwestern Ethiopia. But by neglecting its responsibility to provide prophylactic medicines to assist resettlers to combat diseases such as malaria, the Dergue condemned hundreds of thousands of people to death. Government field workers witnessed the death of "hundreds" of infants, the elderly, and the weak in the course of this state policy, which Giorgis has characterized as "genocide of helpless people."[48]

CRIMINALIZING MASS DEPORTATION

Jason Clay and Bonnie Holcomb have argued that the Dergue purposefully used resettlement as a tool to stifle the survival of the Oromo, the largest ethnic group in Ethiopia, which, according to them, had posed "the most serious threat" to the Ethiopian state since the nineteenth century.[49] Clay and Holcomb overstretch the facts. The resettlement of Oromos and Amharas from Wollo, Tigrayans and other ethnic groups from Tigray, in the North, Amharas and Oromos from Shoa, in central Ethiopia, Kembatas and Hadiyas from Keffa province, in the Southeast, and vagrants in Addis Ababa and other urban areas, undermines Clay and Holcomb's argument that the Dergue's resettlement program was deliberately designed to destroy a particular ethnic group. People who were resettled between 1978 and 1986 in Ethiopia were not relocated on the basis of their ethnicity but rather their material condition and were perceived as potential recruits for armed opponents of the Dergue.[50] Moreover, when a genocidal intent to

---

46 Author's interviews with Zegeye Asfaw, minister of settlement in the Dergue administration, Addis Ababa, May 29, 1995, and peasants at Mersa, North Wollo Administrative Zone, Ethiopia, October 20, 1995. See also Giorgis, *Red Tears*, 271, 300–1.
47 Giorgis, *Red Tears*, 272.   48 Ibid., 118.
49 Clay and Holcomb, *Politics and the Ethiopian Famine*, 25–26.
50 Author's taped interviews with Amhara and Oromo resettlees at Pawe resettlement villages 14 and 23, Pawe, East Gojjam Administrative Region, October 1, 1995, and with Tesfaye Mekasha Amare,

exterminate a group exists, the perpetrator usually blocks the flight of the victims to safety. That is exactly what the Khmer Rouge did, but not the Dergue. The Khmer Rouge massacred ethnic Vietnamese whom they had ordered expelled from Cambodia and who were on their way to Vietnam. They also prevented other Vietnamese from fleeing Cambodia and later massacred them.[51] But in Ethiopia, once the victims of resettlement began to migrate toward state-controlled areas, the Dergue facilitated their movements. Similarly, the Dergue's armed political opponents aided peasants and resettlers in state-controlled areas who wished to emigrate to territories under their control.[52]

The Dergue's resettlement program was not a tool of genocide against the Oromo ethnic group as Clay and Holcomb suggest. It was intended as a counterinsurgency measure to intimidate and isolate potential soldiers of the TPLF and EPLF.[53] The Dergue must have also been motivated by suspicion that unpublicized external relief assistance and other support from international nongovernmental organizations (NGOs) helped the TPLF and EPLF to escape state control and use relief aid to recruit peasants.[54] This suspicion was reinforced when the Dergue impounded an Australian ship, the *Golden Venture*, at Assab port in January 1985. The vessel, which was bound for Port Sudan, in the Republic of Sudan, and had mistakenly berthed at Assab, in Ethiopia, contained relief cargo clearly marked for delivery to the EPLF and TPLF.[55] The incident confirmed long-held suspicions of the Dergue that international sympathy for antigovernment groups increased the flow of resources to their relief organs, thus strengthening their resolve to overthrow the revolutionary military regime. Here, Barbara Harff and Ted Robert Gurr are correct in arguing that war becomes a vehicle for genocide when one group in the conflict perceives that external supporters are assisting its opponents.[56]

former vice minister of foreign affairs in the imperial government, Addis Ababa, November 16, 1995.

51 Kiernan, *The Pol Pot Regime*, 26.

52 Author's taped interviews with Amhara, Oromo, and Kembatta resettlees in Pawe, Gojjam Administrative Region, Ethiopia, October 1, 1995.

53 Author's taped interview with Tesfaye Mekasha Amare, former minister of foreign affairs in the imperial government, Addis Ababa, November 16, 1995. See also Taye Gurmu, Deputy Commissioner of the RRC, to Brother Augustine O'Keefe, CRDA, May 29, 1986, CRDA Archives, Addis Ababa; RRC Files: Reports and Minutes, January 1985–December 1985.

54 RRC, Addis Ababa, *Official Statement*, "A Frustrated Outcry," October 3, 1986, FAO Archives, Addis Ababa, IL 2/2 RRC Files, February 1986–August 1987, January–December 1988.

55 Edward Kissi, "Famine and the Politics of Food Relief in United States' Relations with Ethiopia: 1950–1991," Ph.D. diss., Concordia University, Montreal, 1997, 377.

56 Barbara Harff and Ted Robert Gurr, "Systematic Early Warning of Humanitarian Emergencies," *Journal of Peace Research* 35, 5 (1988): 560.

CONCLUSION

The Dergue was not the same as the Khmer Rouge. The two revolutionary regimes had different visions of revolution. Their crimes also differed in scope and nature. A comparison of revolution in Ethiopia and Cambodia demonstrates that genocide, as defined in the UNGC, is more likely to accompany revolution when an extreme and racist revolutionary movement, such as the Khmer Rouge, succeeds in establishing control over a society without any determined opposition from domestic armed political groups as the Dergue faced. A comparison of the crimes of the Dergue and the Angkar legitimizes Kiernan's argument that the Khmer Rouge leadership was able to "plan such mass murders precisely because of its concentrated power."[57] Arguably, the Dergue's murders could have developed into genocide as defined in the UNGC had the numerous armed groups with opposing ideologies of ethnic secessionism not prevented the military regime from exercising absolute and "concentrated" power.

A comparison of state-organized murder in Ethiopia and Cambodia also bolsters Chalk and Jonassohn's emphasis on the perpetrator's definition of the victim group in the study of genocide. Besides the monks, the Cham Muslims, and ethnic Vietnamese and Chinese whose deaths attest to ethnic and religious murder and, therefore, genocide as strictly defined in the UNGC, some of the Khmer Rouge's victims such as intellectuals, city people, and rich people were also victims of politically motivated murder. They were targeted for destruction because the Khmer Rouge defined them as undesirables in the pure and perfect society it sought to create.

A comparison of revolutionary Ethiopia and Cambodia makes the weaknesses of the UN Genocide Convention even more glaring. Under the convention, the crimes of the Dergue would not constitute genocide because the Dergue targeted those it killed not because of their religious faith, ethnic identity, or even political beliefs, but rather their armed opposition to a military leadership of the Ethiopian revolution.[58] But the Ethiopian case presents a challenge to scholars of genocide studies because in Ethiopian law, the killing of political groups, for whatever reason, is a form of genocide. Under Chalk and Jonassohn's typology of genocide, the Dergue's crimes can be characterized as genocide because the Mengistu regime killed with intent to create terror and implement the state's national unity revolutionary objective. Given the complex history of the Ethiopian revolution, and the culture of political killing in Ethiopia, justice should not be blind to the

---

57 Kiernan, "The Cambodian Genocide – 1975–1979," 352.
58 Harff and Gurr, "Systematic Early Warning of Humanitarian Emergencies," 567.

atrocities of the Dergue's armed opponents. In a world of genocide denials and historical revisionism, it is significant for the court trying the Dergue for genocide to acknowledge that what happened in Ethiopia was not a one-sided mass killing. Opponents – including the TPLF now in power in Addis Ababa – killed unarmed civilians they perceived as assisting their enemies.

15

Modern Genocide in Rwanda

Ideology, Revolution, War, and Mass Murder in an African State

ROBERT MELSON

In April 1994 the world was flooded by grisly images of piles of murdered men, women, and children from Rwanda. Some of the bodies were
discovered in mass graves, some in churches and schools that had become
catacombs for the victims, and some floating along rivers and rotting in lakes.
The slaughter was so extensive that the bodies threatened to clog the rivers
and pollute the lakes. It soon became clear that the world community was
once more confronted with genocide. Indeed, what happened in Rwanda
was no limited massacre or even what the United Nations calls a "genocide-
in-part." This was the real thing: more than a half-million Tutsi murdered –
three-quarters of the population – and the attempt by the Rwandan state
and the Hutu majority to exterminate every last Tutsi. Like the Holocaust
and the Armenian genocide the destruction in Rwanda fits the category
of "total domestic genocide," what the UN calls a "genocide-in-whole."[1]
My aim in this chapter is to demystify the Rwandan genocide and to see it
clearly as an instance of state-sponsored mass murder driven by ideology in
a context of revolution and war that has been a hallmark of our modern era.

A version of this chapter was first presented as a paper at the conference on comparative genocide,
sponsored by the H. F. Guggenheim Foundation, Barcelona, Spain, December 7–10, 2000. I wish to
thank Professor David N. Smith for helpful comments. Of course, I take full responsibility for any
shortcomings in this chapter.

1 According to the widely accepted UN definition formulated in 1948, genocide means actions "committed with intent to destroy in whole or in part a national, ethnical, racial or religious group as such."
By implication the UN recognizes the distinction between the destruction of a group as a "whole"
(genocide-in-whole) from the destruction of its "part" (genocide-in-part), although it uses the same
term for both phenomena. I have emphasized that distinction to differentiate "total" (genocide-in-
whole), like the Holocaust, the Armenian genocide, and Rwanda, from "partial" genocide, like Biafra,
Bosnia, and Kosovo. The significant point here is that the Rwandan genocide was an instance of a
"total" genocide or extermination, which makes it comparable to the Holocaust and the Armenian
genocide. See *Yearbook of the United Nations, 1948–49* (New York, 1949), 959–60. For a more detailed
discussion of these terms, see my *Revolution and Genocide: On the Origins of the Armenian Genocide and
the Holocaust* (1992; Chicago, 1996), 22–30.

In my previous work on the origins of modern genocide I emphasized the role that factors like revolution and war played in creating situations or contexts favorable to a policy of genocide and class destruction.[2] Thus in the Armenian genocide, the Holocaust, and Cambodian genocide, ideologies of nationalism, Nazi racism, and Maoism were crucial for the motivations of leaders and some cadres in the execution of genocide, but it was revolution and war in each of these cases that proved decisive for enabling ideological motivations to be translated into policies of genocide.

In contrast, the recent Rwandan genocide has been viewed by some observers as stemming from "age-old tribal enmities" between Hutu and Tutsi and to have been carried out in a disorganized frenzied manner – an explosion of tribal hatred. Nothing could be further from the truth. There was no "age-old animosity between the Tutsi and Hutu ethnic groups," as the front page of the October 1997 *New York Times* would have it. Indeed, until 1959 when the Hutu revolution broke out, *"there had never been systematic political violence recorded between Hutus and Tutsis – anywhere."*[3]

There was very little that was traditional, primordial, or premodern in the Rwandan genocide. There were no "tribes" invading the land of their enemies in order to capture land, booty, and women, while killing the men or selling them off into slavery. The Rwandan genocide was the product of a postcolonial state, a racialist ideology, a revolution claiming democratic legitimation, and war – all manifestations of the modern world.

I return to this point in the conclusion, after considering how colonialism reconstructed Hutu-Tutsi relations, giving rise to a Tutsi elite hated by a Hutu mass; how the "democratic" Hutu revolution of 1959 excluded Tutsi from the moral order of the Rwandan state and made them available for genocide; and how war between the Rwandan state and the Tutsi-led Rwandan Patriotic Front (RPF) helped to precipitate the genocide.

THE COLONIAL CONSTRUCTION OF HUTU AND TUTSI DIFFERENCES

When first the Germans and then the Belgians came across Rwanda, they were confronted by a complex traditional structure in which kings and their retainers were drawn from among Tutsi cattle herders. The monarch and the aristocracy ruled over a peasantry that was mostly Hutu but included some

---

2 Some of the following discussion derives from my article, "Revolution, War, and Genocide," in Israel Charny (ed.), *The Encyclopedia of Genocide* (Santa Barbara, 1999), 499–501.
3 Philip Gourevitch, *We Wish to Inform You That Tomorrow We Will be Killed with Our Families* (New York, 1998), 59.

Tutsi, and their power extended over a small population of Twa hunters and gatherers.[4] The Tutsi aristocracy was in the process of consolidating its domination even before the arrival of European colonialists, but the Europeans accelerated the process and gave it a racialist cast.[5]

Throughout most of Africa and other parts of the colonial world, even if they had so wished, the colonizers simply lacked the power to reconstruct society from the ground up, so they relied on local rulers who, in effect, became their agents. In Rwanda this meant that first the Germans and then the Belgians came to rely on the Mwami, the Tutsi ruler, and the Tutsi aristocracy to impose their domination. Moreover, the colonizers needed a conceptual framework to comprehend the complexities of African society. Central to it were the notions of "tribe" and "race." No matter how complex and differentiated the African society, it was invariably labeled a "tribe" and its internal differences were viewed as stemming from "race" by the colonizers. With particular variation these terms were applied to the stratification system of Rwanda. Although they probably had a common origin, the Tutsi and Hutu were perceived and labeled as distinct tribes and races by the Europeans.

The fact is that the physiognomy of the aristocratic Tutsi cattle herders differed somewhat from the Hutu peasantry and the nonaristocratic Tutsi pastoralists. The aristocrats in the king's court tended to be taller and slimmer, and their facial features closer to the European ideal of beauty. This apparent physical difference (apparent because some Hutu peasants were tall and some Tutsi pastoralists were short) came to be generalized by the Europeans as indicating that all Tutsi were of a different and superior race from the Hutu.[6] It was a racial difference that was further elaborated by Belgian administrators and anthropologists who argued – in what came to be known as the "Hamitic Hypothesis" – that the Tutsi were conquerors

---

4 From 1897 to 1916, Rwanda was under German rule, and from 1916–62 under Belgian colonialism. The country was declared a republic on January 28, 1961, and it became independent on July 1, 1962. In a population of roughly 7 million, by 1989, 85 percent were Hutu, 14 percent Tutsi, and 1 percent Twa. The area of the country is 10,169 square miles.

5 Catherine Newbury, *The Cohesion of Oppression: Clientship and Ethnicity in Rwanda, 1860–1960* (New York, 1988). In a private correspondence David Norman Smith notes: "Actually, the Tutsi monarchy and nobility had been fully in control for quite some time before the Germans arrived, and the finishing touches on the regime's bureaucracy were applied during the reign of Yuhi Gandihiro in the late 18th century. The Belgians *reconfigured* 'Tutsi' power radically, transforming what had been a lacework hierarchy into a flattened labor-control mechanism. The Mwami was turned into a ceremonial figure, de facto and then de jure, and the majority of pre-colonial Tutsi nobles were given substantially reduced roles as well."

6 David Newbury and Catherine Newbury, "Bringing the Peasants Back In: Agrarian Themes in the Construction and Corrosion of Statist Historiography in Rwanda," *American Historical Review* 105, 3 (June 2000): 839.

who had originated in Ethiopia (closer to Europe!) and that the Hutu were a conquered inferior tribe of local provenance.[7]

The fact of the matter is that the somatic difference between Tutsi aristocratic cattle herders and the population of Hutu cultivators can be just as well attributed to selective inbreeding, wherein "most people married within the occupational group in which they had been raised."[8] Upper-class differences in Rwanda resulted over centuries in somatic distinctions just as they have among castes in India and upper and lower classes in Great Britain, but for the European colonizers the apparent coincidence between body type and social status was irresistible and they recast it in racial terms. Thus Pierre Ryckmans, a Belgian administrator from the 1920s, noted: "The Batutsi were meant to reign. Their fine [racial] presence is in itself enough to give them a great prestige vis-à-vis the inferior races which surround [them]. . . . It is not surprising that those good Bahutu, less intelligent, more simple, more spontaneous, more trusting have let themselves be enslaved without ever daring to revolt."[9]

The Belgians, like the Germans before them, decided to rule through the Tutsi and, in so doing, they favored them in every way. In the traditional system there had been three types of chiefs, with the chief of the land being a Hutu. However, the Belgians abolished this tripartite division, centralizing chiefly powers in one man, usually a Tutsi. By 1959 forty-three out of forty-five chiefs were Tutsi and only two were Hutu.[10] The Belgians also initiated and made widespread a draconian system of forced labor, wherein mostly Hutu where drafted to work for the state without pay. Most important, they refused to view the land as belonging to native lineages, allowing the state to dispose of Hutu land after paying out compensation to the owners. But compensation was often inadequate and Tutsi personalities, who were

---

7 According to the early European explorers like John Hanning Speke (see his *Journal of the Discovery of the Source of the Nile* [London, 1863], ch. 9), the Tutsi were viewed as a superior race who probably originated in Ethiopia. Speke thought they were related to the Oromo or Galla. Other Europeans traced Tutsi origins to the ancient Egyptians, the Greeks, the Jews, to the lost continent of Atlantis, even to Eden. See Gerard Prunier, *The Rwanda Crisis: History of a Genocide* (New York, 1995), 7–8.

8 Alison Des Forges, *Leave None to Tell the Story: Genocide in Rwanda* (New York, 1999), 33. A judicious discussion of the apparent Hutu-Tutsi difference is provided by Mahmood Mamdani who suggests that the origins of the two groups are difficult to discern and have become politically charged and controversial. His own take on the distinction is that in the precolonial period the term "Tutsi" came to stand for rulers and "Hutu" for subjects. As Tutsi expanded from a core area, the conquered peoples were called "Hutu," while those individuals and lineages that could be incorporated into the ruling group were renamed as "Tutsi." See his *When Victims Become Executioners: Colonialism, Nativism, and the Genocide in Rwanda* (Princeton, 2001), 41–75. Whatever the true origins of the terms "Tutsi" and "Hutu" may be, it was their political significance in the colonial and postcolonial periods that became crucial to the genocide of 1994.

9 Prunier, *The Rwanda Crisis*, 11.   10 Ibid., 27.

close to the Belgian administration, often profited from such deals. The *ubuhake* system, a traditional social contract entailing subordination between Hutu and Tutsi, wherein some Hutu were able to rise to Tutsi rank, was undermined by the privatization of the land, and, inadvertently, its passing also reinforced the Hutu-Tutsi split.

Primary and secondary education was in the hands of the Belgian priests who favored the Tutsi. As the Tutsi realized that Belgian "reforms" could in fact benefit them, they began to convert to Catholicism and to attend mission schools in order to improve their social position. In 1932, at the elite Astrida College (now Butare) out of 54 students 45 were of Tutsi origins. Even in 1959, on the eve of the revolution, out of 422 students, 279 were Tutsi.[11]

In sum, during the colonial period, the Belgians cast all Tutsis, both aristocrats and nonaristocrats, in the role of the natural elite of Rwanda, whose origins lay in Egypt or Ethiopia and who in effect constituted a superior race. Such flattering constructions were not rejected by the Tutsi, especially since they dovetailed with Belgian policies that favored them. By the same token, the Hutu, who were pauperized and deprived of all political power by the Belgian authorities, came to hate the Tutsis as racial enemies and foreign interlopers. At the same time as they identified all Tutsi, even those who were poor and powerless, with the dominant race, they turned hatred into self-hatred and suffered agonies of bruised self-esteem and inferiority.[12]

It was tragic, given future events, that the indigenous peoples came to believe the European version of their origins and social structure. Indeed, the more educated the Rwandan, the more likely he or she was to appropriate and to internalize European ethnic and racial categories and to view the differences between the Tutsis and the Hutu in essentialist terms. Not surprisingly some Tutsi took pride in their alleged racial superiority, which the Hutu resented, and the Hutu came to view all Tutsis as foreign conquerors and interlopers. Thus a racialist conception or ideology of Tutsi-Hutu differences was crucial to the ensuing genocide. Prunier summarizes this point well: "Ideas and myths can kill, and their manipulation by elite leaders for their own material benefit does not change the fact that in order to operate they first have to be implanted in the souls of men."[13] But ideas and myths can kill only under special circumstances; in Rwanda, as elsewhere, these were revolution and war.

11 Ibid., 33.
13 Ibid., 40.

12 Ibid., 39.

THE HUTU REVOLUTION

The Belgians, who had helped to create and freeze a caste system, and who gave it a racial definition preceding World War II, made matters still worse by trying to dismantle it after the war. Capitalism as introduced by colonialism had undermined traditional relations between Hutu and Tutsi, while indirect rule reinforced and crystallized Tutsi hegemony. Ironically, however, to make matters still worse, by the 1950s the Belgian authorities, including the church, tried to "democratize" the colonial system. A new class of Belgian priests and civil servants came to power in the church and the colonial administration that was apparently much more sympathetic to the "downtrodden" Hutu. The churchmen feared being replaced by Tutsi priests, while the administrators were increasingly open to egalitarian ideas that promoted the lowly Hutu over the Tutsi upper class and aristocracy. By initiating policies favoring the Hutu after the war, the Belgians were bound to encourage a Hutu revolt and Tutsi reaction.

By 1957 there emerged Hutu-led political movements demanding an end to Hutu subordination and the overthrow of Tutsi hegemony. Significantly they referred to the Tutsi as an alien race, not as an indigenous upper class. In an important _Bahutu Manifesto_ of the period it was said that, "the problem is basically that of the political monopoly of one race, the Mututsi."[14] But the manifesto did not call for a new order based on equality for all. In effect it called for the replacement of one system of domination with another. Significantly, it demanded that the racial categories be maintained in identity papers, thereby reifying such labels with deadly consequences for the 1994 genocide. "In order to monitor this race monopoly we are strongly opposed at least for the time being, to removing the labels 'Mututsi,' 'Muhutu' and 'Mutwa' from identity papers. Their suppression would create a risk of _preventing the statistical law from establishing the reality of facts._"[15] In other words, the manifesto wanted to perpetuate the Hutu-Tutsi distinction and have it reflected in identity papers, believing quite rightly that such documents would help to identify and isolate the Tutsi in the postcolonial era. Indeed, such papers did during the genocide: when genocidal killers were in doubt about the identity of their victims,

---

14 The _Bahutu Manifesto_ was the popular name given to a document, "Notes on the Social Aspect of the Racial Native Problem in Rwanda." The full text appears in F. Nkundabagenzi, _Le Rwanda politique (1958–1960)_ (Brussels, 1961), 20–29. Cited in Prunier, _The Rwanda Crisis_, 45.

15 Prunier, _The Rwanda Crisis_, 46. Meanwhile, with anticolonial movements taking off after World War II, ironically, it was the Tutsi – the best educated – who were most likely to articulate African nationalist sentiments and a desire for independence from Belgian rule, but for the most part they opposed Hutu equality.

they relied on colonial-era documents that had labeled people as Tutsi or Hutu.

As independence neared, both European administrators and Hutu intellectuals argued that the new "democratic" state had to rest on the Hutu majority. The Tutsi would be relegated to a tolerated "minority." In 1959, with the aid of Belgian administrators, political movements led by Hutu elites revolted against their Tutsi overlords and displaced one "ethnocracy" with another. In Rwanda, where formerly the Belgians had ruled with the aid of some Tutsi frontmen, now Hutu called the shots.

Commencing on November 1, 1959, Hutu violence spread throughout the country. Colonel Guy Logiest, commander of the Belgian troops, approved of the violence and actively encouraged it. Blind to the irony of his position, Logiest recalled, "It was without a doubt the will to give the people back their dignity. And it was probably just as much the desire to put down the arrogance and expose the duplicity of a basically oppressive and unjust aristocracy."[16] Four months previous to the Hutu uprising, the Mwami, the king who was a living symbol of Tutsi-Hutu unity, had collapsed and died after having been treated by a Belgian doctor. The suspicion lingers that he had been assassinated in preparation for the "Hutu revolution."

In October 1960 Gregoire Kayibanda, one of the authors of the *Bahutu Manifesto*, headed a provisional government and declared, "Democracy has vanquished feudalism."[17] The implications of that slogan were clear: Hutu "democracy" had abolished Tutsi "feudalism." In January 1961 the monarchy was abolished, and Rwanda was declared a republic. The republic was granted full independence in 1962, with Kayibanda as president. In this manner the revolution of 1959 transformed Rwanda from a Belgian colony that had utilized a Tutsi elite as a subterfuge for Belgian power into a Hutu ethnocracy dressed up as a populist majoritarian democracy that excluded the "Tutsi race" from the political order. Indeed, at a recent conference sponsored by Ibuka, a Tutsi survivors' association (Kigali, Rwanda, November 25–December 1, 2002), most survivors dated the origins of the 1994 genocide to the 1959 revolution, when they were made second-class citizens in a racially polarized state.

WAR AND GENOCIDE

The violence against the Tutsi minority following the Rwandan revolution prompted thousands of Tutsi refugees to flee to neighboring countries,

16 Gourevitch, *We Wish to Inform You*, 60.   17 Ibid., 61.

especially Burundi and Uganda. By 1962 there were 120,000 such refugees. Two years later that number had exploded to 336,000.[18] The Tutsi diaspora provided the manpower for guerrilla forces that attacked Rwanda from abroad. As a result of such attacks, the Tutsis who had stayed in Rwanda were further demonized as traitors and periodically massacred.

One of the long-run effects of the Rwandan revolution was to set off a vicious spiral of ever increasing violence between Tutsi guerrilla forces operating abroad and the Rwandan state, as well as a government-sponsored campaign against domestic Rwandan Tutsis that culminated in the genocide of 1994. But that was not all. The revolution also had consequences for Burundi – Rwanda's neighbor and twin, whose social structure paralleled Rwanda's but where the Tutsi-led army was able to cling to power.

Warned by events in Rwanda, the Tutsi-dominated Burundian army subverted popular elections that would have brought the Hutu majority to power. In 1972, and periodically later as well, the Burundian army, fearing the results of national elections, launched major operations culminating in massacres against the Hutu. The Burundian army had learned the lessons of the 1959 Hutu-led revolution in Rwanda only too well and was determined to prevent the rise of a Hutu ethnocracy in Burundi.[19]

The violence in Burundi was not lost on Hutu leaders in Rwanda. As a reaction to the events in 1972 in Burundi, Kayibanda and his army chief of staff, Jouvenal Habyarimana, organized anti-Tutsi pogroms. By July 1973 Habyarimana staged a coup. Declaring himself president of the Second Republic, he organized a one-party dictatorship under his leadership and that of the MRND (National Revolutionary Movement for Development).

Having consolidated his power, Habyarimana modulated violence against the Tutsi for the first few years, but Rwandan freedoms were severely curtailed and discrimination against the Tutsi minority became institutionalized. Then in the 1980s the economy suffered a downturn, and the Habyarimana regime became increasingly vulnerable to liberalizing pressures from donors from abroad. In June 1990, following a meeting with French President Mitterand, Habyarimana announced that Rwanda would become a

---

18 Prunier, *The Rwanda Crisis*, 61–62.

19 Until the Rwandan genocide of 1994, when most people thought of genocide in the area, they pointed to the events in 1972 in Burundi where nearly 100,000 Hutu were slaughtered by an army dominated by the Tutsis. See Rene Lemarchand, *Burundi: Ethnic Conflict and Genocide* (Cambridge, 1995). Indeed, events in Rwanda and Burundi had powerful blowback effects in each country. Like Rwanda, Burundi, a country of some 5 million, was divided along similar Tutsi-Hutu-Twa lines in similar proportions. It too experienced German and Belgian colonialism. Hence Rwanda and Burundi became nightmarish mirror images of each other, with Tutsi massacred in Rwanda and Hutu in Burundi. However, the genocide in Rwanda in 1994 was qualitatively different: it was an attempt at exterminating the Tutsi minority in a manner not paralleled in Burundi.

multiparty system, allowing for the formation of other parties to compete with the MRND, but such reforms were too little and too late to affect the situation of the Tutsi minority.

On October 1, 1990, the Rwandan Patriotic Front, a Tutsi-dominated force based in Uganda, commenced operations that would ultimately lead to the invasion of the country. The RPF invasion as well as domestic competition for power provided Hutu chauvinists in the Rwandan government with the rationale for a vicious anti-Tutsi campaign of calumny and dehumanization. When Habyarimana's plane was shot out of the sky on April 6, 1994 – he was returning from peace talks with the RPF that had been held in Arusha, Tanzania – "Hutu Power" gave the signal and the extermination of the Tutsi commenced.

THE GENOCIDAL CAMPAIGN

The "genocidal campaign" was initiated and orchestrated by a radical Hutu elite at the center of government, calling itself "Hutu Power," that had close ties to President Habyarimana, the army, the police, the party structure, and the mass media. "The genocide resulted from the deliberate choice of a modern elite to foster hatred and fear to keep itself in power," but that elite found a ready willingness on the part of the Hutu masses to join in the slaughter.[20]

Initiated in Kigali, the capital, the genocidal campaign spread to every prefecture, commune, sector, and village. It utilized the mass media to vilify the Tutsi minority as well as the Hutu opposition. Both were said to be traitors in league with the invading RPF. Rwandan Tutsis were demonized and accused of harboring murderous intentions against all Hutu. They were labeled *ibyitso* (traitors) and *inyenzi* (cockroaches). It was a case of "kill or be killed." With a 66 percent rate of literacy and a 29 percent rate of radio ownership (59 percent in the cities), Rwanda was a setting where the mass media proved very effective as tools of mobilization and propaganda.[21]

But even before April 1994 and the actual genocide, Hutu Power's campaign also relied on direct action to make the case for Tutsi perfidy and to frighten and involve ordinary Hutu. Thus on October 4–5, 1990, it

20 See Des Forges, *Leave None to Tell the Story*, 1. The concept of "genocidal campaign" and much of the argument below derives from her work. Some of the following also appears in my review of Des Forges's book in the *Institute for Genocide Studies Newsletter* 25 (Fall 2000): 16–19.

21 Des Forges, *Leave None to Tell the Story*, 65–96. See also Frank Chalk, "Radio Broadcasting in the Incitement and Interdiction of Gross Violations of Human Rights Including Genocide," in Roger W. Smith (ed.), *Genocide: Essays toward Understanding, Early-Warning, and Prevention* (Williamsburg, Va., 1999), 185–203.

staged a phony attack on Kigali, which it blamed on the RPF. It initiated very real massacres of Tutsis as reprisals for RPF incursions and as a way of habituating ordinary people to violence. And during the genocide it used traditional means of mobilization in the villages, such as calling people out to do communal work, *umuganda*, but in this case "work" meant mass murder.

Starting as reprisal for the RPF's invasion from Uganda in 1990, Hutu Power's campaign to prepare people for genocide was so successful that by 1994 – when the order came down to start the killing – the speed with which people were slaughtered in Rwanda surpassed that of any other genocide in the modern era. If not for the military victory of the RPF no Tutsis or moderate Hutus (those who opposed the genocide) would likely have survived.

The concept of a "genocidal campaign" is important for an understanding of what happened in Rwanda, but it leaves some questions unanswered. For the distinctiveness of the Rwandan genocide lies not only in its organization and speed; it lies also in the extent of its mass participation. Tens of thousands of ordinary Hutu peasants and workers wielding machetes, clubs, hoes, or other farming implements massacred their Tutsi neighbors, sometimes in a joyful, festive, manner. Priests, pastors, and ministers turned on their flocks, as did husbands on their wives and wives on their husbands. It should also be well noted, however, that many refused to get involved, and some even hid and attempted to save people targeted for death. Where did the tens of thousands of killers come from? What was going through their minds as they joined the campaign of mass murder?

No doubt the propensity of ordinary "law-abiding" people to do as they are told by their leaders played a role, as did the endless propaganda of Radio Milles Collines, which could use the war to make it appear as if all Tutsi were in league with the RPF invaders whose main goal was to kill or subjugate the Hutu. Greed for land and property no doubt played an important role in the motivations of poverty-stricken villagers, but what is missing is their voice. What did ordinary Hutu make of their Tutsi neighbors, of Habyarimana, of the RPF?

Some indication of underlying popular attitudes may be gleaned from the pioneering work of Liisa Malkki. Studying Hutu refugees from the Burundian massacres of 1972, she demonstrates how pervasive the "Hamitic Hypothesis" and racialist views of Tutsis had become. In the popular Hutu mind, the Tutsis were demonized by an ideology (which she calls a "mythico-history") that viewed them as foreign invaders from Ethiopia or Somalia who had arrived in Burundi (Rwanda) centuries before and were bent on subjugating or destroying the Hutu and stealing their land.[22] Although the informants were Hutu peasants fleeing the violence in Burundi, there is good reason to believe that similar views were held by Rwandan Hutu participating in the genocide. The seeds of colonial racism had fallen on receptive ground in Rwanda: revolution and war provided the context for the genocide that was already implicit in the "Hamitic Hypothesis."

CONCLUSION: REVOLUTION, WAR, AND GENOCIDE

In the introduction I made the claim that the Rwandan genocide was an instance of modern genocide among which the Holocaust, the Armenian genocide, and the Cambodian genocide are prime examples. What links all of these instances and makes them "modern" are the role of ideology and the circumstances of revolution and war.

No doubt the intentions of the killers are essential for an understanding of the causes of genocide. Indeed, how could we begin to understand the Holocaust without an analysis of Nazism or the Armenian genocide without Pan-Turkism, or the Cambodian genocide without Maoism, or, indeed, the Rwandan genocide without the "Hamitic Hypothesis." However, in any society, including liberal peaceful democracies, there are people who harbor murderous thoughts against national, ethnic, religious, racial, and other groups, but because they do not have the power to act on their intentions their murderous projects are mostly stillborn. The question therefore arises, What are the circumstances under which genocidal killers might be able to gain power in order to act on their intentions? In some important cases the circumstances of revolution and war made it possible for genocidal killers to come to power and to implement their policies. And it is this point that I wish to stress in the remainder of this conclusion.

The Young Turks came to power in a disintegrating Ottoman Empire in 1908. They tried to implement radical changes, and started the deportations of the Armenians under the circumstances of the First World War. The Nazis came to power in 1933 after the destruction of the old regime of imperial Germany and the collapse of the Weimar Republic. They put into effect their "final solution," under the circumstances of the Second World

---

22 For example, one of Malkki's respondents characterized the Tutsi following the Hamitic Hypothesis as follows: "One fault of the Tutsi, let us say that it is theft.... What have they stolen from us? First of all our country. *The Tutsi are of nilotic provenance* [emphasis added]. They come from Somalia. And then [they stole] that which exists in [our] country – the livestock, cows, chickens, domestic animals.... All the wealth of the country, you understand, was ours. Because we were the natives of the country. They came perhaps four or five hundred years ago.... They stole all that." Liisa Malkki, *Purity and Exile* (Chicago, 1995), 67.

War. The Khmer Rouge came to power on April 17, 1975, after years of struggling first against the Sihanouk and then the Lon Nol regimes under the circumstances of the wider war for the former Indochina. Having seized power the revolutionaries destroyed the Khmer middle and upper classes and committed genocide against the Chams and the Vietnamese. And, as we have seen, the Rwandan genocide was a product both of the revolution of 1959 and the war against the RPF that the revolution spawned. In these four instances, all of which are culturally and historically independent of each other, the revolutionary regime was governed by an ideology that identified certain groups as the enemies of society, it was at war with foreign and domestic enemies – some of them of its own making – and, under those circumstances, it sought to destroy what it called "the enemies of the revolution."

Why do some revolutions lead to genocide? When revolutionary vanguards come to power in a situation where most institutions have been undermined and the identity of the political community is in question, they need to reconstruct society, revitalize support for the state by way of a new system of legitimation, and forge new identities. Under revolutionary circumstances they will redefine the identity of a subset of the political community as "the people," "the nation," "the race," "the religion," or "the class." These are the group or groups that are celebrated by the ideology of the revolutionaries and from whom they hope to draw their support. In Turkey it was the Muslim Turks, in Germany it was the "Aryans," in Cambodia it was the Khmer peasantry, and in Rwanda it was the Hutu.

However, groups that are not included and are singled out as racial, national, religious, or class enemies run the danger of being defined as "the enemies of the revolution and the people." And it is such groups that may become the victims of repression or genocide. In Turkey it was the Armenians, in Germany it was the Jews, in Cambodia it was the Khmer middle and upper classes as well as the Chams and the Vietnamese, and in Rwanda it was the Tutsis.

At its founding a revolutionary regime seeks not only to reshape the domestic social structure and redefine the identity of its people; it also aims to alter the state's international situation. Indeed, for many revolutionaries it was their country's relative weakness in the international arena that prompted them to challenge the old regime in the first place. Thus revolutions are often the products of war and lead to further war. It is under the circumstances of revolution that leads to war that genocide is most likely to be committed. The Armenian genocide occurred in World War I, the Holocaust in the midst of World War II, the Cambodian genocide in a war over Indochina, and the Rwandan genocide in a war against the RPF.

There are three ways in which revolutionary war is closely linked to genocide. First, it gives rise to feelings of vulnerability and to paranoid fears that link supposed domestic "enemies" to external aggressors. The victims of all of the major genocides were said to be in league in a nefarious plot with the enemies of the revolutionary state: the Armenians with the Russians, the Jews with the Bolsheviks, the Khmer upper classes with the American imperialists, and the Rwandan Tutsis with the RPF. Second, war increases the autonomy of the state from internal social forces, including public opinion, public opposition, and its moral constraints. Third, war closes off other policy options of dealing with "internal enemies." The expulsion of "internal enemies" may not be possible, while their assimilation and/or segregation may take too long and may not be feasible in a wartime situation. Thus it is that revolutions, and especially revolutions that lead to wars, can provide the circumstances for genocide.

This is not to suggest that all revolutions lead to genocide, or that all genocides are the products of revolution. Indeed, the French and the American revolutions did not lead to genocide; moreover, invasions, colonialism, and religious revivals are among some other circumstances that can promote genocide. What is essential as well is the ideology of the revolutionaries, as discussed earlier.

Finally, the Rwandan genocide was a total domestic genocide, what the UN would call a "genocide-in-whole" as against a "genocide-in-part," and as such it was the African version of the Holocaust. There are some apparent similarities to the Holocaust among which an official racism and the hierarchically organized dictatorial state stand out. There are also some features unique to the Rwandan genocide, most notably the scale of popular participation in the killing. Never before was a majority of a population mobilized by the state to become the "willing executioners" of a minority. Thousands of ordinary Hutu men, women, and children followed the dictates and orders of government functionaries and managed to slaughter the Tutsi minority at a rate much faster than the Holocaust.[23]

Scholars of genocide are now left to ponder not only the extraordinary features of the Holocaust but those of the Rwandan genocide as well.

23 See Christian P. Scherrer, *Genocide and Crisis in Central Africa* (Westport, Conn., 2002), 125.

Why did the Nazis truly believe that there was a World Jewish Conspiracy aimed at the German people and that Jews the world over were their enemies? How was it possible for so many ordinary Rwandans to respond to the appeals of Hutu Power, and, seizing any weapon at hand, go forth to murder their Tutsi neighbors with whom they had lived in peace for centuries? Such are some of the insights and questions raised by the Rwandan genocide.

16

History, Motive, Law, Intent

Combining Historical and Legal Methods in Understanding Guatemala's 1981–1983 Genocide

GREG GRANDIN

For a small country, Guatemala has had an impressive history. Its 1944 October Revolution was one of the first efforts in Latin America to try to make good on the social democratic promise offered by the Allied victory in World War II. In 1954 it had the unfortunate distinction to suffer the first Latin American Cold War coup. That U.S.-sponsored event, in turn, led to two important consequences: throughout the rest of his life, Che Guevara, who was in Guatemala at the time, cited the intervention as a key moment in his political radicalization, and the United States, seven years later, would try to replicate its Guatemalan success in Cuba with the Bay of Pigs intervention. In the 1960s, following the Cuban Revolution, Guatemala was one of the first Latin American countries to develop both a socialist insurgency *and* an anticommunist counterinsurgency. Practices the United States rehearsed in Guatemala would be applied throughout Latin America in the coming decades.[1] In the 1980s, the final escalation of the superpower conflict turned Guatemala, along with Nicaragua and El Salvador, into one of the Cold War's final battlefields.

In February 1999 the United Nations–administered Historical Clarification Commission (CEH) released the results of its investigation into the political repression that underwrote this history. The commission not only ruled that the state bore overwhelming responsibility for more than 200,000 political murders but that during a particularly brutal period between 1981 and 1983 it had committed acts of genocide against its Mayan population, who makes up 60 percent of a population of 10 million people. The CEH also condemned both the United States government for financially, technically, and materially supporting Guatemalan security forces and

---

1 Martha K. Huggins, *Political Policing: The United States and Latin America* (Durham, N.C., 1998).

U.S. businesses for "maintaining archaic and unjust social and economic relations."[2]

These forceful conclusions, uncharacteristic of the usually conciliatory tone of truth commissions, was made possible by the CEH's unique use of historical analysis and narrative. Despite the fact that they exercised no power to indict, prosecute, or punish, past truth commissions in Argentina, Chile, and El Salvador focused primarily on a juridical interpretation of human rights violations – inquiries that judged individual transgressions in light of national and international legal doctrine, limiting themselves to asking "who did what to whom and how." Other than providing hazy descriptions of political polarization, these commissions studiously avoided asking why repression took place. Confronted with the inability of liberal jurisprudence to represent adequately the horrors of a four-decade civil war, the CEH broke with past Latin American commissions and placed human rights violations at the end of a historical narrative that in effect begins with the Spanish conquest.[3] Yet rather than dilute institutional responsibility (the commission was prohibited from identifying individual violators) in abstract structural causes, the CEH joined historical and juridical analysis in a manner that strengthened legal doctrine. The application of history to law allowed the commission to rule that the Guatemalan state committed acts of genocide against its Mayan population, for genocide, while defined by intent – a psychological state most comfortably fitted to individuals – is always a social crime, collective in execution and consequence.

A STATE RACIST IN THEORY AND PRACTICE

The CEH was established in a series of United Nations–brokered agreements between the military and rebels that in 1996 ended one of the longest and most bloody civil conflicts in the world. Like other accords negotiated by an enervated guerrilla leadership and a victorious military, it angered national and international human rights organizations. The CEH did not have the power to subpoena witnesses or records and its final report could not "individualize responsibility" nor have "legal effects."[4] The agreement,

---

2 See the summary by Christian Tomuschat, the CEH's president, given at the presentation of the report <http://www.c.net.gt/ceg/doctos/tomu0225.html>.

3 I discuss some of the philosophical questions raised by the CEH's historical methodology in Greg Grandin, "Chronicles of a Guatemalan Genocide Foretold: Violence, Trauma, and the Limits of Historical Inquiry," *Nepantla* 1, 2 (2000): 391–412.

4 The accord is in the commission's final report. Comisión para el Esclarecimiento Histórico (CEH), *Guatemala: Memoria del silencio*, 12 vols. (Guatemala City, 1999), 1:23–26. The report is available on-line at <www.hrdata.aaas.org>.

however, in a strategic avoidance of potentially deal-breaking specifics, left vague other aspects of the commission's work. Unlike the strict mandates of the Argentine and Chilean truth commissions, which limited the time period and violations to be investigated, the CEH accord did not define the crimes to be examined, the period to be considered, or the commission's methodology.

A number of factors led the commission – comprised of German human rights law expert Christian Tomuschat, and Guatemalans Otilia Lux de Cotí, a Mayan educator, and Alfredo Balsells, another law professor – to apply a more critical historical method than did previous commissions. The duration and brutality of the violence, an unrepentant military and oligarchy, an indifferent state, and profound social and racial cleavages undercut the argument that future deterrence could be brought about by an affirmation of shared social values – an argument usually made to support a more open-ended historical interpretation of the causes of human rights violations. The ambiguity of the accord allowed the commissioners to interpret its mandate broadly: "To address the historical causes of this most tragic epoch ... implies dealing with conditions that developed over time and whose effects have accumulated influence on human conduct and social practice.... Guatemalan history chronicles manifold, enduring forms of violence that affect segments of the population. This violence is clearly reflected in political life, in social relations, and in the realm of work, and its origins are of an economic, political, ideological, religious, and ethnic character."[5]

Based on the collection of over 8,000 testimonies from victims and their relatives, the CEH concluded that the state was responsible for 93 percent of the violations and that the military committed 626 massacres. The guerrillas were assigned responsibility for 3 percent of the violations and 32 collective killings. During the course of the conflict, the military and its allied agents killed or "disappeared" over 200,000 Guatemalans. Yet *Memoria del silencio*, as the final report is titled, goes well beyond divvying out responsibility for the violence to the state and the guerrillas. Starting with an introduction that lays out staggering statistical evidence of social inequality – the country's health, education, literacy, and nutritional indicators are among the most unjust in the world despite an abundance of national wealth – the CEH spends the rest of its first volume chronicling the "causes and origins" of Guatemala's armed conflict. It is a damning account that indicts not just the nation's ruling elite but its culture and history as well.

5 Ibid., 82.

The CEH focuses a good part of its analysis on the political intolerance brought about by a deterioration of liberal state institutions. A weak state could not fulfill even the most rudimentary redistributionist function, which contributed to a "political culture where intolerance defined the totality of social interaction."[6] Yet in contrast to past truth commission reports, the CEH describes intolerance and polarization as effects, not wellsprings, of social relations and political actions. Nor, despite its harsh criticisms of the United States, does it attempt to displace blame onto the foreign powers: "[I]t is not possible to present simple explanations that presents the armed conflict as a manifestation of the Cold War confrontation between the East and the West. . . . If the most visible actors of the conflict were the military and the insurgency, the historical investigation conducted by the CEH provides evidence of the responsibility and participation, in different forms, of segments of the economic elite, political parties, and diverse sectors of civil society. . . . In this sense, any reduction [of the conflict] to the logic of two actors is not only insufficient, but misleading."[7]

The CEH identifies three mutually dependent "structural" or "historical" causes of state violence: economic exclusion, racism, and political authoritarianism. Its analysis rests heavily on "theories of authoritarianism," elaborated by Southern Cone social scientists, that see Cold War military regimes as emerging from a particular path of dependent economic development.[8] Yet while these explanations tend toward abstraction, the CEH carefully unfolds its narrative in close chronology, particularly in its description of Guatemala's post-1954 history. The transition to coffee cultivation at the end of the nineteenth century intensified colonial exploitation, racism, and authoritarianism. Guatemala's plantation elites gobbled up vast amounts of land and came to rely on the state – "racist in theory and practice" – to ensure the cheap supply of labor, mostly Mayans from highland communities. A series of forced labor laws combined with land loss to "increase the economic subordination" of Mayans and poor Ladinos (Guatemalans not considered Mayan). This model of coercive development in turn militarized the state, which focused its energies on enforcing policies, particularly the acquisition of labor through debt and vagrancy laws, that benefited

---

6 Ibid., 79.   7 Ibid., 80.

8 See, e.g., Guillermo O'Donnell, *Modernization and Bureaucratic-Authoritarianism* (Berkeley, 1973), and "Tensions in the Bureaucratic-Authoritarian State and the Question of Democracy," in David Collier (ed.), *The New Authoritarianism in Latin America* (Princeton, 1979), and Fernando Henrique Cardoso, *Autoritarismo e democratização* (Rio de Janeiro, 1975). See also the essays in Kees Koonings and Dirk Kruijt (eds.), *Societies of Fear: The Legacy of Civil War, Violence and Terror in Latin America* (London, 1999). See Idelber Avelar's important discussion on these theories in *The Untimely Present: Postdictatorial Latin American Fiction and the Task of Mourning* (Durham, N.C., 1999), ch. 2.

the coffee oligarchy.[9] Since the end of the nineteenth century, "the landed class," writes the CEH, "especially the sector connected to the cultivation of coffee ... imposed its economic interests on the state and society."[10]

The CEH identifies political actions taken either in response to social exploitation or in defense of entrenched interests as the mainspring of the Guatemalan conflict: "State violence has been fundamentally aimed against the excluded, the poor, and the Maya, as well as those who struggled in favor of just and more equitable society.... Thus a vicious circle was created in which social injustice led to protest and subsequently to political instability, to which there were always only two responses: repression or military coups."[11] Confronted with movements demanding "economic, political, social, or cultural change, the state increasingly resorted to violence and terror in order to maintain social control. Political violence was thus a direct expression of structural violence."[12]

This dynamic eased and even reversed for a ten-year period when, following a democratic revolution in 1944, two reformist administrations curtailed many of the prerogatives and privileges of the coffee oligarchy. The CEH identifies this period as an "immediate antecedent" for the civil war. The new governments ratified a social democratic constitution, ended forced labor, legalized unions, enacted a labor code, expanded the vote, and passed a far-reaching land reform. These measures "increased ideological polarization and internal political struggle within an international context that was increasingly charged by the tensions of the east-west struggle."[13] An "archaic judicial structure" that could not deal with the conflicts generated by the rapid expansion of new rights, including those granted by the land and labor reforms, aggravated social tensions and deepened polarization. While the "defenders of the established order" quickly mobilized against the state, opposition came from other sectors as well.[14] Rural peasant and indigenous mobilization along with the legalization and growing influence of the Communist Party reinforced an anticommunism that had deep roots among the middle-class, Catholic Church, and military. In turn, resistance to reform both radicalized and divided revolutionary parties.

This democratic decade, according to the CEH, "awoke the energies and hopes" of Guatemalans who had "yearned to overcome the past."

---

9 Many historians share this assessment. For Guatemala, see David McCreery, *Rural Guatemala, 1760–1940* (Stanford, 1994). For Guatemala's transition to export capitalism compared with Mexico, see Alan Knight, "Debt Bondage in Latin America," in Leonie Archer (ed.), *Slavery and Other Forms of Unfree Labour* (New York, 1989).

10 CEH, *Guatemala: Memoria del silencio*, 1:81. 11 Ibid., 5:21–22.
12 Ibid. 13 Ibid., 1:100.
14 Ibid., 103–5.

This awakening took place in a larger global context in which "the world was entering a new political period with the defeat of fascism and the promise offered by capitalist economic development." The CEH describes the U.S.-orchestrated 1954 counterrevolution as a national "trauma" that had a "collective political effect" on a generation of young, reform-minded Guatemalans: "So drastic was the closing of channels of participation and so extensive was the recourse to violence that it is considered one of the factors that led to the guerilla insurgency of 1960."[15] Expectations raised and struggles fought during this period resonated throughout Guatemala's subsequent civil war. In the countryside, many of the land conflicts that fueled peasant participation in political movements and the insurgency date back to the Arbenz land reform of 1953.

The U.S. intervention reinitiated the "exclusivist dynamic." The state once again put "itself at the bidding of a minority at the expense of the majority."[16] It also led to two new consequences important to understanding the development of Cold War political violence. First, Cold War tensions and anticommunism energized nationalist racism and reinvigorated old forms and justifications of domination. A racially divided and economically stratified Guatemala was a tinderbox; counterinsurgent fear was the match. "What happened during the period of armed conflict," writes the CEH, "can be summed up as a process by which the radius of exclusion and the notion of an internal enemy" was extended and intensified through the whole of society.[17] Second, the Cold War radically transformed the possibilities of political alliances. In the past, the state responded to demands made by political movements not only with repression but with concessions and negotiations as well. The triumph of the 1944 revolution was the highpoint of this pattern. Following 1954 and intensifying after the 1959 Cuban Revolution, Guatemalan elites increasingly turned to the United States in order to confront domestic threats to their power. The balance tipped in the state's favor and repression gave way to full-scale terror.

COUNTERINSURGENT MOTIVES, GENOCIDAL INTENT

The CEH's marriage of history and law was more than one of convenience. Beyond providing a fulsome description of the conditions that give rise to political terror, the CEH's historical method proved indispensable to its ruling on genocide, a difficult crime to define under liberal jurisprudence.

---

15 Ibid., 107. 16 Ibid., 86.
17 Ibid., 83.

Most recent attempts to judge cases of genocide use the definition established by the 1948 United Nations Convention on the Prevention and Punishment of the Crime of Genocide, which defines genocide as one of a series of acts committed with the "intent to destroy, in whole or in part, a national, ethnical, racial, or religious group, as such."[18] While genocide is defined by intent – a psychological state associated with an individual – its collective nature challenges the very premise by which intent is defined.

Intent can be defined two ways. Specific intent attaches to "perpetrators whose actual aim or purpose is to realize certain forbidden consequences." General intent describes the state of mind governing the actions of individuals who "knew to a practical certainty what the consequences of those actions would be, regardless of whether or not they deliberately sought to realize those consequences." In the first case, the act is committed with the *purpose* that the consequence would occur. In the second, it is the *knowledge* that a particular act would have a certain consequence.[19] In the formulation, x killed y because x was jealous, *intent* is used to describe the psychological state of whether x knew that his or her actions would lead to the death of y, whereas *motive* is used to describe the reason, jealousy, for the actions. In most cases, the relationship between motive and intent is corroborative, that is, unveiling the motive makes more certain a charge that an individual intended a particular act. In legal proceedings, motive is usually always supplementary, whereas intent is essential in establishing guilt.[20] The separation between motive and intent is a juridical artifice, used to cull out responsibility for a particular act from a larger historical sequence of action and meaning. Liberal jurisprudence, of course, recognizes that individuals, actions, and psychological states exist within a larger constellation of moral and political relations and over the course of time has produced a series

18 Convention on the Prevention and Punishment of the Crime of Genocide, December 9, 1948, 102 Stat. 3045, 78 U.N.T.S. 277, U.N. G.A. Res. 260, U.N. GAOR, 3d Sess., 179th plen. mtg. at 174, U.N. Doc. A/810 (1948). The recently adopted Rome Statute of the International Criminal Court, the body that will, if instituted, judge future cases of genocide, adopted the following definition of intent: "[A] person has intent where a) In relation to conduct, that person means to engage in the conduct; b) In relation to consequence, that person means to cause that consequence or is aware that it will occur in the ordinary course of events." See Mahnoush H. Arsanjani, "The Rome Statute of the International Criminal Court," *American Journal of International Law* 93, 1 (1999): 22.

19 Alexander K. A. Greenawalt, "Rethinking Genocidal Intent: The Case for a Knowledge-Based Interpretation," *Columbia Law Review* (December 1999): 2266.

20 Consider this distinction between motive and intent found in a standard law text: "Intent relates to the means and motive to the ends, but ... where the end is the means to yet another end, then the medial end may also be considered in terms of intent. Thus, when A breaks into B's house in order to get money to pay his debts, it is appropriate to characterize the purpose of taking money as the intent and the desire to pay his debts as the motive." Wayne R. LaFave and Austin W. Scott Jr., *Criminal Law*, 2nd ed. (St. Paul, 1986), 228, cited in Greenawalt, "Rethinking Genocidal Intent."

of doctrines to account for a diffusion of responsibility and still retain the authority to punish a given act. Crimes committed by more than one person or as a result of a chain of command and actions taken in pursuit of a greater good – either in self- or social defense – are all defined and judged accordingly.

Genocide, however, poses a challenge to liberal jurisprudence to address collective crimes, for it is collective in two ways. First, the victim category is not simply a group of individuals but rather a racial, religious, or ethnic group. Second, it would often be practically impossible to conclude an act was committed with genocidal intent by an examination of an isolated act.[21] In order to establish that a particular act was committed with genocidal intent, that is, in order to prove that the perpetrators had either knowledge or purpose that their actions would result in the destruction in whole or in part of a defined group, it is perhaps essential, not just corroborative, to establish motive. Motive both links individual acts within a larger campaign and furthers an argument that the victims were understood in racial or ethnic terms.

Yet the introduction of motive as a probative requirement undermines the very definition of genocide. Just as lawyers often fear an appeal to history will be used to exonerate individuals from the consequences of their actions, a search for motive can dilute the racial content of a crime, *for race is never just race*. Racial, ethnic, and religious identity intertwine in all aspects of social life and national history. The motives that drive genocidal campaigns may not be understood in racial terms at all or may be justified in terms that emphasize a greater good. This is true even in a case as extreme as the Jewish Holocaust, the historical standard on which rest commonsensical understandings of genocide. In no other genocidal event, it seems, has motive mapped onto intent as seamlessly as it did during the Holocaust. The Nazis intended to destroy Jews because they were Jews. But even in this case, debate inevitably arises when historians attempt to situate intent within a larger array of social, political, and economic relations. Was Nazi intent to eliminate Jews a reaction to being pushed back on the eastern front? What was its relationship to other ideological motivations – to nationalism or anticommunism? Were genocidal acts committed to establish an emotional bond with the Führer? What is the relationship between those who executed and those who ordered genocidal acts?[22]

---

21 Except perhaps in the case of Hiroshima or Nagasaki.
22 Ron Rosenbaum, *Explaining Hitler: The Search for the Origins of His Evil* (New York, 1998), and Christopher R. Browning, *Fateful Months: Essays on the Emergence of the Final Solution* (New York, 1985).

In the Guatemalan case, the question that confronted the CEH was this: despite the massive violence visited upon indigenous communities by the military between 1981 and 1983, were Mayans killed because they were Mayan, or because they represented the real or perceived support base of the insurgency? The fact that the army did not inflict the same terror on indigenous communities that did not support the rebels lent weight to the claim that the violence was not genocidal but rather counterinsurgent. Indeed, Guatemalan president Alvaro Arzú's rejected the CEH's genocide ruling in such terms: "I do not believe that this macabre episode of thirty-six years was genocide. Genocide is the desire to exterminate an ethnic group, a race, and this was not the reason for this brutal conflict."[23] From the same assumptions, many on the left who were members of the insurgency or affiliated social movements were uncomfortable with the charge of genocide. For them, the description of the repression as genocide risked overshadowing the fact that the state was being challenged by a powerful, multiethnic coalition demanding economic and political reform. Many felt that by purportedly denying indigenous participation in the popular movement, the claim of genocide risked reducing the history of the repression to a simplified tale of Ladino violence heaped on defenseless Indians.

The CEH avoided this dilemma by carefully interpreting the UN's convention on genocide to differentiate motive from intent. "It is important to distinguish," wrote the CEH, "between 'the *intent* to destroy [a group], in whole or in part' . . . from the motives for such intention. In order to rule genocide, the intention to destroy the group is enough, whatever be the motives. For example, if the motive to intend to kill an ethnic group is not racist, but military, the crime is still genocide."[24] Once it made this foray into a more historically grounded understanding of genocide – unavoidable considering the development of events under consideration – the CEH had to contend with the potential for the consideration of motive to exonerate the perpetrators. The repressive state *was* threatened by a powerful insurgency. Mayans *did* participate in massive numbers in social movements and in the

---

23 *El Periódico*, June 30, 1999, 3.
24 CEH, *Guatemala: Memoria del silencio*, 3:316. A review of the history of the drafting of the convention confirms the CEH's distinction between intent and motive. The Soviet delegate attempted to insert language that would make "the qualifying fact" of genocide "not simply the destruction of certain groups but destruction for the reason that the people in them belonged to a given race or nationality, or had specific religious beliefs." The majority of delegates, however, rejected such a definition on the grounds that such wording would too narrowly limit the definition's application. The Siamese delegate, for instance, voted for the convention because it did not specifically define motives. See the discussion in Greenawalt, "Rethinking Genocidal Intent."

insurgency. The military *did* principally target indigenous communities that supported the guerrillas.

The CEH neutralized the potential of motive to absolve by using historical analysis to reveal the racialized assumptions of military strategy. In its "causes and origins" section, the commission described how patterns of rule and resistance developed along distinct racial lines. Unlike what occurred, for instance, in neighboring Mexico, the deepening of capitalist relations strengthened ethnic affiliation in Guatemala. In Mexico, particularly in the central valley, a vibrant colonial economy broke down indigenous ethnicity into a more homogeneous, but still racially marked, peasant identity.[25] In contrast, Guatemala's peripheral colonial and early republican economy buffered the consolidation and endurance of distinct indigenous identities centered around residential communities. With the introduction of coffee in the mid-nineteenth century, the creation of Guatemala's agrarian proletariat took place along clearly defined ethnic lines.

Guatemala's liberal coffee state was "characterized by its contradictions."[26] It "eliminated the juridical distinctions between Indians and non-Indians" but also "abolished [corporate] social protections," such as the right to land and political autonomy.[27] On the one hand, the state promoted assimilation into a single national identity. On the other hand, it enforced labor and tax policies that maintained Mayans as a distinct group. Mayans were singled out as obvious sources of labor and, when wages proved insufficient to attract a voluntary work force, the state enacted a series of extraeconomic "incentives" to secure workers, including forced labor drafts, debt peonage, and vagrancy laws. At times, whole communities became the captive work force of specific planters. Furthermore, unable to support a full-time labor force, coffee production relied on the ongoing existence of Indian communities to supply the subsistence needs of their seasonal workers. At the same time, Mayans used the wages they did receive to strengthen community institutions and traditions threatened by a shrinking subsistence land base due to population growth and commercial agricultural production. Guatemalan colonialism and capitalism did not create indigenous culture, but the particular form colonialism and capitalism took provided Indians space in which to survive *as* Indians.

Guatemala's nineteenth-century political trajectory likewise reinforced ethnic identity. As in Mexico, Indians and peasants allied themselves with nonindigenous political elites as their interests and identifications dictated.

---

25 See Alan Knight, "Racism, Revolution and Indigenismo: Mexico, 1910–1940," in Richard Graham (ed.), *The Idea of Race in Latin America, 1870–1940* (Austin, 1994), 78.
26 CEH, *Guatemala: Memoria del silencio*, 1:91.   27 Ibid., 92.

Unlike in Mexico, however, indigenous peasants usually supported conservative opposition to liberal reforms, which, on the whole, tended to undermine indigenous political authority and land rights. When coffee planters took control of the state and its ideological apparatus in 1871, Mayan political participation was either denied or portrayed as reactionary and ahistorical. Nationalists constantly blamed their political failures on indigenous reaction, and nearly uniformly wrote Indians out of their narration of national progress and destiny. The fall of the first independent liberal regime in 1838, the failure of the Central American Federation in 1840, and the endurance of a long postcolonial conservative regime (1839–71) were all blamed on Indians.[28]

The period between 1944 and 1954 saw a brief respite from this dynamic. But with the revolution's overthrow, "old forms of exploitation, of forced labor, of land appropriation against Indians and in favor of large landowners started again."[29] During the Cold War, the friend-enemy distinction that drives anticommunism easily took root in this fertile, race soil: "Patterns of violence within a society tend to generalize," the CEH writes, "they are copied and imitated and defuse throughout the social body and are reproduced across generations. Racism, conscious or unconscious, is an important factor in the explanation of many of the excessive acts of violence committed during the history of Guatemala and the armed conflict. For a racist mentality, any form of indigenous mobilization brings to mind an atavistic uprising. In this way, it can be considered that racism was present in the most bloody moments of the armed conflict, when the indigenous population was punished as an enemy that needed to be vanquished."[30]

In order to prove genocide, the CEH applied its historical analysis to the logic of the military's 1981–82 scorched earth campaign. Officers drew on long-held assumptions regarding indigenous culture to "single out [Maya] as the internal enemy ... both a real and potential support base for the guerrillas."[31] As one 1972 intelligence manual put it, "the enemy has the same sociological traits as the inhabitants of our highlands."[32] Guatemalan military analysts focused on what they identified as the "closed," castelike isolation of highland indigenous communities as the reason for the supposed collective susceptibility of Mayans to communism: "[T]he existence

---

28 For still the best account of indigenous support of conservative movements, see Hazel Ingersoll, "The War of the Mountain: A Study in Reactionary Peasant Insurgency in Guatemala, 1837–1873," Ph.D. diss., George Washington University, 1972. For the ideological consequences of indigenous political participation, see Greg Grandin, *The Blood of Guatemala: A History of Race and Nation* (Durham, N.C., 2000), chs. 3 and 6.

29 CEH, *Guatemala: Memoria del silencio*, 1:92.   30 Ibid., 93.

31 Ibid., 5:49.   32 Ibid., 3:322.

of diverse ethnic groups, with different languages and dialects, demonstrates the partial nature of national integration due to a lack of a common identity."[33] Mayans, wrote another military analyst, "have joined the guerrilla due to a lack of communication with the state."[34] To these assumptions, strategists added the Ladino tendency to interpret all indigenous political mobilization – on the rise since the 1960s – as the product of outside manipulation.

The military's scorched earth campaign, therefore, was designed to respond to this caste threat. It brutally cut off communities from the insurgency and broke down the communal structures that military analysts identified as seedbeds of guerrilla support. This explains the singularly savage nature of the Guatemalan counterinsurgency, which targeted not just individuals. In the majority of massacres, the CEH found "evidence of multiple ferocious acts that preceded, accompanied, and followed the killing of the victims. The assassination of children, often by beating them against the wall or by throwing them alive into graves to be later crushed by the bodies of dead adults; amputation of limbs; impaling victims; pouring gasoline on people and burning them alive; extraction of organs; removal of fetuses from pregnant women. . . . The military destroyed ceremonial sites, sacred places, and cultural symbols. Indigenous language and dress were repressed. . . . Legitimate authority of the communities was destroyed."[35] Mayans were identified as the enemy and killed *qua* Mayans, even if the *motivation* was to beat the insurgency.

Official responses to the report and the genocide charge have been disappointing. Unlike in Chile where President Patricio Aylwin formally apologized on behalf of the state for the crimes committed during the Pinochet years, the Guatemalan government has not claimed the CEH report as its own. During the official presentation of *Memoria del silencio* in Guatemala's National Theater, victims, their relatives, and members of popular and human rights organizations greeted the report's conclusions with clamorous applause. Guatemala's president, Alvaro Arzú, his close advisors, and military officers, however, appeared stunned. Arzú did not personally receive the report, instead delegating the government's secretary of peace to the stage. In the days that followed, official reactions were ambiguous at best. While the president begged for time to "read, analyze, and study in meticulous detail each and every word" before he would make an official statement (Arzú finished his term without issuing an official response), his secretary

33 Ibid. 34 Ibid.
35 Ibid., 5:43.

immediately reminded the press that while the work of the commission was laudable, it was important to keep in mind that "those responsible for the massacres will not be brought to justice."[36] Guatemala's minister of defense remarked that the report was "a partial truth, since its version of history is nothing more than the point of view of the commission." The head of Guatemala's official tourist institute complained that the report would result in more "damage than reconciliation" because its negative portrayal of Guatemala would cause foreign tourists to cancel their travel plans.[37]

While the report's findings are not legally binding, *Memoria del silencio* called for the full application of Guatemala's 1996 Law of National Reconciliation. This law allowed human rights violators to apply for amnesty for crimes committed during the civil war but not for acts of genocide, torture, and forced disappearances. By ruling that aspects of the military's 1981–83 scorched earth campaign were genocidal, the CEH hypothetically opened the door to prosecution, calling for the prosecution of "those crimes that the law does not exempt."[38] It is doubtful that anyone responsible for the terror will be charged in a national court anytime soon. In Argentina and Chile, recent efforts to prosecute violators of human rights in foreign courts have energized and strengthened domestic judicial systems. In Guatemala, the first flush of defensiveness on the part of the state tapered off into silence and neither the government, the military, nor the oligarchy have the will or desire to confront the past in a court of law.

CONCLUSION

Historical analysis not only supported the legal reasoning that backed the CEH's genocide ruling but provided historians with a way of distinguishing Cold War political terror from larger patterns of mobilization and repression. The CEH's analysis suggests that Mayan participation in the revolutionary movement of the 1970s and early 1980s marked a change from past indigenous strategies of dealing with the state. Through the colonial period and into the republican period, indigenous communities viewed the state as an arbiter of social relations, capable of mediating pacts, alliances, and conflicts between various social blocs.[39] Following 1954, rapid economic growth, a violent breakdown of a governing consensus among Ladino elites, U.S. intervention, and escalating state repression joined to undercut the power of

36 Radio broadcast *Guatemala Flash*, March 2, 1999; Radio broadcast, *Noti-7*, February 25, 1999.
37 *El Periódico*, February 26, 1999; Radio broadcast, *Noti-7*, March 2, 1999.
38 CEH, *Guatemala: Memoria del silencio*, 5:72.
39 See the conclusion to Grandin, *Blood*, for a more detailed discussion.

indigenous elites to fulfill their role as brokers between local, regional, and national interests. Stripped of their ability to negotiate political relations, community leaders in the 1970s "confronted the state head on."[40] According to the CEH, starting in the 1970s, Mayans joined other "citizens from broad sectors of society ... in [a] growing social mobilization and political opposition to the continuity of the country's established order."[41] The army's 1981–83 genocidal campaign can be understood in military terms as a strategic reaction to this shift in the balance governing relations of rule and resistance. In 1983, following the worst of the massacres, the military quickly decentralized the responsibility of social control to civil patrols and other local institutions run by selected Mayans. In effect, this phase of the military's counterinsurgency campaign was a return to older tactics of dealing with indigenous communities. Colonial, conservative, and even liberal regimes had invested a significant amount of authority in indigenous leaders in exchange for their cooperation in administering political relations, including, when needed, pacification of unruly subjects and communities.

The CEH's innovative use of history not only distinguished motive from intent but prevented counterinsurgent justifications from mitigating the severity of the charges of military atrocities. Historical analysis explained the apparent contradiction between the particularly savage nature of the Guatemalan counterinsurgency and the fact that once the surviving Indians were perceived to be under control, once the military felt it had substituted itself for the insurgency, the killing stopped. Only history could make sense of the perverse logic of Guatemalan president General Efraín Ríos Montt's remark made at the height of the slaughter he directed: "Naturally, if a subversive operation exists in which the Indians are involved with the guerrilla, the Indians are also going to die. However, the army's philosophy is not to kill the Indians, but to win them back, to help them."[42]

---

40 Víctor Gálvez Borrell, Claudia Dary Fuentes, Edgar Esquit Choy, and Isabel Rodas, *¿Qué sociedad queremos? Una mirada desde el movimiento y las organizaciones mayas* (Guatemala City, 1997), 63–66.
41 CEH, *Guatemala: Memoria del silencio*, 5:22.
42 Foreign Broadcast Information Service, Central America, "Rios Montt's Views on Peasant Killings, Communism," June 2, 1982.

17

Analysis of a Mass Crime

Ethnic Cleansing in the Former Yugoslavia, 1991–1999

JACQUES SEMELIN

We know it: Man is reasonable. But what about men?

Raymond Aron

Since Raphael Lemkin's pioneer work,[1] several scholars have published comparative studies on genocides. The works of Leo Kuper,[2] Helen Fein,[3] Frank Chalk and Kurt Jonassohn[4] are among the best known. However, they have not been able to agree on a definition of the concept of genocide. Researchers go from a sweeping approach – such as the one favored by the *Encyclopedia of Genocide*[5] – to a more restricted one, based on the United Nations 1948 Convention on the Prevention and Punishment of the Crime of Genocide, favored by Ben Kiernan, the founder of the Genocide Studies Program at Yale University.[6]

Considering that the UN definition is both too narrow and too restrictive, other scholars have introduced new terminology, such as "politicide"[7] or "democide."[8] The 1990s saw a growing number of comparative studies on "massacres" that distanced themselves from former studies on genocides: among them, the works of Brenda Uekert,[9] Denis Crouzet,[10] Mark

1 Raphael Lemkin, *Axis Rule in Occupied Europe* (Washington, D.C., 1944).
2 Leo Kuper, *Genocide: Its Political Use in the Twentieth Century* (New Haven, 1981).
3 Helen Fein, "Genocide: A Sociological Perspective," *Current Sociology* 38, 1 (Spring 1990): 1–126.
4 Frank Chalk and Kurt Jonassohn, *The History and Sociology of Genocide* (New Haven, 1990).
5 Israel Charny (ed.), *The Encyclopedia of Genocide*, 2 vols. (Santa Barbara, Denver, and Oxford, 1999).
6 Ben Kiernan, "Sur la notion de genocide," *Le Débat*, no. 104 (March–April 1999): 179–92.
7 Barbara Harff and Ted Robert Gurr, "Toward Empirical Theory of Genocides and Politicides: Identification and Measurement of Cases since 1945," *International Studies Quarterly*, no. 32 (1988): 369–81.
8 Rudolph J. Rummel, *Death by Government* (New York, 1997).
9 Brenda K. Uekert, *Rivers of Blood: A Comparative Study of Government Massacres* (Wesport, Conn., 1995).
10 Denis Crouzet, *La nuit de la Saint-Barthélemy, Un rêve perdu de la renaissance* (Paris, 1994).

Levene,[11] Stahtis Kalivas, Luis Martinez, and myself.[12] In some of them, the dividing line between "genocide" and "massacre" disappeared, leading such authors as Brenda Uekert[13] or Yves Ternon[14] to use the expression "genocidal massacres." In addition, Mark Levene gave a definition of "massacre" that is close to the definition of "genocide" given by other scholars, that is, "one-sided killings."[15]

And yet, it is essential that the words "massacre" and "genocide" be clearly and precisely differentiated, if only for one reason, that "genocide" comes under international law. A massacre is in no way a genocide, whereas a genocide always implies one or more massacres. This raises another question: which parameters will define the escalation from massacres to genocide, as has often been the case in past history? Robert Melson has come up with what he calls a genocidal continuum that goes from partial massacre to total genocide.[16]

Obviously, debates on terminology will be going on for a while. I, for one, am trying to elaborate a specific typology called "mass crime" that would differentiate between several scenarios, such as "massacre" and "genocide." But finding the right terminology is by no means as essential as building comparative analytical frames that will permit us to study "mass crime"; this is notably the purpose of the *Journal of Genocide Research*. In particular, these comparative studies should demonstrate how "ordinary" individuals come to act out extreme violence. I study mass crime within the frame of the ethnic cleansing that took place in the former Yugoslavia in the 1990s.

A DEFINITION OF MASS CRIME

Mass crime does not constitute a "basic" human rights violation by a specific power against a minority, nor is it an outrageous economic exploitation; rather, it is characterized by the destruction of large segments of a civilian population, often accompanied by atrocities, which would first appear to be random or without purpose. Yet, beyond the murderous frenzy of men,

---

11 Mark Levene and Penny Roberts (eds.), *The Massacre in History* (New York, 1999).
12 See the papers presented for the conference on Political Uses of Massacres, Centre d'Etudes de relations Internationales (CERI), Paris, November 16, 1999, in the *Revue Internationale de Politique comparée*, December 2000. In particular Stathis Kalyvas, "Problèmes méthodologiques de l'étude des massacres. Le cas de la guerre civile en Grèce (1943–1949)," Luis Martinez, "Les massacres en Algérie: Trois approches," and Jacques Semelin, "Penser les massacres."
13 Uekert, *Rivers of Blood,* introduction.
14 Yves Ternon, *L'etat criminel. Les génocides au XXème siècle* (Paris, 1995).
15 Ibid.
16 Robert Melson, "Problèmes soulevés par la comparaison entre le génocide arménien et l'holocauste," in *L'actualité du Génocide arménien* (Créteil, 1999), 373–85.

which we often hold responsible for such crimes, "mass crime" follows a certain "rationality," albeit a delirious one.

I prefer the expression "mass crime" to the more frequently used "mass murder" because the notion of "crime" covers broader actions. Mass crime does not imply only the killing of great numbers of people; its goal might be to deport them, or to force them to flee far away from their family roots. This uprooting, through terror and force that either precedes or accompanies massacre, is already a crime. Mass murder can also be preceded by the dehumanization of the potential victims, in itself a crime. In the end, mass crime leads to mass murder. Therefore the notion of crime not only encompasses the end result (death) but everything that precedes or follows death (such as atrocities performed on the victims, mutilation of corpses, etc.). The notion of crime also emphasizes the true signification of the act: the transgression of the "You shall not kill" law that universally governs life within a group (whatever the religion may be).

In other words, mass crime denies some segments of population their status as members of a society. Here the notion of "mass" is particularly relevant. Mass does not only imply quantification, a number of victims, which as we all know, can reach the hundreds of thousands, even millions. The "mass" concept implies hunting, starving, murdering a group of individuals that falls under a global criterion (nationality, ethnicity, political, or religious beliefs), without any consideration for personal characteristics. It implies eliminating an amorphous group of people, who, because they have lost all specific traits, has been reified into some sort of threatening globality.

The historical and political contexts in which mass crimes took place vary from one country to another. However, in light of the objectives pursued in each particular situation, and despite the diversity of contexts, we can observe two fundamental dynamics of mass crimes: submission of a group and eradication of a group.

Submission of a Group

The goal is to annihilate part of a group to force the rest into submission. The perpetrators count on the impact of terror to reach their objectives. This dynamic, of a terrorist nature, can take two different orientations: it aims at the capitulation of the group in order to impose a political will, as in the case of the civil war in Guatemala in the early 1980s; or once the submission of the group is attained, the organizers engage in a program of reeducation of the surviving members of the group, and the relationship between terror and ideology becomes a central factor, as in Stalin's USSR or Mao's China.

Eradication of the Group

The goal is no longer the submission of the group, but rather its elimination from a territory more or less substantial in size. Here, the question is one of "cleansing" a territory from the presence of a group deemed undesirable, and/or dangerous. This criminal strategy, based on issues of identity, can also be subdivided into two categories. First, the goal is to annihilate a part of the group so that the rest is forced to flee. Terror, in this case, aims at provoking and later accelerating a migration. Depending on the case, these forced population movements can be organized, in the form of forced marches, convoys, and the like. Ethnic cleansing in the former Yugoslavia is a recent example. Second, the goal is to annihilate the group completely, without any possibility of escape. In this case, the aim is to round up all the members of the group, wherever they may be, in order to eliminate them. The notion of "cleansing a territory" becomes secondary to that of annihilation. The extermination of the Jews by the Nazis during World War II is the best example.

These two dynamics – submission and eradication – can coexist in the same historical situation, one being predominant and the other secondary. Whatever its objectives, the logic of mass crime is related to the logic of war. It is based on the creation of an image of the enemy (foreign or national) to be subdued or annihilated. Mass crime thus develops out of the radical polarization of the society into the dialectic pair "friend-foe," which, Carl Schmitt maintains, constitutes the very essence of politics and of war.[17] Mass crime is indeed different from war crimes, and yet there is some relationship between the two. Mass crime can be integrated in the act of war; combined with war; or quasi-autonomous.

Integrated into the Act of War. Mass crime is an extension of war or of the practice of war. For instance, the massacre at Oradour-sur-Glane in France by a division of the SS on June 10, 1944, when the military killed the population of a village is an example of mass crime in the context of a *classical war*, whereas in Spain in 1936 mass crime took place during a *civil war*, when each side killed civilians who were presumably supporting the enemy camp. The dynamic of confrontation itself drives opposing armies to commit atrocities against civilian populations.

17 Carl Schmitt, *La notion de politique* (Paris, 1992).

Combined with War. Mass crime takes place in the context of military confrontation. Here, mass crime is not an extension of the act of war: its perpetration does not play a role in the outcome of the conflict, but rather, the conflict creates "favorable" conditions for mass crime, with an increase of the violence in social intercourse in the context of a war. This was notably the case with the Armenians in Turkey during World War I, and the Jews and Gypsies during World War II.

Quasi-Autonomous. Mass crime tends to detach itself almost entirely from the practice, or even from the context, of war. To be sure, mass crime is still justified by its perpetrators as a reaction to a perceived threat, and consequently as an act of war. However, on the so-called "battlefield," mass crime is the only act of war. Ethnic cleansing in the former Yugoslavia (1991–99) is a typical example.

How can we explain the development of the Yugoslav situation in the European context at the end of the 1980s? I would like to emphasize the notion of "delirious rationality" mentioned earlier. Basically, my hypothesis is that fear, exploited by propaganda, played a fundamental role in the construction of this criminal project, a project that was later carried out with carefully thought out methodology and organization. However, once set in motion, crime obeys a range of variants, including contextual factors, on which it leans in order to attain its one and only goal: ethnic cleansing of a given territory.

THE DEVELOPMENT OF COLLECTIVE PSYCHOSIS

Fear has played a fundamental role in the history of the Balkans. Underlying the way each population in the region collectively thinks about itself and its neighbors, there is fear: hidden or obvious, subtly spread or grossly orchestrated, fear remains present in every mind. Where does it come from? Obviously, from the series of massacres that were perpetrated on the Balkan people over the past two centuries. The will to create homogeneous states in a region where populations are heavily mixed often led to insidious or brutal decisions meant to displace or eliminate "undesirable" groups of people.

This policy of "homogenization" first derived from religious criteria. In the eighteenth century, as they regained land from the Turks, the Catholic powers, such as Austria and Venice, drove the Muslims out of Hungary, Slavonia, Dalmatia, and neighboring regions. In the nineteenth century, the national factor became predominant. New states, namely Serbia, Greece, and Montenegro, as they took shape and expanded, expelled former Muslim oppressors from their land.

In the twentieth century, the Balkan wars, and later, the war between Greece and Turkey, generated new massacres of civilians. "The burning of villages and the exodus of the defeated population is a normal and traditional event of all Balkan wars and insurrections," as the Carnegie commission already reported in 1914.[18] The worst occurred during World War II. As Gypsies and Jews were exterminated by Nazis, the Ustase led by Ante Pavelic in the new Croatian state proceeded to eliminate Serbian populations in Croatia and Serbia. At nearly the same time, Serb nationalists, the Chetniks, started perpetrating massacres in Croatian and Muslim villages. Tito's partisans themselves can be held responsible for many exactions against Chetniks. What has been taking place in the former Yugoslavia since 1991 belongs to the same chain of events. Each segment of population can feel potentially threatened, as a group, by another segment that, in a recent or distant past, perpetrated acts of violence against it.

Therefore, a vague feeling of fear survives, that feeds itself on the collective memory of massacres, and is used as the basis for nationalistic propaganda. For this kind of propaganda grows on the fertile soil of ancient fears. It tries to stir them up, to exploit them when they could remain latent, painful memories. Tito's regime apparently managed to silence nationalistic passions by calling for "brotherhood" and "unity" among the various Yugoslav peoples.[19] The Yugoslav media reported some of the atrocities of the time, such as the massacres of Ustase and Chetniks; those perpetrated by the partisans, however, were rigorously censored. These massacres were described in conformity with the official ideology, often in general terms, paying homage to "victims of fascism." But such biased reporting could not satisfy those who, in Serbia, wanted it to be known that Ustase, who were Croats, had killed Serbs, not because they had joined the Allied forces, but because they were Serbs. In each group of people, a memory survived, different from the official one, a memory that could not express itself openly but that was kept alive in the families.

After Tito's death in 1980, cracks started to appear in the official system. At the same time, the economic crisis that hit the country became a powerful element in the increasing collective worry. Harold Lydall writes: "[T]he decline in the standards of living [is such] that it is difficult to imagine

---

18 Carnegie Endowment for International Peace, *Reports of the International Commission to Inquire into the Causes and Conduct of the Balkan Wars* (Washington, D.C., 1914), 73.
19 Ivo Banac, *The National Question in Yugoslavia* (Ithaca, 1984).

another country that would not have reacted to the situation with either drastic political changes, or even with a revolution."[20] In the early 1980s, in Serbia, as reported by Paul Garde, one could hear that "ethnic Albanians demand an ethnically clean Kosovo."[21] Was it a rumor, or was it incipient propaganda by Serb nationalists? These few words achieved their aim because they meant that ethnic Albanians wished to eliminate Serbs from a province (Kosovo) that many Serbs considered the sacred land of their ancestors. Consequently, the expression "an ethnically clean Kosovo" was bound to stir up the Serbian fear of a new "genocide."

Serbs have historically disliked ethnic Albanian populations, sometimes aggressively so.[22] In the 1980s, this hostility grew visibly, as analyzed by Muhamedin Kullashi. In Serb papers, articles warn against their "diabolical proliferation." This fear of demographic growth, long rooted in Serb minds, seems founded because ethnic Albanians are now roughly 90 percent of the population in Kosovo. Some Serbs in Serbia and in Kosovo try to defuse this collective psychosis, bringing forth evidence of the fairly good relations between ethnic Albanians and Serbs, some of which appears on certain television shows. But, over a few years, "propaganda has been proving frighteningly efficient," using the media more and more openly, based on a "demonization of ethnic Albanians that overcame reluctance, common sense and objectivity."[23]

However, to be effective, propaganda cannot solely rely on the impact of its messages. It also relies, primarily maybe, on the receptivity of its targets and on their willingness to accept its messages as conveying the truth. Even if the information is not credible, it is accepted as credible. Fear and propaganda find themselves dialectically related. Historically entrenched feelings of fear offer a good soil on which to drop the seeds of propaganda, even coarse propaganda. Fear of being destroyed turns an irrational discourse into a credible one. Vice-versa, propaganda itself, with its repetition of anxiety-provoking messages, increases fears in a worried population. Propaganda polarizes the threatened group and triggers hate against what that group perceives as mortal danger. In 1986 a memorandum on the Yugoslav situation by the Academy of Sciences in Belgrade lent some intellectual credit to the argument. Inspired by Dobrica Cosic, a nationalistic writer, the report is an indictment against Tito's system and, in its second

20 Harold Lydall, *Yugoslavia in Crisis* (Oxford, 1989), 9.
21 Interview with Paul Garde, Paris, September 5, 1999.
22 Michel Roux, *Les Albanais en Yougoslavie. Minorité nationale, territoire et développement* (Paris, 1992).
23 Muhameddin Kullashi, "1981–1990: La production de la haine," in Antoine Garapon and Olivier Mongin (eds.), *Kosovo. Un drame annoncé* (Paris, 1999), 35–63, 52, 54.

section, denounces "the physical, political, juridical and cultural genocide of the Serbs in Kosovo."[24] The report denounces Slovenia and Croatia as politically dominating Serbia, and points at the federal system in Yugoslavia as the cause of "discrimination against Serbs within the Federation." This report, first circulated under cover, justified the fears of the population and was therefore readily accepted. What was being rumored, what had sometimes appeared in the press, was now "summarized" in a report emanating from a prestigious scientific institution. As the winds of reform started to blow in the East, the report offered a new approach, undoubtedly very different from Gorbachev's glasnost, but an approach that appealed to the Serbs. The report was an overt incitement to defend themselves, underscoring that "the greatest calamity for the Serbs is that they do not have a State like any other people."[25]

After 1987 Slobodan Milosevic turned the memorandum's perspectives into a real political strategy. He was one of the rare members of the communist apparatus who did not openly criticize the report. Tim Judah portrayed him as an "opportunistic leader," changing his speeches according to the different audiences.[26] As a former apparatchik, Milosevic soon turned into a first-class nationalist leader. In 1989, at the same time as the communist regimes in Prague and Warsaw were collapsing, Milosevic was taking a different route away from communism. In order to do so, Milosevic capitalized on nationalism. The various stages that allowed him to seize power are well known and need not be expanded upon.[27] Milosevic has often been described, and rightly so, as an astute tactician and an excellent propagandist. But what has rarely been told is that, while he reached the presidency by maneuvering well enough to gain control of the whole apparatus, including the media,[28] he was also the product of the evolution of Serb society in the 1980s. Therefore, fear and propaganda, plus power obtained by using them cleverly, were part of the flow of history. Free elections, held for the first time in December 1990, were Milosevic's reward for his political strategy of the previous three years. His party won by a landslide, and Milosevic's goals took on a new legitimacy.

---

24 Mirko Grmek et al. (eds.), *Le nettoyage ethnique. Documents historiques sur une idéologie serbe* (Paris, 1993), 251.

25 Ibid., 266.

26 Tim Judah, *The Serbs: History, Myth and the Destruction of Yugoslavia* (New Haven, 1997), 160.

27 Paul Garde, *Vie et mort de la Yougoslavie* (Paris, 1993). See also the recent biography of Milosevic written by Vidosav Stevanovic: *Milosevic, une épitaphe* (Paris, 2000).

28 See Rade Veljanovski, "Le revirement des médias audiovisuals," in N. Popov (ed.), *Radiographie d'un nationalisme. Les racines serbes du conflit yougoslave* (Paris, 1998), 299–326.

Whether the new Serb authority was called "national communist" or "ethno-nationalist,"[29] its goal remained the same: the defense of Serb identity, wherever the Serbs are, against the "dangers that plague it." In other words, the creation of a nation for the Serbs, within the frame of a "Greater Serbia." The new power fed itself on aggressiveness: the destruction of whatever was not Serb. Of course, this idea was not clearly spelled out. The memorandum kept silent on the subject. Those who practiced ethnic cleansing in the Balkans, whether they were Serbs, Croats, or others, did not talk about it. They just acted. People remembered massacres perpetrated against their own people; they did not talk about those they perpetrated in turn, and even less about those they were about to perpetrate. Milosevic's authority was part of the tradition. As the incarnation of the collective psychosis that brought him forth, he rose to crush what had been defined, even before his birth, as "the threat." This is why Milosevic's power, in its very conception itself, was ready for crime.

ACTING OUT

Fear of death is one of the most powerful motivations behind violence. In war, the risk of death is a real threat; one must kill before one gets killed. In mass crime, on the other hand, death is not a real threat, because the "enemy" is unarmed – thus, the puzzling aspect of this type of "war" against civilians. How does one evolve toward criminal activity, how does one transform fantasy into action, how does one evolve from fear of being destroyed to a decision to destroy defenseless civilians? Irrational violence can develop quite rationally. The perpetrator calculates, prepares his moves, selects the best moment to act. To annihilate one's fear of being destroyed, one has to hit before being hit. One must hunt and kill "preventively" those who are the threat. As such, ethnic cleansing is a process that is not only premeditated but long and carefully prepared.

Will the records of such preparation ever be found in Serbia? In any case, UN reports, especially the works of Tadeusz Mazowiecki and Cherif Bassiouni, unanimously describe a "systematical effort." An effort such as this one implies organization, implication of the state at its highest levels, involvement of the police, of the administration, of special services and militias. Did all these personalities take part in the preparation and implementation

---

29 Pierre Birnbaum, "Dimensions du nationalisme," in P. Birnbaum (ed.), *Sociologie des nationalisms* (Paris, 1997), 1–33.

of these plans? Will someone, one day, write how Serb government officials and civil servants complied with, or rebelled against, ethnic cleansing? Whatever the case, the conviction that they were serving the highest interests of the Serb nation, the political legitimacy of its leader, and the process of submission to authority[30] are among the factors that explain how the vast majority agreed to participate in such mass crime.

Now comes the time to find out when mass crime precisely starts. The downfall of the Soviet empire in general, and, more particularly, of the Yugoslav federation plays a fundamental role, as suggested by the works of K. Holsti.[31] In 1991 and 1992 declarations of independence by Slovenia, Croatia, and Bosnia provided a legitimate pretext for Milosevic to "come to the rescue of Serb minorities" living in those republics. It is now known that the said minorities had been armed by Belgrade.[32] In Slovenia, war stopped fairly rapidly. In Croatia, the first ethnic cleansing operations started in July 1991. They foreshadowed a total war against a population threatened with "memorycide," to use Mirko Grmek's terminology,[33] as well as "Urbicide," a fundamental dimension of this memorycide, as Bogdan Bogdanovic put it.[34] The goal was not only to kill or drive out populations who were deemed undesirable on the territory to be "cleansed" but to destroy anything that could be a reminder of their presence (churches, schools, etc.). Here, ethnic cleansing is definitely a form of mass crime that aims at the eradication of a population group from a specific territory.

The passivity of the rest of the world plays a key role in the pursuit of the aggression. The Great Powers' delays and procrastination, Pierre Hassner says, were interpreted by Belgrade as a green light to pursue their ethnic cleansing campaign.[35] Serb authorities were watching out for any international reactions that could have thwarted it. Serbia took the Western governments' passivity on the Croatian situation as an encouragement to engage in the same kind of campaign in Bosnia.

---

30 I refer here to Stanley Milgram's well-known study translated in French under the title *La soumission à l'autorité* (Paris, 1974).
31 K. V. Holsti, *The State War and the State of War* (Cambridge, 1996).
32 For example, the Bassiouni report notes that, in the Prijedor district, a parallel administration and a Serb armed guard were secretly created, at least six months before the beginning of the attack against Bosnia. These two bodies were immediately operational and worked together with the Serbian army.
33 Mirko Grmek, "Un mémoricide," *Le Figaro*, December 19, 1991.
34 Bogdan Bogdanovic, "L'urbicide ritualize," in Véronique Nahoum-Grappe (ed.), *Vukovar-Sarajevo. La guerre en ex-Yougoslavie* (Paris, 1993), 33–37.
35 Pierre Hassner, "Les impuissances de la communauté internationale," in Nahoum-Grappe, *Vukovar-Sarajevo*, 86–118, and "Institutions, États, sociétés: Une culpabilité partagée," in Agnès Nordman et al. (eds.), *L'ex-Yougoslavie en Europe. De la faillite des démocraties au processus de paix* (Paris, 1997), 45–58.

This third attack, launched on April 6, 1992, was the bloodiest and the most barbaric. As a result, ethnic cleansing operations became widespread. As early as 1992, Croats, under their nationalist leader, Franjo Tudjman, engaged in ethnic cleansing against Muslims of Bosnia-Herzegovina.[36] Following their victory in the Serbian enclave of Krajina, Croatian troops rampaged and burned Serbian villages. Bosnians, in turn, committed atrocities against both Serbs and Croats. The massacre fever spread, as if by contagion, and all the protagonists seemed to be joining in the same "dance of death."[37] As David Rieff also noted, "everything seemed to get worse all the time."[38] Does History repeat itself? Bosnia, which had been the stage for incredible atrocities during World War II, was hit by horror again. Fifty years later, killings were taking place often in the same villages. At the end of 1995, as the Dayton accords – whose aim was to put an end to the conflict – were being negotiated, war had already caused approximately 250,000 deaths.

The chronology of events is surprising: why was ethnic cleansing against ethnic Albanians in Kosovo never considered a priority? Propaganda against ethnic Albanians triggered the rebirth of Serb nationalism. Logically, they should have been the first victims. Indeed, since the 1980s ethnic Albanians had been submitted to a "differentiation" regime that soon turned to real apartheid in 1990 after both the Parliament and the government were suspended. Very few observers noticed it.[39] While some reports started denouncing violations of human rights and systematic use of torture in Kosovo,[40] these exactions had not yet reached the degree of violence and barbarity that had devastated Bosnia.

How can one explain the delay in Kosovar massacres? Let's go back to the notion of fear that allowed Milosevic's accession to power. Feeding itself on the perception of a threat, Milosevic's government paid close attention to the development of threatening environments and showed deep understanding of the context used them to justify launching his operations.[41] In the early 1990s, Croatia, rather than Kosovo, triggered such action. Zagreb's declaration of independence led to the Serbs' aggression, and the beginning of ethnic cleansing of the coveted territories. Ultranationalistic speeches by the

36 Regarding Tudjman's coming to power, see Marcus Tanner, *Croatia: A Nation Forged in War* (New Haven, 1997), 221–40.
37 Xavier Bougarel, *Bosnie. Anatomie d'un conflit* (Paris, 1996), 13.
38 David Rieff, *Slaughterhouse: Bosnia and the Failure of the West* (London, 1995), 171.
39 In France, the first paper that drew attention to their situation was that of Antoine Garapon in *Le Monde diplomatique*, November 1989.
40 See the reports of the Fédération internationale des droits de l'homme in September 1989 and April 1990.
41 The notion of threat in the shaping of ethnic conflict is the central issue of Dov Ronen's work, *The Challenge of Ethnic Conflict: Democracy and Self-Determination in Central Europe* (London, 1997).

Croatian president Franjo Tudjman provided Belgrade with an opening to come to the Serb community's rescue. At the same time, Kosovo was in a totally different situation. Ethnic Albanians had started a kind of civil resistance against the Serbs, a form of quiet resistance that is quite exceptional in a violent land where vendetta still rules.[42] Under the aegis of Ibrahim Rugova, ethnic Albanians wanted to resist without violence.[43] Were the same pacific winds that knocked down the Berlin Wall blowing over the Balkans? Was it the fear of impending death that convinced the majority of ethnic Albanians that it was safer not to provoke the Serbs? Indeed, it can be said that their pacific resistance gave no valid reason to launch an ethnic cleansing campaign in the province.[44] As Howard Clark summed up: "In extremely difficult conditions, civil resistance managed to postpone war, to maintain the integrity of the Albanian community in Kosovo and its way of life, to counter Serbian pressure on Albanians to leave, and to enlist international sympathy."[45]

In 1998–99, the context turned to Belgrade's advantage: more and more ethnic Albanians were supporting the UCK (Liberation Army of Kosovo) and their plans. The first operations of this newborn "army" triggered disproportionate repression from the Serbs, in 1998, in the Drenica valley.[46] War and terror hit the province. More ethnic Albanians joined the ranks of the UCK, "justifying" reprisals by the Serbian army against Albanian villages. Under the pretext that it was fighting UCK terrorists, Belgrade launched its ethnic cleansing campaign. Because the conflict might spread to other regions, and because of the horrified reactions in public opinion, the Great Powers started worrying about the fate of Kosovar Albanians, unfortunately forgotten by the Dayton accords.[47] The first NATO air strikes

42 As Serbian terror developed and spread, ethnic Albanians seemed to reconcile between themselves, a reconciliation instigated by Anton Ceta, a sociologist. Starting in spring 1990, Albanian families solemnly and publicly renounced blood feud. One of the most important public meetings was held in the Decani valley, where an estimated 500,000 people assembled. In a country, where whole families still kill each other, such a phenomenon is extraordinary and its political and sociological impact should definitely be scrutinized. One of the rare interviews Anton Ceta (who died in 1995) gave in French can be read in "La Resistance Civile au Kosovo," in *Rapport de Mission de la Délégation du Mouvement pour une Alternative Non Violente* (Paris, August 1993).
43 Ibrahim Rugova explains the roots of his struggle in an important book, *La question du Kosovo*, with Marie-Françoise Allain and Xavier Galmiche (Paris, 1994).
44 Concerning issues about this kind of resistance, which the media have difficulty in qualifying ("passive resistance," "pacific resistance," and "non-violent resistance" are used indiscriminately), see Jacques Semelin, "De la force des faibles. Lecture critique des travaux sur la résistance civile et l'action non violente," *Revue française de science politique*, no. 6 (December 1998): 773–82.
45 Howard Clark, *Civil Resistance in Kosovo* (London, 2000), 187.
46 On the history of Albanian resistance and the creation of KLA, see also Nathalie Duclos, "Le conflit du Kosovo à la lumière des séparatismes ouest-européens," in Xavier Crettiez and Jérôme Ferret (eds.), *Le silence des armes? L'Europe à l'épreuve des séparatismes violents* (Paris, 2006), 286–306.
47 See the analyses and recommendations of the Carnegie commission regarding Kosovo, published after Dayton: Leo Tindemans, Lloyd Cutler, Bronislaw Geremek, and John Roper, *Unfinished Peace:*

on March 24, 1999, whose admitted purpose was to force Serbia to sign the accords at Rambouillet, indeed reinforced the war climate that would allow the development of mass crime. Milosevic, who appeared more preoccupied by the success of his ethnic cleansing policy, used the strikes to accelerate its implementation. As in Bosnia, seven years earlier, massacres and expulsions could now be organized on a large scale.

PERPETRATION OF THE CRIME

Massacres seem to have been carefully organized, as the most important one, in Srebrenica (July 13–15, 1995), attests.[48] In Bosnia or, later, in Kosovo, a massacre implied coordination between four players: the Serbian army, the Serbian police, paramilitaries from Serbia, and neighboring Serbian civilians. Reports invariably prove the convergence of several factors – which could be called "the basic system for mass crime" – before mass crime starts. Mass crime operations are rationally organized and based on:

1. *A hierarchy in the structure of command between the actors and their respective tasks:*[49] Both play an essential role, not only for reasons of technical efficiency, but also because the hierarchical model and the fragmenting of tasks are classical techniques to make individuals feel less responsible as they sink deeper into criminal action.
2. *A sealed up theater of operations*: The area where the action is due to take place becomes off limits. In that restricted area, everything becomes possible and violence can become boundless. The "huis clos" (closed door) becomes a condition of barbarity. Obviously, the question of witnesses becomes fundamental. Who will be able to testify to having seen what will have happened? Will they be credible? Who will believe them?[50]
3. *A culture of impunity*: Protected by their hierarchy, sheltered from witnesses, perpetrators know they can do "anything" with their victims, now held at their mercy. Survivors have said it again and again: "They could do anything they wanted to us." Assumed impunity kills whichever inhibitions might exist, and violence can reach extremes.

Such an operation is based on the abolition of regular social order, with its rules and taboos. It generates an awkward relationship between

---

Report of the International Commission on the Balkans, Carnegie Endowment for International Peace (Washington, D.C., 1996), 112–19.

48 David Rohde led a remarkable inquiry into the Srebrenica tragedy, which can be considered as the largest massacre of civilian people in Europe since World War II (approximately 7,000 dead): David Rohde, *Le grand massacre, Srebrenica juillet 1995* (Paris, 1998).

49 Usually, the army goes in first, bombing the village and encircling it. Then, paramilitary forces take over, helped by civilians.

50 On this question of witnesses, see the useful Roy Gutman, *Bosnie: Témoin du genocide* (Paris, 1994). On the same topic, see also Samuel Totten, William S. Parsons, and Israel W. Charny (eds.), *Century of Genocide: Eyewitness Accounts and Critical Views* (New York, 1997), and Renaud Dulong, *Le témoin occulaire. Les conditions sociales de l'attestation personnelle*, ed. E.H.E.S.S. (Paris, 1998).

the persecutors and their victims. The "huis clos" situation and the total dependence of victims on their persecutors deeply modifies their relations to the world. On the persecutor's side, the feeling of unrestricted power is at its highest: "Nothing, nobody, neither Allah, nor the United Nations can help you out. I now am your God." Thus spoke General Mladic to the Muslims of Zepa he intended to wipe out.[51] Time, for the victims, has now stopped: "I live in another world," the mayor of Prijedor wrote, after being arrested. "What's happening seems inconceivable. . . . I have the impression that I have never been alive."[52]

But the operation, at this stage, only defines the frame within which crime will be committed. All kinds of techniques and devices aim at stimulating the perpetration of murder. First, propaganda and criminal actions are now simultaneous: to wit, a tract that circulated within the ranks of the Serbian army in 1992: "Under the warm sun of the Balkans, they have spit-roasted people, they have run bayonets through the bodies of children, to add to the folklore of the enemies of Serbian people."[53] In other words, what they have done to Serbs, you may, you must do yourself. Following instructions given to them before their attacks on Muslim houses in Bosnian villages, Croatian troops used similar methods. Excerpts from the orders that preceded the attack on Zenica were quoted by judges of the International Tribunal for the Former Yugoslavia: "The enemy continues to murder Croats in Zenica, where Muslim forces shoot at people, crush them under their tanks, while being fully aware that they are mainly women and children." The orders emphatically concluded: "Live up to your historical responsibilities."[54] Atrocities committed by Muslims "justified" the use of similar atrocities by Croats. But Muslim violence here was complete fabrication, and the purpose of the orders was to instill imaginary fears in Croatian soldiers that would make it easier for them to act out extreme violence. Propaganda, once more, attempted to strike fear in Croats and provoke them to take revenge. Believing they were victims, Croats became aggressors and yet were convinced that they were only doing their duty.

Did propaganda prove sufficient provocation to kill? More concrete than the psychological manipulation of men, the lure of important benefits (from looting) was one of the primary motivations for ethnic cleansing. According to John Mueler, warlords were composed of 20 percent fanatic Serbian nationalists and 80 percent prison inmates whom Milosevic had released with

---

51 John Pomfret, "Serbs Drive Thousands from Zepa Enclave," *Washington Post*, July 27, 1995.
52 Quoted by Gutman, *Bosnie*, 197.   53 Ibid., 28.
54 *Jugement du général Tihomir Blaskic*, Tribunal International, The Hague, March 3, 2000, United Nations (n. IT-95–14-T), 219.

the promise that they could help themselves to the possessions of the victims they were instructed to kill and/or chase. Therefore, "the relationship of such behavior to 'nationalism' and to 'ethnic hatred,' ancient or otherwise, is less than clear. Its relation to common criminality, however, is quite evident."[55] For others, members of the army or the police, career expectations ("come with us, and you'll be promoted") may have been the motivation; as may have been the possibility of sexual violence, as encouraged by officers (mass rape). These various factors can increase the number of individuals involved in the process of mass crime.[56] Mass crime aims at the expansion of crime.

Pressure from the group, while generating emulation, contributes to the escalation of violence. The most determined men watch closely over those who appear to waver and force them into barbarous action. Each man must prove his own toughness to the others. Philippe Zimbardo's experiences[57] on the relationship between prisoners and wardens, as well as Elias Canetti's analyses[58] on "mass" have proved the power of such dynamics. In fact, in crime, everyone must be like everyone else. What Christopher Browning calls the "conformism of killers" is an important factor in how criminals become undifferentiated.[59] If mass crime first implies dehumanization of the victims, it also provokes the killers' dehumanization. By destroying their victims, they self-destroy. And if that is not enough, then alcohol and drugs can help break the last taboos. Self-exhilaration leads to murderous intoxication.

This is why mass crime can be committed and repeated. The different ways of giving death belong to historical tradition. The practice of cutting throats (from the back and with the victim down on his knees) was used by Chetniks during World War II. Killers assert themselves with nationalist songs sung while they kill. This is symptomatic of the ethnic cleansing process. Words heard in Kosovo, such as "you have burned our hearts, we'll burn your houses" are also very significant. They reflect the delirious rationality of crime, at the very time it is perpetrated, in its swing from the fantasy of destruction to the act of destruction itself.

---

55 John Mueler, "The Rise, Decline, Shallowness and Banality of Militant Nationalism in Europe: Hobbes, Thugs, 'Ethnic Conflict' and the Future of Warfare," paper presented at the 1999 meeting of the American Political Science Association, Atlanta, 17.

56 On the analysis of violence against women, see Alexandra Stiglmayer (ed.), *Mass Rape: The War against Women in Bosnia-Herzegovina,* trans. M. Faber (Lincoln, 2000).

57 Haney Banks and Philippe Zimbardo, "Interpersonal Dynamics in a Simulated Prison," *International Journal of Criminology and Penology* 1 (1983): 49–97.

58 Elias Canetti, *Masse et puissance* (Paris, 1966).

59 For a full discussion, see Christopher R. Browning, *Ordinary Men: Reserve Police Battalion 101 and the Final Solution in Poland* (New York, 1992), 159–89.

Killers' terminology can also negate the victims' identity. It seems that, at the time of execution, the killer wants to offer some justification. Thus, the frequently used insult "son of a Turk" puts the death of the victim within the context of the century-old battle, with its political and religious connotations. The identity of the victims can also be "militarized." When they tell their victims "NATO did sure forget you!" the criminals put their action under the aegis of military power. At the last moment, mass crime masquerades as an act of war.

WHY ATROCITIES?

The definition of mass crime cannot be reduced to large-scale murder. It often implies to kill "atrociously." Ethnic cleansing operations are preceded and accompanied by an astonishing level of barbarity as proved by what took place during the first days of the aggression against Croatia and, similarly, by what Primo Levi has called "futile violence" spread in the concentration camps of Bosnia.[60] In those camps, killing was just not enough, inflicting pain was just not enough. One had to reach a certain level of abjectness. In the villages of Bosnia and Kosovo, massacres were accompanied by the most horrific scenes of rape, mutilation, and castration. A few cases of cannibalism were even reported. After the killing, bodies might be torn apart, cut into pieces or burned. Such atrocities are hard to understand.

All the individuals who commit such atrocities are not psychopaths. Some of them may have perverse or sadistic personalities, but most of them do not. Individuals are not monsters as such; they become monsters when they get caught in the terrifying dynamics of mass crime. In this context, Hannah Arendt's notion of "the banality of evil" is particularly enlightening.

Some guidelines may shed some light on the interpretation of the relationship between the ordinary and the extraordinary in the carrying out of atrocities. Using the concept of crime's "delirious rationality," one can argue that atrocities, far from being perceived by criminals as "senseless," are indeed perceived as necessary. Mass atrocities would thus be used to further one or more political goals.[61] Ideology therefore carries a great weight: it is because an individual is personally convinced that horror is necessary that he will resort to crime. His cruelest acts are justified, in his own eyes, by what he believes to be a transcendent goal. Because he considers his victim

---

60 Primo Levi, "La violence inutile," in *Les naufragés et les rescapés* (Paris, 1989), 104–19.

61 Luis Martinez and I took this hypothesis, as the basic issue of the conference we organized on the The Political Use of Massacres, Centre d'Etudes et de Relations Internationales, Paris, November 16, 1999.

as being less a man than an animal, a piece of detritus, he can subject him or her to the worst abuse. The more defenseless beings he kills, the more he persuades himself that he is killing in the name of values or plans that demand it. Hannah Arendt's views on totalitarianism are based precisely on the analysis of this very dialectic between terror and ideology.[62]

Other scholars have explored the relationship between violence and identity. They show how important it is for a given group to give a manipulative interpretation of the identity of the group that they are seeking to eliminate. Jean François Bayart, for instance, underscores the role of "the imaginary" in the perpetration of crime.[63] Ethnic cleansing in the former Yugoslavia illustrates this approach perfectly. Along those lines, the anthropologist Veronique Nahoum-Grappe offers an original interpretation of what she calls "the political use of cruelty."[64] Taking the Serbs' "imaginary" and their vision of what is pure or impure as a starting point, she explains how "the enemy is defined by his blood ties that can go as far as race ties." Physical destruction of the members of a group will therefore not fulfill the stated goal of eradication. As such, mass rape and the profanation of graves are particularly revealing of ethnic cleansing considered as a way of destroying the enemy's identity. "The profanation of graves, the ransacking of historical buildings," she writes, "are mirror answers to the rape of women, the cutting of men's throats."[65] For Florence Hartmann, atrocities have a strategic signification for the longer term: the goal of ethnic cleansing is not to eliminate all Croats or all Muslims, but to annihilate all efforts by the different communities to live peacefully together. "To separate Serbs and Croats, enough atrocities had to be committed that would feed a century of hatred."[66]

These functional interpretations of mass atrocities are perhaps simply an effort to give significance to atrocities when in fact they have none. Wolfgang Sofsky's works on "extreme violence" argue that the perpetration of atrocities has no other goal than itself. Sofsky's analysis of the role of terror in Nazi concentration camps is remarkable.[67] Ideology does not play such an important role in the unleashing of extreme violence because a power that has to legitimize its actions is a weakened one. Absolute power can only rely on itself. Cruelty becomes a goal in itself. Sofsky suggests that massacre, as a

---

62 Hanna Arendt, *Le système totalitaire. Les origines du totalitarisme* (Paris, 1972), 203–33.
63 Jean-François Bayart, *L'illusion identitaire* (Paris, 1996).
64 Véronique Nahoum-Grappe, "L'usage politique de la cruauté: L'épuration ethnique (ex-Yougoslavie, 1991–1995)," in *De la violence*, Séminaire de Françoise Héritier (Paris, 1996), 273–323.
65 Ibid., 284.
66 Florence Hartman, *La diagonale du fou* (Paris, 1999), 21.
67 Wolfgang Sofsky, *L'organisation de la terreur* (Paris, 1995), 34.

collective act, follows "invariants" that he outlines in his *Traité de la violence.*[68]
The same forms of cruelty, which we think apply to the Balkans only, can
be found in many other countries. The scenario that leads to a massacre
is nearly always the same: unexpected offensive, encirclement, separation
of men and women, waiting period, atrocities and rapes, beginning of the
killings, the ransacking of homes, mutilation of corpses, and arson. All in
all, for Sofsky, the uniformity of massacres does not reflect the similarity of
objectives but rather the universal dynamic of extreme violence.[69]

These two interpretations are based on conflicting points of view. One
argues that atrocities have a meaning whereas the other argues that they
do not. One emphasizes the functional utility of horror as viewed by the
criminals, the other entirely separates atrocity in its undertaking from the
action in its finality. Could the historical authenticity of mass crime be
sustained by these contradictory interpretations? Could the perpetration of
atrocities be seen as preparatory, preliminary work leading to mass crime?
When asked, "Since you were going to kill them all, why these humilia-
tions?" Franz Stangl, the former commander of Treblinka, answered: "To
condition those who would have to carry out the executions, to make it
possible for them to do what they would be asked to do."[70] In other words,
atrocities clearly had a functional role: they conditioned future executioners.
In other circumstances, atrocities will be the result of an extreme violence
that finds itself without purpose. In civil war, for example, massacre is first
used as intimidative and coercive tactics against civilian populations. But
repeated perpetration of massacre tends to destabilize perpetrators, adding
a "mad" dimension to their behavior.

At this point, we do not know enough about mass crimes to endorse
fairly one or the other of the theories. The complexity and the foreign
nature of the phenomena under study call for a multidisciplinary approach.
Psychology, history, sociology, and anthropology are the first disciplines that
come to mind. However, the odds are that these works, however necessary
to explain political facts and increase the knowledge of humankind, will
perhaps never be able to fathom the enigma of our own barbarity.

---

68 Wolfgang Sofsky, *Traité de la violence* (Paris, 1998).
69 Ibid.,159.
70 Quoted by Lévi, *Les naufragés et les rescapés*, 124.

Conclusions

18

Investigating Genocide

ROBERT GELLATELY AND BEN KIERNAN

The specter of genocide, unleashed with a vengeance in the twentieth century, now haunts the globe.[1] For several decades, daily newspapers and nightly television news have regularly featured stories about genocide and other mass violence. Killing continues almost under our noses. New and horrific mass crimes and violence seem only around the corner. For these reasons and more, scholars from many disciplines and writers of all kinds have immersed themselves in the tasks of researching past and ongoing cases of mass murder. The terrorist attacks of September 2001 on the World Trade Center in New York will certainly stimulate more such research.

Our sense of the multiplying violence around us is reinforced by the plethora of new evidence about past atrocities, partly from the post–Cold War opening of formerly secret Soviet archives, but also elsewhere. The discovery of the chilling security archives of the Khmer Rouge, revelations of Italian wartime crimes against humanity in the Balkans and Africa, new evidence of French official crimes during the Algerian War in the memoirs of General Paul Aussaresses, and documentation of the Western Hemisphere–wide "Thirty Years' Dirty War" against leftists in Latin America have all brought heretofore hidden mass murders to public attention.[2] Even lost Nazi

---

1 Jonathan Steele, "It Will be Remembered as the Age of Barbarism," *Guardian Weekly* (London), December 30, 1999, 3; Ryszard Kapuscinski, "Genocide in the Modern Age: Man's Inhumanity to Man," *Monde diplomatique* (Paris), April 2001, 14–15.
2 Rory Carroll, "Dirty Secrets," *Guardian Weekly* (London), July 5, 2001; Paul Aussaresses, *Services spéciaux Algérie 1955–57: Mon témoignage sur la torture* (Paris, 2001); Claire Mauss-Copeaux, *Appelés en Algérie* (Paris, 1999); John Henley, "UN Urged to Save Archives of Pinochet's Terror," *Guardian Weekly*, November 11–17, 1999, 5; J. Patrice McSherry, "Operation Condor: Deciphering the US Role," Crimes of War website, June 2001 <www.crimesofwar.org/special/condor.html>; Pierre Abramovici, "Latin America: The 30 Years Dirty War," *Monde diplomatique*, August 2001.

documents continue to surface, and historians are producing new studies of the Holocaust based on them.[3]

Concern about recent genocides, denial of earlier ones, worry that such horrors might recur, and new opportunities to document and punish them, have all been met by a number of official and semiofficial initiatives around the globe. For their part, universities and colleges in North America and elsewhere have created new centers for Holocaust and genocide studies. It is common for these institutions to offer courses on genocide, and in some places it is now possible to earn a Ph.D. in this area of study.[4] A similar trend can also be found in Europe, Australia, and elsewhere. Not only have students, academics, and journalists grown more interested in the topic of genocide, but several influential politicians and jurists in the United States and in other countries have taken up the cause.[5] As we write, a new International Criminal Court is being established before which the world can try future perpetrators of genocide and other mass crimes. It is our hope that this book will contribute to the ongoing discussion and stimulate further study, including research on genocide prevention.

On the Thai-Cambodian border in 1979, a young Khmer Rouge company commander remembered the U.S. aerial bombardment of his native village eight years before. Of the 350 villagers, 200 were killed, he said. The twelve-year-old survivor ran terrified into the jungle. Khmer Rouge guerrillas gave him a gun. They told him the "killing birds" had come "from Phnom Penh." Urban dwellers were the enemy. After victory in 1975, this boy murdered 200 "enemies." Asked what it felt like to kill so many people, he patted his right shoulder. "It hurts, here," he said, recalling the kickback from his rifle butt.[6] In mid-2001, as many as 300,000 children under eighteen were participating in armed conflicts in forty-one countries.[7] How many of these young victims could become future war criminals?

Long-term genocide prediction and prevention require understanding of the societal nutrients that fertilize the seedbeds of mass murder. Popular historical grievances, previous social traumas, ingrained poverty, educational deprivation, sudden political or economic destabilization, colonial

3 For new studies that build on this documentation, see Christian Gerlach, *Kalkulierte Morde: Die deutsche Wirtschafts- und Vernichtungspolitik in Weissrussland 1941 bis 1944* (Hamburg, 1999), and Michael Wildt, *Generation des Unbedingten: Das Fuehrungskorps des Reichssicherheitshauptamtes* (Hamburg, 2002).

4 Karen Springen, "Studying to Prevent the Past," *Newsweek*, April 29, 2002, 14.

5 For instance Michael Naumann, "Wachdienst für die Weltgemeinschaft," *Frankfurter Rundschau*, January 29, 2000.

6 Staffan Hildebrand, personal communication to Ben Kiernan, Stockholm, August 1979.

7 Peter Moszynski, "Hostilities in Forty-one Countries Force Children into War," *Guardian Weekly*, June 21–27, 2001; Pierre Conesa, "Small Forgotten Conflicts: Places of No Importance," *Monde diplomatique*, March 2001.

occupation, and war are just some of the conditions that foster the growth of sociopathic political movements. For example, modern warfare, exacerbated by the spread of the technology of industrial slaughter from the late nineteenth century, has been a breeding ground for genocidal movements, even as it provides a cover for their crimes. The Young Turks, the Nazis, the Khmer Rouge, and others were all spawned in wartime atmospheres of crisis. The destabilization of entire societies through mass destruction, death, forced migration, and trauma opens up vast new possibilities for radical extremists not only to nurse paranoias about the enemy but also to project them on others, recruit supporters, seize power, and put their deadly goals into practice behind screens of war censorship and emergency military justification. Over the longer term, mass poverty, falling living standards, and rapid economic destabilization, including widespread land dispossession, have spread a similar sense of social crisis and often led to war, further encouraging simple solutions to complex socioeconomic problems. The targeting of easily visible, unarmed, and vulnerable victim groups follows.

But not every sustained or sudden social or historical crisis leads to genocide and mass murder. A second essential element is human agency – criminal decisions by leaders of extremist and violent political sects or regimes. Groups likely to implement such decisions must be identified in advance of their ascendancy, in order to block their path to power. Along with the historical and social environments in which they flourish, the ideological notions and inimical preoccupations of such groups must be studied and compared from one case to another, if we are to understand the political conditions for acts of genocide.

Such work can be usefully interdisciplinary. The emerging field of comparative genocide studies was pioneered by sociologists: Leo Kuper, Irving L. Horowitz, Helen Fein, Kurt Jonassohn, and Vahakn Dadrian. Rarer work by historians such as Frank Chalk, and by political scientists such as Colin Tatz, Robert Melson, and Roger Smith, has been of great value. It is important to build on this work, as well as on studies like Norman Naimark's account of "ethnic cleansing" in modern Europe. More research is needed on the history, anthropology, economics, demography, literature, law, and psychology of genocide, and its perpetrators, victims, bystanders, and survivors.

The events of September 11, 2001, brought home to the people in the United States that they were by no means immune to attacks on their "home front." That attack led the president to declare a war on terror, but it should also stimulate broader examination of human rights abuses and mass murder around the globe, including in those countries with which the

United States is allied. The 1999 report of the UN-administered Historical Clarification Commission, which found that Guatemalan security forces enjoying U.S. support had committed genocide against indigenous Mayan groups in 1981–83, deserves to be studied, and at least translated and published in English.[8] It is unfortunate to see the Bush administration attempting to undermine the embryonic International Criminal Court, a new forum for the prosecution and enforcement of international law that aims to further the cause of genocide prevention and deterrence.[9] U.S. and European insistence on the arrest and prosecution of Slobodan Milosevic and his deputies for genocide and other crimes in the Former Yugoslavia resulted in a historic development: the first international genocide trials and some of the first convictions for such crimes since World War II.[10] The first person ever convicted for genocide in an international tribunal was Jean-Paul Akayesu, former mayor of Taba in Rwanda, who was found guilty in September 1998. Captured Al Qaeda leaders such as Abu Zubaydah should also be tried, possibly before an international tribunal.[11]

The United Nations should not depend on Indonesian courts to deliver justice to the East Timorese.[12] The Security Council must establish an Ad Hoc International Criminal Tribunal similar to those sitting in judgment over the genocides in the Former Yugoslavia and Rwanda. Nor should the UN abandon the tribunal that Cambodia is bound by the Genocide Convention to establish for the judgment of the crimes of the Khmer Rouge. Rather, the UN should return to the negotiating table and use its presence to improve the defective Cambodian justice system. The United States

8 A one-volume edited version (in English and Spanish) of the Report's thirteen volumes is being prepared by Daniel Rothenberg, as *Memory of Silence: The Guatemalan Truth Commission Report*. The report's executive summary is available in English at <http://hrdata.aaas.org/ceh/report/english/>. It is not widely known that U.S. President Ronald Reagan asserted on a visit to Guatemala in 1982 that the head of the perpetrator regime was "totally committed to democracy" and receiving a "bum rap" from critics. Quoted in Edward S. Herman and Noam Chomsky, *Manufacturing Consent: The Political Economy of the Mass Media* (New York, 1988), 73. The killings in Guatemala are not even mentioned in the index of Samantha Power, *"A Problem from Hell": America and the Age of Genocide* (New York, 2002).

9 Barbara Crossette, "U.S. Opposition to Tribunal Worries European Supporters," *New York Times*, July 14, 2001, and Neil A. Lewis, "U.S. Rejects All Support for New Court on Atrocities," *New York Times*, May 7, 2002.

10 Keith B. Richburg, "Tribunal Finds Serb Guilty of Genocide," *Guardian Weekly*, August 9–15, 2001, 27; Ian Fisher, "Power Drove Milosevic to Crime, Prosecutors Say as Trial Opens," *New York Times*, February 13, 2002, 1, 16. In September 1998, Jean-Paul Akayesu, former mayor of Taba in Rwanda, became the first person ever convicted for genocide in an international tribunal.

11 Slavoj Zizek, "Are We in a War? Do We Have an Enemy," *London Review of Books* 23 (May 2002): 3–6.

12 Joel Rubin, "Justice Delayed in East Timor," Crimes of War website <www.crimesofwar.org/mag_timor.html>, May–June 2001.

and Australia, too, should support Cambodia in establishing a tribunal, as Washington and Canberra promised to do in 1991.[13]

As the essays in this book illustrate, the investigation of genocide and other mass crimes is yielding important findings. However, given the sheer complexity of the murderous events we are trying to understand and explain, controversies and debates have also emerged. Perhaps the thorniest issue concerns how to define the term "genocide" and its relationship to other crimes against humanity and war crimes.

A common complaint in discussions about genocide is that the term has been overused to the point that it has become hopelessly debased. It is worth pointing to how historians and others have used the concept in the past several decades. If one surveys all the definitions used in the specialist literature, we can arrange them along a continuum, running from narrow and restrictive, all the way to broad and inclusive. This also applies to various specific issues: which groups should be legally protected, whether only racial or religious groups or social and even political groups as well; whether a group's intentional destruction in whole or in part constitutes genocide; whether the crime requires killing or can be perpetrated by nonviolent, coerced dispersal (destruction of a "group, as such"). Those who insist on narrower definitions often also advocate studying historically specific cases, whereas scholars adopting broader definitions are more likely to suggest the importance of carrying out comparative studies. Whatever approach we take, however, we do not really get around the issue of what should count as genocide by creating a series of more expansive neologisms loosely linked to or meant to imply genocide, terms like "ethnocide," "linguicide," "planeticide," and so on. The new terms do not solve the problem. Rather, they multiply it by either eliding distinct concepts or limiting analysis of mass murders and other kinds of abuses to their specific historical contexts. Despite the proliferation of other terms and definitions of genocide, the UN Convention's legal definition is finally gathering force from its recent application by the courts. We believe it also provides the best conceptual tool to distinguish varying historical cases, whether or not one chooses to regard them all as genocides.

Far more is involved than the law or the language. Subsumed in the concept of genocide is a set of extremely complex issues and areas of dispute and

13 Secretary of State James A. Baker stated: "Cambodia and the US are both signatories to the Genocide Convention and we will support efforts to bring to justice those responsible for the mass murders of the 1970s if the new Cambodian government chooses to pursue this path" (*New York Times*, October 24, 1991, A16). Australian Foreign Minister Evans added: "We would give strong support to an incoming Cambodian government to set in train such a war crimes process" (*Melbourne Age*, October 24, 1991, 1).

contention. There are debates between those who stress popular participation in genocides, and those emphasizing state or elite coercion.[14] Scholars who insist on documentary evidence disagree with those favoring the legitimate contribution of oral history.[15] Another debate weighs historical continuity against change. Simply put, is genocide as old as biblical Am'alek?[16] Or something very new? Is it a throwback, a hangover from the past, or essentially "modern"? In this volume, many writers point to modernity as a culprit. Several link genocide explicitly to specific historical developments, particularly in Europe, that began in the nineteenth century and were aggravated by the "new imperialism" and the First World War. In this reading, the modernity of genocide becomes not only its most chilling, but also its quintessential characteristic and one that sets it apart from mass murder in earlier times and other places. This argument is a cogent and plausible one.

Nevertheless, a number of scholars argue that there were genocidal acts well before the twentieth century, including in North, Central, and South America.[17] In the 1770s the North Carolina delegation to the United States Continental Congress even proclaimed that "the duties of a Christian" included such determined action against the Cherokee Indians as "to extinguish the very race of them and scarce to leave enough of their existence to be a vestige in proof that the Cherokee nation once was."[18] In *Rivers of Blood, Rivers of Gold*, Mark Cocker shows dramatically how Spanish Conquistadors exterminated Mexican peoples, how British settlers eliminated Tasmania's indigenous people from their island, how U.S. settlers dispossessed the Apaches – and he compares their fates with that of the Herero of South West Africa at the hands of German soldiers in 1904–8.[19] We could cite multiple cases before 1900 for which convincing arguments could be made that mass murder and intentional extermination policies and practices were used in efforts to destroy the whole or a substantial part of a group of people or a nation.[20] Publication of *Le livre noir du colonialisme*,

---

14 This is a common theme of scholarly dispute in the Holocaust literature. See also "Fierce Debate Divides Scholars of the 1994 Rwandan Genocide," *Chronicle of Higher Education*, August 3, 2001, 16–19.
15 For an elegant attempt to reconcile these two camps, see Inge Clendinnen, "Every Single Document," *London Review of Books*, May 23, 2002, 7–8.
16 "And the Lord said to Moses, 'Write this as a memorial in a book and recite it in the ears of Joshua, that I will utterly blot out the remembrance of Am'alek from under heaven.'" Exodus 17:14.
17 See, e.g., David E. Stannard, *American Holocaust: The Conquest of the New World* (New York, 1992).
18 Quoted in Thomas Hatley, *The Dividing Paths: Cherokees and South Carolinians Through the Era of Revolution* (New York, 1993), 193.
19 Mark Cocker, *Rivers of Blood, Rivers of Gold: Europe's Conquest of Indigenous Peoples* (New York, 1998).
20 See Kurt Jonassohn with Karin Solveig Bjornson, *Genocide and Gross Human Rights Violations in Comparative Perspective* (New Brunswick, N.J., 1998), chs. 17–20; Frank Chalk and Kurt Jonassohn, *The History and Sociology of Genocide* (New Haven, 1990), 58–229.

with its indictment of brutal European conquests, has complemented the catalog of twentieth-century mass murder in *Le livre noir du communisme*.[21]

All students of "genocide," therefore, are faced with a dilemma. Lemkin invented the term in a specific time and place, to describe what had happened to the Armenians and the Jews. But was the tragedy of genocide a new phenomenon? And how can what has since been inflicted on other peoples in different ways be compared to what happened to the Armenians and the Jews? These are complex issues, and we need to keep the discussion going in the hope of finding new and effective ways of addressing them.

The question as to what should count as genocide and whether it is new or eternal also relates to a whole series of contemporary social issues. One of the most controversial of these deals with what can be termed the politics of recognition for the survivors of genocidal or other murderous regimes. The process by which individuals and groups seek to establish their identity and worth occurs on two levels. According to philosopher Charles Taylor, the first level has to do with the intimate or personal sphere "where we understand the formation of identity and the self as taking place in a continuing dialogue and struggle" with friends and family.[22] The second level is the public sphere, where, for example, individuals not only claim equal rights, but also have a need to have their suffering recognized. In the context of a discussion of genocide, demands for recognition made by people who were intended victims mean that they might ask for the right to be recognized for having suffered from the worst crime, that is, from genocide. If one were to reject such claims and to suggest that a persecuted group – be they Armenians or Sinti and Roma (or "Gypsies") or some others – did not face a "real genocide," then these people may regard themselves as being denied rightful recognition of their suffering and grievances. To deny them the recognition that they have suffered the worst crime runs the risk of diminishing their grievances. Clearly, the issues of survivor recognition are crucial, and possibly beyond the limits of historical research. Historians are constrained in their understanding by the rules of evidence.

But scholars also have a responsibility to the victims of any crime to exercise care when appearing to circumscribe legal rights and jurisdictions. To contest categorization of a genocide may even serve to deny victims of

---

21 Stéphane Courtois et al., *The Black Book of Communism: Crimes, Terror, Repression*, trans. J. Murphy and M. Kramer (Cambridge, Mass., 1999); Marc Ferro (ed.), *Le livre noir du colonialisme* (Paris, 2002).

22 Charles Taylor, "The Politics of Recognition," in Amy Gutman (ed.), *Multiculturalism: Examining the Politics of Recognition* (Princeton, 1994), 25–73. The volume contains a number of other interesting comments and essays, including ones by K. Anthony Appiah and Jürgen Habermas.

such an event the legal remedy to which they have legitimate resort. Unlike crimes against humanity and even war crimes, international law on genocide has the clear-cut statutory authority of the convention. For this reason, we suggest that scholars who disagree with the breadth of the UN definition of genocide, in describing a particular case as a tragedy falling short of genocide, should make clear that they are not exercising a legal judgment that might diminish the rights of redress on the part of the victims. And scholars who find the UN definition too narrow may also wish to allow for the possible ongoing development of the law by the courts, as judges, called upon for the first time to implement the Genocide Convention, make decisions on its applicability to the large number of new cases. The Rwanda International Tribunal has already set a legal precedent with its judgment in one case that violent sexual crimes against women constituted genocide.[23] We do not suggest that the specter of genocide can finally be banished merely by pronouncing its name. But if even scholars fail to speak out clearly, or mumble prevarications, victims will continue to suffer unheard, and the unspeakable will haunt our species in a new century of genocide.

---

23 "Human Rights Watch Applauds Rwanda Rape Verdict: Sets International Precedent for Punishing Sexual Violence as a War Crime," Human Rights Watch, New York, September 2, 1998 <www.hrw.org/french/press/akay-fr.htm>.

Convention on the Prevention and Punishment of the Crime of Genocide

Adopted by Resolution 260 (III) A of the U.N. General Assembly on December 9, 1948. Entry into force: January 12, 1951.

The Contracting Parties,

Having considered the declaration made by the General Assembly of the United Nations in its resolution 96 (I) dated 11 December 1946 that genocide is a crime under international law, contrary to the spirit and aims of the United Nations and condemned by the civilized world,

Recognizing that at all periods of history genocide has inflicted great losses on humanity, and

Being convinced that, in order to liberate mankind from such an odious scourge, international co-operation is required,

Hereby agree as hereinafter provided:

Article I: The Contracting Parties confirm that genocide, whether committed in time of peace or in time of war, is a crime under international law which they undertake to prevent and to punish.

Article II: In the present Convention, genocide means any of the following acts committed with intent to destroy, in whole or in part, a national, ethnical, racial or religious group, as such:

    (a) Killing members of the group;

    (b) Causing serious bodily or mental harm to members of the group;

    (c) Deliberately inflicting on the group conditions of life calculated to bring about its physical destruction in whole or in part;

For a list of parties to the convention, see <http://www.unhchr.ch/html/menu3/b/treaty1gen.htm>.

(d) Imposing measures intended to prevent births within the group;

(e) Forcibly transferring children of the group to another group.

Article III: The following acts shall be punishable:

(a) Genocide;

(b) Conspiracy to commit genocide;

(c) Direct and public incitement to commit genocide;

(d) Attempt to commit genocide;

(e) Complicity in genocide.

Article IV: Persons committing genocide or any of the other acts enumerated in article III shall be punished, whether they are constitutionally responsible rulers, public officials or private individuals.

Article V: The Contracting Parties undertake to enact, in accordance with their respective Constitutions, the necessary legislation to give effect to the provisions of the present Convention, and, in particular, to provide effective penalties for persons guilty of genocide or any of the other acts enumerated in article III.

Article VI: Persons charged with genocide or any of the other acts enumerated in article III shall be tried by a competent tribunal of the State in the territory of which the act was committed, or by such international penal tribunal as may have jurisdiction with respect to those Contracting Parties which shall have accepted its jurisdiction.

Article VII: Genocide and the other acts enumerated in article III shall not be considered as political crimes for the purpose of extradition.

The Contracting Parties pledge themselves in such cases to grant extradition in accordance with their laws and treaties in force.

Article VIII: Any Contracting Party may call upon the competent organs of the United Nations to take such action under the Charter of the United Nations as they consider appropriate for the prevention and suppression of acts of genocide or any of the other acts enumerated in article III.

Article IX: Disputes between the Contracting Parties relating to the interpretation, application or fulfilment of the present Convention, including those relating to the responsibility of a State for genocide or for any of the other acts enumerated in article III, shall be submitted to the International Court of Justice at the request of any of the parties to the dispute.

Article X: The present Convention, of which the Chinese, English, French, Russian and Spanish texts are equally authentic, shall bear the date of 9 December 1948.

Article XI: The present Convention shall be open until 31 December 1949 for signature on behalf of any Member of the United Nations and of any nonmember State to which an invitation to sign has been addressed by the General Assembly.

The present Convention shall be ratified, and the instruments of ratification shall be deposited with the Secretary-General of the United Nations.

After 1 January 1950, the present Convention may be acceded to on behalf of any Member of the United Nations and of any non-member State which has received an invitation as aforesaid. Instruments of accession shall be deposited with the Secretary-General of the United Nations.

Article XII: Any Contracting Party may at any time, by notification addressed to the Secretary-General of the United Nations, extend the application of the present Convention to all or any of the territories for the conduct of whose foreign relations that Contracting Party is responsible.

Article XIII: On the day when the first twenty instruments of ratification or accession have been deposited, the Secretary-General shall draw up a proces-verbal and transmit a copy thereof to each Member of the United Nations and to each of the non-member States contemplated in article XI.

The present Convention shall come into force on the ninetieth day following the date of deposit of the twentieth instrument of ratification or accession.

Any ratification or accession effected, subsequent to the latter date shall become effective on the ninetieth day following the deposit of the instrument of ratification or accession.

Article XIV: The present Convention shall remain in effect for a period of ten years as from the date of its coming into force.

It shall thereafter remain in force for successive periods of five years for such Contracting Parties as have not denounced it at least six months before the expiration of the current period.

Denunciation shall be effected by a written notification addressed to the Secretary-General of the United Nations.

Article XV: If, as a result of denunciations, the number of Parties to the present Convention should become less than sixteen, the Convention shall cease to be in force as from the date on which the last of these denunciations shall become effective.

Article XVI: A request for the revision of the present Convention may be made at any time by any Contracting Party by means of a notification in writing addressed to the Secretary-General.

The General Assembly shall decide upon the steps, if any, to be taken in respect of such request.

Article XVII: The Secretary-General of the United Nations shall notify all Members of the United Nations and the non-member States contemplated in article XI of the following:
- (a) Signatures, ratifications and accessions received in accordance with article XI;
- (b) Notifications received in accordance with article XII;
- (c) The date upon which the present Convention comes into force in accordance with article XIII;
- (d) Denunciations received in accordance with article XIV;
- (e) The abrogation of the Convention in accordance with article XV;
- (f) Notifications received in accordance with article XVI.

Article XVIII: The original of the present Convention shall be deposited in the archives of the United Nations.

A certified copy of the Convention shall be transmitted to each Member of the United Nations and to each of the non-member States contemplated in article XI.

Article XIX: The present Convention shall be registered by the Secretary-General of the United Nations on the date of its coming into force.

Index